CW01163771

WAR AND GOVERNMENT
IN THE MIDDLE AGES

WAR AND GOVERNMENT
IN THE MIDDLE AGES

ESSAYS IN HONOUR OF J.O. PRESTWICH

Edited by John Gillingham and J.C. Holt

THE BOYDELL PRESS · BARNES & NOBLE

© Contributors 1984

First published in 1984 by
D.S. Brewer
240 Hills Road, Cambridge
an imprint of Boydell & Brewer Ltd
PO Box 9, Woodbridge, Suffolk IP12 3DF
and by Barnes and Noble Books
81 Adams Drive, Totowa, New Jersey 07512

Reprinted 1984
Reprinted 1986

ISBN 0 85115 404 2

British Library Cataloguing in Publication Data

War and government in the Middle Ages
1. Europe — History — 476-1492
I. Gillingham, John   II. Holt, J.C.
III. Prestwich, J.O.
940.1'8   D117

ISBN 0-85115-404-2

Printed in Great Britain by
Short Run Press Ltd, Exeter, Devon

CONTENTS

LIST OF MAPS AND TABLES	vi
ABBREVIATIONS	vii

J.O.P.
John Edwards — ix

The Basques in Aquitaine and Navarre: Problems of Frontier Government
Roger Collins — 3

The Status of the Norman Knight
R. Allen Brown — 18

Policy and Visions. The case of the Holy Lance at Antioch
Colin Morris — 33

Lords of the Norman Vexin
Judith Green — 47

Strongbow, Henry II and Anglo-Norman intervention in Ireland
Marie-Therese Flanagan — 62

Richard I and the Science of War in the Middle Ages
John Gillingham — 78

The Loss of Normandy and Royal Finance
J.C. Holt — 92

What Happened in 1258?
D.A. Carpenter — 106

The Lord Edward's Crusade, 1270—2: its setting and significance
Simon Lloyd — 120

The Gascon Nobility and the Anglo-French War 1294—98
M.G.A. Vale — 134

Cavalry Service in Early Fourteenth Century England
Michael Prestwich — 147

The Jurisdiction and Origins of the Constable's Court
Maurice Keen — 159

Sed Nihil Fecit? The Last Capetians and the Recovery of the Holy Land
C.J. Tyerman — 170

The Financial Position of Richard, Duke of York
J.M.W. Bean — 182

LIST OF MAPS

Vasconia	4
The Vexin	46
Gascony in the late thirteenth century	following p. 135

LIST OF GENEALOGICAL TABLES

Lords of the Norman Vexin between pp. 61 and 62

I.   The Crispin Family
II.   The Lords of Baudemont
III.   The Lords of Gisors
IV.   The family of Chaumont, lords of Guitry

ABBREVIATIONS

BIHR	*Bulletin of the Institute of Historical Research*
BL	British Library
BN	Bibliothèque Nationale
BT	*The Bayeux Tapestry*, ed. F.M. Stenton, 2nd ed. London 1965
CCR	*Calendar of Close Rolls*
C Ch R	*Calendar of Charter Rolls*
Cal. Docs. France	*Calendar of Documents preserved in France* . . . i, 918—1216, ed. J.H. Round, H.M.S.O. 1899
CFR	*Calendar of Fine Rolls*
CIPM	*Calendar of Inquisitions Post Mortem*
CLR	*Calendar of Liberate Rolls*
CPR	*Calendar of Patent Rolls*
CR	*Close Rolls*
De Gestis Regum	William of Malmesbury, *De gestis regum Anglorum*, ed. W. Stubbs, RS 1887
Domesday Book	*Domesday Book, seu liber censualis* . . . ed. A. Farley, 2 vols., 'Record Commission', 1783
Dudo	*De Moribus et actis primorum Normanniae Ducum Auctore Dudone Sancti Quintini Decano*, ed. J. Lair, Société des Antiquaires de Normandie, 1865
EHD	*English Historical Documents*, ii, ed. D.C. Douglas, 2nd edn, London 1981
EHR	*English Historical Review*
Fauroux	*Recueil des actes des ducs de Normandie* (911—1066), ed M. Fauroux, Mémoires de la Société des Antiquaires de Normandie, xxxvi, 1961
Foedera	*Foedera, conventiones, litterae et cujuscunque generis acta publica*, ed. T. Rymer, 4 vols. Record Commission, London 1816—69.
GEC	*Complete Peerage of England, Scotland, Ireland, Great Britain and the United Kingdom*, 13 vols. in 14, London 1910—59
Gesta Guillelmi	William of Poitiers, *Gesta Guillelmi* . . . ed. R. Foreville, Paris 1952
Jumièges	William of Jumièges, *Gesta Normannorum Ducum*, ed. J. Marx, Société de l'histoire de Normandie, 1914
MGH	*Monumenta Germaniae Historica*
ns	New Series
Orderic	Ordericus Vitalis, *Historia Ecclesiastica*, ed. M. Chibnall, Oxford Medieval Texts, 1969
PRO	Public Record Office

Procs. BA	*Proceedings of the British Academy*
Regesta	*Regesta Regum Anglo-Normannorum*, i. ed. H.W.C. Davis, Oxford 1913; ii, ed. C. Johnson, H.A. Cronne, Oxford 1956; iii, ed. H.A. Cronne, R.H.C. Davis, Oxford 1968
RHC Occ.	*Recueil des historiens des Croisades. Historiens occidentaux.*
RS	Rolls Series, London
RP	*Rotuli Parliamentorum* London 1783—1832
ser.	series
Trans.	Transactions
TRHS	*Transactions of the Royal Historical Society*
Statutes	Statutes of the Realm 11 vols, Record Commission, London 1810—28
VCH	Victoria County History
Vita Herluini	ed. J. Armitage Robinson in his *Gilbert Crispin abbot of Westminster*, Cambridge 1911

J.O.P.

John Edwards

For those who arrived on the scene comparatively late in his career, it is hard to imagine a time when J.O.P. was not a leading figure, both in Queen's itself and in the Modern History Faculty. He did, indeed, achieve eminence very quickly. After graduating from Hertford College in 1936, he spent only a year as a Magdalen Prize Fellow before being elected to the Michel Fellowship and Praelectorship at Queen's which he held for the rest of his teaching career.

The new History Fellow had little opportunity to establish himself before war broke out. He began his military service in the Ox and Bucks Light Infantry, but was soon seconded to Intelligence. A colleague at Bletchley speaks warmly of John's work as a military adviser in Hut 3, from 1941. The German 'Ultra' code was deciphered from the summer of 1940 onwards, with immeasurable consequences for the Allied war effort. John and his colleagues worked eight-hour shifts, day and night. It is suggested that his training as a medievalist helped him to develop his extraordinary gift of extracting the full meaning from apparently baffling scraps of intelligence, and also of drafting clear, concise and unambiguous signals to commands abroad. Those who used its results testify to the value of Bletchley's work, which, in 1944, John was sent to share with staff at the Pentagon, as they struggled with Japanese codes.

Between 1939 and 1945, Queen's history was largely in the hands of what some may regard as an ill-assorted pair, John's own wife, Menna, and Rev. Dr Norman Sykes, who had been evacuated from Westfield College. At the end of the war, Sykes left to become Dixie Professor of Ecclesiastical History at Cambridge. John himself returned in 1945 to a massive teaching load. He took charge of English History Papers 1 and 2, Political Thought, Stubbs' Charters, medieval foreign periods and the special subject on the Crusades. Eventually, English History Paper 2 was shed, thanks to the arrival of R.A.C. Parker, but in other respects his teaching commitments changed little over the years, while the modernists, Dell, Pelling and Morgan, succeeded one another. Menna, of course, continued to provide academic as well as personal support, teaching early modern history to dozens of Queensmen.

The accounts of pupils in the early postwar years in many respects ring true to later generations. There were, of course, peculiar austerities in the period up to 1951, and some admit that they still associate medieval history with minuscule fires, which barely altered the room temperature all day. Some found John severe in his manner as well as his scholarship. Others wondered how he could possibly have acquired such mastery of the printed sources, when his career had been so interrupted by war. After 1945, he supervised graduates whose contribution to the subject is well known to all. He might at times appear aloof, at others more obviously friendly, but he has been unfailingly loyal, and generous with help and advice on academic matters.

Oxford filled up, after the war, with ex-servicemen as both undergraduates and dons. John clearly revelled in helping to revitalise a History Faculty which, in his eyes, contained too many clergymen and rather tired teachers. For him, the 'Age of Faith' had little appeal, and his stoutly secularist approach clearly inspired many, just as his lectures, both at that time and later on, attracted large and faithful audiences, which appreciated his clarity of thought, lucidity of expression, and care to ensure, even if only by means of the famous cough, that undergraduates had the chance to keep up in their note-taking.

John demanded a great deal of his tutorial pupils, and was prepared to give as much and more in return. In the late sixties, a whole prelim. tutorial group might have been observed on the book-strewn floor of his study, crawling round a map of Anglo-Saxon England, in an attempt to unravel the doings recorded in Bede's *History*. Sometimes, tutorial pupils might wish that this same floor would open to receive them, when a piercingly detailed question was asked about twelfth-century England. Often, John's generosity with his time would cause the last pupil before dinner to forfeit his soup, though generally in return for a glass of sherry. Tutorials could well be two-part affairs, playing havoc with individual schedules, but also vividly demonstrating one of John's most treasured characteristics, his concern for his pupils' humanity, as well as their historical scholarship. After a piece of scathing criticism, the word 'Sorry!' would always be added, indicating, in a way which many who were not Prestwich pupils seem not to understand, the vital difference between going for the man and going for the ball. If there is one phrase from tutorials, though, which encapsulates John's approach to history, it is 'What's your evidence?'.

In view of his gifts, freely offered to so many, it is sad that the Prestwich achievement is not available on a larger scale in print. He has clearly not seen the need, either to acquire new-fangled doctorates in exchange for theses, or to display his wares in garishly-covered volumes in bookshops. Thus, much of his precious, painstakingly-acquired knowledge has been passed on in lectures and tutorials. Nonetheless, although his Domesday thesis has not seen the light of day, he has given a series of fine articles to the reading public. His acute analysis of historical debates and controversies is well displayed in 'Anglo-Norman feudalism and the problem of continuity' (*Past and Present*, xxvi, 1963, 39—57), and his mastery of detail in 'King Aethelhere and the battle of the Winwaed' (*EHR*, lxxxiii, 1968, 89—95). However, his most important contribution to medieval history must surely be his work on war finance in the Anglo-Norman monarchy. His seminal article, 'War and finance in the Anglo-Norman state' (*TRHS*, 5th ser., iv, 1954, 19—43) and his more recent 'The military household of the Norman kings' (*EHR*, xcvi, 1—35) have ensured that he is widely known for his original insights, both into the detailed evidence and into the real meaning and value of the concepts of 'feudalism' and 'bastard feudalism', which are often misused by minds less precise and rigorous than his. Indeed, the sheer brilliance of his mind should never be obscured by an excessive concentration on his mastery of detail. His qualities were never better displayed than when he expounded, to his Political Thought pupils, the products of Thomas Hobbes's robust intellect. All those whom he taught, both Queensmen and others, including the ladies of St Hilda's, have cause to be grateful for John's refusal to tolerate either ignorance or sloppy thinking. During the upheavals of 1968, more than one undergraduate from another School was reduced to silence by his insistence on the accurate definition of the fashionable phrases of the moment, such as the 'affirmation' of 'rights'.

Indeed, despite the importance of his massive scholarship, it would be wrong to disregard the qualities which he has shown as a social being, both in Queen's and outside. A powerful figure in College affairs, who gave strength and confidence to his protégés, John was also a humane presence, a graceful holder of the office of Senior Fellow, who helped Common Room occasions to run more smoothly than they would otherwise have done, and, in the early seventies, even secured a croquet set for the diversion of the junior fellows, beholding with a benevolent eye some of the resulting revels. His concern also followed his pupils when they moved from the College to other pastures. It was, however, a recognition of his talents and achievements in circles beyond the confines of Oxford which resulted in an invitation from the British Academy, in 1980, to lecture to the Accademia Nazionale dei Lincei in Rome, on 'Richard Coeur de Lion: *rex bellicosus*' (*Accademia Nazionale dei Lincei. Problemi attuali di scienza e di cultura*, 253, 1981, 3—15). On this occasion, John represented British scholarship, together with his former pupils, Holt and Gillingham, who quickly became known as 'l'Équipe Prestwich'. The Oxford History Faculty itself paid its own tribute by inviting J.O.P. to give the 1983 Ford lectures. Once again, an enormous audience of dons and undergraduates was treated to a display of John's finest qualities as a historian. Some of the less experienced listeners may not have grasped all the witty and acute references to current controversies which delighted his colleagues, but all must have benefited from his clarity and learning. It is to be hoped that John will not be offended or embarrassed to be told not only of the esteem but also of the affection in which he is held by his pupils, including those who offer him this volume.

WAR AND GOVERNMENT
IN THE MIDDLE AGES

THE BASQUES IN AQUITAINE AND NAVARRE: PROBLEMS OF FRONTIER GOVERNMENT

Roger Collins

'Les Basques sont commes les femmes honêtes; ils n'ont pas d'histoire' was the, doubtless despairing, comment of one French *savant* when faced with the intractable problems of the origins and early history of the Basques. Questions of the genesis of that enigmatic people revolve around purely linguistic arguments, and look, for the moment at least, to be ultimately insoluble, although hypotheses abound.[1] For the Early Medieval historian, the total absence of any internal evidence relating to the social organisation and culture of the Basques, and the resulting necessary dependence upon fragmentary and often apparently contradictory scraps of external evidence, in the form of brief annalistic entries and notices occasionally afforded them by the chroniclers of their hostile neighbours, can prove equally demoralising. However, the contemporary importance of the Basques in respect of both Spain and France, and their modern political aspirations, and sense of separate racial and cultural identity, would alone justify an attempt to understand something of their history in the sixth to tenth centuries; in which period they both start to make, for the first time, a clear impression in the historical records of those neighbouring peoples, who sought to dominate or to contain them, and also establish their distinctive presence, not only in the Western Pyrenees, but also in Aquitaine south of the Garonne, the future Gascony. In addition, their history at this time well illustrates the character and problems of a frontier zone, difficult in its terrain but important for its routes of communication, placed between two generally antagonistic and expansionary powers: the Visigothic monarchy and then the Umayyad Amirate of Córdoba to the south in the Iberian peninsula, and the Merovingian and Carolingian rulers of Francia to the north.

It is possible, to plot, using toponyms, albeit approximately, the areas occupied by Basque speaking tribes, who might generically be entitled the *Vascones*, in the period before the Arab conquest of Spain in the early eighth century. There are some dangers here, particularly in respect of the possible foundation of new settlements by Basque speakers at a later period. Thus for example, the colonisation of Castille and the Rioja in the ninth and tenth centuries may have introduced new settlement names of Basque origin into those regions.[2] However, the existence of Basque names for such natural features as mountains and rivers, generally of greater antiquity than those of settlements,

---

[1] Julio Caro Baroja, *Sobre la Lengua Vasca*, San Sebastian N.D.; Ramon Menéndez Pidal, *En torno a la Lengua Vasca*, Buenos Aires 1962; On these controversies, and for the origins and early history of the Basques see in general Roger Collins, *The Basques*, Oxford, forthcoming.
[2] Jose J.B. Merino Urrutia, *La Lengua Vasca en La Rioja y Burgos*, Logroño 1978, 12—13.

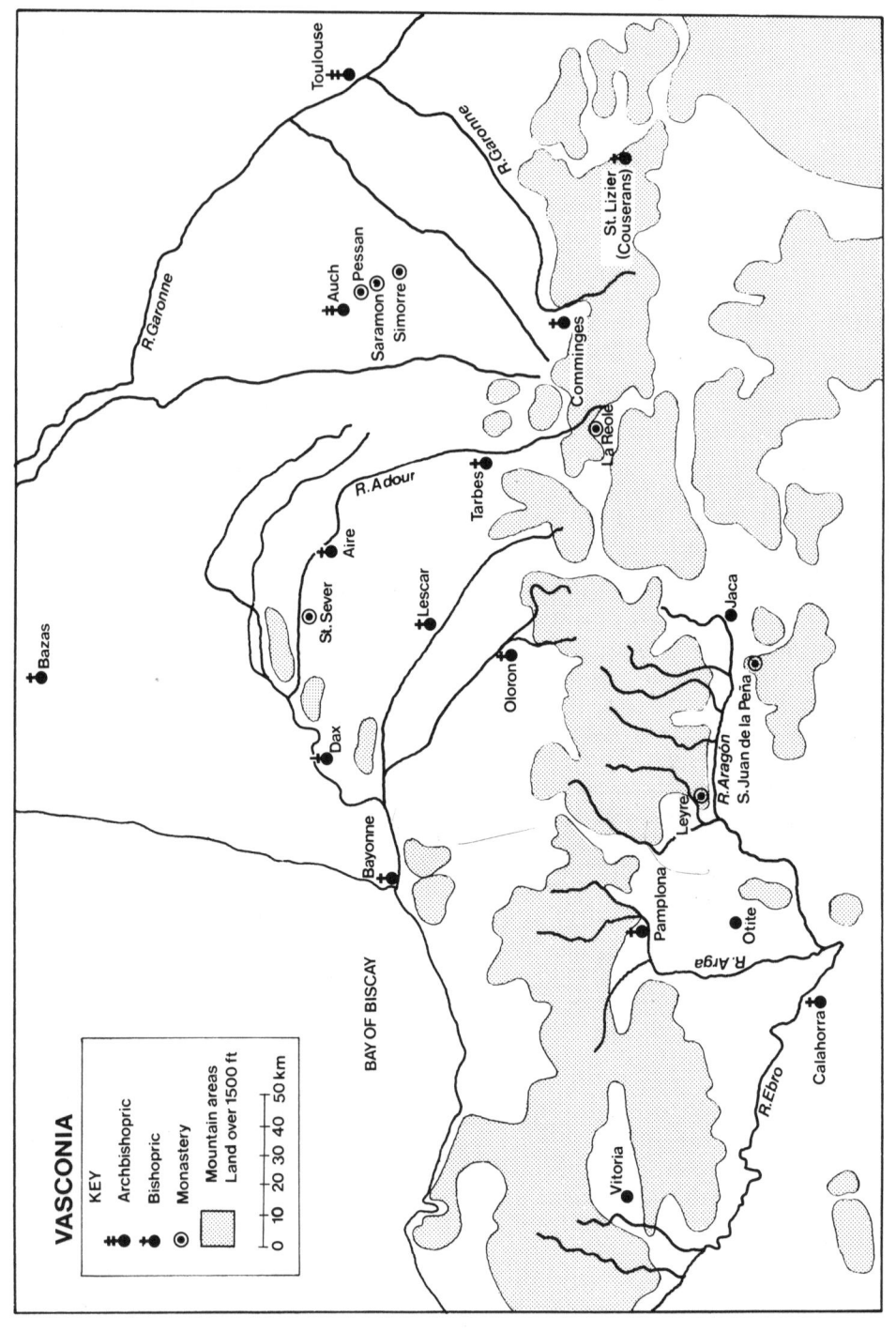

can provide a corrective. The results suggest a distribution of Basque tribes, not only in the area of the modern Spanish provinces of Vizcaya, Alava and Guipuzcoa, but also over the whole of the middle Pyrenees and upper Ebro valley, the nuclei of the kingdoms of Navarre and Aragón, and also over the western fringes of Castille, in the modern province of Burgos. As for the extension northwards over the Pyrenees into southern Aquitaine, while clearly Basque settlement names could date from the documented period of their occupation, beginning in the late sixth century, the lack of impact on the names of natural features beyond the fringes of the mountains would substantiate the belief that their penetration of the area was relatively recent.[3]

The existence of basically mountain dwelling tribes all along the northern coastal region of the Iberian peninsula, from Galicia to the central Pyrenees, presented the greatest military threat that had to be faced by the Roman administration in Spain and across the western Pyrenees in the province of *Novempopulana*, or southern Aquitaine.[4] The depredations of the largely unassimilated and unpacified mountain tribes against the settled regions, to the south in the Meseta and the Ebro valley, and to the north in the area of the future Gascony, necessitated the maintenance of military forces in these parts right up to the ending of effective Roman rule in Spain and Aquitaine in the early fifth century.[5]

The greater attention to this interior frontier, and the main thrust of Roman military and colonizing activity, was directed against the western end of this long series of mountain ranges and their inhabitants, probably as a result of their greater potential economic value to the Empire. The Asturias was a major source of silver, as well as of recruits for the army, during the early imperial centuries.[6] On the other hand, apart from the needs of the defence of the civilian settlements of the upper Ebro and the maintaining of the route across the mountains to Aquitaine, the Romans showed much less interest in the Pyrenean regions; perhaps largely as a result of the even less tractable nature of the terrain, but also because it had less to offer them materially.

Christianity seems to have failed to penetrate the Basque region during the Roman period, and indeed was fairly slow to develop in the adjacent mountainous areas of the west.[7] Bishoprics did come into existence in Lugo, Astorga, León and some other Roman settlements in the fourth and fifth centuries, but there is no evidence of one at Pamplona before 589, and that was probably intended to serve the needs of the inhabitants of the upper Ebro valley, rather than of the mountains to the north.[8] In Novempopulana, on the other hand, all of the major *Civitates* listed in the *Notitia Galliarum* seem to

---

3 Luis Michelena, 'Toponomia', *Fontes Linguae Vasconum, Studia et Documenta*, Pamplona 1971; for place names in Gascony see below notes 29 and 30.
4 Abilio Barbero and Marcelo Vigil, *Sobre los Orígenes Sociales de la Reconquista*, Barcelona 1974, 13—51.
5 *Notitia Dignitatum* Oc. XLII, 18—19, 26, ed. Otto Seeck, Frankfurt am Main 1962 (reprint of 1876 edition), 216.
6 Alberto Balil, *Historia Social y Económica de la España Romana (Siglos I—III)*, Madrid 1975, 73—6.
7 Manual C. Díaz y Díaz, 'Early Christianity in Lugo', *Classical Folia*, xxxii, 1978, 243—59.
8 Acts of the Third Council of Toledo (589): *Concilios Visigóticos e Hispano Romanos*, ed. José Vives, Barcelona-Madrid 1963, 138; Bishops of Pamplona or their deputies also signed the *acta* of the Synod of Toledo (610), XIII Toledo (683) and XVI Toledo (693), 407, 434, 521; José Goñi Gaztambide, *Historia de los Obispos de Pamplona*, Pamplona 1979, vol. I, 41—54.

have had bishoprics, at least by the early sixth century, and a group of them, Conserans, Comminges, Bigorre, Oloron and Béarn were to be found along the northern fringes of the Pyrenees.[9] A diocese was also created at *Lapurdum* (Bayonne), but the date of this is unclear and no bishop is attested for the see before the tenth century.[10]

With the removal of the Roman imperial army from the Iberian peninsula the control of the *Limes* confronting the Asturian and Cantabrian mountains seems to have been entrusted to some of the migratory Germanic tribes, notable the Sueves and Hasding Vandals, who forced their way into Spain in the autumn of 409.[11] This arrangement, whereby the Germans were established as federates along the former military frontier in the north, was probably made with the regime of the usurping emperor Maximus and hardly survived his fall in 411. A similar but initially more stable agreement was made between the legitimate emperor Honorius, or rather the military dictator Constantius, and the Visigoths in 418, whereby they were established as federates in southern Aquitaine, with their capital at Toulouse. This has been interpreted as a move intended to protect the Roman provincials against the threat presented by the *Bagaudae*, a not easily defined group of largely peasant rebels who were active in *Armorica* (Brittany) in the years 411—17 and again in the 430s and 440s.[12] On such a view it is hard to understand why the Visigothic military presence was established so far to the south, and Bordeaux might have been expected to have made a more convenient centre for action directed against a threat coming from the north, from Brittany, than Toulouse. It might be more reasonable to assume that the danger was foreseen as coming from the south, from the Pyrenees, and take the form of the raids of the *Vascones*, rather than those of the more distant and probably less formidable *Bagaudae*.

The creation of what rapidly became an independent Visigothic kingdom in south western Gaul and its extension from 456 onwards into Spain once again united these areas under a common authority, and also put an end to a period of considerable turmoil in the peninsula. Amongst the brief annals of the only contemporary Spanish chronicle of that time is a reference to the Suevic king Rechiarius' expedition into *Vasconia* in 449, part of his ill-fated attempt to bring the Ebro valley under his authority.[13] The Visigothic invasion of Spain in 456 and the subsequent transfer of many of their number into the peninsula to settle there, recorded as taking place in the 490s, must have given renewed importance to the Pyrenean passes.[14] Sometime after 466 a Visigothic army

---

9 *Notitia Galliarum* ed. Otto Seeck, Frankfurt am Main 1962, 271-2; Louis Duchesne, *Fastes Episcopaux de l'Ancienne Gaule*, 2nd. ed. Paris 1910, II, 89—102.

10 Duchesne 89; A. Oïhenart, *Notitia Utriusque Vasconiae*, Paris 1638, 545—6. Even this depends upon a highly suspect charter: *Le Livre d'or de Bayonne* ed. J. Bidache, Pau 1906, doc. I, 1—3.

11 Orosius, *Historiarum adversus Paganos Libri VII*, VII, xl, ed. C. Zangemeister, Hildesheim 1967, 548—52; E.A. Thompson, 'The End of Roman Spain I', *Nottingham Medieval Studies*, xx, 1976, 18—28, but see the arguments of R.J.H. Collins, *Early Medieval Spain*, London 1983, ch. I.

12 E.A. Thompson, 'The Settlement of the Barbarians in Southern Gaul', *Journal of Roman Studies*, xlvi, 1956, 65—75.

13 Hydatius, *Chronicle* s.a. 449, ed. Alain Tranoy, *Sources Chrétiennes* 218, Paris 1974, 142.

14 *Chronicorum Caesaraugustanorum Reliquiae* s.a. 494, 497, ed. Theodor Mommsen, *MGH, Auctores Antiquissimi* XI, Berlin 1894, 222.

came, probably via Roncesvalles, to occupy Pamplona on its way to take Zaragoza and add the whole of the Ebro valley to the rapidly expanding Hispano-Gallic kingdom of its monarch Euric (466—84).[15] However, the defeat of his son Alaric II by the Franks at Vouillé in 507, and the resulting loss of all the Visigothic territories in Gaul, other than Septimania, turned the Pyrenees once more into a frontier zone between hostile realms.

Sources are far from plentiful for this period, and apart from the few details to be found in the work of the Galician chronicler Bishop Hydatius, which ends in 469, information about the Basques and their region is entirely lacking until the late sixth century, from when onwards they start to make almost regular appearances in both Frankish and Visigothic chronicles and histories. But it is clear that a significant development has taken place in the intervening period: a large-scale expansion of the Basques to the north of the Pyrenees into Aquitaine below the Garonne had certainly got under way by the second half of the sixth century. Gregory of Tours in his *Histories* records the defeats in 581 and 587 of two Frankish expeditions against the *Vascones*, the first in 'Vasconia' and the second, significantly, on the plains of Aquitaine.[16] From the same period comes a poem of Venantius Fortunatus dedicated to a Count Galactorius, who is praised for his defence of Aquitaine against *Cantabri* and *Vascones*.[17] By 602 the Basques had clearly established a grip on at least some of the lands that were to be the later Gascony; for in that year those north of the Pyrenees were defeated by the forces of the Frankish kings Theodebert II and Theoderic II, and were then subjected to the authority of a *Dux* called Genial, probably not himself a Basque, and were obliged to render annual tribute to the fisc.[18] It is notable that there seems to have been no question of driving them back into the mountains, and by 628 an area of southern Aquitaine is, for the first time, being called 'Wasconia' in Frankish sources.

It has been suggested that this process of migration and occupation, despite military defeat, by the Basques of the area of the former Roman province of Novempopulana resulted from the pressure then being put upon them in their Pyrenean homelands by the Visigothic king Leovigild (569—86) and some of his successors.[19] Thus in 581, the year of their victory over the Frankish *Dux* Bladast, the *Vascones* were themselves subjected to attack by the Visigothic king, who penetrated into the mountains and celebrated his triumph there by the foundation of the town of Victoriacum.[20] His son Reccared also campaigned in *Vasconia*, as did the forces of two later kings Sisebut (612—21) and Suinthila (621—31), the latter of whom is also attributed with the foundation

---

15 Isidore of Seville, *Historia Gothorum* xxxiv, ed. Theodor Mommsen, *MGH, Auctores Antiquissimi* XI, Berlin 1894, 281.
16 Gregory of Tours, *Libri Historiarum Decem* VI, xii, and IX, vii, ed. Bruno Krusch and Wilhelm Levison, *MGH, Scriptores Rerum Merovingicarum* I (re-edition), Hanover 1951, 283, 420—1.
17 Venantius Fortunatus, *Opera Poetica* X, xix, ed. F. Leo, *MGH, Auctores Antiquissimi* IV, i, Berlin 1881, 251—2.
18 *The Fourth Book of the Chronicle of Fredegar* 21, ed. J.M. Wallace-Hadrill, London 1960, 14.
19 Barbero and Vigil 52—8.
20 John of Biclar, *Chronica* s.a. 581, ed. Theodor Mommsen, *MGH, Auctores Antiquissimi* XI, Berlin 1894, 216; often identified with the modern Vitoria (prov. of Alava), but the latter only received its name in 1081, in a grant of *Fueros* by Sancho VI.

of a town in the region.[21] However, it would be unwise to regard the Basque tribes at this time as having much homogeneity. Events on one side of the Pyrenees might but would not necessarily have to affect those on the other. Moreover it might as reasonably be argued that the cause of the military successes of the Visigothic kings was the prior migration of some of the tribes into southern Aquitaine; nor is it likely that a defeated population driven from its mountain homeland would have been able so successfully to resist the pressure of the Frankish assaults. It is quite possible that their tenacity resulted from a slightly longer occupation of the area of Gascony than our sources can now indicate. Indeed the removal of the Visigothic military presence from southern Aquitaine after the disaster of Vouillé, which was not compensated for by comparable Frankish involvement in the area before the 580s, may have provided the opportunity for the Basques to obtain that grip on the region, which could not be shaken by the campaigns directed against them in the early seventh century.

The Franks may have had other interests, apart from the need to curb the expansion into their territory of the Basque tribes, in concentrating their attentions at this time on the western Pyrenees. The weakened Visigothic kingdom created in Spain after Vouillé had been subjected to continuing Frankish attack in the sixth century before the accession of Leovigild, largely directed at Septimania and around the eastern flanks of the Pyrenees. The virtual unification of the peninsula and the revitalisation of the Visigothic monarchy by that king affected the balance of power betweeen the kingdoms.[22] Further, the divisions and feuds between the Frankish monarchs led to the development of more active diplomatic interchange between some of them and the Visigothic realm.[23] Communication across the Pyrenees grew in importance in the later sixth century, and for the Neustrian, and conceivably the Austrasian Frankish kingdoms, this will have meant via the western passes such as Roncesvalles, rather than through the Burgundian kingdom and the eastern route around the mountains. In addition, with the Visigothic grip on Septimania strengthened during the reigns of Leovigild and Reccared, a military presence in the western Pyrenees gave the Franks control of the only alternative route of entry into the Iberian peninsula.

That they had such a presence is indicated by a statement in the work of the mid-seventh century Burgundian chronicler known as Fredegar. He refers to the Visigothic king Sisebut regaining control of *Cantabria*, which he records as having been for a few years previously under the rule of the Franks, led by the *Dux* Francio.[24] This claim by Fredegar has been derided, and on the face of it with good reason.[25] Cantabria, as it is known today, is roughly the central part of the mountainous region of northern Spain, and it might well be wondered what the Franks were doing there and how they got themselves to such parts. The problem is one of shifting geographical terminology. Late sixth and early seventh century Spanish sources also refer to *Cantabria*. The chronicler John

21 Isidore lxiii, 292—3; the city was *Ologicus* (Olite).
22 E.A. Thompson, *The Goths in Spain*, Oxford 1969, 60—4, 74—6.
23 The letters of Count Bulgar, *Epistolae* X—XVI in *Miscellanea Wisigothica*, ed. Juan Gil, Seville 1972, 30—44; Fredegar IV, 30—1, 20—1.
24 Fredegar IV, 33, 21.
25 Fredegar IV, 33, 21 note 3.

of Biclar records the subjection of such a region and the destruction of its ruling body, the *Senatus Cantabriae*, by Leovigild in 574.[26] Again, by itself, it might by thought that this reference is to the area of the modern region, between the Asturias and the Basque provinces. However, the same episode is referred to in the *Vita Sancti Aemiliani*, written by Bishop Braulio of Zaragoza in the early seventh century. Its subject, the hermit Aemilian, had various encounters with members of that *Senatus Cantabriae*, and indeed prophesied its violent fate.[27] It is equally clear, however, that Aemilian's activities, which extended into the 580s, were confined exclusively to the Rioja, and thus it must have been in that region that this body was established, and to which the term *Cantabrica* or *Cantabria* was at that time applied. It should be noticed, too, that the poem of Venantius Fortunatus to Galactorius refers to the ravages of the *Cantabri* as well as the *Vascones*, and again this makes renewed sense if it can be taken that the people thus referred to came from the western Pyrenees rather than from northern Spain. Thus it is possible to restore Fredegar's credibility, in this respect at least, and believe that the Franks did cross the Pyrenees, quite possibly in the wake of their campaign in 602, and occupied a part or all of the upper Ebro valley, until expelled by the generals of King Sisebut about a decade later.

It has proved virtually impossible to assess the effects on the region as a whole or even the extent and distribution of the Basque settlement of Aquitaine south of the Garonne. Archaeology has not been able to help, nor are place names an unambiguous guide.[28] Some have argued that what appear to be Basque toponyms are in fact names from a pre-Roman and non-Celtic Aquitainian language, closely akin to that of the *Vascones*.[29] This, it is held, serves to show the limited character of the Romanisation of the area, indicated by the survival of these archaic names, rather than the pattern of settlement of the Basque invaders of the sixth century. Such a disputed interpretation leaves the problem almost insoluble, though the balance of probability may favour the Basque rather than ancient Aquitainian viewpoint.[30] However, neither place name nor any other form of evidence can corroborate a few generalised statements in the writings of Fredegar and the seventh century Cosmographer of Ravenna that imply Basque control of all of Aquitaine, right up to the river Loire.[31] Details of events in which they participated, and the somewhat treacherous toponyms, would seem to limit their areas of activity to the south of the Garonne.

Their social impact on the region at this time is almost incalculable. The only extant evidence relating to the towns of the former *Novempopulana* is both limited and negative. Some of the several episcopal sees of the area that had been in existence in the early sixth century were still recorded in the late

26 John of Biclar s.a. 574, 213.
27 Braulio of Zaragoza, *Vita Sancti Aemiliani* xxvi, ed. Luis Vázquez de Parga, Madrid 1943, 34; Cantabria = Rioja, see Oïhenart 16—18.
28 Edward James, *The Merovingian Archaeology of South-West Gaul*, 2 vols. Oxford 1977, 207—10.
29 J. Séguy, 'La Colonisation Romaine et Préromaine en Gascogne et en Aragon' in his *Studien zur romanischen Namenkunde*, Munich 1956, 103—113.
30 See the examples cited in Charles Rostaing, *Les Noms de Lieux*, 9th ed. Paris 1980, 122—4.
31 *Ravennatis Anonymi Cosmographia* IV, 40—1, ed. J. Schnetz, Leipzig 1940, 77—8; for Fredegar, see examples cited below in notes 53 and 54.

seventh. A number of their bishops signed the acts of an ecclesiastical council held at Bordeaux in the reign of Childeric II (662—675).[32] That those from other sees of the region such as Dax or Bigorre did not, is far from implying that those bishoprics were no longer functioning, let alone that their towns had or had not ceased to exist. It is possible that archaeology may be able to be of service here in the future, but relevant historical records are too scanty to support even the most provisional of reconstructions.

On the Spanish side of the Pyrenees, the Basques were still described as being pagans in the middle of the seventh century, but it has been suggested that this period saw the first serious inroads being made by Christianity amongst those to the north of the mountains, and that this resulted from the activities of St Amandus.[33] This Amandus was an Aquitainian noble, who, after a short time spent as a hermit at Bourges, had a vision of St Peter, who instructed him to preach the Gospel to the pagans, and thenceforth he seems to have acted as an itinerant missionary, attempting to evangelize the Frisians, the Slavs, the Franks themselves, and, at an early stage in his career, the Basques. His activities extended from the 630s until his death in 684, and in the first part of his career, having served at court, he enjoyed the patronage of the Frankish king Dagobert I (623—639).[34] However, the only evidence relating to his attempted proselytising of the Basques comes from his *Vita*, written after his death by his disciple the monk Baudemund, and which is far from giving the impression that he was successful.[35] The encounter between Amandus and the Basques, as described by Baudemund in the twentieth chapter of his work, was clearly brief and fruitless. Indeed the worthy man's only satisfaction in the episode seems to have come from seeing one of the Basques, who had abused him more forcefully than the rest, seized by demonic possession and die in a fit.

The problem of the Christianizing of the Basques, and with it inevitably their acceptance of a measure of the common Latin culture of their Gallo-Roman and Visigothic neighbours, thus remains, like so much else, incapable of precise resolution. For the Spanish side of the Pyrenees, it has been suggested that the decisive influence may well have been that exercised by hermits establishing themselves in cave dwellings in the Basque mountain regions.[36] Braulio's *Life of Aemilian* certainly records the activities of one such figure, and the stories of his miraculous cures and interventions show something of his dealings with the indigenous inhabitants of the probably largely Basque Rioja countryside. The existence of cave churches in the mountains in the province of Santander, that are dated to the seventh century, indicate that he was by no means unique.[37] The career and writings of the late seventh century priest and hermit Valerius give evidence for a similar development further west, in the Bierzo.[38]

32 *Concilium Modogarnomense seu Burdegalense* in *Concilia Galliae*, ed. C. de Clercq, *Corpus Christianorum Series Latina* CXLVIII A, Turnholt 1963, 312—3.
33 Barbero and Vigil 94 and note 154.
34 Carl Albrecht Bernoulli, *Die Heiligen der Merowinger*, Tübingen 1900, 147—9.
35 Baudemund, *Vita Sancti Amandi Episcopi Traiectensis*, ed. Bruno Krusch, *MGH, Scriptores Rerum Merovingicarum* V, Berlin 1910, 428—49, especially 443—4.
36 Barbero and Vigil 188—90.
37 J. González Echegaray, *Los Cántabros*, Madrid 1966, 236—7.
38 Consuelo M. Aherne, *Valerio of Bierzo*, Washington D.C. 1949, especially the texts, 68—159.

The Frankish approach may have been initially more direct, and it is possible, though not stated by Baudemund, that Amandus' unsuccessful attempt at conversion of the Basques was deliberately prompted by King Dagobert, and should be linked to his attempt to impose political organisation on the tribes, and to bring them within the orbit of the Frankish administrative system. On the death of their father, Chlotar II (584—629), Dagobert established his brother Charibert II (629—632) as king in Aquitaine, with his seat at Toulouse.[39] This marked the first effort by the Merovingians to impose effective royal authority in the area, and may mark a response to the Aquitainians' sense of separate identity, as well as to the problems posed by the establishment of the Basques in 'Wasconia'.[40] It was certainly with this latter that the new king sought to deal, or rather his advisers did, for the monarch himself was reputedly half-witted.[41] In 630 or 631 his armies overran *Wasconia*, and thus, as Fredegar put it 'somewhat extended his kingdom'.[42] It is perhaps worthy of note that at this time, in 631, his brother Dagobert promoted the successful usurpation of the Visigothic throne by Sisenand (631—6), thus replacing King Suinthila who had recently been campaigning, perhaps too effectively, in the Basque territories to the south of the Pyrenees.[43]

The death of Charibert II and the replacement of his regime by that of Dagobert was followed by a large scale revolt by the Basques against the newly imposed Frankish domination. In 635 Dagobert's generals were successful in crushing Basque resistance, despite one reverse that they suffered, and furious reprisals were directed against the rebels, driven to seek refuge in the Pyrenees. One of the victors, a Saxon called Aighyna, formerly an opponent of the advisers of King Charibert, was imposed on the re-subjugated Basques as *Dux*. He may have based his administration at Bordeaux, but as well as having responsibility for the military overseeing of the region, he also acted as intermediary for its inhabitants with the king. Fredegar's account of the Basque embassy to Dagobert in 636, which Aighyna led, refers to the *Seniores* of the region.[44] That the tribal leaders of the people are thereby indicated would seem a reasonable guess, but no further details survive that could illuminate the character of Basque society, government or law at this period.

Despite the oaths of loyalty taken by the Basque leaders to the King, his sons and to the Frankish kingdom, Fredegar implies that their subjection proved short-lived.[45] References from later in the century indicate that Gascony became a convenient and secure place of refuge for political exiles from the Frankish kingdoms, and in the eighth century a valuable source of military manpower for the rulers of Aquitaine in their attempts to secure and maintain their independence.[46] Across the Pyrenees, in the Visigothic kingdom, the

---

39 Fredegar IV, 57, 47—8.
40 M. Rouche, *L'Aquitaine des Wisigoths aux Arabes*, 2 vols. Lille 1977, 75—100; I cannot follow Rouche in seeing the reign of Chramn and the usurpation of Gondovald as early experiments in the creation of an Aquitainian monarchy.
41 Fredegar IV, 56, 47.
42 Fredegar IV, 57, 48 (editor's translation).
43 Fredegar IV, 73.
44 Fredegar IV, 78, 65—7.
45 Fredegar IV, 78, 67.
46 Continuations of Fredegar 2, 10, 25, ed. J.M. Wallace-Hadrill, *The Fourth Book of the Chronicle of Fredegar*, London 1960, 82, 89, 98.

campaigns of the early seventh century proved equally unavailing in bringing the Basques to heel and bringing them to accept royal authority. They took advantage of a revolt against King Reccesuinth (649—72) in the Ebro valley in c. 654 to ravage the area around Zaragoza, and Wamba (672—80) was campaigning against them when faced by the rebellion of Paul in the province of Narbonne in the first year of his reign.[47] Similarly the last of the Visigothic kings, Roderic (710—11), was absent in the north, having taken the field against the Basques, when the Arabs landed in Spain.[48] One of the all too few personal records to be found in the sparse records relating to this period is the verse epitaph of a certain Oppila, probably a member of the Gothic aristocracy, which reports his death at the hands of the *Vascones* in the year 642.[49]

The first half of the eighth century saw a considerable alteration in the importance of the western Pyrenean regions and of Gascony. This resulted firstly from the rise in Aquitaine of a line of independent Dukes, who may have accorded themselves a royal title, and secondly from the establishment of the Arabs in Spain. The use of Basque armies by the Duke Eudo (d. 735) may explain the extension of the term *Wasconia* to cover the whole of his realm of Aquitaine, and his achievement up till 732 of a considerable measure of autonomy for the region. However, Eudo was threatened on two sides, and initially the more serious danger was to be anticipated from the south. After their relatively speedy subjugation of Spain, the Arabs and their Berber mercenaries were directed in a series of raids across the Pyrenees by successive governors. Whilst the main thrust of these was aimed around the eastern edge of the mountains into the former Visigothic *Septimania*, where an independent kingdom briefly survived until 720, and then on into Provence, some went via Pamplona over the western end of the Pyrenees into Aquitaine.[50]

Eudo's attempt in 729 to block at least some of the routes of access into his territories by an alliance with Munnuz, one of the Berber leaders in Spain, who had been established in the frontier region of Cerdanya, had fatal consequences.[51] Racial and cultural antagonism between the Arabs and the indigenous Berbers in North Africa created repercussions in *Al-Andalus*, or Arab-ruled Spain, and it was as the result of ill-treatment of his people in Africa that Munnuz, who may well have been a Christian, rebelled against the Arab governor. His speedy suppression exposed his erstwhile ally Duke Eudo to reprisals, which took the form of a large scale raid on Aquitaine by the governor Abd al-Rahman ibn Abd-Allah al-Ghefeki in 732. The Aquitainian (and Basque?) forces were routed on the Garonne, and Eudo was forced to appeal for aid to the Arnulfing Mayor of the Palace, Charles 'Martel'. The significance of the resulting Frankish victory over the Arab army at Poitiers

---

47 Taio, *In Libri Sententiarum Praefatio, Epistula ad Quiricum Barcinonensem, Patrologia Latina* LXXX, Paris 1863, 727; Julian of Toledo, *Historia Wambae* 9, ed. Theodor Mommsen, *Corpus Christianorum Series Latina* CXV, Turnholt 1976, 224.
48 Al-Makkari, *History of the Mohammedan Dynasties in Spain* IV, 2, tr. Pascual de Gayangos, 2 vols. London 1840—3, 268.
49 *Inscripciones Cristianas de la España Romana y Visigoda* 287, ed. José Vives, 2nd. ed. Barcelona 1969, 90—1.
50 Rouche 101—24.
51 *Chronica Muzarabica* 65, ed. Juan Gil, *Corpus Scriptorum Muzarabicorum*, 2 vols. Madrid 1973, I, 41—3.

has been greatly exaggerated, and the internal disturbances in *Al-Andalus* during the course of the next three decades probably played a more important role in putting an end to the danger of Arab expansion across the Pyrenees.[52] However, its real consequences may rather have been a fatal weakening of Aquitainian military strength and the eventual subjugation of the region by the Arnulfing Mayors, who in 751 transformed themselves into the new Carolingian royal dynasty.

A series of campaigns in the 760s by Pepin 'the Short' and completed by his son Charlemagne, put an end to the authority of the heirs of Eudo.[53] None of these, however, was directed across the Garonne, but the resistance put up by one of the earlier independent Dukes, Chunoald I (735—45), is said to have been supported by the *Wascones* in Aquitaine, in a context that appears to distinguish them from the other elements in the population, called rather anachronistically the *Romani*.[54] The lack of any other evidence makes it impossible to determine how much reliance should be placed upon this apparent ethnographic division. Were there substantial Basque settlements now to be found north of the Garonne? Or is the terminology of this author, the continuator of Fredegar, who was not a native of the region, merely inexact?

The period of Carolingian domination in Aquitaine, when for the first time since the early seventh century Frankish power was extended across the Pyrenees, vitally affected the political organisation of the western Pyrenean area, in that it became once more a frontier region between two relatively sophisticated and powerful states. Initial Frankish intervention was illconceived and premature, occurring even before Aquitaine had been assimilated; for Charlemagne's expedition to the Ebro valley in 778 in support of Berber and *Muwallad* rebels in Zaragoza can be characterised as little more than a fiasco, with the Basques destroying his rearguard in the course of the retreat via the pass of Roncesvalles.[55]

The emergence of an independent kingdom based upon Pamplona, that was to be the nucleus of the later realm of Navarre, is one of the obscurest and yet most controverted developments in the Franco-Spanish frontier regions in the ninth century.[56] It must be admitted that its Basque character is open to question, although its first ruling dynasty was clearly so.[57] Although virtually all of the scant evidence concerning its history in the first two centuries of its existence relates to the areas to the south of the city of Pamplona, that is the upper Ebro valley stretching towards but not including Tudela and Huesca, which region had long been under Roman and then Visigothic domination, it is clear that the kingdom owed its origin largely to the interrelationship of Basques and Franks on the Pyrenean March, and that its authority, when established, extended over some of the Basque mountain areas to the north. The office of

---

52 Collins ch. V; Jean Deviosse, *Charles Martel*, Paris 1978, 159—78.
53 Continuations of Fredegar 41—52, 109—20.
54 Continuations of Fredegar 25, 98.
55 Eginhard, *Vita Caroli Magni Imperatoris* 9, ed. Louis Halphen, Paris 1967, 28—30; *Annales Regni Francorum* s.a. 778, ed. F. Kurze, *MGH, Scriptores Rerum Germanicarum*, Hanover 1895, 50—1.
56 Justo Pérez de Urbel, 'Lo viejo y lo nuevo sobre el origen del Reino de Pamplona'; *Al-Andalus* xix, Granada 1954, 1—42; Claudio Sánchez-Albornoz, 'Problemas de la Historia Navarra del siglo IX', *Cuadernos de Historia de España* xxv-xxvi, Buenos Aires 1957, 5—82.
57 Manuel Ilarri Zabala, *La Tierra Natal de Iñigo Arista*, Bilbao 1980.

Comes Vizcayae, subordinate to the kings of Pamplona, is recorded in the tenth century, and the region between the city and the pass of Roncesvalles appears to have gone under the peculiarly archaic and anachronistic title of *Gallia Comata*.[58] Other Basques further to the west were subjected to the authority of the kings of the Asturias from the middle of the eighth century, and a fluctuating frontier existed between that realm and Pamplona.[59]

Effective Carolingian intervention in the areas south of the Pyrenees began in the aftermath of Charlemagne's establishment of his son Louis as King of Aquitaine in 781, although all of the military undertakings of the new monarch were conducted by Charlemagne's sanction or on his command. As far as Spain was concerned these were largely directed, with initial success, at the eastern end of the Pyrenees, and a new March was created by the conquest of Barcelona in 801.[60] It is unlikely that Frankish intentions in the area went much beyond the establishment, largely by repopulation, of a defensive and self-supporting frontier zone, that would be capable of containing the raids by land and sea directed by the Arab, Berber and *Muwallad* marcher lords of the Ebro valley against the Frankish possessions north of the Pyrenees. This is certainly what the 'Spanish March' became after the failure of King Louis' attempts to take and hold Tarragona and Tortosa between 808 and 810.[61]

That a similar purpose directed Frankish activity in the western Pyrenees at this time is most probable. Pamplona had been occupied by Charlemagne in 778, and its walls were destroyed by him in the course of his retreat to Roncesvalles.[62] In 806 the city was again brought under Frankish rule.[63] In the meantime it had again been subjected to the Umayyad Amirs of Córdoba, but had rebelled against them in 799.[64] There is reason to believe that its leaders soon after formed an alliance with the equally rebellious Banu Kasim, a *Muwallad* family centred around Tudela, who dominated the upper Ebro for most of the ninth century.[65] The return of Frankish power was probably accompanied by the incorporating of the region around Pamplona into the

---

58 Eulogius of Córdoba, *Epistola ad Wiliesindum Pampilonensis Episcopi*, 1, ed. Juan Gil, *Corpus Scriptorum Muzarabicorum*, 2 vols. Madrid 1973, II, 497—8; various theories as to the location of this region are discussed in Claudio Sánchez-Albornoz, 'Sobre la probable localización de la *Gallia Comata*' in his *Orígenes de la Nación Española* III, Oviedo 1975, 651—54; For *Comes Vizcayae*; José M. Lacarra, 'Textos navarros del Códice de Roda', *Estudios de Edad Media de la Corona de Aragón* I, Zaragoza 1945, 238 and note 17.
59 Claudio Sánchez-Albornoz, 'Los Vascos y los Arabes durante los dos primeros siglos de la Reconquista', *Boletín del Instituto Americano de Estudios Vascos* iii, Buenos Aires 1952, 65—79; *Crónica de Alfonso III* s. Alfonso I and Fruela I, ed. Antonio Ubieto Arteta, Valencia 1971, 36—9.
60 Leonce Auzias, *L'Aquitaine Carolingienne*, Toulouse 1937, 1—67; on the success of the Carolingians in the eastern Pyrenees, see Roger Collins, 'Charles the Bald and Wifred the Hairy' in *Charles the Bald: Court and Kingdom*, ed. Margaret Gibson and Janet Nelson, Oxford 1981, 169—89.
61 'Astronomer', *Vita Hludovici Imperatoris* 14—16, ed. R. Rau, *Quellen zur karolingischen Reichsgeschichte* I, Darmstadt 1974, 276—82; but for the Arab accounts of these events: Ibn el-Athir, *Annales du Maghreb et de l'Espagne* tr. E. Fagnan, Algiers 1904, 172; Al-Makkari 104.
62 *Annales Regni Francorum* s.a. 778.
63 *Annales Regni Francorum* s.a. 806.
64 *Muktabis* of Ibn Hayyān, ed. and tr. E. Lévi-Provençal and E. Garcia Gomez, 'Textos inéditos del Muqtabis de Ibn Hayyān sobre los orígenes del Reino de Pamplona', *Al-Andalus* xix, 1954, 296—7.
65 Sánchez-Albornoz, 'Problemas', 273—83.

administrative structure, then being developed, of a western Pyrenean March, possibly under the authority of a *Marchio* based at Toulouse. The Basques in Gascony are again recorded as being under the direction of a royally appointed official, the *Comes Wasconiae*, who, in the ninth century, generally appears to have been of Basque origin.[66] Whether his authority was extended to cover the 'Pamplonans and Navarrese', as the Franks called them, or they were given a Count of their own, is not known.[67] A county certainly existed in the valley of the river Aragón by the middle of the ninth century, which, although linked to the newly emerged Kingdom of Pamplona, continued to refer to the Frankish kings in its charters, and it may have originally been a Carolingian creation.[68]

Unlike Catalonia, the March in the western Pyrenees failed to survive, or to display any loyalty to the Frankish dynasty. In 813 King Louis, having forced Basque rebels north of the mountains to submit at Dax, crossed to Pamplona, where, as the author of the anonymous *Vita Hludovici* rather lamely put it, 'he settled matters'. During his return he took precautions so as not to be ambushed in the passes.[69] The next Frankish expedition was less wary, and when in 824 an army led by Counts Aeblus and Asinar, having suppressed a rebellion in Pamplona, was withdrawing via Roncesvalles, it was set upon and almost totally destroyed. This second battle of Roncesvalles, unlike the first, had significant consequences in that it marked the end of Carolingian attempts to establish a permanent presence across the western Pyrenees. Instead an independent kingdom of Pamplona or Navarre came into being, which, in reaction to the Frankish threat and the danger presented by the expansion of its western neighbour, the Kingdom of the Asturias, tended to ally with the powerful Banu Kasim, or on occasion with the Umayyad Amirs. Indeed after the battle at Roncesvalles the captive Count Aeblus was sent as a present to Córdoba. Asinar, as a fellow Basque, was released.[70].

It is noteworthy that the army sent to Pamplona in 824 was largely Basque in composition, and later, when Ordoño I (850—66) of the Asturias purchased their aid, Basque forces from Gascony fought for him against the Banu Kasim and their ally King Garcia of Pamplona.[71] Despite such acts as the freeing of Count Asinar, based upon racial identity, the Basques were clearly happy to fight each other. Nor was their political loyalty consistent. The Count of the Basques in Gascony, Sancho, probably brother of that Count Asinar defeated in 824, opposed King Pepin II of Aquitaine (838—48) in his struggles against his uncle Charles the Bald, King of West Francia, then seems to have afforded him refuge after final defeat in 848, only to hand him over to the victor in 852.[72] The existence of a Kingdom of Aquitaine, north of the Garonne, made

66 *Annales Bertiniani* s.a. 836, ed. R. Rau, *Quellen zur karolingischen Reichsgeschichte* II, Darmstadt 1972, 30.
67 *Annales Regni Francorum* s.a. 806. 'Navarrese' and 'Navarre' are not found in Spanish sources until a much later date. The Kingdom is first so called in the eleventh century.
68 *Cartulário de Siresa* 1, ed. Antonio Ubierto Arteta, Valencia 1960; also *Cartulário de Obarra*, Madrid: Archivo Historico Nacional, Códices 1048B, doc. 1.
69 *Vita Hludovici* 18, 282—4.
70 *Annales Regni Francorum* s.a. 824; *Vita Hludovici* 37, 320.
71 *Annales Regni Francorum* s.a. 824; Auzias 266—7 and notes 59—60.
72 *Annales Bertiniani* s.a. 836, 852; Auzias 263—7.

the Basques natural allies of its enemies, but they were equally hostile to any power that replaced it. They were quick to take advantage of Frankish weakness, and in the tenth century at least, willing to collaborate with Viking raiders. When Bishop Leo of Bayonne was fleeing from a Viking attack, Basques drove him back into the town to his death (c. 900 A.D.).[73]

The history of Gascony in the ninth and tenth centuries is if anything even obscurer than that of the neighbouring kingdom of Navarre. By the later ninth century the Counts, nominally Frankish royal appointees, had been replaced by a line of hereditary Dukes, whose dynasty was to extend into the eleventh century, when by genealogical accident it was replaced by that of the Dukes of Aquitaine.[74] Little more than the names of the Dukes is now known, and that is thanks to the survival in the few cartularies of the region of a handful of tenth century documents. It is quite conceivable that these Dukes are of the same family as at least some of the earlier Counts, but the later legend of the origin of their dynasty also portrays the first of the line, Sancho 'Mitarra' (c. 870) as being elected by the Basques and recalled from Castille, of which his father was Count.[75] This mythical episode divorces the Duchy from its more probable origin in Frankish royal creation and relates the ducal family both to that of the later famous Counts of Castille, Fernan Gonzalez and his line, and through them to the royal dynasty of Navarre. Such myth-making, as clearly evidenced in the twelfth century 'Black Cartulary' of Auch, is important for the insight it gives into the historical perceptions of Gascons in subsequent centuries, but it is perhaps more likely that the Duchy derived from the deliberate devolution of royal powers, that in this region at least had rarely been more than theoretical, by the Carolingian monarchs; a process that can be paralleled and more clearly demonstrated as occurring in Catalonia at this same period.[76]

In the tenth century the Duchy of Gascony, which extended as far as Bordeaux and the Garonne to the north and into the middle Pyrenees (the region of Béarn) in the south and east, may have exceeded the area of Basque settlement in its size. The dividing up of this substantial area between subordinate Counts and Viscounts, in the persons of members of the cadet branches of the ducal family, can be shown to have taken place in the early tenth century, principally in the times of Dukes Garcia II (c. 920) and Sancho IV (c. 930), and is perhaps indicative of more settled and sophisticated administration of the Duchy.[77] Significant monastic foundation only commences in the late tenth century, despite spurious claims to antiquity made by some of the houses, and is largely confined to Béarn and an area close to the metropolitan

---

73 *Acta Sanctorum, Martii* I (1668), 93—7, L'Abbé Menjoulet: *Saint Léon, Apôtre de Bayonne*, Bayonne 1876.
74 Jean de Jaurgain, *La Vasconie* 2 vols. Pau 1898, 1902; vol. I, 195—219; genealogical table *ibid* 394.
75 'Cartulaire Noir' doc. II: *De Consulibus Guasconiae* in C. Lacave La Plagne Barris ed. *Cartulaires du Chapitre de l'Eglise Metropolitaine Sainte-Marie d'Auch* Paris-Auch 1899, 6. This story is taken at face value by Jaurgain, op. cit. II, 8, and in the other classic histories of Gascony. See also the *Nomina Comitum Guasconiensium*, Lacarra 248—50.
76 Collins, 'Charles the Bald and Wifred the Hairy', 176—7.
77 'Cartulaire Noir d'Auch docs. III—V, 7—8. Jaurgain, *op cit.* vol. II lists all of these office holders, their family relationships and the evidence for their chronology. However, some of the charters upon which his deductions are based require fuller and more critical examination.

church of Auch.[78] The restoration of bishoprics and diocesan organisation at the heart of the Basque region, along the northern fringes of the Pyrenees, is not recorded before c. 1054. Before that an itinerant 'Bishop of the Gascons', without fixed see, is only known for the period c. 980—1054.[79]

During the whole of the first millenium A.D. the Basques of the western Pyrenees thus successfully resisted domination and assimilation by powerful and sophisticated neighbours, expanded the limits of their own areas of settlement, in the case of southern Aquitaine very substantially so, and presented a constant problem of defence to successive rulers of Spain and France. Culturally they were gradually affected as a result of the attempts to contain them by those whom they threatened, though it is by no means clear that the majority of them were Christians by the end of the tenth century. More tangible are the political changes to which they became subject, again largely as the result of brief periods of alien rule. It is quite possible that some clan identity survived, but larger units of political authority existed in the form of rule of the Kings in Pamplona, and the Counts and Dukes in Gascony. The effects of the Basque preservation of a sense of separate identity through this period, which saw so much more substantial change in most other parts of Europe, continue to be felt up to the present.

---

78 For distribution of monasteries see *Grosser historischer Weltatlas* II, Munich 1979, map 26; for monastic foundations see Louis-Clément de Brugèles, *Chroniques Ecclesiastiques du Diocèse d'Auch*, Toulouse 1746, 34—9, 42—43, 47—8, 180—193, 249, 333—48. For spurious antiquity *ibid*. 180, 187, also 'Cartulaire Noir d'Auch' doc. LXXVII, 77—86. All of these texts need reappraisal.
79 See the episcopal lists and evidences in D. Sammarthani, *Gallia Christiana* I Paris 1715, 965—1330: *Provincia Auxitana*, also the *Instrumenta* 159—204. For the 'Bishops of the Basques' see Estanislao Jaime de Labayra y Goicoechea, *Historia General del Señorio de Bizcaya*, 3 vols, Bilbao—Madrid 1895, vol. I, 179—81.

THE STATUS OF THE NORMAN KNIGHT

R. Allen Brown

At a memorable dinner at The Queen's College, given for his former research pupils on the eve of his retirement, Mr J.O. Prestwich made, as the occasion demanded, an admirable speech. In this he first divided his guests into 'old' historians and 'new' historians, and then, deftly reshuffling and redealing the pack, showed that those who were 'old' were nevertheless sometimes 'new', and those who were 'new' were sometimes not as new as they thought. For myself, I was well pleased to be dealt first as an old historian, and I am quite sure that subsequent illustration of my occasional inadvertent lapses into newness were meant in the kindest fashion. Certainly as an historian I have always been as old as possible, and I become unrepentantly older as time passes and fashions change. Certainly, also, I have never felt older than of late in contemplating knights, and Norman knights especially, in the middle and second half of the eleventh century — a period of some consequence as that of the great Norman expansion into Maine, England and Britain, Italy, and Antioch on the First Crusade. One might, after all, in not too old-fashioned a spirit, call this the particular achievement of the Norman knights. We really ought to know what manner of men these were (not even the most avant-garde have yet made them women) and how they conducted themselves both on the field and off it, in peace as well as war. In fact, perhaps because élites are now out of fashion in the age of the Common Man (and Woman), these supermen have, amongst historians in our time, suffered 'a number of setbacks' and 'a loss of prestige', a severe social demotion, as, for example, Tony Hunt seeks to show in an heroic survey and summary of recent literature upon the subject.[1] The demotion, as it turns out, has been particularly severe in England and among English historians, ever suspicious, it would seem, of foreign (and right wing) things like feudalism, so that, while the good Old English thegn remains as illustrious as ever (five hides and all that), and not even elbowed out of the social scene by housecarls, the alien Norman knight has in some quarters been put firmly in his place as a man of peasant status or none. It seems to me it is high time that he was reasserted as the dominant figure in that society which in fact he did dominate after his resounding victory at Hastings, as he dominated also Normandy, southern Italy and Antioch. In saying this I do not at all wish to be controversial, but merely hope, in an old-fashioned way, that all right-thinking persons will agree with me when I say it.

I had intended to write this paper, on which I have been necessarily brooding for a number of years, without any preliminary reading for the

---

1 Tony Hunt, 'The Emergence of the Knight in France and England, 1000—1200' in *Knighthood in Medieval Literature*, ed. W.H. Jackson, Woodbridge 1981.

occasion, lest I might lose sight of the wood for all the innumerable trees and saplings — in Jolliffe-fashion, one might almost say, for that great man of one's youth always gave the impression of writing what he knew he had to say with very little reference to anybody else. In the event, my courage failed me, and I have tried to read or re-read everything relevant both old and new, upon which I could lay my hands. It has proved a mixed blessing. The best part has been to experience againt the excitement with which I first read Guilhiermoz[2] and Marc Bloch[3] many years ago (the fact that I once read Bloch by candlelight shows how old an historian I am), for the sheer erudition of the one and the continuous perception of the other beggar all description — which is not to say that neither had the other virtue. To begin by bowing the knee — better, doing homage — to both, seems to me appropriate when both are out of fashion, and Guilhiermoz almost vanished even from the footnotes of those who should know better.

Elsewhere, to my relief, things might be worse, at least upon the Continent. Germany, or the German-speaking lands of the German kingdom and Empire, it is agreed, were different and behind the times because of the survival of ancient Carolingian monarchy[4] (like England before 1066), but in France, which matters most as the cradle and very patrimony of feudalism, the knight is still — or, rather, has become again — a person of some consequence in the eleventh century. Though we are no longer allowed to believe with Guilhiermoz and Bloch (and Sir Richard Southern[5]) in the New Men taking over from a former Carolingian nobility in the disintegrating kingdom of the West Franks in the tenth century[6] (the absence of evidence for the lineage of the former being evidently a mere historical accident), the new military élite of knights has nevertheless socially arrived by the mid-eleventh century, when, in the Mâconais and elsewhere, the word *miles* has become a synonym for 'noble', and nobles, their lineage notwithstanding, are content to take it as a title.[7] There is nothing here, therefore, to persuade us to demote those Norman knights (with others from neighbouring lands) who fought and won at Hastings, or those who stayed (and those who came over to join them) to become the new secular ruling class and upper class in England and beyond. Indeed, since no-one on either side of the Channel or Atlantic has yet denied

---

2 P. Guilhiermoz, *Essai sur l'origine de la noblesse en France au moyen âge*, Paris 1902.
3 Marc Bloch, *La société féodale*, Paris 1939—40; *Feudal Society*, trans. L.A. Manyon, London 1961.
4 Thus the polite but firm rebuttal, as applicable to France, of Léopold Génicot's findings (in the second volume of his *L'économie namuroise au bas moyen age: Les hommes, la noblesse*, Louvain 1960) by Georges Duby, 'The nobility in medieval France' (1961), in his *Chivalrous Society*, 96—8. Duby, of course, has in recent years come to dominate this subject. Wherever possible reference will be given here to the collection and translation (by Cynthia Postan) of his more important essays published in this country as *The Chivalrous Society*, London 1977. That most useful volume provides a key to the original French publications (pp. 226—7) and the original date of the French publication will be noted here in parenthesis.
5 See especially the splendid passage in R.W. Southern, *The Making of the Middle Ages*, London 1953, 82 ff.
6 Duby, 98 ff: Jane Martindale, 'The French aristocracy in the early Middle Ages, a reappraisal', *Past and Present* No. 75, 1977.
7 Thus Duby, 'Lineage, nobility and knighthood' (1972); also e.g. 'The history and sociology of the medieval west' (1970), and 'The origins of knighthood' (1967); *Chivalrous Society*, 76—7, 85—6, 158 ff. For Normandy, however, cf. Musset and Bates, cited n. 8 below.

that all nobles or magnates in Normandy itself were New Men at least from 911 if not later,[8] we could almost, as Anglo-Normans, accept the whole Bloch thesis of a new military élite becoming a new social élite to form an aristocracy of knights, and all this before 1066. We can also be more relaxed than our French colleagues on the issue of nobility, since it is generally agreed that in post-Conquest England there was not one, *i.e.* in the strict sense of a closed and hereditary social class with privileges enshrined in law. For my part, all I want is for our knights to be Top People, upper class, real or potential, as I am sure they were, both in their own eyes and in those of others.

However, knights in England in and after 1066 have been far more savagely demoted by English historians than they have been on the Continent; which may at once suggest that something is wrong with us, since they are most unlikely to have lowered their status or diminished their military skills in crossing the Channel — quite the reverse, in fact. Thirty years ago Richard Glover[9] reduced the military potential of the Norman knights at Hastings to mere 'mounted javelineers' indulging in 'infantile' cavalry tactics and, as often as not, 'happily mixing it in on foot'. For all of this, though God may forgive him, I never shall; but meanwhile there are many who, evidently ignorant of the still neglected yet crucial subject of medieval warfare, are more than content to accept and repeat his misapprehensions. Twelve years ago Sally Harvey claimed that an analysis of Domesday Book 'reveals the normal landed basis of the eleventh-century knight to be about 1½ hides' which 'puts him only just above most well-to-do peasants',[10] and these views, too, now find much favour among the *avant-garde*. Very recently indeed John Gillingham found, once more again, little if any difference between the knight and thegn[11] — though perhaps that makes the former more socially respectable. There is no doubt that these are very serious matters, and we may well ask how these views have come about, clean contrary as they are not only to the opinions of past historians but also to those of most of our present Continental colleagues.

We will begin with status since that is very much the present concern of 'new' historians especially, and of their 'demography' (which seems to be the application of the dubious methods of sociology to the past) — though one would do well at the outset to insist with Guilhiermoz and Bloch that in the world of the mid-eleventh century status in secular society was intimately bound up with fighting. Oddly enough, F.M. Stenton, whom most would accept as an old historian, and whom I revere as is appropriate to one in a sense brought up by him and his lady wife, seems in this century to have begun the demotion of the knight in the England of 1066 and after. In 1932 in his

---

8 Cf. Lucien Musset who, while accepting a new aristocracy, keeps his knights humble at least until the mid-eleventh century; and David Bates who has his Norman knight even in 1066 'usually a simple soldier', and seeks to make his contemporary aristocracy a good deal less new than usual, all in accordance with the latest fashion. See Musset, 'L'aristocratie normande au xie siècle' in *La Noblesse au Moyen Age xie—xv^{e}s: Essais à la mémoire de Robert Boutruche*, ed. Ph. Contamine, Paris 1976; Bates, *Normandy before 1066*, London and New York 1982 (e.g. 106—11, 125, 134—5). The latter work fortunately appeared too late for me to read before first writing this paper.
9 'English Warfare in 1066', *EHR* lxvii, 1952.
10 'The knight and the knight's fee in England', *Past and Present* No. 49, 1970, 15.
11 *Proceedings of the Battle Conference in Anglo-Norman Studies*, henceforth *Anglo-Norman Studies*, iv, 1981, 52.

First Century of English Feudalism he wrote that 'although knighthood in the eleventh century implied military proficiency, it carried no social distinction', and went on to call attention both to the rarity of the use of the word *miles* as a mark of distinction in twelfth-century charters, and to the *milites* in Domesday Book 'of a very inferior condition, whose holdings were small, and whose names were not thought worth the recording'.[12] In due course, in *Anglo-Saxon England*, first published in 1943 and which, one hopes, undergraduates still read, he wrote again that 'The ordinary knight of the eleventh century was a person of small means and insignificant condition'.[13] Since then matters have gone much further, as we have already seen, with Stenton's 'meagre knights' of the Domesday Survey, but let us consider first the matter of the use of *miles* as a title in charters, since Stenton's point of its rarity before the thirteenth century is also made by Sally Harvey.[14] The point is obviously of some consequence, for so long as *miles* retained its classical meaning of ordinary, common, soldier, no-one was likely to attach it to a personal name as a quasi-title or distinction.

Whatever may be the case in England (and Normandy?) in the twelfth century — and no-one knew his charters better than Sir Frank Stenton — there is no doubt whatever that in Norman charters of the eleventh century, and the tenth, and indeed from the beginning, the word *miles* is so used, attached to the names of witnesses and donors and others. The very first and earliest authentic charter in Marie Fauroux's splendid edition of the ducal *acta* of pre-Conquest Normandy[15] (dare one say still not appreciated in this country?), dating from 965 and the reign of Richard I, has Teofredus *miles* amongst its signatories, sandwiched between the count of Dreux and the duke of Normandy. Indeed this remarkable charter is almost sufficient evidence in itself for the conventional view of the elevated status of knighthood and vassalage alike, and of the feudalization of Norman society, even at this early date — which in the circumstances of Norman history, beginning in 911, is even earlier. The duke subscribes and thus confirms the deed whereby Walter count of Dreux himself approves the grant by his noble vassal Teodfredus (*nobilis vassallus Teodfredus*) of a church of the latter's benefice (*beneficii ipsius*) to St Peter at Chartres. And in the subscriptions, as we have seen, Teodfredus the noble vassal is Teodfredus, knight. From then on, *i.e.* for the whole of this period for which we have record, printed and well edited, knights, *milites*, as signatories or witnesses, and as donors, are common; and in the latter case, it is, of course, to be noted that they have lands (frequently allods) to give.[16] We may note in particular, perhaps, the two knight-signatories of a charter of Richard II, Osbern and Anfridus, who are in fact his brothers-in-law;[17] duke Robert subscribing *cum suis episcopis et militibus . . . atque aliis nobilibus*;[18] or duke William *cum omnibus suis militibus concedente* — which is evidently

12 First edn., Oxford 1932 (hereafter cited), 142—3.
13 Second edn., Oxford 1947, 628.
14 Harvey, 42.
15 Fauroux, no. 2. Charters subscribed by the duke as well as those issued in his name are included in her edition.
16 Fauroux, e.g. nos. 13, 16, 18, 24, 30, 43, 44, 69, 80, 86, 94, 107, 110 and, indeed, *passim*.
17 No. 44.
18 No. 43.

synonymous with the same duke William *et baronibus suis concedentibus*,[19] and also to be compared with the phraseology of the notification which informs us how William was brought to St.-Léger de Préaux, to make a confirmation of its property, *cum magno comitatu militum*.[20] There are knights of bishops and other magnates as well as of the duke.[21] Amongst them all we must certainly note the William, knight, who holds the castle of Moulins[22] (*Ego Willelmus miles, filius Walteri, qui castrum teneo de Molendinis . . .*), and we must also note that a man called *miles* in one document may not be so specified in another, for these documents are written by individual scribes, in no way writing for our benefit, and thus in no way amenable to a statistical approach. But, with the exception of one or two instances[23] — a clerk who appears in a list of knights (an error? a joke? a nick-name?) and five enigmatic *liberi milites* who raise more questions than they answer — the overwhelming impression one acquires from reading through the ducal charters of pre-Conquest Normandy is of an aristocracy of warrior knights, pre-eminently comprising men such as Richard [de Reviers], a knight of duke William and *vir quidam clarus genere seculari milicia deditus* who, campaigning with the duke against Henry I of France, was sent to take over the castle of Thimert near Chartres;[24] or John de Laval, a native of Maine, who when almost 30, *jam virilis esset et militari sub habitu, vir quippe ex illustri prosapia ortus degeret*, like Herluin wearied of the world of arms and gave himself as a monk with his land to Marmoutier[25] — which at this date is, one fears, a rather aristocratic thing to do.

What, then, are we to do with our Domesday *milites*, or, rather, those of Stenton and Sally Harvey? Not modes or medians or even histograms will convince me of the latter's contention that their alleged average holding of 1½ hides and prosperous peasant level of subsistence show any sort of norm for the knight in England in 1086.[26] One can, of course, emphasize the hazards of Domesday Book itself (to read the later Welldon-Finn is gloomily to conclude that no generalization at all may be made therefrom); the particular hazards of translating or interpreting Domesday nomenclature, in this case *miles*; and the especial hazards of a statistical approach to the Great Survey, or any other medieval record impatient of it. Duby cites with evident approval the propensity of the new historians and demographers to count 'everything capable of being counted in a continuous documentation', but he also remarks, as well he might, that such quantification influences the questions asked.[27] Of course Round was right to say that 'Much labour has been vainly spent on attempts to determine the true area of a knight's fee',[28] and Stenton was also right to point

---

19 Nos. 106, 107.
20 No. 149.
21 Fauroux, e.g. nos. 48, 130, 140, 202, 208, 227, 229.
22 No. 225.
23 Nos. 85, 199.
24 Fauroux, no. 147. The castle was under anathema and Richard, falling mortally ill, sent urgently to the bishop for his absolution and gave his land of Bourbesville (dép. Manche) to St. Peter at Chartres, to the subsequent irritation of his brothers.
25 No. 137.
26 Harvey, 15, and above.
27 'The history and sociology of the medieval west' (1970); *Chivalrous Society*, 82.
28 *Feudal England*, London 1909, 293. He also observed that 'Wonderful are the things that people look for in the pages of the great survey', 229. Cf. Harvey, 3.

out that the very concept of the knight's fee as the unit of land (or rather, land value) appropriate to a knight without vassals of his own was slow to form, as also such fees themselves were often the result of piecemeal accumulation.[29] Indeed, one might go further to suggest that it is an almost exclusive concentration upon the fee or fief, common to many historians, which has produced the curiosity of Sally Harvey's humble knight of prosperous peasant status. Our word 'feudal' (for 'feudalism' we have to wait until the nineteenth century) may have been coined from the Latin *feudum* meaning fief, but that was in the seventeenth century when the reality was largely gone. In the mid-eleventh century the reality was knights, and castles, rather than the fief which may or may not have supported both.

One might go even further yet and say that, if there was no real concept of the knight's fee in the England of 1086, so also, there or anywhere else, it was difficult to be just a knight, as a single isolated figure, *tout court* and by yourself. In reality you had to be the knight of someone else, to owe service to or take service with a lord, and serve with him and your peers in a group however small, to be of use and integrated in society. It is the absence of the household, the *familia* as one should say, recently set before us in all its fundamental importance by J.O. Prestwich,[30] that seems to me one worrying *lacuna* in Sally Harvey's highly intellectual exercise. To become a knight, to get on as a knight, and the way to the top if you were good and lucky and found favour, in that world was to take service with a lord. It might well not be easy to find a place if you or your family were undistinguished. At the age of 12 or 13 according to Suger,[31] a boy, *puer*, seeking a career in arms and the necessary military education which could be obtained nowhere else, would need to be placed by his father or other relative. Lords had standards, as duke Richard II of Normandy, we are told, liked to have gentlemen about him,[32] and the initiative of recruitment might be the other way about, as Henry I is said to have been on the look out for likely young men anywhere on this side of the Alps.[33] But of course there were other households than the king's or duke's, to which only the best connected or outstanding could aspire: you did the best you could or that could be done for you, rather like choosing schools some years ago. Once in and once a knight, a young man might feel, as a young man should, that the world was at his feet — and so it might be, for William Marshal rose from the household of Henry II's son to become earl of Pembroke and *rector regis et regni*. Worldly success through service was, of course, the acquisition of a fief or an heiress. Those Domesday *milites*, if they really only had 1½ hides of land, or, rather, rents therefrom, may well have just put a foot on the first rung of the ladder,[34] and it is certainly unwise to assume that they had no other means of livelihood or support.

We are approaching here the idea of the 'poor knight', which has, I believe,

---

29 *First Century*, 157 *et seq.*, and thus 'the twelfth century was far advanced before the clerks who wrote charters . . . allowed themselves the free use of the words *feudum militis*', 164.
30 'The military household of the Norman kings', *EHR* xcvi, 1981. See also Marjorie Chibnall, 'Mercenaries and the *Familia Regis* under Henry I', *History* lxii, 1977.
31 Guilhiermoz, 425.
32 D.C. Douglas, *EHR* lxi, 1946, 147.
33 Thus Walter Map, cited by Prestwich, 8.
34 Sally Harvey recognizes the possibility (p. 24), but for her they are poor knights none the less.

in our money-based and materialistic world, come to mean something very different among historians than it ever did among contemporaries. Before we leave the household, therefore, let us note that such glimpses of it as we have are aristocratic or gentlemanly at least. It is difficult in any case to suppose that erks and country bumpkins figured prominently among the household and the *familiares* of the king, or of any other lord, and when the young count Waleran of Meulan, before his defeat at Bourgthéroulde in 1124, hot-headed and 'anxious to prove his knighthood' (*militiae cupidus*), haughtily called the king's knights who opposed him *pagenses et gregarios* he did so as an insult and not a sociological observations.[35] The most precious and prolonged glimpse of the household of a great lord is that of count Gilbert of Brionne in the opening section of Gilbert Crispin's *Life of Herluin*. There we see for a while the household knights, clean-shaven and their hair cut like good Normans, all of them, I would suppose, 'noble' like Herluin himself, endlessly pursuing a round of gentlemanly activities, practising arms, riding on the count's business, acting on his behalf in law-suits, and dining in the hall.[36] The Bayeux Tapestry also, surely, shows us the household knights of count Guy of Ponthieu and of duke William similarly employed, armed, well-dressed and superbly mounted.[37] And the rewards of service could be great. Orderic tells us that Hugh, earl of Chester, in the Conqueror's England had a household more like an army, and was more prodigal than simply generous,[38] and William of Malmesbury says that William fitz Osbern, the Conqueror's closest friend, was so prodigal to his multitude of knights as to irritate the king.[39]

We approach the poor knight also via the wholly modern concept of the two levels of feudalism, spelt out specifically by Joseph R. Strayer in 1967[40] and widely prevalent. By this a yawning gap or gulf is fixed between those lords who had households of their own and the humble, simple and poor knights who served them. Though Strayer had his two levels becoming assimilated in the eleventh century, others have been slower,[41] and in Sally Harvey's work on her Domesday *milites* we find the concept of two levels given an altogether new dimension. Throughout we read not only of poor knights and lesser knights, but also of 'professional knights', 'active knights', 'serving knights' and 'fighting knights', all employed as synonymous terms and opposed to 'nominal knights' and even 'belted knights' *i.e.* their social superiors, the lords and substantial mesne tenants, who evidently seldom if ever fought at all.[42]

35 Orderic, vi, 350.
36 *Vita Herluini*, 87—91. For Herluin, see below, p. 26.
37 *BT*, Pls. 9—14.
38 Orderic, ii, 260.
39 *De Gestis Regum*, ii, 314.
40 'The Two Levels of Feudalism', in R.S. Hoyt (ed.), *Life and Thought in the early Middle Ages*, Minneapolis 1967, 51—65.
41 Cf Hunt, 'The Emergence of the Knight in France and England', 3.
42 Were I John Horace Round (who should be living at this hour) I would set out passages in my text in column and with much use of italics. But though some magnates do go on campaigns (p. 28), this seems the meaning or the implication of her text. Thus we read of 'two completely different social and tenurial classes, the influential knightly sub-tenants and the professional knights' (p. 5); and that, 'The important vassals did not themselves perform the military service due to the tenants-in-chief' (p. 12); or that, 'Disentangled from the nominal knights we are now free to follow up the position of the fighting professional' (p. 14). There seem to be three overlapping stages of the argument and its assumptions: (1) a study and analysis of the Domesday *milites*

One would rather suppose that in the secular society of the eleventh century (and earlier and later) with its wholly military ethos, the higher you stood socially the better you were expected to fight and the more martial you were supposed to be. The role of the king himself as war leader (to go no further down the social scale), before and after the feudal period as well as during it, is a fundamental in history. One must insist, I think, that the concept of the two levels of feudalism, and of knighthood, though it may have its uses, is simply misleading if it is forced into some kind of sociological pattern and imposed upon the protesting past. If one must measure status in crude materialistic terms of mere wealth and possessions, as contemporaries did not ('Rich in the abundance of poverty'[43] would make a fine contemporary concept on which to preach a sermon or give a lecture), than an infinite gradation of resources among the members of the knightly class, all of whom were a substantial cut above the peasants they despised, would be the way to do it. Of course not all knights were magnates and great lords, but all great lords and magnates, and kings and princes too, were knights, and that ensured as well as proves the social superiority of knighthood. Duke William himself was knighted in his youth according to William of Poitiers, who is not likely to be wrong in this though he characteristically adds that at the news a tremor ran through all France,[44] and the Bayeux Tapestry provides a superb illustration of the same duke's knighting of earl Harold.[45] It is clear from the pages of Orderic Vitalis and elsewhere that already by the mid-eleventh century knighthood was a distinction and a rank, given after long and sufficient training, both military and social, in the household, by the conferment of arms, and that it confirmed and established a protective and loyal relationship between the two parties.[46] The relationship between Herluin and his lord, count Gilbert, in Gilbert Crispin's *Life*, is not one between master and servant.[47] Duby writes perceptively of a common vocation of arms[48] which explains much, and vassalic commendation, we know, was an honourable bond between two men equally free. The notion of honourable service is another we have almost lost, together with the abundance of poverty. The young knights, if they had no place or fief, went off in companies of *juvenes*, 'bachelors',[49] in search of both, and of

---

(2) that there are no other *milites* in Domesday Book except those so specified (3) that all knights in England in 1086 conform to this alleged type, *i.e.* of the poor, 'professional' and 'fighting' knights *etc.*, as opposed to the occasionally mentioned 'nominal' knights and 'belted' knights, who are apparently the magnates and men of substance. Magnates and men of substance, indeed, are almost entirely absent from her consideration: hence the extraordinary statement that an analysis of Domesday Book reveals 'scarcely any instance of a knight holding the whole of a manor' (p. 21 — The king? All those tenants-in-chief?); or that cap. 11 of Henry I's Charter of Liberties (W. Stubbs, *Select Charters*, 9th edition, Oxford 1921, 119), which old historians like me, brought up on Stubb's *Charters*, had always been taught of considerable 'constitutional' importance, is 'explicitly confined to the serving knights', representatives evidently of 'professional classes of low birth', and thus of great annoyance to the magnates (p. 26).

43 Cf. Jonathan Sumption, *Pilgrimage: an image of medieval religion*, London 1975, 127.
44 *Gesta Guillelmi*, 13.
45 *BT*, Pl. 27.
46 See Brown, *The Normans and the Norman Conquest*, London 1969, 47; Duby, *Chivalrous Society*, index *sub* 'dubbing'; Guilhiermoz, especially 346—8, 393—421; Bloch, 312 ff.
47 *Vita Herluini*, 87—91.
48 *Chivalrous Society*, 79.
49 See especially Duby, 'Youth in aristocratic society' (1964); *Chivalrous Society*, 112 ff.

adventure and heiresses, 'happy and joyful on their horses' as Aimé of Monte Cassino described the Norman knights errant outside Venosa in Italy,[50] when all the world was young. *Per diversa loca militariter lucrum quaerentes* — 'seeking wealth as knights in many places' — is Geoffrey of Malaterra's description of the Hauteville brothers[51] amongst the Norman knights in southern Italy, and the mention of those dusty warriors reminds us again that the rewards of mere knighthood, without any extensive patrimony to start out from, could be huge. Of all the surplus Norman knights who sought their fortune in Italy in the course of the eleventh century, many lost their lives, but, of the rest, most gained fiefs, some principalities, and the son of one a kingdom. Of course not all knights made it to the top everywhere and anywhere, not even in Italy, or among the rich pickings of England, or in the hard-fought and harsh terrain of Antioch; any society, any class, any career-structure, has its failures as well as its successes; but to be a knight was to be potentially a lord or lordling, and the indispensable pre-condition of a worth-while career at arms and of social preferment. Beyond doubt, the ultimate degradation, and a fate worse than death, was to set one's hand to the plough. And if in this paragraph I have waxed a little romantic, that is necessary, for there is more to medieval history and knighthood than the statistical analysis of the returns of the Domesday commissioners compressed into Domesday book.

For myself, I have sometimes wondered of late if there ever was such a thing as a poor knight. Poverty is comparative, and subjective. I have no doubt there were many landless knights, and some enfeoffed, who thought themselves impoverished by the standard of their betters or their own ambition, but I doubt if Hod the peasant pitied them as they rode by (as they always did), any more than today's agricultural worker has much sympathy for the poverty-stricken student. None of those superbly armed and mounted knights on the Bayeux Tapestry look poor to me, and they seem unlikely to become poorer once the conquered provinces of England lie beneath the hooves of their horses. Did any knight, albeit landless and without a hide or acre to his name, really lead an impoverished life in the household of any lord, albeit not of the first rank? It must be remembered, too, that a lord's reputation will depend upon the turn-out and deportment of his men. The poor knight is certainly very elusive in the evidence which we have, and it is worth noting that the best known poor knight in Anglo-Norman history, Herluin the founder of Bec, grows considerably in status and in wealth if regarded at all closely. His biographer, Gilbert Crispin (scion of a knightly family and writing, of course, later, some time after 1093), in those invaluable early pages of his *Life*,[52] makes him as noble as he can, his mother related to the counts of Flanders. He is very well placed, in the household of count Gilbert of Brionne, who was himself the grandson of duke Richard I, and the count treats him with particular favour amongst those who are called the nobles (*primates*) of the household (*curia*). We are told that he was well connected with all the best families in Normandy, and it is made clear that a particular difficulty of

---

50 Amatus of Monte Cassino, *Storia de' Normanni*, ed. V. de Bartholomaeis, Rome 1935, 78—9.
51 Gaufridus Malaterra, *Historia Sicula*, I, v. ed. Migne, *Patrologia Latina*, t. 149, cols. 1103—4.
52 *Vita Herluini*, 87—91. See also C. Harper-Bill, 'Herluin, abbot of Bec, and his biographer', *Studies in Church History* xv, 1978.

Herluin in gaining his release from his lord's service to follow a life of religion is that he sought the release of his lands as well as himself. On one occasion, in breach with his lord and withdrawn from the household, he was nevertheless able to come to Gilbert's aid on campaign with twenty chosen knights (*delectos milites*). However humble Herluin's eventual foundation may have been in origin, it is clear that the poverty of the founder was very relative indeed. We may also, perhaps, turn to another well-known and contemporary poor or very moderate knight, though one this time land-holding. Tancred of Hauteville is almost invariably described as a petty (or the equivalent) baron in eleventh-century Normandy, although Geoffrey of Malaterra says that he served in the duke's household with ten knights under him (*in curia comitis decem milites sub se habens*) — which sounds very much like a *conroi* or Round's *constabularia*. He also tells us that, having twelve sons (by two wives) he had all of them trained and educated as knights from their adolescence, which may be thought almost the equivalent of sending them all to public schools. The Hauteville patrimony being obviously insufficient for such a brood once graduated, eight of them went off to Italy in turn, as from about 1035, *militariter lucrum quaerentes*.[53] And how, one may finally ask, did they and all those other poor knights from Normandy ever get there? I feel sure they did not walk, and they probably took a servant or two with them.

The time has come, indeed, to insert into this debate a measure of reality, the reality of war and tactics, horses and weapons, largely neglected by the *avant-garde*, even Duby, though not by Bloch or Guilhiermoz before them.[54] Whenever it was that the Franks developed heavy cavalry as the spearhead of their armies and the *corps d'élite*, remains as important a date in European history as ever it was in Brunner's classic thesis of the origins of feudalism[55] (so too does Lynn White's stirrup remain crucial, whenever it was exploited, for you cannot be a knight without it[56]). Such warfare and tactics, and more specifically those who practised them, were of necessity more expensive and more professional than infantry and foot-soldiers of whatever rank, and the central point of Brunner, Guilhiermoz and Bloch therefore remains, that the new military élite became inevitably in the circumstances of the age a social élite also. Like aerial warfare in 1940, more particularly that waged by Fighter Command and its German equivalent, this was a type of warfare in which only gentlemen could engage. One need have no doubt that it was first adopted by

---

53 Malaterra, I, iv, v. For Round's *constabularia*, see *Feudal England*, 259. For the *conroi*, see J.F. Verbruggan, 'La tactique militaire des armés de chevaliers', *Revue du Nord* xxix, 1947; Brown, 'Battle of Hastings', *Anglo-Norman Studies* iii, 1980, 16.
54 Cf. Colin Morris, '*Equestris Ordo*: chivalry as a vocation in the twelfth century', *Studies in Church History* xv, 89, 'We are dealing, not only or not primarily with the emergence of a new social class, but with a new style of fighting and above all of changing sensitivities'.
55 See B.S. Bachrach, 'Charles Martel, mounted shock combat, the stirrup and feudalism', *Studies in Medieval and Renaissance History* vii, 1970, and below, p. 30. The thesis is Heinrich Brunner, 'Der Reiterdienst und die Anfänge des Lehnswesens', in *Zeitschrift der Savigny-Stiftung für Rechtsgeschichte, Germanistische Abtheilung* viii, 1887, 1—38; reprinted in Brunner, *Forschungen zur Geschichte des deutschen und französischen Rechts*, Stuttgart 1894, 39—74.
56 Lynn T. White, *Medieval Technology and Social Change*, Oxford 1962, 1—38, 135—53. His chapter on 'The Stirrup' has also become something of a classic thesis, though Marc Bloch had pointed out the importance of the stirrup (and the horseshoe) long before him. For criticism, which does not at all affect the importance of the device, see R.H. Hilton and P.H. Sawyer in *Past and Present* xxiv, 1963.

rich nobles, as most good things in life descend from the top downwards. But nobles needed, as they always had needed, armed retainers of the best about them, and these now mounted warriors were obtained, trained and retained, not by central government raising cavalry regiments from public funds as in the modern period, but by lordship and vassalage and by the integrating and overlapping institutions of the household and the fief. Like J.O. Prestwich, I do not see my military household and *familia* as exclusively an early phase of feudalism giving way to enfiefment.[57] The alleged sociological pattern of the landless household knight being replaced by the enfiefed knight is as false, I would suggest, as exaggerated versions of the 'two levels of feudalism'. Each generation needs the household, and each generation has its sons and younger sons to fill it.

As Marc Bloch observed in a sentence whose simplicity is profound, 'in order to possess a warhorse and to equip oneself from head to foot, it was necessary to be fairly well-off or else to be assisted by someone richer than oneself'.[58] The arms and armour necessary for knighthood were or came to be lance and sword, shield, helmet and the hauberk, the long coat of mail which, as the distinguishing feature of the armed knight, comes to have almost mystical properties in an age of symbolism. The cost of it all, but more especially the sword and hauberk, was very heavy. Marc Bloch cites a landowner in Suabia in 761 exchanging his ancestral fields and a slave for a horse and sword and a Norman charter of 1043—8 refers to a hauberk worth seven *livres*.[59] Beyond doubt much more work is required on these vital matters, but meanwhile a friend of mine, learned in arms and armour and who practises what he teaches,[60] tells me that it may take him some 140 hours to make a hauberk (and even so not one of the finest quality but with rings merely butted as opposed to rivetted) and up to 200 hours to make a sword of eleventh-century pattern (though even so without any inscription, inlay or any other decoration). And then there were the horses. Not any horse will do for the battlefield, and more particularly for the shock-combat of the knights, as Sally Harvey and John Gillingham seem to think.[61] The warhorse, specially bred and trained for what it had to do, the prince of horses in the field, was enormously expensive. I do not know what significance Sally Harvey wishes us to attach to her £1 Domesday sumpter horses (*i.e.* pack horses) which she mentions in connection with her Domesday *milites*[62], but no one I know would wish to ride one at Hastings, and in the mid-eleventh century Gilbert Crispin obtained from the abbot of Jumièges a horse worth 20 *livres* and Roger of Montgomery one worth 30.[63] Nor is this necessarily all. Knights engaged at Hastings would presumably need more than one war-horse to be effective (as they were) in a battle which began at 9 a.m. and went on until after dusk. (One nowadays

---

57 Cf. therefore Duby where the notion is explicit and implicit, e.g. *Chivalrous Society*, 83, 86—7.
58 *Feudal Society*, 152.
59 *Feudal Society*, 152; Fauroux, no. 113.
60 Mr Ian Peirce of Battle, Sussex.
61 Harvey, 20; Gillingham, *Anglo-Norman Studies* iv, 53. Those who will have no difference between Norman knights and Old English thegns are bound to close their eyes to this difference too.
62 Harvey, 40.
63 Fauroux, nos. 113, 188.

needs a string of polo ponies for an afternoon's engagement on Smiths Lawn). Nor would a war-horse ridden the seven miles from the new Hastings castle to the battlefield be in the best condition on arrival. It is thought that the warhorse — *destrier, dextrarius* — gets its name from being led by the right-hand (*O.E.D.*) and one should envisage the eleventh-century equivalent of racehorses in horse-boxes on the road to Newmarket. In such a case, one will need another horse to ride (the palfrey?) for one does not walk (perish the thought!). Therefore one soon needs a boy, esquire, or servant, to look after these horses, and he must ride also to keep up, and to keep up one's own status (the rouncey or common hack will do for him, no doubt).[64] The upkeep of all these horses by the household in which the knights served must have been a problem, and has even been suggested as one motivation for enfiefment. Occasionally we may hear an echo of this particular reality, as when, in a charter of c. 1066 to the abbey of Beaumont-lès-Tours,[65] Roger de Malfillastre carefully reserves the pasture of his horses and of the horses of his knights (*equitum*), or when, soon after the Conquest, Robert de Curzon, with the leave of the Norman sheriff Roger Bigod, invaded the demesne manor of the monks of St Edmund at Southwold in Suffolk to obtain pasture for his horses.[66]

The expense of knighthood, however, is not confined to the sheer cost of horses, armour and weapons and the maintenance of all three. (The aethling Athelstan's sword-polisher in Ethelred II's will (c. 1014)[67] held no sinecure, for blades then corroded very easily, while the thought of a hauberk in the rain would make any batman blanch.) Far greater was the cost of professionalism. By this I mean that mounted warfare required a life-time's dedication from an early age, in order especially to acquire the horsemanship necessary to manage those great stallion warhorses in the heat and noise of battle, to deliver from the brute's heaving back all those accurate sword strokes which the *chansons* endlessly admire, above all to take part effectively in the shock-tactic of the charge. If, as I never cease to say in lectures, it demands a life-time's dedication to produce the equestrian skills of Harvey Smith, or, a better analogy perhaps, H.R.H. the Princess Anne, by how much more would this be necessary when life itself, and honour, were at stake? Hence the Carolingian maxim later echoed by the poet, and duly quoted by Marc Bloch: 'You can make a horseman of a lad at puberty; after that, never'; and again, 'He who has stayed at school till the age of twelve, and never ridden a horse, is fit only to be a priest'.[68] For all this it was necessary to be released from, and elevated above, the sordid necessity of earning a livelihood by any other means; and the

---

64 See Guilhiermoz, 466 *et seq*. In their rule, admittedly compiled in the thirteenth century, the Knights of the Temple were limited to three horses each and one esquire, because of their poverty. For Templar practice and information about contemporary horses I am much indebted to my pupil Mr Matthew Bennett.
65 Fauroux, no. 227.
66 *Memorials of St. Edmund's Abbey*, ed. Thomas Arnold, RS, i (1890), 79. I owe this reference to Antonia Gransden; cf. her paper on 'Baldwin, abbot of Bury St. Edmunds', *Anglo-Norman Studies* iv, 68.
67 *Anglo-Norman Wills*, ed. Dorothy Whitelock, Cambridge 1930, no. 20, p. 61. For another sword polisher see Alfred's laws, cap. 19. 3 (F.L. Attenborough, *Laws of the Earliest English Kings*, Cambridge 1922, 74; Whitelock, *EHD* i, first edn., London 1955, 376). I owe these references to Dr A.R. Rumble.
68 *Feudal Society*, 152, 293—4.

answer was the household and the fief. The result was not only the knight, and the superb fighting machine of trained and disciplined man and horse, but also the pride of professionalism, the happy warrior, and the élan of an élite. Georges Duby has called for a social history of the horse[69] (does the innate social superiority of the man on the horse start here?), but there are not many horsy figures among academics, any more than the sheer love of war — 'fresh and joyful war'[70] — and physical achievement finds much sympathy in academe.

I am very well aware that inherent in all I am saying is the vital question of date. I seek to establish the status of knights, and Norman knights in particular, as a secular upper class, real or potential, in the second half of the eleventh century, and to do it I have tried to confine myself to contemporary evidence. This is necessary because it is very generally held that the knight became (yet) more socially elevated, exclusive and aristocratic in the course of the twelfth century. Be that as it may, the larger question is surely that of origins. For me the central and fundamental element in feudalism is the knight, and the mystery of feudal history is when, and also why, the Franks began to develop cavalry, more particularly heavy cavalry, as their main military arm. The conventional reason given, that the idea came to Charles Martel at or after the battle of Poitiers in 732 against the Muslims, is anything but convincing, nor does an alleged military revolution at that time seem to fit the facts of Carolingian military history in so far as they are known or studied.[71] Clearly there must have been a beginning, when things were neither so developed nor so sophisticated as they became. But it is certain that by the mid-eleventh century Norman knights at least (and let us therefore add those allied knights from neighbouring regions whom the Conqueror took into his service in 1066) were a military élite, and therefore a social élite, and that in particular they were already developing, or had developed, their most devastating tactic of the couched lance and the charge.[72] This alone may explain much. This is what Anna Comnena had in mind when she wrote of the Frankish chivalry at the time of the First Crusade that the charging knight would pierce the walls of Babylon.[73] This, too, made knightly warfare even more exclusive, and did wonders for morale. Those endless Norman victories in the eleventh century across the breadth of the known world gave them that headiest of all feelings, that God is on our side. By the twelfth century they could believe that they held victory as a fief from God.[74] One needs some better explanation for all those feats of arms than that the Normans were good fighters, or even were a new Chosen People blessed by God in Holy War. It was the Norman heavy cavalry of knights, of course combined with infantry in set engagements, and their charge, of course controlled by discipline and

---

69 *Chivalrous Society*, 163.
70 Bloch, 293.
71 Bachrach, *Studies in Medieval and Renaissance History* vii, 49ff. Cf. David Bullough, *The Age of Charlemagne*, London 1965, 36.
72 See D.J.A. Ross, 'L'originalité de "Turoldus": le maniement de lance', *Cahiers de civilisation médiévale* vi, 1963; Brown, 'Battle of Hastings', *Anglo-Norman Studies* iii, 12—13. Do not see Glover, 'English Warfare in 1066', *EHR* lxvii, 1952.
73 *Alexiad of Anna Comnena*, ed. and trans. E.R.A. Sewter, Harmondsworth 1969, 416.
74 See J. Le Patourel, *The Norman Empire*, Oxford 1976, 353—4. Cf. Ailred of Rievaulx in *Chronicles of the Reigns of Stephen, Henry II and Richard I*, ed. R. Howlett, RS iii, 1896, 185—6.

training to be delivered at the right moment (clean contrary to the idiot myth of feudal warfare propagated by Oman), that carried all before it in this age. Nothing is more impressive as one reads, for example, of the amazing exploits of the Normans in southern Italy, making all due allowance for the proud exaggerations of the chroniclers, than the way in which comparatively small numbers of invariably outnumbered knights, rode through their enemies, Greek or Lombard, like a knife through butter. With his initial 200 knights obtained as the marriage portion of his first wife Aubrey, Robert Guiscard, one candidate for the most outstanding of the Hautevilles, became from his first castle of San Marco Argentano the lord of all Calabria. So on to Sicily, to which they shipped their horses with them, and where on a May morning in 1061, Roger of Hauteville took the city of Messina with an advance party of less than 500 knights, before his elder brother Robert had crossed with the main army.

If in the course of the twelfth century, knights in the Anglo-Norman and Angevin dominions as elsewhere became more aristocratic, more exclusive, fewer, as it seems generally to be agreed, we need to know the reasons for it. Perhaps some are to be found in inflation, though Duby eschews it,[75] and I as an 'old historian' cannot be expected to understand it. In England some may also lie in constant overseas campaigning, though that did not deter duke William's knights in 1066. Perhaps the last remark provides a clue, pointing to an explanation of an almost demographic kind. In the great days of Norman expansion as many knights as possible were needed and there were opportunities on every hand. In the twelfth century demand diminished, and the endless source of fiefs to reward and breed knights dried up, as earlier generations became established in England and Wales and southern Scotland and Ireland, in Italy and Sicily and Antioch. What I do know is that there was no soaring cost, save via inflation, of a knight's equipment in the twelfth century to explain it, and therein no basic change. On seals and in sculpture and illumination the familiar representation of the knight remains the same in all essentials until the surcoat and the pot-helm of Richard I's day. Neither of those can be thought to cause much increase in expense, and if plate armour did, we have to wait until the fourteenth century for its full adoption.[76] In any case if knights a century after Hastings, for whatever cause, were becoming even more exclusive, that does not make their predecessors lower-class. The élitism was already there when duke William sailed for England in 1066. The ideas and ideals, it is agreed, of the Peace and Truce of God,[77] of the Three Orders ordained by God, clergy, knights and peasants,[78] and of Holy War,[79] all developed in the course of the eleventh century and all of them elevated

---

75 *Chivalrous Society*, 183.
76 Cf. therefore Harvey, 39, 40; Tony Hunt, 'The emergence of the knight in France and England', 11'; Duby, *Chivalrous Society*, 184.
77 Bloch, 412ff; Morris, '*Equestris Ordo*'; Duby, 'Laity and the peace of God' (1966); *Chivalrous Society*, 123ff.
78 Guilhiermoz, 357—8; Bloch, 291—2; Morris, '*Equestris Ordo*'; Duby, 'The origins of a system of social classification' (1972), *Chivalrous Society*, 88ff, and his book, *The Three Orders*, trans. A. Goldhammer, Chicago and London 1980 (original French Edition, 1978)
79 See especially D.C. Douglas (not least for the Norman contribution), *The Norman Achievement*, London 1969, 89ff. See also J.M. Wallace-Hadrill, 'War and peace in the earlier Middle Ages', *TRHS* (5) xxv, 1975.

knighthood in society. One does not have to wait for St. Bernard for knights to be respectable. We might obtain a new dimension to our studies by investigating contemporary art, especially sculpture, which affords not only invaluable technical information about arms and armour but also a measure of the prestige of knighthood, and the appeal of chivalry to the imagination of men and women second only to such favourite Biblical scenes as the Annunciation or the Nativity, the Flight into Egypt or Doubting Thomas. I speak very much as an amateur, but a celebration of knighthood relevant to this paper seems to run from, let us say, the jousting knights of St.-Georges-de-Boscherville in Normandy (thought to be reset from an earlier building) to the knights representing Virtues overcoming Vices at Aulnay.[80] In the real world room must be found, no doubt, for failures and drop-outs, and even for enigmatic Norman *vavassores*,[81] survivors, it seems, from earlier generations; but if we wish to know about the Norman knight, his prowess and his status, in England in the second half of the eleventh century, we do not, *pace* Sally Harvey, 'abandon our hindsight view of the splendidly equipped figure . . . afforded by the late medieval knight'[82] but look at the splendidly equipped and mounted figures on the contemporary Bayeux Tapestry.

80 If the great typanum of comparable date (c. 1130?) on the west front at Conques shows amongst many other scenes a knight being dragged down to Hell, that emphasizes scarcely less a knightly dominance of society.
81 See H. Navel, 'L'enquête de 1133 sur les fiefs de l'Evéché de Bayeux', *Bulletin de la Soc. des Antiquaires de Normandie* xlii, 1934, 51—2, 60, 70 ff. Cf. Bloch, 177.
82 Harvey, 4.

POLICY AND VISIONS

The case of the Holy Lance at Antioch

Colin Morris

It is natural for historians to explain the political and military decisions of medieval rulers in terms which are familiar in the modern world. Such an attempt is fraught with danger, because decisions in the twelfth century were shaped by assumptions which seem strange, or at least strangely expressed, in the twentieth-century context. One of the now unfamiliar features of medieval politics is the importance which was attached to supernatural or religious considerations, which might have a powerful influence on public opinion and the making of decisions. The discovery of the holy lance at Antioch, at a crucial point in the history of the first crusade, is an outstanding example of the entanglement of politics and visions.[1] We are fortunate in that the evidence is good, or as good as we can hope in face of such complex phenomena, for several accounts were written within a year or two by observers who were close to the events. The finding of the holy lance also proved to be the centre-piece of a spectacularly wide range of happenings. The story includes, not only the discovery of one of Christendom's most sacred relics, but also a long and elaborate sequence of visions, many of them with a political content, instructions about a variety of ritual observances, and an ordeal by fire to conclude the drama with a satisfyingly ambiguous final scene.

There were special reasons why the crusaders were sensitive to such phenomena. They had reached the neighbourhood of Antioch in September 1097, about a year after the main contingents had left western Europe, and it proved to be the beginning of a long delay. Indeed, of the three years which were spent on the expedition, almost half was consumed by the stay in northern Syria, and the holy lance episode was born from the military perils and quarrels about policy which marked their sojourn there. The capture of Antioch by the Franks on 3 June 1098 was paradoxically the moment of greatest danger, for they found themselves enclosed in a city by a powerful army under Kerbogha, while their supply situation was critical and the citadel was still in

---

1 The episode has been studied by S. Runciman 'The Holy Lance found at Antioch', *Analecta Bollandiana* 68, 1950, 197—209, and the nature of the relic is considered in F. de Mély, 'La Sainte Lance', vol. III of P. Riant, *Exuviae Sacrae Constantinopolitanae*, Paris 1904. In addition there are commentaries or discussions with editions of the sources. In particular, see H. Hagenmeyer, *Anonymi Gesta Francorum*, Heidelberg 1890; C. Klein, *Raimund von Aguilers. Quellenstudie zur Geschichte des ersten Kreuzzuges*, Berlin 1892. Also there are three works by J.H. and L.L. Hill, *Raymond IV, Count of Toulouse*, Syracuse 1962; *Le Liber de Raymond d'Aguilers*, Paris 1969 (an edition), and Raymond d'Aguilers, *Historia Francorum qui ceperunt Iherusalem*, Philadelphia 1968, (a translation). I have not been able to consult L.F. Sheffy, 'The Use of the Holy Lance in the First Crusade', Master's thesis, Univ. of Texas 1915.

Moslem hands. Prominent crusaders began to flee the city seeking the relative safety of the ships at Saint Simeon, and the early visions reflect this situation of extreme crisis. The priest Stephen of Valence, for example, was at prayer in the church of Saint Mary, 'weeping because he was expecting to die there with his companions'.[2] The finding of the holy lance, along with some helpful advice from Saint Andrew, largely inspired the victory over Kerbogha on 28 June 1098, which restored military security to the expedition. This, however, was not the end of the visions, because these were now required as guidance in a political crisis occasioned by the deep divisions which became apparent among the crusaders. The basis of organisation of the army, which consisted of a series of contingents each with its own princely leader or leaders, meant that there was no single head, and the princes now found themselves facing a series of policy decisions: what should be done with Antioch, which they had captured without the promised help of the Byzantine Emperor, Alexius Comnenus? when should the march to Jerusalem be resumed? Two major antagonists emerged among the princes, Bohemond of Taranto (the leader of the Norman army from southern Italy) and Raymond of Saint-Gilles (the leader of the Provençal contingent). The conflict of interest among the leaders was complicated by a division of another kind. The circumstances of the long expedition had given to its ordinary members a common purpose and organisation which the lower classes did not normally possess, and the 'poor' now emerged as an important political influence. The relationship of their demands to the conflict of policy among the leaders was not a simple one. In many ways count Raymond was the more sympathetic to their desire to press on to Jerusalem, while Bohemond gave priority to securing his position in Antioch; but the rank-and-file crusaders seem to have been fiercely hostile to the Greeks, as Bohemond himself was. These cross-currents can be observed in the visions of 1098—9. Visionaries quite often in medieval society functioned as critics whose messages shaped public opinion and directly influenced decisions; at Antioch, they had a field day.[3]

The cohesion of the expedition was further disrupted by the death on 1 August 1098 of bishop Adhemar of Le Puy, whom Urban II had appointed his legate with the crusade. Some contemporaries stressed his role as peace-maker and spiritual leader. When Stephen of Valence was asked by Christ, 'who is lord in the army?' he gave the reply, 'there was never one single lord there, but they trust most in the bishop'.[4] The chronicler Raymond of Aguilers thought that Adhemar's death was the crucial event which led to the dispersion of the crusaders: 'How useful he had been to the army of God and the princes was shown after his death, when the princes were divided from one another, with Bohemond returning to *Romania* and the duke of Lorraine leaving for Edessa'.[5] Historians have doubted whether Adhemar was so influential, and it

2 Raymond 72 (References are to the edition by J.H. and L.L. Hill, as above).
3 The crucial nature of the decisions of policy is examined by J. France, 'The Crisis of the First Crusade: from the Defeat of Kerbogah to the Departure from Arqa', *Byzantion* 40, 1970, 276—308. France does not consider the holy lance affair in detail, but it is interesting that his definition of the period of crisis coincides almost exactly with its course from the discovery of the lance to the ordeal at Arqa.
4 Raymond 73. The Latin (*magis episcopo credunt*) is clumsy, and perhaps means 'they mostly trust the bishop'.
5 Raymond 84. Guibert of Nogent, writing in the west ten years after the end of the crusade,

is difficult to judge his potential importance for the crusade, because the situation in which the princes found themselves in the summer of 1098 was a new one. They had not previously been faced with policy decisions of this magnitude.[6] Whether Adhemar's role was myth or fact, it came to be accepted that he had been a centre of unity which must somehow be replaced. On 11 September 1098 the leaders wrote to ask Urban II to come in person to lead the expedition.[7] One of the themes in the prolonged visions was the guidance provided to the crusade in the shape of advice from Adhemar beyond the grave. The variety of interpretations which the sources offer us reflects the importance of the phenomena as an influence on the conflict of interests and policies.

The holy lance was central to the sequence of events. Its existence was revealed to the Provençal Peter Bartholomew in a series of visions, and subsequently others (notable Stephen of Valence and Peter Desiderius) received supplementary revelations, but the crucial authentication of these was found in the discovery of the holy lance in the church of Saint Peter at Antioch. In Saint John's Gospel the story is told of a soldier who thrust a spear or lance into the side of Christ on the cross, apparently to make sure that he was dead: 'But when they came to Jesus and saw that he was already dead, they did not break his legs. But one of the soldiers pierced his side with a spear, and at once there came out blood and water.' (John xix. 33—4). The soldier became known in western legend by the name Longinus, presumably derived from the Greek word for a lance, λογχη, and he appeared on almost all portrayals of the crucifixion. The significance of the lance must have been known to all Christians, even those most poorly instructed, and it is not surprising that a number of lances appeared in relic collections. Not all were even supposed to be 'the Dominical lance', as crusading chroniclers usually called it. The one with the most respectable ancestry was at Constantinople, having originally been discovered by the Empress Helena. At the time of the first crusade it was preserved in the chapel of the Pharos. Although it is natural to suppose that the crusaders would have become aware of such a major relic of the passion during their stay at Constantinople, none of the sources mentions the existence of a rival, and it is interesting to observe that the lance is not included in a lengthy list of relics detailed by the emperor Alexius in his supposed letter to count Robert of Flanders.[8] The accounts make it clear that what was found at

---

described Adhemar as 'specialis pater et dux' and pointed to his death as the occasion for the outbreak of disputes among the princes and the poor: 'coepere inter principes simultates aliquotiens ac insolentiae oboriri; apud mediocres praeterea et vulgares, licentiae quas non omnino deceret haberi'. *Gesta Dei per Francos* vi. 22 (*RHC Occ* IV, 217).

6 The importance of bishop Adhemar is discussed by J.H. and L.L. Hill, 'Contemporary Accounts of the Later Reputation of Adhemar, Bishop of Puy', *Medievalia et Humanistica* 9, 1955, 30—8; H.E. Mayer, 'Zur Beurteilung Adhemars von Le Puy', *Deutsches Archiv* 16, 1960, 547—52; and J.A. Brundage, 'Adhemar of Puy. The Bishop and his Critics', *Speculum* 34, 1959, 201—12.

7 H. Hagenmeyer, *Epistulae et chartae ad historiam primi belli sacri spectantes*, Innsbruck 1901, letter XVI p. 164. Raoul of Caen described the death-bed appointment of Arnulf, the chaplain of duke Robert of Normandy, as his successor: *Gesta Tancredi* xciv (*RHC Occ* III, 673). This is most improbable, but it reflects the importance felt later at Antioch for the maintenance of the succession to Adhemar as spiritual leader of the expedition.

8 Hagenmeyer, *Epistulae et chartae*, letter I, p. 134. Whatever the origin of this strange letter, the list of relics is sufficiently accurate to suggest a genuine acquaintanceship with the Constantinople

Antioch was taken to be a spear-head or lance-point, and that it was claimed that this belonged to the Dominical lance itself.[9]

The accounts written by contemporaries, or near-contemporaries, give us three quite different versions of what happened. The first is the 'official' story, communicated to the west by the leaders in the summer of 1098. The sequence of events in these letters is a simple one of divine favour, shown at a time of grave peril by the revelation of the holy lance. There is no indication of doubt or criticism. This is clear in the letter of 11 September 1098, addressed by all the princes, but composed in the household of Bohemond:

> But meanwhile the most merciful compassion of Almighty God came to our aid and cared for our needs. Saint Andrew the apostle three times revealed to a certain servant of God the lance of the Lord, by which our Saviour's side was pierced by the hands of Longinus, and showed him the place where the lance was; and we found it in the church of Saint Peter, the prince of the apostles. By the discovery of this and many divine revelations, we were so comforted and strengthened that, whereas we had previously been timid and afflicted we now urged one another to battle boldly and eagerly.[10]

This simple acceptance of the revelation as a sign of God's protection is expressed in a hymn, *Ierusalem, laetare*, which appears to have been composed for the festival of the capture of the city shortly after the end of the crusade:

> Lancea regis caeli
> Genti datur fideli,
> Ut sit mors infideli.[11]

This official account, formulated within a month or less of finding the lance, received a fuller statement in the *Gesta Francorum*, which was written by a clerk who had travelled to the east in Bohemond's company. Hagenmeyer suggested that the anonymous author of the *Gesta* had also prepared the letter from Bohemond and the other princes dated 11 September, and in that case the *Gesta* would be following this account in a very precise sense.[12] It is unquestionably a fuller version of the story told in the letters. The

---

collections. If the letter was constructed after 1100, as some scholars have suggested, the lance could have been dropped from the list because of the claims of the Antioch lance, but in my own view it is probable that the whole composition pre-dates the first crusade. In that case, the absence of the lance suggests that the westerners were unaware that their relic had a rival claimant. For the problems posed by the letter of Alexius, see E. Joranson, 'The spurious letter of the emperor Alexius to the count of Flanders', *Amer. Hist. Rev.* 55, 1950, 811—32, and M. de Waha, 'La lettre d'Alexis I Comnène à Robert I le Frison', *Byzantion*, 47, 1977, 113—25.

9 There is no way of determining what was actually found. Raoul of Caen, as we shall see, thought it was a lance-head fraudulently smuggled into the hole. It is in fact not surprising that a dozen men, digging for a whole day under the floor of a cathedral, found a piece of metal which could plausibly be seen as a lance-head, and perhaps no further explanation is necessary. The later fate of the lance, after the end of the crusade, is discussed in the article by Runciman, cited above.

10 Hagenmeyer, Letter XVI, p. 163, Cf. Letters XV, pp. 159—6; XVII, pp. 166—7.

11 C. Blume and G.M. Dreves, *Analecta Hymnica* 45b, 1904, no. 95, pp. 76—8, stanza 16. The same confidence was expressed in a letter of Paschal II dated 28 April 1100: 'illud vero quanti gaudii, quanti potest miraculi aestimari, quod sacrosancti lateris sui vulneratricem lanceam et vivificae crucis partem vestris oculis revelavit'. Hagenmeyer, Letter XXII, p. 178.

12 On the authorship of the *Gesta Francorum*, see H. Hagenmeyer, *Anonymi Gesta Francorum*,

Policy and Visions

author tells of two visions reported to the leaders of the crusade. One was that of a priest (whose name we can supply from other accounts as Stephen of Valence) in the church of Saint Mary at Antioch, who saw Christ, Mary and Peter. He was promised by Christ that the crusaders would receive great help within five days. The priest offered to prove the authenticity of his vision by undergoing an unusual ordeal, throwing himself from a tower, but bishop Adhemar was content to exact an oath from the leaders that none of them would abandon the army in its perilous situation. There was a further revelation to 'a certain pilgrim whose name was Peter' (Peter Bartholomew). Saint Andrew appeared to him and showed him where the lance was hidden in the ground in the cathedral of Saint Peter; and later returned to complain that he had not reported the vision. This time Andrew promised that a sign would be given within five days and would encourage the Christians to wage a victorious battle. Thirteen men then dug all day, and Peter found the lance. 'From that hour' a plan of attack was decided and an embassy sent to deliver an ultimatum to Kerbogha. The besieging army was crushed outside the walls of the city on 28 June, in a battle in which bishop Adhemar carried the holy lance and celestial forces assisted the Franks. This account is fuller than the letters, but it tallies with them and may be accepted as an accurate account of the beliefs of the army after the great victory.[13] Remarkably, the *Gesta Francorum*, in continuing the narrative up to the capture of Jerusalem, made no mention of an ordeal in April 1099, and indeed never indicates that there was a party which doubted the lance.[14] Its influence on later writers was so strong that it generated a tradition of historiography. Some of the writers who followed the *Gesta Francorum* knew of the ordeal, but they accepted the lance as a sign of God's favour to the crusaders and regarded Adhemar as its firm champion.[15]

The second version of the finding of the lance provides a fierce polemic against the one which we have considered so far. The *Gesta Tancredi* of Raoul of Caen records the events as they were remembered in Norman circles some twenty years later.[16] Raoul explains that the whole affair was rooted in the

---

Heidelberg 1890, 1—10. The theory that its author was a knight appears to me to rest on faulty deductions from the 'we' passages in the chronicle. All we can say with certainty is that the author had received a competent clerical education. This does not exclude the possibility of someone educated for ordination, who had nevertheless transferred to lay life, but a clerical writer is more probable. The letter of 11 September would presumably be composed by a clerk (but not, surely, by a knight?) in Bohemond's service, and this leaves open the way to Hagenmeyer's hypothesis that the same man wrote the letter and the chronicle. The stylistic similarities found by Hagenmeyer, however, do not seem to me strong. See *Epistulae et chartae* pp. 96—7.

13 R. Hill, *Gesta Francorum*, Oxford 1962/1972, 57—60, 65—6. The two latter pages suggest that the crusaders acted immediately on finding the lance, but the chronology of Raymond of Aguilers, which seems reasonable at this point, indicates a delay of 14 days.

14 The treatment of the lance becomes more comprehensible if we suppose that the *Gesta Francorum* was written in at least two campaigns. The author would thus be describing events at Antioch without knowing about the later ordeal. We can only speculate why he did not incorporate the ordeal in his account of the march to Jerusalem, but this is relatively brief and does not give much space to conflicting parties among the crusaders.

15 Guibert vi. 22 and vii. 34 (*RHC Occ* IV, 217—8 and 252)

16 *RHC Occ* III, 675—8, 682—3; see A.C. Krey, *The First Crusade*, Gloucester Mass. 1958, 237—41. Raoul was a former pupil of Arnulf, a Norman scholar who went on the first crusade and who eventually became patriarch of Jerusalem. Raoul himself came to the east about 1107 and entered the service of Tancred. Between 1112 and 1118 he wrote the *Gesta Tancredi* and dedicated the work to Arnulf.

quarrel between the contingents of Bohemond and Raymond which began even before the fall of Antioch. All the southern French sympathised with Raymond and the Provençal party, while the northern French, and the Normans in particular, were on the Apulian side. The visions were devised by a member of Raymond's army, 'a versatile fabricator of lies, Peter'. The discovery of the lance was a fraud, for this same Peter had found an Arabic spear point, which was unfamiliar to the Franks by its form, and claimed in the darkness to have discovered it during the excavation in the cathedral. Count Raymond had stage-managed the discovery (although Raoul hints, rather than states, that he was party to the fraud) and the Provençals became the champions of the lance saying that 'the glory of the triumph should be ascribed to the lance, which was borne ahead in battle, as if it were a trophy'. Bohemond, however, was immediately aware of the trick and argued passionately against it. Saint Andrew would hardly have appeared to a man who was often drunk and disorderly; the original lance would hardly be under the cathedral floor at Antioch; and the circumstances of its discovery were highly suspicious.[17] Bohemond, who rarely put a foot wrong when it came to expressions of piety, declared that victory came from God, and not from a piece of iron. A conspiracy by Raymond, who stirred up the people against Bohemond, was only defeated as a result of its premature discovery by Arnulf, who appears as a strong sympathiser of Bohemond and who was able to warn him. Matters stood there until a few months later, when at the siege of Arqa the dispute over the authenticity of the lance flared up again. This time, the leaders decided to settle the matter by the most solemn of ordeals, the ordeal by fire. Peter had to take nine steps between two flaming pyres, emerged terribly burned, and died the following day. The people, penitent, recognised Peter as a deceiver, although Raymond and the Provençals plotted against Arnulf, 'the chief discoverer, of the fraud' and continued to defend the supposed revelation.

Medieval scepticism needs to be treated as critically as medieval superstition, and there is a good deal in Raoul of Caen's account which is hard to accept. The story about the fraudulent introduction of the spearhead into the cathedral at Antioch, although a similar tale is told by the Moslem historian Ibn al-Athir, is a plausible speculation, but cannot rest upon knowledge. More dubious is the assertion that Bohemond was already challenging the authenticity of the lance at Antioch, immediately after its discovery. In reality the letter to Urban II and the *Gesta Francorum*, writings with a special connection with Bohemond, seem to have been interpreting it at that stage as a sign of God's pleasure. We shall also see shortly that the visionaries in the early days seem to have supported Bohemond's claim to Antioch. There is no reason to suppose that the Normans rejected the holy lance in the summer of 1098.

The two versions which have been considered so far make clear the link

---

17 The omissions in the polemic are as interesting as the arguments. There is no mention of the fact that the Greeks had a relic at Constantinople which they had long identified as the lance; it seems that the Normans simply did not know this. Nor, even more strikingly, is there any mention of doubts on the part of bishop Adhemar, for whom Raoul had considerable respect. The only mention of a lance at Constantinople appears in the *Gesta Francorum Iherusalem Expugnantium*, a later compilation which indicates that it was mentioned in the dispute at Arqa (*RHC Occ*, III, 507).

between the lance and political and military events, but their account is simplistic. The finding of the lance was a proof of divine favour (*Gesta Francorum*) or it was a fraud (Raoul of Caen). The scene changes totally when we open the pages of Raymond of Aguilers. As chaplain of count Raymond, he was basically an exponent of the Provençal point of view, but he was not uncritical about the count's policy, and he also preserved a great mass of reports of visions which reflect the conflicts over political and religious interests and over the holy lance itself. His chronicle, which was written close to the events, is an interweaving of a narrative and a book of visions, a sort of *Visiones Lanceae Dominicae*.[18] This is not the type of source-material which modern writers regard with enthusiasm and it is not surprising that Raymond has had a bad press. He has been described as 'a sneaking scoundrel and unscrupulous fraud', 'a medieval Baron Munchausen', and a 'spinner of tall crusading tales'.[19] It is true that medieval readers were lovers of tall tales, which were sometimes incorporated even into sober narratives, and Raymond is not wholly free from far-fetched stories which came to him at third hand.[20] These apart, he was reporting statements by people he knew, which contained as a rule a relatively sober report of a vision, with a message relating to the situation of the crusaders. The relationship between a visionary and his reporter was a complex one, for the statement by the visionary would be shaped by the expectations of his audience and the sort of questions he was asked.[21] There is no reason to suppose that Raymond invented these accounts *ab initio*. Can we

---

18 This is not the place to discuss the problem about authorship and date of the chronicle. In this discussion, I am assuming that the present work as a whole was composed by Raymond of Aguilers, the chaplain, who is therefore identical with the canon of Le Puy in the dedicatory letter. I believe that it was completed by the end of 1099, and the account of events at Antioch may well have been written in the course of the crusade. Most of these views are controversial, but a different account of the process of composition, although it would require some changes in the article, would not fundamentally alter its conclusions.

19 'ein schleichender Schurke und gewissenloser Betrüger' (Klein, cited Hagenmeyer, *Epistulae et chartae* 332); J.L. and L.L. Hill, in their translation, p. 5. In their study of *Raymond IV*, p. 90, the Hills credit Raymond of Aguilers with 'the extension and amplification of the visions' and say that 'the pronouncements of the saints inherit from him the homiletic myopia of a bookish priest'. In contrast, Sir Steven Runciman used Raymond's reports as the basis for his narrative and regarded him as 'within his limits . . . sincere and well informed'. S. Runciman, *A History of the Crusades*, I, Cambridge 1951, 241ff, 328.

20 An example is the evidence given by the priest Ebrard before the ordeal in April 1099 (Raymond pp. 117—8). The use of stories or *exempla* of a far-fetched kind is discussed in J.-Th. Welter, *L'Exemplum dans la littérature religieuse et didactique du Moyen Âge*, Paris-Toulouse 1927, reprint 1973.

21 The study of vision-literature has developed greatly in recent years. For good introductions, see C.J. Holdsworth, 'Visions and visionaries in the Middle Ages', *History* 48, 1963, 141—53, and Peter Dinzelbacher, *Vision und Visionsliteratur im Mittelalter*, Stuttgart 1981. The experiences on the first crusade do not fall strictly within the category of 'visions' as Dinzelbacher defines it, but are in his terms 'appearances'. The book nevertheless has much valuable information about the background to these experiences. Crusading sources apply words cognate with both 'vision' and 'appearance' indiscriminately: *visio, visum, apparuit* etc. An interesting account of the relationship of visionary and redactor is to be found in P.G. Schmidt, 'The Vision of Thurkill', *Journal of the Warburg and Courtauld Institutes*, 41, 1978, 50—62; see p. 51 for the case of Alberic of Montecassino who later discovered that the reporter had described *quod a nobis numquam audivit*. The social content of earlier visions is discussed by M. Aubrun in *Cahiers de Civilisation Médiévale* 23, 1980, 109—30.

form any impression whether, given an element of shaping and selection, he was preserving a roughly correct account of what was said by Peter Bartholomew and his colleagues?

Raymond was well placed to obtain information; not only was he the chaplain of count Raymond, but he was present at the finding of the lance, was responsible for its keeping and was present at least at one of the visions. In a few cases the vision may already have been recorded, so that Raymond was incorporating a document into his text, but in general we must see him as the redactor of the visionaries' statements, in the same situation as the clerks who produced other twelfth-century *Libri Visionum*.[22] He had the information needed for a correct report, and it is interesting to find that there are marked similarities between the experiences of Peter Bartholomew and those described in the slightly later collections of Orm, Tundal or Thurkill. True, these may sometimes be the result of Raymond's own embellishment, but as a whole they suggest that the visions of the holy lance were rooted in the same mentality as the other collections. Common features include the visionary's humble origin (he is often a layman with little learning); the shaping of the eidetic image from material suggested by painting or sculpture; the special importance attached to the vision of Christ, and even more of the crucifix; and the use of visions to authenticate a relic. References to contemporaries and to political issues are also characteristic. Another feature is the frequency of self-criticism or self-doubt, and of scepticism on the part of the audience.[23] This does not exclude the assumption that Raymond of Aguilers retold the visions to such an extent that the originals are irrecoverable. Our judgement of that must turn on the extent to which they have been refashioned to express Raymond's own ideas. Some of them, as we shall see, are dominated by views different from his, emerging from another part of the crusading army. One striking illustration of this is his report of visions which indicate bishop Adhemar's doubts about the lance. Although there are some problems about this, discussed in the Appendix below, it is highly unlikely that Raymond, the champion of the lance and admirer of Adhemar, is here inventing an embarrassing story which was not in his sources. Modern critics of the chronicle have started from the present-day assumption that a vision can be doctored to mean almost anything. The twelfth-century assumption was the opposite. Once a message was accepted as divinely-given, it was more difficult to explain away than an event or an ordeal, and as a result we have a number of blocks of raw material which have, to all appearances, not been processed by the chronicler, but which remain as

---

22 When Peter Bartholomew reported a sequence of visions to count Raymond and bishop Adhemar, they inquired about the *revelationis et iussionis apostolice ordinem*, a phrase which could indicate the preparation of a record (p. 68). A clearer example is the vision of 5 April 1099, which is discussed later. In both cases, if a document had been prepared separately from the chronicle, Raymond of Aguilers may well have been its scribe.

23 To substantiate the parallels in detail would require an article to itself, but the basis exists in Peter Dinzelbacher's excellent discussion of the changing patterns of visions in their cultural setting. Similarly for reasons of space, I have not considered to what extent the visionaries' experience was (in our way of thinking) para-normal or illusory, and how far, conversely, they were merely assessing according to their own valuation dreams and other experiences which we would categorise as normal. There is valuable material about the political content of visions generally in E. Dünninger, 'Politische und geschichtliche Elemente in mittelalterlichen Jenseitsvisionen', Diss Würzburg 1962.

unusually informative evidence of public opinion.

The material came to Raymond from a number of different visionaries, who by no means all had the same attitudes, but the most productive of them all was Peter Bartholomew. Peter is described by Raymond as 'a poor peasant . . . of Provençal origin',[24] and his low social origin was a matter for reproach during the final quarrel at Arqa in April 1099: 'some began to say that they would never believe that God would speak to that sort of person, and pass over princes and bishops and show Himself to a peasant'.[25] Peter Bartholomew had a foot in three camps, if the phrase may be allowed, because in addition to being associated with the Provençal party and the poor he had some knowledge of letters. Even when he was miraculously deprived of this, he still knew the Lord's Prayer, Creed, Magnificat and Benedictus — well above par for an ordinary peasant.[26] Peter Bartholomew's messages, not surprisingly, are varyingly reminiscent of the Provençal, the poor man, and the clerk. With so much more material at his disposal, Raymond's narrative differs greatly from other accounts of the lance. The revelation begins, as in the *Gesta*, in the dark days at Antioch, with Kerbogha outside the gates, early in June 1098. The leaders heard that Saint Andrew had appeared to the poor pilgrim, Peter Bartholomew, to show him the location of the holy lance, and that Christ had appeared to the priest, Stephen of Valence, with a promise of help for the oppressed crusaders. The leaders as a result found the lance beneath the cathedral on 14 June. In all important respects, the *Gesta*, the Letters and Raymond are united in this account. At this point, however, Raymond goes on his own line with no confirmation from the other authorities. In his account, the visions and messages did not stop; and this is plausible, because the holy lance had not in fact achieved victory yet, and still less had it united the crusaders on the march to Jerusalem. We must examine the content of these further messages, which are reported by Raymond alone.

The first major concern of these continuing visions was the elevation of the holy lance, which was at once the bringer of divine aid and guarantee of Peter's reliability. Immediately after the discovery of the lance Saint Andrew gave instructions for its annual commemoration.[27] It would seem, however, that the discovery of the lance did not have the galvanising effect upon morale which is indicated in the 'official' account. There was a gap of fourteen days before Franks emerged from the city to fight Kerbogha, and it was necessary for Saint Andrew to appear again. This time a new note was struck with the provision of detailed instructions; it is the first truly 'political' vision.[28] These included, not only the performance of specific penances, but military measures as well: the army was to accept the plan agreed by the princes, not to delay the battle, and not to be diverted to the enemy's tents in hope of booty. In the

---

24 'pauperem quendam rusticum . . . provincialem genere', Raymond 68. Cf. Bruno of Lucca, Letter XVII p. 166: 'quidam pauperrimus et omnium fere abiectissimus, Provincialis genere'.
25 Raymond 116, reading *episcopos*.
26 Raymond 76. Presumably because of this smattering of Latin learning, Peter Bartholomew was believed by Albert of Aachen and William of Tyre to be a clerk.
27 Raymond 76. The payment of proper ceremonial respect to the lance was the subject of a further message to Stephen of Valence several months later (p. 127).
28 'quomodo ante bellum et in bello agere deberemus Beatus Andreai per iuvenem illum qui de lancea dixerat edocuit' (pp. 77—8).

subsequent battle of 28 June, among many signs of divine favour, the holy lance, which was carried by Raymond the chaplain in person, protected the bishop's contingent from all harm.

It proved in the event that the victory over Kerbogha did not fulfil the hopes of those who had discovered the lance, because the princes, torn by disagreement about what was to be done with Antioch, decided 'against God's command' to postpone the renewal of the march until 1 November.[29] The death of Adhemar on 1 August increased the likelihood of continued dissension, and immediately after his burial Adhemar and Saint Andrew appeared to Peter Bartholomew, probably on 3/4 August. Bishop Adhemar promised his continued presence with the crusaders: 'I will be with them, and so will all my brothers who, like me, have ended their lives; and I will appear to them and advise them much better than before.' Then in a long speech the apostle presented a political package which is the fullest statement we have of the hopes of the poorer participants of the crusade.[30] He dismissed with contempt the interests of the Greeks; the visions nowhere contain any trace of pope Urban's intention to bring help to the eastern brethren. It was disgraceful, the princes were told, that they had not retained Nicaea, which God had given them, and count Raymond must now seek out the man who wanted to be lord over Antioch and discover what sort of lordship he intended to exercise. The apostle stressed the need for concord between the count and Bohemond, and ordered that a Latin patriarch (*qui sit de vestra lege*) should be appointed. The rich were to assist their poor dependents (*de cognatione sua*). The unnamed claimant to the city, whose title is thus approved, must be Bohemond, and it is clear that at this stage, although the lance had been found by a Provençal prophecy and was kept in count Raymond's entourage, Peter Bartholomew was by no means in complete sympathy with the count's policy. On the contrary, he stood for concord among the princes, the grant of Antioch to Bohemond, and the resumption of the crusade — a programme which in all probability expressed the ideals of the ordinary members of the expedition.

The attitude of Peter Bartholomew to the Provençal leaders was, at this stage, ambiguous. The possession of the lance had established count Raymond's special position as 'standard-bearer of the army',[31] but this honour had been given him to lead the people to Jerusalem. At Chastel-Rouge towards the end of September 1098 Peter Bartholomew was telling the count to his face that Saint Andrew wanted him to dismiss his advisers and advance on Jerusalem without delay.[32] The pressure reached its height about Christmas 1098. By this time, Bohemond was refusing to participate in continuing the expedition until the following spring, and was openly ridiculing the messages from Peter Bartholomew. Led by the bishop of Albara and a few nobles, the knights and people asked that count Raymond should act as *ductor et dominus exercitus* or give the lance to the people, who would continue to Jerusalem under the Lord's leadership. The Christmas meeting marked the point at which popular hopes finally abandoned Bohemond and became fixed on Raymond who, however reluctantly, had accepted the duty implicit in his

29 Raymond 84.
30 Raymond 84—8.
31 Raymond 75, vision of 15 June 1098, after discovery of the lance.
32 Raymond 91.

position as custodian of the lance.[33]

The separation of the crusade into two factions, now openly for and against the authenticity of the lance and its visions, came to a crisis in the siege of Arqa. On 5 April Peter Bartholomew experienced the most carefully recorded of all his visions.[34] For the first time, he saw Christ on the crucifix, and it is plain from his description that in composing the image his imagination was drawing on sculptures and paintings of the crucifixion. To this vision was added a meditation which, in truth, had little to do with it and which plainly expressed the visionary's own anxieties. The five wounds reminded him of the five ranks in the army, ranging from those who were prepared to accompany the Lord to Jerusalem, to those who were ready like Judas to betray him. Christ's instructions were to draw up the army for battle, and the doubters, who were reluctant to fight, should be put to death. Covered by only the thinnest veil of prophetic language, the threat to the enemies of the lance was clear. Christ himself had condemned those who would not go to Jerusalem and those who doubted the lance, the two groups being implicitly identified. The Norman party reacted sharply under the leadership of Arnulf, the principal critic of the lance, and a judicial process was instituted, with a long series of witnesses who reported visions in support of the lance, and finally the ordeal on Good Friday, 8 April 1099. Ordeals were frequently ambiguous, and Raymond imposed his own interpretation upon what happened: Peter Bartholomew passed unscathed through the fire, thus validating the lance as a true relic, but he was then mobbed by a crowd wanting to secure pieces of his garments as relics, and severely injured. He died a few days later, but the lance continued to be revered by the Provençal party and their sympathisers.

There are thus three accounts of the impact of the holy lance upon the politics of the crusade. The 'official' view as we have called it, stated by the letters of the princes and elaborated in the *Gesta Francorum* and Guibert of Nogent, acknowledged the holy lance as a sign of divine favour and pledge of victory. It contained no acknowledgement of doubt about the authenticity of the relic and no mention of the ordeal. The later Norman tradition recorded by Raoul of Caen was equally simple, in an opposite direction, and saw the lance as a fraud, exposed by the ordeal. Only in Raymond of Aguilers do we obtain a glimpse of the complexity of the situation. It is true that Raymond had his own strong interests in the subject, as chaplain of count Raymond and himself responsible for the lance, and his account of events is slanted, especially in the description of the final ordeal. Nevertheless, the visions which he records do not always tally with his own views and it is reasonable to think that he was often reporting, with fair accuracy, the words of the visionaries. Through these we can obtain a glimpse of the aspirations of some of the ordinary

---

33 A similarly ambivalent attitude is shown by the visionaries to the other great leader from southern France, bishop Adhemar of Le Puy. Since this raises some acute critical problems, and is not directly germane to the conduct of policy on the crusade, I consider this in an appendix.

34 Raymond 112—5. This record has the form of a deposition by Peter Bartholomew, who reports his vision in the first person. It is highly probably that it was prepared by Raymond the chaplain, in quasi-legal form, for the trial which follows. It may be that there was a formal procedure, leading up to the ordeal, and in that case the deposition must have been prepared immediately after 5 April. It is also possible that the original proceedings were far more disorderly, and that Raymond subsequently produced *pastiche* depositions in order to make a trial out of what originally had been a tumult.

crusaders, who (in a fairly familiar medieval style) used the utterances of saints and seers to shape the politics of princes.

Appendix: The Doubts of Bishop Adhemar

Bishop Adhemar of Le Puy was regarded with respect by many of the participants in the crusade, and in a real sense as a moral leader and centre of unity. His role was emphasised, as we have already seen, both by Raymond of Aguilers and by Stephen of Valence in his vision before the finding of the lance.[35] Raymond preserves indications of a current of criticism of Adhemar within the army which deserves some attention. We first encounter it when Peter Bartholomew reports his early visions to the leaders in Antioch. In one of these, Saint Andrew instructed him to ask why the bishop was neglecting his duty to preach, to admonish and to bless.[36] No details were given (was there some censorship by Raymond as editor at this point?) but it is reasonable to suppose that this comment represents dissatisfaction among the poor with Adhemar as a spiritual leader, and it may have some connection with the complaints in other visions about evil living among the crusaders. However this may be, this particular criticism was not mentioned again, and Peter Bartholomew received a vision in which Adhemar promised to continue his guidance from beyond the grave.[37]

Its place was taken by a different criticism: bishop Adhemar doubted the lance. Raymond is the only writer with first-hand knowledge to provide this information, and at first sight it is so unlikely that he would have invented it that it has been generally accepted by historians. It does, however, have worrying features, because Raymond provided no circumstantial detail and gave no reason for Adhemar's doubts. The only direct historical statement which Raymond makes about Adhemar's attitude in his life-time is that, when Peter Bartholomew first told the story of his visions, the bishop thought there was nothing in it: *episcopus autem nichil esse preter verba putavit*.[38] Thereafter, the chronicler steadfastly distanced Adhemar from the lance, and did not record his attitude to it. He did not mention his reaction to the vision of the priest Stephen, nor to the oath to stay with the army which the magnates took as a result. He did not comment on Adhemar's reaction to the discovery of the lance, nor associate him with the inquiry about Peter's literacy which followed the issue of complicated liturgical instructions; and he recorded, in his account of the battle of 28 June, only that he (Raymond personally) carried the lance in

---

35 Adhemar's function as legate is particularly examined by H.E. Mayer, art. cit. (note 6 above).
36 Raymond 69.
37 Raymond 85. 'eis apparebo et multo melius quam actenus consiliabor eis'. In view of the preceding criticism, these words may have a sharp edge.
38 Raymond 72.

the bishop's ranks. Raymond is being evasive. Bishop Adhemar must have been responsible for requiring Stephen to swear on the cross to the truth of his vision and indeed Raymond records that the message was directed to Adhemar and that Adhemar was active in preventing the flight of demoralised members of the expedition. Nor could the lance have been carried in Adhemar's contingent without his permission. On both these occasions, the straightforward account of the *Gesta Francorum* appears preferable: the bishop required an oath from Stephen on the Gospels and Cross, and carried the lance in battle.[39] In Raymond's account, the attitude of Adhemar is only made absolutely clear after his death; then, immediately after his funeral, Peter Bartholomew saw him with his face and head burned because of his sins after the discovery of the lance, which obliged him to spend the time between his death and burial in hell. This theme is renewed at Arqa in the following April, when Raymond reports that Arnulf invoked Adhemar's doubts as the authority for his own, and in response the story of Adhemar's punishment was repeated, this time in a vision ascribed to Peter Desiderius.[40]

Why was Raymond of Aguilers so vague, or rather so evasive, in reporting Adhemar's attitude to the discovery of the lance? One possible reason is his discomfort at having to report the scepticism of so eminent an authority about the relic to which Raymond was so committed. The information at his disposal forced him to acknowledge the doubts, but they were unwelcome to him and he forced them to the side-lines. He knew that Adhemar had been systematically sceptical, but limited his reference to the first appearance on the scene of Peter Bartholomew, suppressing all mention of other indications of opposition. This view would contradict the clear evidence of the *Gesta Francorum*, and makes it hard to reconstruct the course of events: it would not have been possible for the leaders to act upon the revelation to Stephen of Valence, or to carry the lance in battle, without the approval of the legate. There is another, and quite different possibility: the evidence on which Raymond was relying was the information provided by the visions. It is not uncommon for medieval historians to use visions as a source, and to incorporate their content into the narrative; and this was what Raymond was doing. On this assumption, he had no information at all, from Adhemar's last few weeks, which indicated doubt about the lance, or (alternatively) his doubts were limited to Peter Bartholomew's original claims, before they were validated by the message of Stephen of Valence and the finding of the lance. Raymond was faced by a conflict of evidence between the historical knowledge of Adhemar as authenticating the holy lance and the visionary revelation that he was a doubter at heart. Such visions were provoked either by the memory of Adhemar's initial hesitation or simply by the current of criticism towards him which existed among the pilgrims. On this reconstruction, the truth about Adhemar's doubt is that they were confined to the initial phase of the business, or even (and this may well be the fact of the matter) that he had no doubts at all.

39 *Gesta Francorum* 58—9, 68. The phrase *portans secum lanceam Saluatoris* need not mean that Adhemar carried the lance personally and does not contradict Raymond's statement. Hagenmeyer believed that Raymond knew the account in the *Gesta*, and there are certainly close similarities at this point. If he were right, Raymond's evasiveness would be even clearer, because he would then be re-writing one of his sources so as to efface Adhemar's responsibility for what happened.
40 Raymond 84—5. 116—7.

The Vexin

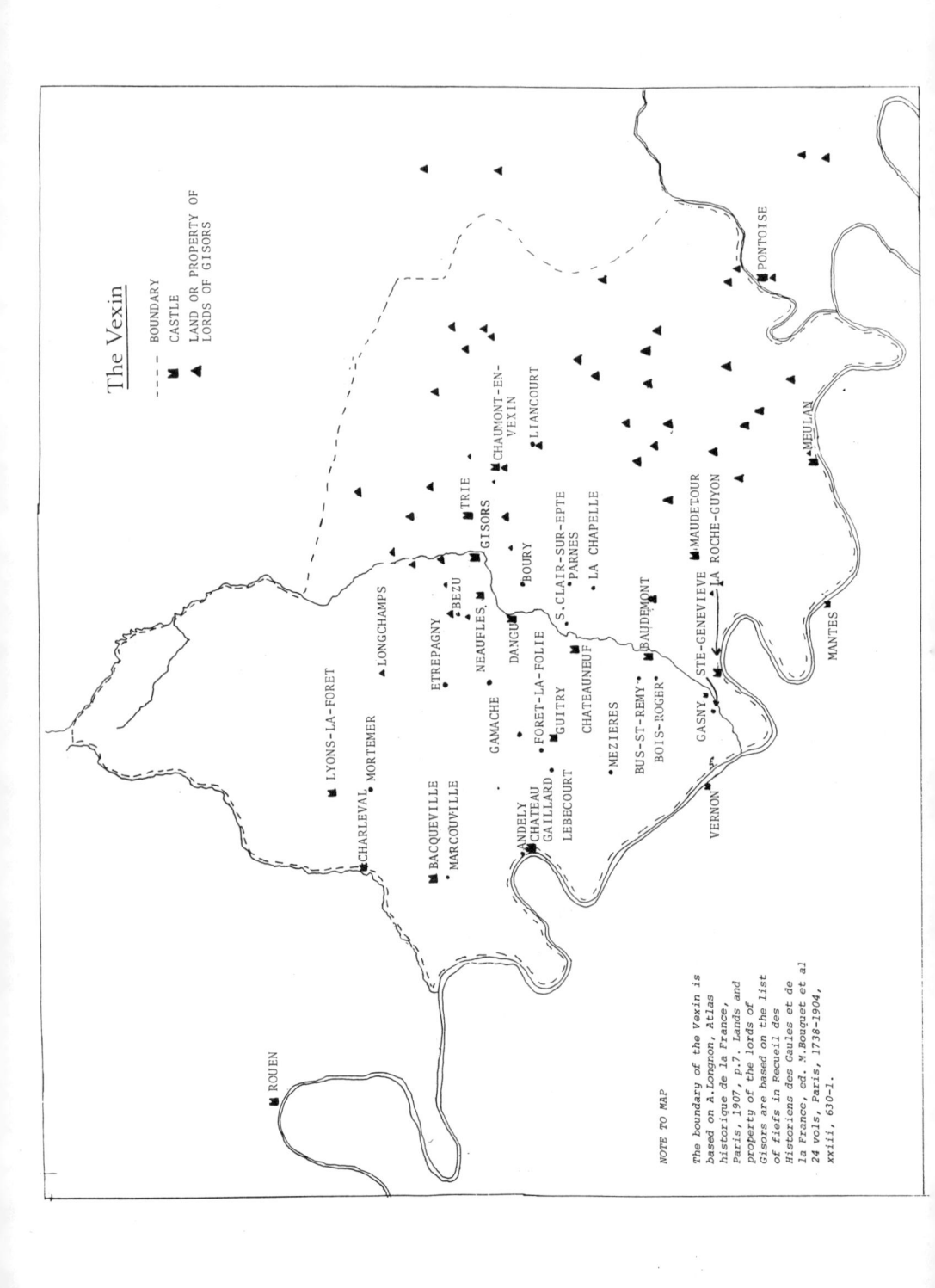

- - - - BOUNDARY
▬ CASTLE
▲ LAND OR PROPERTY OF LORDS OF GISORS

ROUEN

PONTOISE
MEULAN
CHAUMONT-EN-VEXIN
LIANCOURT
TRIE
GISORS
BEZU
BOURY
NEAUFLES
S.CLAIR-SUR-EPTE
PARNES
LA CHAPELLE
MAUDETOUR
LA ROCHE-GUYON
LONGCHAMPS
ETREPAGNY
DANGU
FORET-LA-FOLIE
GAMACHE
GUITRY
CHATEAUNEUF
BAUDEMONT
MEZIERES
BUS-ST-REMY
BOIS-ROGER
GASNY
STE-GENEVIEVE
LYONS-LA-FORET
MORTEMER
BACQUEVILLE
MARCOUVILLE
ANDELY
CHATEAU GAILLARD
LEBECOURT
CHARLEVAL
VERNON
MANTES

NOTE TO MAP

The boundary of the Vexin is based on A.Longnon, Atlas historique de la France, Paris, 1907, p.7. Lands and property of the lords of Gisors are based on the list of fiefs in Recueil des Historiens des Gaules et de la France, ed. M.Bouquet et al 24 vols, Paris, 1738-1904, xxiii, 630-1.

LORDS OF THE NORMAN VEXIN

Judith A. Green

In the work of establishing or extending frontiers in the middle ages the aristocracy had a crucial role to play, at its most dramatic perhaps on the fringes of Christendom, in Spain, Germany, and the Holy Land, but also vital in maintaining boundaries between Christian powers. Life in a frontier region had certain attractions for aristocratic families. Their allegiance was particularly important to a ruler, and might well be recognized by the grant of lands or privileges. Such families, situated as they were on the periphery of a territory, were often granted or aggregated greater control over their lands than those whose estates were closer to the ruler's power base: the Marcher Lordships of Wales where the king's writ did not run provide a famous example. Frontier regions were also often bandit country with little effective control by any ruler, where local lords could pursue their own independent interests. A notable eleventh-century example is provided by the lords of Bellême, who built up a lordship in the no man's land between France, Maine, and Normandy, and were able to play off their overlords against each other.[1] Yet allegiance to more than one lord could be problematic if overlords went to war. Life in frontier areas was obviously exposed to risk, and frontier lords had to be prepared to fight. This was nowhere more true than in that section of the frontiers of Normandy in the eleventh and twelfth centuries which lay along the river Epte. The frequent wars here have usually been discussed, if at all, from the standpoint of the rulers of Normandy and France. An alternative approach is through the history of the local aristocracy which not only provides a fresh angle, but adds to our detailed knowledge of Norman politics, and helps to illustrate some of the advantages and disadvantages of frontier life. In order to understand that history, however, it is necessary to look first at the character of war in this area, and, secondly, at the role in it of the aristocracy.

The river Epte is one of the oldest provincial boundaries in France. It was established as the frontier between the newly created duchy of Normandy and France as early as 911, according to Dudo of St. Quentin.[2] It left its mark not

---

The author would like to thank Mr. David Crouch and Dr. Ian Green for their helpful comments on earlier drafts of this article; also the Research Fund of the Queen's University, Belfast, for financial assistance; and the librarians of Queen's University for their efforts in obtaining rare books.

1 J. Boussard, 'La seigneurie de Bellême aux Xe et XIe siècles', *Mélanges d'Histoire du Moyen Age dediés à L. Halphen*, Paris 1915, 43—55.
2 Dudo 169; for the Norman frontiers in general see J.-F. Lemarignier, *Recherches sur L'Hommage en Marche et les Frontières Féodales*, Lille 1945.

just on politics and administration but also on customary law and even dialect.³ From the later eleventh century until the fall of Normandy to Philip Augustus it was a bitterly contested boundary, not just because its proximity both to Rouen and Paris made it likely that Norman or French attacks would be launched across this frontier, but for additional, more complicated reasons. The establishment of the Norman frontier at the river Epte had bisected an older unit of administration, the *pagus* of the Vexin, thereafter divided into the Norman Vexin and the French Vexin. Until 1077 the French Vexin was ruled by a count. Under Count Dreux (?1018—35) relations with Normandy appear to have been cordial; there was a later story that Dreux had accepted the overlordship of Robert duke of Normandy, and that this situation had been recognised by Henry I of France.⁴ Such a belief may well have provided the justification for William Rufus' attacks on the French Vexin in 1097 and 1098. After the last count of the Vexin retired into a monastery in 1077, the French Vexin was ruled by the king of France, as a fief of the abbey of Saint-Denis, as it was thought in the twelfth century. The link between the monarchy, the abbey, and the French Vexin was greatly strengthened when in 1124 Louis VI in his capacity as count of the Vexin received from the hands of the abbot a standard, which came to be identified with the *oriflamme*, the banner of Charlemagne.⁵ The role of Saint-Denis and particularly Abbot Suger in fostering the image and the reality of Capetian monarchy is well known; what needs emphasis here is its particular association with the French Vexin. In the later twelfth century it was the Norman Vexin that became a bone of contention between Normandy and France. Geoffrey of Anjou had ceded it to Louis VII in 1151 as the price of recognition of his son's homage for the duchy;⁶ Henry had repossessed it in 1160, and afterwards the French kings made repeated attempts to recover it. It was not just a question of conflicting political interests, however, for there was the additional problem that the ecclesiastical boundary in this region did not follow the Epte, as the Norman archdiocese of Rouen took in the whole of the Vexin, both Norman and French, and the archbishops thus had the unenviable task of trying to maintain their authority in territory subject to another, often hostile, ruler.⁷

The Epte frontier, therefore, became a battleground for Norman and French troops for more than a century. Warfare was frequent, ranging from

---

There is also an unpublished thesis on the Norman Vexin to which I was unable to gain access, E. Willemsens, 'Le Vexin Normand de 911 à 1204', summarized in *Bibliothèque de l'Ecole des Chartes, Positions des thèses*, 1900, 153—9.
3 M. Bloch, *The Ile-de-France*, trans. J.E. Anderson, London 1971, 5, 28—9.
4 Orderic, iv, xxx—xxxiv.
5 R. Barroux, 'L'abbé Suger et la vassalité du Vexin en 1124', *Le Moyen Age*, lxiv, 1958, 1—26.
6 The narrative sources are not wholly clear about the date when the Norman Vexin was ceded to Louis VII. According to the 'Historia Gaufridi Ducis', Geoffrey of Anjou conquered all Normandy except Gisors in 1144, and this seems likely in view of the attestations of Goscelin Crispin and Baudry de Bosco to his charter for the citizens of Rouen, *Chroniques des Comtes d'Anjou et des Seigneurs d'Amboise*, ed. L. Halphen and R. Poupardin, Paris 1913, 71—2; *Regesta*, iii, no. 729. The 'Historia Gloriosi Regis Ludovici VII' states that the Norman Vexin was ceded after Louis had accepted Henry's homage for the duchy, *Recueil des Historiens des Gaules et de la France*, ed. M. Bouquet and others, 24 vols., Paris 1738—1904, xii, 127. Robert of Torigny implies that Geoffrey promised the Norman Vexin to Louis VII after Henry I's death, *Chronicles of the Reigns of Stephen, Henry II and Richard I*, ed. R. Howlett, RS, iv, 149, 169.
7 Lemarignier, 47—55.

cross-border raids, only casually mentioned in the sources, to full-blooded campaigns. As a result the frontier eventually bristled with castles on both sides. Some, like Meulan and Mantes, were evidently in existence at an early date, whereas others were built in the course of the wars. By 1100 there were castles at la Roche-Guyon, Chaumont, Maudétour, Trie, and Pontoise, in the French Vexin, whilst in the Norman Vexin Neaufles and Vernon date back to the Conqueror's reign, supplemented later by Châteauneuf-sur-Epte and Gisors, the key to Normandy.[8] In the early twelfth century Henry I built castles at Lyons-la-Forêt and at Charleval on the river Andelle, whilst Louis VI fortified Gasny.[9] The most famous addition to Norman defences later in the twelfth century was Richard I's Château Gaillard, built to guard the approaches to Rouen.[10] On the Norman side the key fortresses along the river Epte were kept in ducal custody from the early twelfth century, but there were other castles controlled by the local families at Baudemont, Gamaches, Bacqueville, Guitry, and Etrepagny.[11] The number and strength of castles — and this is by no means an exhaustive list — is a clear reflection of the impact of war on the region, a war in which the local aristocracy inevitably had an important part to play.

The leading aristocratic families on both sides of the frontier can be seen emerging from obscurity during the early eleventh century. In the Norman Vexin the critical period seems to have been the early years of Duke William's rule. It was he who was responsible for sending William Crispin to guard the castle of Neaufles against incursions by Count Walter of the Vexin, an appointment which must have occurred after 1035, the year when Walter became count, and probably before 1054, when William Crispin is mentioned as one of the Norman lords fighting against the French at the battle of Mortemer.[12] William came from a leading aristocratic family, related to the ducal house through his mother Gunnor. He and his brother Gilbert both witness the duke's charters, and Gilbert also was entrusted with a border command, in his case the castle of Tillières.[13] William's position at Neaufles was that of *vicomte* of the Vexin, an office which became hereditary in his family. The office was extremely powerful, combining financial and judicial responsibilities, and would in effect have made him the duke's key representative in that area.[14] His establishment at Neaufles was evidently on land belonging to

---

8 There is no comprehensive guide to castles in the Vexin, but see M. de Dion, 'Exploration des Châteaux du Vexin', *Bulletin Monumental*, xxxiii, 1867, 330—66; J. Yver, 'Les châteaux forts en Normandie jusqu'au milieu du XIIe siècle, *Bulletin de la Société des Antiquaires de Normandie*, liii, 1957 for 1955—6, 28—115, 604—9. . For Meulan see E. Réaux, *Histoire du Comté de Meulan*, 2nd edn., Meulan 1873, 78; for Mantes, Orderic, iv, 74; for la Roche-Guyon, Chaumont, Trie, and Maudétour, Orderic, v, 214, 216; Pontoise was in existence by 1092, *Cartulaire de l'Abbaye de Saint-Martin de Pontoise*, J. Depoin, Publications de la Société Historique du Vexin, 1895, no. 19; for Neaufles, 'Quo B. Maria subvenit Guillelmo Crispino Seniori', *Patrologiae cursus completus, series latina*, ed. J.-P. Migne, 221 vols., Paris 1844—55, cl, 737; for Vernon, *Gesta Guillelmi*, 17; for Châteauneuf-sur-Epte and Gisors, Orderic, vi, 232, 214—16.
9 Orderic, vi, 234, 218, 234, 184.
10 F.M. Powicke, *The Loss of Normandy*, Manchester, 1913, *passim*.
11 'Historia . . . Ludovici VII', *Recueil des Historiens de France*, xii, 127; Robert of Torigny, 169.
12 'Quo B. Maria . . .', *Patrologiae latina*, cl, 737; *Gesta Guillelmi*, 73.
13 Fauroux, nos. 105, 110, 156; Jumièges, 117.
14 C.H. Haskins, *Norman Institutions*, New York 1918, 41—8.

the archbishop of Rouen, for this was one of the properties recognised as belonging to the archbishop in a charter issued by Duke Robert between 1028 and 1033.[15]

A second important aristocratic family in the Norman Vexin, the lords of Baudemont, may also have been established on archiepiscopal land at about the same time. The earliest clearly identifiable member of the family was Baudry, called 'de Bosco' from the hamlet of Bus-Saint-Rémy near Baudemont, who was actively involved in the wars of Henry I's reign. It seems likely that he was descended from Nicholas of Bacqueville, who witnessed a charter for the nunnery of Saint-Amand at Rouen, issued between 1042 and 1066.[16] Baudry gave land at Ecraketuit, a hamlet of Bacqueville, to the nunnery of Saint-Amand, and he is presumably related to, or identifiable with, the Baudry who quitclaimed to Saint-Amand the service of two knights at Bacqueville until he had paid them thirty pounds in return for the reception of his sister into the nunnery.[17] The Nicholas who witnessed for Saint-Amand was presumably the Nicholas of Bacqueville who was a son of Baudry the German.[18] Bacqueville, Mézières, and Marcouville, all later in the possession of the Baudemont family, had been archiepiscopal property at the time of Duke Robert's charter, and it is likely that the family had been established there at much the same time as William Crispin at Neaufles, possibly during Duke William's minority, when the Norman aristocracy enriched itself at the expense of the church.

The Crispins and the Baudemonts were the two most important families whose interests lay on the Norman side of the frontier, but here as in other border regions there were families with lands on both sides. In this case the two to be reckoned with were the lords of Gisors and of Guitry. The earliest lord of Gisors to have been identified is Hugh, who apparently came from the Touraine, and was well established at Gisors by the middle of the eleventh century, when he gave to the abbey of Marmoutier a place at Gisors called Saint-Ouen, which he said belonged to him by hereditary right.[19] He also gave the church of Saint-Gervase and Saint-Protase, and subsequently Archbishop John of Rouen confirmed to Saint-Ouen for the use of Marmoutier all that which it held at Gisors by the gift of Hugh and his wife, whose dowry this was.[20] It was demonstrated at an inquest in the early thirteenth century that all the family's land at Gisors and at Gamaches was held of the archbishopric of

---

15 Fauroux, nos. 66, 67.
16 Fauroux, no. 187.
17 A. le Prévost, *Mémoires et Notes pour servir à l'histoire du département de L'Eure*, 3 vols., Evreux 1862—9, i, 166; Haskins, 20.
18 Orderic, ii, 82; according to Robert of Torigny's interpolations to the chronicle of William of Jumièges, Nicholas de Bacqueville married a niece of Duchess Gunnor, but this Nicholas is said to have been the ancestor of William Martel, lord of Bacqueville near Dieppe, Jumièges, 328; *Cal. Docs. Fr.*, 356. Baudry de Bosco must be distinguished from Baudry de Bocquencé, tenant of St. Evroul. If the reconstruction above is correct, Baudry de Bosco was the nephew of Baudry de Bocquencé. A further question arises as to the identity of Nicholas son of Baudry, Lord of Guitry, see below n. 26. It is entirely feasible that he was the same man as Nicholas de Bacqueville, though proof of this is lacking.
19 Depoin, no. 3, also p. 407 for the statement that the family came from the Touraine. It has not been possible to trace the communication by Depoin mentioned there.
20 Depoin, no. 4; *Magni Rotuli Scaccarii Normanniae*, ed. T. Stapleton, 2 vols., London 1840—4, ii, xxxvi—xxxvii.

Rouen.[21] Here then was a third family established on archiepiscopal land, but in this case the timing and the method are not so clear. Archbishop John's confirmation suggests that Hugh's land at Gisors was his wife's dowry: she is known to have been related to the *vicomtes* of Chaumont, but when and how they obtained the land is unknown. Gisors was leased for life by Archbishop Maurilius (1055—1067) to Count Ralf of the Vexin, whose son Simon subsequently restored it to the then archbishop.[22] It is tempting to place the enfeoffment during that period, except that it is rather late bearing in mind the timing of Hugh's gifts to Marmoutier.

A second cross-border lordship was established at about the same time, and the method in this case was apparently through marriage. Robert 'the eloquent' of Poissy is thought to have been a prévôt at Chaumont, subordinate to the *vicomte* there.[23] His name indicates his place of origin as Poissy, and Orderic identifies him as lord of Parnes in the French Vexin, where Saint-Evroul founded a priory.[24] He married a daughter of Nicholas son of Baudry, through whom he is said to have acquired Guitry in the Norman Vexin.[25] It is possible that this Nicholas son of Baudry is the Nicholas de Bacqueville mentioned earlier — certainly Bacqueville and Guitry are not far apart — but no evidence has been found for the identification.

Situations of dual allegiance were by no means uncommon in border regions, in some instances reflecting the inability of rulers to prevent them, in others because they were encouraged as a means of extending a ruler's influence into neighbouring territory. The dukes of Normandy were by no means averse to such tactics in the eleventh century, seeking to establish overlordship over neighbouring territories and permitting Normans to marry into families beyond the frontiers of the duchy. In the time of Duke William the marriage of Roger of Beaumont to Adeline, daughter of Waleran count of Meulan, eventually united in the hands of their son Robert vast estates in Normandy and England as well as the county of Meulan.[26] However, as far as the two cross-border lordships discussed above are concerned, there is no evidence to indicate whether they had come into being with the dukes' blessing, or against their wishes.

Such cross-border lordships on the fringes of Normandy were more likely to come into being in the eleventh century than later for a number of reasons. As territorial states grew stronger, their rulers were better able to control the marriages of their vassals, and to prevent them if necessary from becoming vassals of other rulers. In the Vexin the dangers of dual allegiance must have become obvious during the protracted periods of war between Normandy and France.

---

21 *Cartulaire Normand de Philippe-Auguste, Louis VIII, Saint-Louis et Philippe le Hardi*, L. Delisle, Caen 1882, no. 202.
22 Paris BN ms. nouv. acq. lat. 1243, f.161, no. cxiii. Mr. David Crouch kindly drew my attention to this document and supplied me with a copy. There is a French translation in Dom F. Pommeraye, *Histoire de l'église cathédrale de Rouen*, Rouen 1686, 569—70.
23 Depoin, 368.
24 Orderic, ii, 132, 154.
25 Depoin, 368—9. Depoin gives no evidence for this marriage, and he cites an act showing that Nicholas had a son named Roger who held Guitry. He also had other sons, possibly by his marriage to Gertrude, whom Depoin thinks was his second wife, though again Depoin gives no evidence for this belief.
26 Réaux, 119; GEC, vii, 521—37; xii.ii, 357—64, 829—38.

Some writers show an awareness of the problems of dual allegiance. Orderic Vitalis in particular refers to it in a number of contexts: in relation to the separation of England and Normandy under different rulers after 1087 and the problems this created for the magnates; in the French contribution to William Rufus' attack on the French Vexin in 1097—8; and in connexion with the transfer of homage of William count of Evreux from Robert Curthose to Henry I.[27] 'No man can serve two masters' is a recurring theme in Orderic's history; he may well have felt particularly strongly on the subject in reaction to the political events of his own lifetime. By the end of the twelfth century the difficulties posed by dual allegiance, especially in this region, must have been uppermost. William the Breton, for example, in his poem the *Philippide*, celebrating the achievements of Philip Augustus, writes of the dilemma war between Plantagenet and Capetian created for Robert, count of Meulan, forced to choose between his overlords. This was à propos of the siege of Vendôme in 1188 when Robert sent forces to the aid of Henry II, only to see them captured by Philip Augustus.[28]

As the outlines of political geography clarified in the Norman Vexin, a similar process was happening in the French Vexin. Under the overlordship of the counts of the Vexin powerful aristocratic families established themselves in the main centres, at Meulan, Mantes, Chaumont, Trie, Maudétour, and la Roche-Guyon. Here as elsewhere in the Ile-de-France, possession of a castle was a key factor in their dominance, and their local power made them a tough proposition to control. Yet from the reign of Louis VI the Capetian kings do not appear to have had as much difficulty with the French Vexin as did the rulers of Normandy with the Norman Vexin. Louis VI, who had held the French Vexin before his father's death, drew on the families there for support, and the alliance forged at that time does not appear to have broken down seriously afterwards.[29]

Families from both sides of the frontier were drawn into the fighting of the eleventh and twelfth centuries. There are incidental references to their members being killed or wounded, but the most vivid picture of a whole society at war is that which springs from the pages of Orderic Vitalis and Suger, both of whom describe the wars of the late eleventh and early twelfth centuries in a way that clearly demonstrates the role of the local aristocracy. Orderic was well informed about the Vexin thanks to Saint-Evroul's priory at Parnes, and although he recorded the Norman viewpoint he wrote with a certain sympathy of the defence put up by the castellans of the French Vexin in 1098:

> 'In that region there are a great number of distinguished knights, whose gallantry and great courage is inborn. They did not wish the high honour of the French to be tarnished, and fought the enemy to the death for the

---

27 Orderic, iv, 120—4; v, 214; vi, 58.
28 Depoin, 324 n. 63 prints the relevant extract, and also discusses the fate of Count Robert, who lost all his lands after the conquest of Normandy by Philip Augustus.
29 J. Lemarignier, *Le Gouvernement Royal aux Premiers Temps Capétiens*, Paris 1965, 121—3; E. Bournazel, *Le Gouvernement Capétien au XIIe siècle, 1108—80*, Limoges 1975, especially 51—3, 70—80, 86, 98, 113. One exception to this alliance is the quarrel between Louis VII and Theobald of Gisors, see below n. 72. Depoin's notes on the families of the French Vexin provide a useful introduction.

defence of their country and the glory of their people'.[30]

In that war Theobald Payn of Gisors fought on the Norman side, whilst the French defence was led by Robert of Maudétour, Otmund of Chaumont, Walberg of Boury and his brother Richard, Godfrey of Serans and his brother Peter.

The Vexin bore the brunt of the fighting between Henry I and Louis VI. The archbishop of Rouen's fortified manor at Andely was captured and garrisoned by French knights who used it as a base from which to ravage the Norman Vexin. Lords of the Norman Vexin later fought with the French against Henry I's forces. The war culminated in a battle at Brémule in 1119, in which William Crispin III, fighting on the French side, distinguished himself by hitting Henry I on the head, before being captured.[31] Nothing deterred, William, Theobald Payn of Gisors, and Baudry de Bosco, all joined the rebellion of 1123—4 under the leadership of Waleran, count of Meulan, and Amaury, count of Evreux in Normandy and lord of Montfort l'Amaury in France. Men from the French Vexin were to be found in the garrison of the rebels at Pontaudemer, and at Waleran's castle of Beaumont-le-Roger. Meanwhile, Amaury de Montfort and William Crispin, his kinsman as Orderic points out, tried to ambush King Henry's castellan at Gisors, but the plot miscarried and in the ensuing panic much of the town was burned down.[32] There is much less circumstantial detail for these families fighting in the later twelfth century, and it may be that the heyday of their participation had passed, but clearly they could not ignore the later campaigns and would have had to defend their own lands and castles when necessary.

As far as the lords of the Norman Vexin are concerned, not only were they often involved in war, but they were frequently fighting against the rulers of Normandy. Some rulers were notably better than others in keeping the support of these men, but although the tide of support ebbed and flowed, it never looked particularly strong. Rufus evidently had some support here and in the French Vexin, which both Orderic and Suger attribute to his financial resources.[33] Henry I by contrast might almost be said to have held the Norman Vexin in spite of rather than because of the local lords. He did have one huge advantage in the unwavering support of Robert of Meulan, but for the rest he was consistently opposed by Baudry de Bosco, William Crispin, and Theobald Payn of Gisors. Geoffrey of Anjou seems to have been more successful in his dealings with these lords. He had the support of William Crispin, and William's son Goscelin witnessed Geoffrey's charter for the citizens of Rouen, as did Baudry de Bosco.[34] Baudry may well have been prepared to support, or at least acquiesce in, the Angevin conquest of Normandy because of the influence of Waleran of Meulan, who in 1141 had been induced to transfer his allegiance from King Stephen to Geoffrey, and evidently drew other men into

---

30 Orderic, v, 216; cf. Suger, *Vie de Louis VI le Gros*, ed. and trans. H. Waquet, Paris 1964, 4—12.
31 Orderic, vi, 184—248; Suger, 182—200.
32 Orderic, vi, 330—358; Suger's account of this war is dominated by the threat from the emperor and Louis' heroic defence of France, having received the standard from the abbot of Saint-Denis.
33 Orderic, v, 214; Suger, 8.
34 *Regesta*, iii, no. 729.

his orbit.[35] Waleran himself subsequently managed to negotiate the political hurdles presented by his allegiance both to the dukes of Normandy and to Louis VII of France, though it would appear that his relations with the former took a downward turn from the late 1140s.[36] Under Henry II the situation of his grandfather's reign was recreated, for in the great rebellion of 1173—4 both Goscelin Crispin and Baudry de Baudemont were mentioned as participants.[37] When the Norman baronage was finally faced with the decision of choosing between John and Philip Augustus, William Crispin, John of Gisors, and William de Chaumont, all opted for French allegiance, as, after some vacillation, did the holder of the Baudemont fee, Stephen Longchamps.[38] Viewed from the ruler's position, therefore, the lords of the Norman Vexin look simply like rebellious frontiersmen, but by looking at the histories of the most important families in greater detail, at their lands, marriages, and religious patronage, it is possible to discover how they saw their interests, and how these conditioned their relations with the rulers of Normandy. Each family has some individual features, but it will be suggested that general characteristics emerge.

The Crispin family eventually built up a substantial lordship in the Norman Vexin. Its centres were Neaufles, where William Crispin had originally been established, and Dangu, gained through the marriage of Goscelin Crispin to the daughter and heiress of Robert of Dangu. In 1172 Neaufles owed two knights' service and Dangu one, but in addition to this Goscelin Crispin had another thirty-two knights in his service.[39] The family evidently had land at Etrepagny at an early date, for William Crispin I gave rents here to the abbey of Bec.[40] They also had holdings near the forest of Lyons, for Goscelin and his father-in-law Robert of Dangu gave land at 'Pomeria' and La Mesangère to the abbey of Mortemer.[41] Goscelin may already have had land in this area, or it may have come to him through marriage.

This branch of the Crispin family held land not only in the Vexin, however. A genealogy of the family relates that William I had property in the vicinity of Lisieux, and further details emerge in his charter to the abbey of Bec, to which he gave the church of Blangy and the tithe of his demesne there, the tithe of a ploughland at Le Faulq (near Blangy), the church of Livarot with the tithe of his demesne and mills, revenues from Saint-Marcel near Vernon, and revenues

---

35 Robert of Torigny 142; see also n. 66 below.
36 Waleran's career was traced by G.H. White, 'The Career of Waleran, Count of Meulan and Earl of Worcester (1104—66)', *TRHS*, 4th Series, xvii, 1934, 19—48. Waleran is here portrayed as a faithful supporter of the Angevins after 1141, but Mr. Crouch's doctoral research should present a somewhat different picture of his career.
37 *Gesta Regis Henrici Secundi Benedicti Abbatis: the Chronicle of the Reigns of Henry II and Richard I, A.D. 1169—92* (Roger of Howden), ed. W. Stubbs, 2 vols. RS, 1867, i, 45—7.
38 William Crispin and William de Chaumont kept their Norman lands as the registers of Philip Augustus show, *Recueil des Historiens de France*, xxiii, 621 j, k. For John of Gisors and Stephen Longchamps see Powicke, 492, 489—91.
39 *Red Book of the Exchequer*, ed. H. Hall, RS, ii, 637. Unfortunately it is not possible to identify these fees from the registers of Philip Augustus, where William Crispin only appears as holding Dangu and Neaufles.
40 A.A. le Porée, *Histoire de l'abbaye de Bec*, 2 vols., Evreux 1901, i, 330.
41 Paris BN ms. lat. 18369 f.28—9. This cartulary has been edited by P.F. Gallagher, 'The Monastery of Mortemer-en-Lyons in the Twelfth Century — Its History and Cartulary', unpublished Ph.D. thesis, Univesity of Notre Dame, 1970.

from Pacy. His son added the demesne at Mesnil-Foubert, the church and tithe of Drucourt north-west of Bernay, and half the church and tithe of nearby Bournainville.[42] This branch of the family did not, as far as is known, participate in the Norman invasion of England — the Miles Crispin who was granted land there is thought to have been the nephew of William Crispin I — but at the start of Henry II's reign a Goscelin Crispin, contemporary with the man of that name who held Neaufles, is mentioned in the pipe roll account of Essex.[43] There is no information about his holding in England, and no trace of it afterwards, so it is unlikely to have been substantial.

Of the identifiable marriages of the heirs of this family, one was to a prominent French family, and the other two to local families in the Vexin. William I married Eva, sister of Amaury II, lord of Montfort l'Amaury; William II married Agnes, daughter of Godfrey, lord of Etrepagny;[44] and Goscelin married Isabel of Dangu. Two of these marriages thus consolidated the family's position in the Vexin, whilst the third showed an orientation towards France, rather than towards the top levels of the Norman aristocracy.

The Crispins were particularly associated with two religious houses, both of which were in Normandy. The first was Bec, to which they showed a special affection. One of the sons of William Crispin I, Gilbert, became a monk at Bec and later abbot of Westminster, whilst William's widow Eva was to end her days there.[45] Another son, William II, was one of the Norman lords who fiercely resisted the attempt by Robert of Meulan to bring the abbey under his control, threatening the withdrawal of his family's benefactions if Robert succeeded.[46] William I, William II, and William III were all benefactors of the abbey, and their benefactions were confirmed in 1155 by Goscelin Crispin.[47] The other house to which the family made substantial gifts was the Cistercian Abbey of Mortemer, founded in the forest of Lyons in Henry I's reign. Goscelin Crispin joined his father-in-law in making a grant of land to this house, and it was here that his widow Isabelle, and one of his daughters, Eva de Harcourt, were buried, leaving gifts for the celebration of their anniversaries.[48]

In trying to assess the relationship of the Crispins to the rulers of Normandy, it is hard to avoid the conclusion that it reached its high point during the reign of William the Conqueror. After the death of William Crispin I, his son, and possibly his grandson also, for it is difficult to distinguish between William II and William III in the sources, supported Robert Curthose against Henry I. It is a measure of their estrangement from the royal court that they attested no charters of William Rufus or Henry I. The situation evidently

---

42 Le Porée, i, 330, 490, 656—7.
43 *Pipe Rolls 2—4 Henry II*, ed. J. Hunter for Record Commission, London 1844, 58.
44 J. Armitage Robinson, *Gilbert Crispin*, Cambridge 1911, 13—18.
45 Armitage Robinson, 13—18; 'Quo B. Maria . . .', *Patrologiae latina*, cl, 738—42.
46 'On the liberty of the abbey of Bec', published in translation by S. Vaughn, *The Abbey of Bec and the Anglo-Norman State*, Woodbridge 1981, 134—43.
47 Le Porée, i, 656—7. This is the text of Goscelin Crispin's charter, which makes it clear that there were three William Crispins before Goscelin, as the Crispin genealogy states. Le Prévost was thus incorrect in his belief that there were only two, a belief which he may have derived from Père Ansèlme, Le Prévost, ii, 6, 58; P. Ansèlme, *Histoire généalogique de la maison royale de France*, 3rd edn. revised P. Ange and P. Simplicien, Paris, 1730, vi, 632.
48 Paris BN ms. lat. 18369, f. 11.

improved somewhat in the time of Geoffrey of Anjou: according to the Crispin genealogy, William Crispin III was an intimate of Geoffrey's, to whom indeed he was distantly related, and his son, together with two other members of the Crispin family, occur as witnesses to Geoffrey's charter for the citizens of Rouen.[49] However, Goscelin Crispin hardly seems to have played a leading political role under Henry II, and can only be found in his entourage on the occasion of the grant of a charter to Bec.[50] This aloofness is reflected in the fact that the family does not appear to have benefited from royal patronage to any significant extent, either by grants of lands or privileges. Their lands and their interests lay in Normandy rather than France, but it is impossible to discover any evidence of strong commitment or special reasons for loyalty to the rulers of Normandy.

Unlike the Crispin family, the lords of Baudemont do not appear to have had estates in other parts of Normandy. Their estates in the Norman Vexin were substantial, centred on Bacqueville and Baudemont, at each of which they had a castle.[51] Later these were assessed as three knights' service, but in addition the family had a large number of under-tenants, owing in all more than thirty knights' service according to the returns made in the registers of Philip Augustus.[52] The family also held a modest amount of land in England, going back to the reign of Henry I.[53]

The earliest identifiable marriage of an heir is that of Goel de Baudemont, who married Agnes, sister of Goscelin Crispin, thus allying with the other important local family. Goel was predeceased by his son, also named Baudry, and his lands passed to his daughter Heudeberge, who married Osbert de Cailly, whose lands lay to the north-east of Rouen. When Osbert died his lands passed to his daughters, one of whom married Stephen Longchamps, who held Baudemont in right of his wife.[54] Stephen came from a family of new men who had risen fast through their service to the Plantagenet kings. Their name derived from Longchamps near Lyons-la-Forêt where they had a small estate. Stephen's brother, William Longchamps, entered the church, becoming chancellor to Richard I, bishop of Ely, and co-justiciar of England.[55] Stephen was a steward in King Richard's household, went with him on crusade, and was appointed as one of the governors of Acre.[56] On his return to France he was made one of the guarantors of the peace treaty between Richard and Philip in 1193. His lordship of Baudemont had by then passed into French

---

49 'Quo B. Maria . . .', *Patrologiae latina*, cl, 742; *Regesta*, iii, no. 729. Geoffrey of Anjou's grandmother was Bertrada, daughter of Simon de Montfort, whose daughter by an earlier marriage was the wife of William Crispin I, A. Rhein, 'La Seigneurie de Montfort en Iveline', *Mémoires de la Société Archéologique de Rambouillet*, xxi, Versailles, 1910.
50 *Recueil des Actes d'Henri II, roi d'Angleterre et duc de Normandie, concernant les provinces françaises et les affaires de France*, ed. L. Delisle and E. Berger, 3 vols., Paris 1906—27, ii, 107.
51 See above, n. 11.
52 *Recueil des Historiens de France*, xxiii, 711g, 714b, 717c.
53 Stapleton, ii, cxii—cxviii.
54 The foregoing details are taken from Stapleton, ii, cxii—cxviii, Le Prévost, i, 188; Powicke, 489—91; Goel's son Baudry occurs in a charter for Bec, Le Porée, i, 387. The assumption that he predeceased his father is based partly on that charter and partly on the succession of Goel's daughter Heudeburge.
55 Roger of Howden, *Chronica*, ed. W. Stubbs, 4 vols., RS, 1867, iii, xxxvii—xl.
56 *Gesta Regis Henrici Secundi* (Roger of Howden), ii, 190; see also references in L. Landon, *Itinerary of Richard I*, Pipe Roll Society, New Series, xiii, 1935.

hands, and in the treaty of 1193 it was stipulated that he should be allowed to hold the lordship of King Philip.[57] He evidently held office in Normandy subsequently, for the surviving Norman pipe roll for 1198 shows him accounting for the old farm of the prévôté of Lyons-la-Forêt and for the *ministerium* of Brai and Belvoir, which consisted of the castle of Belvoir and the northern part of the forest of Lyons.[58] On the death of King Richard he followed John to England, but after some hesitation he joined the French allegiance and is said to have died fighting in the French army at the battle of Bouvines.[59]

The Baudemont family were benefactors of a number of religious houses, all within Normandy. Baudry was a benefactor of the priory of Deux-Amants, and he also tried to build a chapel not far from Gasny, which ran into opposition from the monks of Saint-Ouen, who claimed he was building on their land.[60] He and his son Goscelin were benefactors of Mortemer,[61] and his son Goel was also a benefactor of Jumièges, to which he granted a third of the tithes of Bosc-Roger and Mézières. The family is not known to have been benefactors of Jumièges before, but the abbey had vineyards at Mézières, so it was a natural destination for such a gift.[62] Goel also came into contact with the abbey of Bec, to which he made reparations for the damage caused by his son to the abbey's property at Surcy, in return for which the latter was received into fraternity.[63] Finally, towards the end of his life Goel patronised the house of Augustinian canons at Sausseuse. His daughter Heudeberge confirmed his gift, and she also occurs as a benefactress of Saint-Ouen, to which she gave her land at Sainte-Geneviève near Gasny.[64]

For much of the twelfth century the Baudemont family, like the Crispins, held aloof from the royal court. Baudry de Bosco was a persistent adversary of Henry I and did not witness any of his charters, though in his case Henry did make overtures, as the grant of land in England shows. Like Goscelin Crispin, Baudry seems to have been prepared to accept the rule of Geoffrey of Anjou, for he too appeared as a witness of Geoffrey's charter for Rouen.[65] Baudry's decision may have been influenced by Waleran of Meulan, who had opted for the Angevin party in 1141, and whose charters Baudry witnessed in 1141 and 1152.[66] Baudry's son and successor Goel is mentioned in an incident reported by Robert of Torigny in 1153, after the Norman Vexin had been handed over to Louis VII. The latter besieged the castle of Vernon, held by the Norman Richard of Vernon, and, faced with having to withdraw without achieving anything, Louis arranged with Richard that the castle should be handed over

---

57 Landon, 79, 109.
58 Stapleton, ii, 417.
59 Stapleton, ii, cxii.
60 Le Prévost, i, 166; Stapleton, ii, cxiii—cxiv.
61 Paris BN ms. lat. 18369, ff. 38, 40.
62 *Chartes de l'Abbaye de Jumièges*, ed. J.J. Vernier, 2 vols., Société de l'Histoire de Normandie, 1916, i, 223.
63 Le Porée, i, 344.
64 Le Prévost, i, 188.
65 *Regesta*, iii, no. 729.
66 E. Houth, 'Galeran II, comte de Meulan, Catalogue de ses Actes', *Bulletin Philologique et Historique (Jusqu'à 1610) du Comté des Travaux Historiques et Scientifiques*, Paris 1961 for 1960, document no. vi; E. Houth, *Recueil des Chartes de Saint-Nicaise de Meulan*, Publications de la Société Historique de Pontoise et du Vexin, Paris, 1924, no. 13; Réaux, 200.

to Goel de Baudemont who, as the vassal of both men, was an acceptable compromise.[67] Goel seems to have had little to do with the court of Henry II, however, and in 1173—4 his son Baudry was on the side of the rebels.[68] It was only when the honour passed by marriage to Stephen Longchamps, therefore, that this strategically important and wealthy honour passed into the hands of a man whose interests were closely associated with the Plantagenets.

The lords of Gisors are usually mentioned in connexion with Normandy as rebellious frontier lords, yet when the history of their family is examined more closely, they emerge as a French family with some Norman estates, the problem being that these were in a strategically vital area, in and around Gisors. By the early thirteenth century their estates were extensive, stretching from the river Epte to the river Oise and beyond, and southwards to the Seine and the outskirts of Paris. By contrast their Norman property was much smaller, consisting of Gisors, Bézu, Bernoville, Mesnil Gilbert, Mesnil Bencelin, Neaufles, and 'Tigervilla'.[69] Moreover, their lands at Gamaches and Gisors were held as under-tenants of the archbishops of Rouen, and they had control of the castle of Gisors only fleetingly, if at all. The presence of ducal castellans at Gisors would certainly have inhibited their freedom of action. They also acquired some lands in England, dating back to Henry I's reign, when Theobald Payn is known to have held Harting in Sussex. At the time the English estates were finally lost in the early thirteenth century, they consisted of Birling in Sussex and Titchfield in Hampshire.[70]

A study of the connexions of this family through marriage points the same way: they did not marry into Norman families but into those of the French Vexin and surrounding districts. The wife of Hugh de Gisors I is thought to have been related to the *vicomtes* of Chaumont; their son Theobald married a daughter of Geoffrey le Riche, and two of their daughters into the families of Bantelu and Aiguillon of Trie. The family background of Hugh II's wife is unknown, but their son, Theobald II, married Rohais, probably the daughter of Lancelin of Beauvais. In the following generation John of Gisors married Agnes, sister of Walo III of Chaumont, and one of his sisters married William de Garlande.[71]

The distribution of their religious patronage followed a similar pattern, for the houses with which the family was particularly associated lay outside Normandy. Hugh I's benefaction to Marmoutier is explicable in terms of the high reputation of that house in the mid-eleventh century, attracting gifts from a wide area. The family maintained special links with the abbey of Saint-Martin de Pontoise: Theobald Payn entered the community there at the end of his life; his grandson Theobald II took refuge there having quarrelled with Louis VII in 1150, and made several gifts to the community.[72] John of Gisors was a generous patron of a number of religious houses, including Saint-Germer-de-

---

67 Robert of Torigny, 175. Bacqueville and Baudemont were held of the lords of Vernon.
68 *Gesta Regis Henrici Secundi* (Roger of Howden), i, 45—6.
69 *Recueil des Historiens de France*, xxiii, 630—1, 713h.
70 *Red Book of the Exchequer*, ii, 555, 803; *Book of Fees, commonly called Testa de Nevill*, ed. H.C. Maxwell Lyte, 3 vols., London 1920—31, i, 618.
71 Depoin, 407—11.
72 Depoin, 408, nos. clxiv, clxxxiii, clxxxix, cxcix. Note also no. clxiii where Theobald is described as *familiarissimus amicus* of Saint-Martin.

Fly in the Beauvaisis, the abbey of Val Notre-Dame founded by a relative by marriage, and the abbey of Vaux de Cernay.[73]

As the distribution of their lands and family interests suggests, the lords of Gisors moved in the sphere of French rather than Norman politics, insofar as they can be seen to have been involved at all. In 1091 Theobald Payn witnessed a charter of Philip I,[74] and, though he fought against French forces in 1097—8, he subsequently joined them in the wars against Henry I, probably as a result of losing custody of the castle of Gisors.[75] Hugh II and Theobald II like Baudry de Bosco, seem to have come under the influence of Waleran of Meulan, for whom they attested a charter in 1141.[76] As already mentioned, there was a quarrel between Theobald II and Louis VII in 1150, which must have been serious for Theobald to be exiled from his lands, but the breach was evidently not permanent, for Louis addressed a charter to Theobald in cordial terms in 1161.[77] By 1161 Henry II had repossessed the castles of the Norman Vexin, and although he and Richard retained military control of Gisors until 1193, the lords of Gisors stood aloof from their court. When the final decision about allegiance came, John of Gisors opted for Philip Augustus, thus losing his lands in England.

As we have seen, the lords of Chaumont had probably acquired land in Normandy by the marriage of Robert the eloquent to the daughter of Nicholas, lord of Guitry, in the mid-eleventh century. The lordship of Guitry evidently extended as far as Lébécourt, where Nicholas gave land to the abbey of Saint-Wandrille, and at a later date it also extended to Forêt-la-Folie.[78] In the early thirteenth century William II de Chaumont also held one and a half fees at nearby Etrepagny and Mouflaines.[79] Orderic's account of the foundation of the priory at Parnes mentions that Robert the eloquent was overlord of Parnes, and this was presumably part of the knight's fee which the family later held at Saint-Clair-sur-Epte.[80] Robert the eloquent had three sons, of whom Wazo had the toponym de Poissy like his father, whilst the second Otmund, lord of Guitry, was called de Chaumont, where he held the castle.[81] The third son Robert, was called de Beauvais, and became *vidame* of Gerberoy. Otmund's son William married an illegitimate daughter of Louis VI, whose

---

73 Depoin, 409—11; *Cartulaire de l'Abbaye de Notre-Dame des Vaux de Cernay*, ed. L. Merlet and A. Moutié, Paris 1857, 127.
74 *Recueil des Actes de Philippe I, roi de France*, ed. M. Prou, Paris 1908, no. cxxvii for date see introduction, p. lviii; Theobald Payn also witnessed a charter of Louis VI in 1102, A. Luchaire, *Louis VI, Annales de sa vie et de son règne (1081—1137)*, Paris 1890, no. 22.
75 Suger says that Gisors was fortified for Theobald Payn by William Rufus and that the removal of its custody from Theobald Payn was one of the reasons for the outbreak of war in 1109, Suger, 102—4. Orderic mentions that Robert Curthose promised to give Theobald custody of Gisors, Orderic, v, 308.
76 *Chartes de Saint-Nicaise de Meulan* (ed. Houth), no. 13. Gisors does not seem to have been taken by Geoffrey of Anjou, see above note 6. Louis VII wrote to Suger from Antioch in 1148 adjuring him to take the greatest care in guarding Gisors, A. Luchaire, *Etudes sur les actes de Louis VII*, Paris 1885, no. 229.
77 Luchaire, *Louis VII*, no. 454.
78 Le Prévost, ii, 225; in 1180 William de Chaumont accounted at the Norman exchequer for Guitry and Forez (the forest at Guitry), Stapleton, i, 73.
79 *Recueil des Historiens de France*, xxiii, 714a.
80 Orderic, ii, 154; *Recueil des Historiens de France*, xxiii, 624m—625a.
81 Orderic, ii, 154; Depoin, 370.

dowry was land at Liancourt, not far from Chaumont.[82] This marriage is the only one of an heir to have been identified, and it certainly allied the family with Capetian interests. The abbey of Saint-Père de Chartres had a priory at Liancourt, and the lords of Chaumont were its benefactors. Otmund confirmed a grant made by Hugh de Marines, whilst his son William granted the monks free passage across his lands, and his widow at a later date granted them land called *campum Manasserii* which her father had given her, and a *hospes* (a kind of peasant) at Chaumont.[83] The family also maintained the link with Saint-Wandrille in Normandy which went back to the time of Nicholas son of Baudry. Otmund I confirmed Nicholas' grants, and William II gave them the right to take wood for fuel at Guitry, together with a meadow and a garden.[84] Otmund I was also linked with the house of Saint-Germer-de-Fly, where he became a monk.[85]

Rather less is known about this family than the others under consideration, and the evidence relates chiefly to the late eleventh and early twelfth centuries, when they were prominent adherents of Louis VI. Otmund took a leading part in the wars against Rufus and Henry I, and was captured on the battlefield at Brémule.[86] He occurs as a witness to one of Louis' charters, and may have been his chamberlain.[87] His brother Wazo de Poissy was a constable about 1106 or 1107.[88] Otmund's son William also fought against Henry I and was captured at the siege of Tillières. He rose against King Stephen later when the latter burned down the castle of Guitry, which Orderic described as a den of thieves.[89] Orderic clearly had strong feelings about the family, for he called Otmund a wicked old man, who used to plunder pilgrims and poor men, widows, helpless monks and clerks, drawing thus the classic picture of a robber baron.[90] The castle of Guitry was burned again in 1152 by Duke Henry in his attack on the Norman Vexin.[91] There is no sign that the family ever attached itself to the court of the Plantagenets, and on the division of the Norman baronage William II de Chaumont naturally maintained his allegiance to Philip Augustus.

In comparing the history of these four families, some general characteristics emerge. The first is the polarization between the Norman families, who usually married Normans and patronized Norman religious houses, and the two with lands on both sides of the frontier who emerge in fact as French, with lands in Normandy, and who usually married into other French families and patronized French religious houses. This leads on to a second point, namely, the localism of the interests of these families, both in terms of their marriages and religious patronage. With a few exceptions they were not closely associated with the court of the rulers of Normandy, nor a wider network of the Anglo-

---

82 *Cartulaire de l'Abbaye de Saint-Père de Chartres*, ed. B.E.C. Guérard, 2 vols., Paris 1848, ii, 638—9.
83 Guérard, ii, 630—1, 640, 652—3.
84 Depoin, 369, 374.
85 Depoin, 371.
86 Orderic, v, 216; vi, 232—42.
87 Luchaire, *Louis VI*, nos. 136, 9, 141.
88 Depoin, 434—5.
89 Orderic, vi, 242, 490.
90 Orderic, vi, 242.
91 Robert of Torigny, 169.

Norman aristocracy. Moreover, it is difficult to see that they were able to use their frontier position to acquire large estates in Normandy, or in England, or a specially privileged position, like the Marcher Lords in Wales.

These factors throw light on the question of their loyalties and allegiance, and why they were to be found so often in rebellion against the rulers of Normandy. None had any overwhelming reasons for gratitude to those rulers, until in the dying years of Norman rule the lordship of Baudemont came into the hands of Stephen Longchamps. The Crispins and the Baudemonts were generally aloof if not hostile, and the same seems to have been true of the lords of Gisors and Guitry. Only for Stephen Longchamps did the division of the Norman baronage present a real dilemma. He was a Norman by birth, but one whose adherence to the Plantagenets had brought great rewards, as they had to his brothers. Yet in the last resort, with his lands concentrated in the Norman Vexin, he had no choice but to support Philip Augustus.

Studying family history also has implications for our view of Norman rule in this region. In political terms, the rulers of Normandy from the late eleventh century could never count on much support here, with the possible exception of Geoffrey of Anjou. This meant that holding down the frontier would have to be a military operation, and the very strength of ducal castles along the Epte, held by ducal castellans, must have been an irritant to local families, to put it mildly. The loss of custody of Gisors was evidently the reason for Theobald Payn's opposition to Henry I, and custody of Neaufles may have been an issue in William Crispin's opposition. It is possible that the problem of control for the duke was progressive: the harder the region was to control, the more castles were needed in safe hands, which made the families still more intractable.

The lords of the Norman Vexin have been used as an illustration of life on the frontiers of Normandy, but there were other families in a similar situation, such as the lords of Gournay, the counts of Eu and Aumale, the lords of Tosny and the counts of Evreux, and a study of their history would throw further light on frontier politics. It has also been argued that their history, as indeed the history of all families, has to be seen from the internal standpoint of its members, as well as its wider political significance. Most of all, perhaps, it indicates a need for further inquiry into the aristocratic families of Normandy in the eleventh and twelfth centuries to reach beyond generalities to a better understanding of their social and political history.

Lords of the Norman Vexin

I. *The Crispin family*

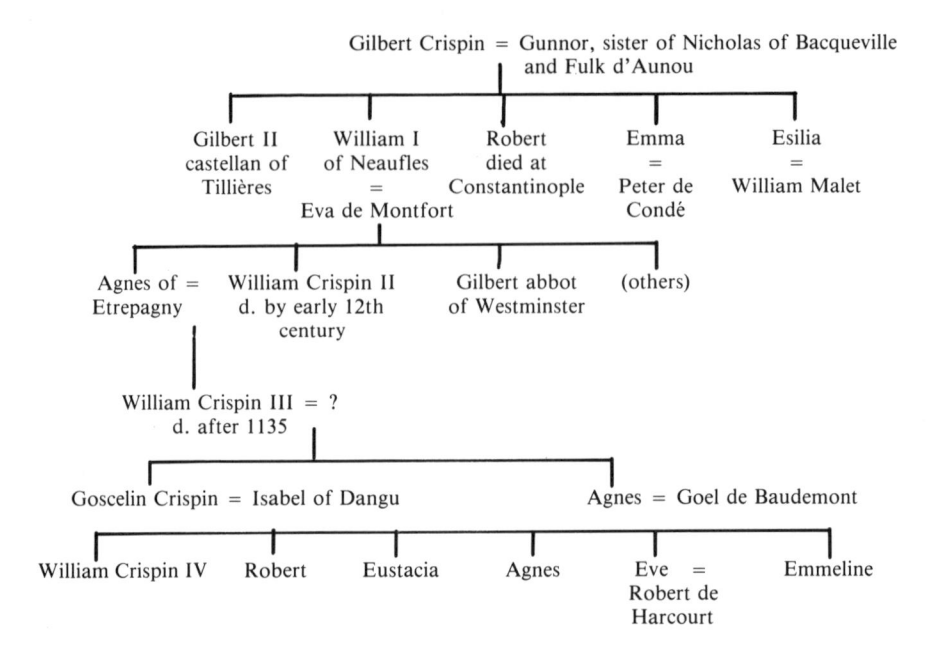

```
              Gilbert Crispin = Gunnor, sister of Nicholas of Bacqueville
                                and Fulk d'Aunou
   ┌──────────────┬──────────────┬──────────────┬──────────────┐
 Gilbert II    William I      Robert         Emma          Esilia
 castellan of  of Neaufles    died at         =              =
 Tillières         =          Constantinople Peter de    William Malet
              Eva de Montfort                Condé
   ┌──────────────┬──────────────┬──────────────┐
 Agnes of =  William Crispin II   Gilbert abbot   (others)
 Etrepagny   d. by early 12th    of Westminster
              century
        │
  William Crispin III = ?
     d. after 1135
   ┌──────────────────────────────┬──────────────────────────────┐
 Goscelin Crispin = Isabel of Dangu         Agnes = Goel de Baudemont
   ┌────────┬────────┬────────┐         ┌────────┬────────┐
 William   Robert  Eustacia  Agnes       Eve   =   Emmeline
 Crispin IV                             Robert de
                                        Harcourt
```

II. *The Lords of Baudemont*

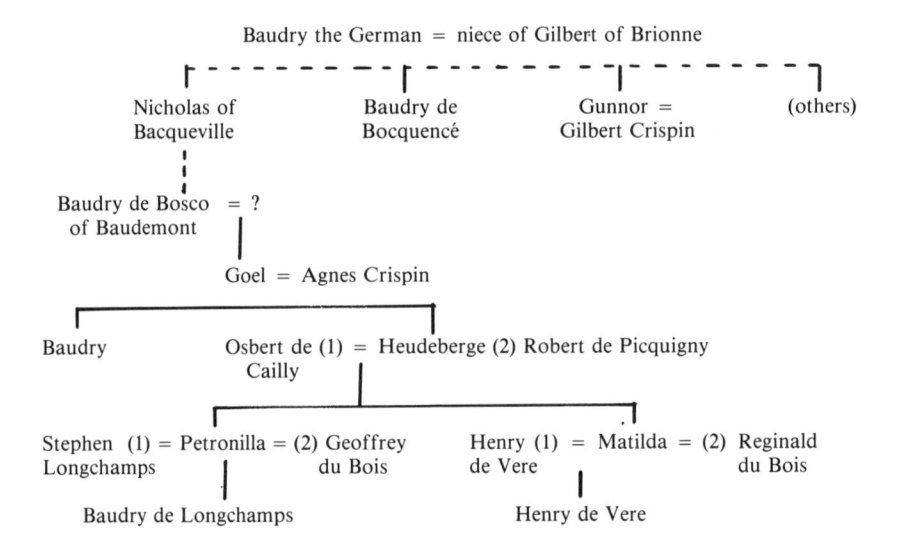

```
              Baudry the German = niece of Gilbert of Brionne
   ┌──────────────┬──────────────┬──────────────┐
 Nicholas of   Baudry de      Gunnor =        (others)
 Bacqueville   Bocquencé      Gilbert Crispin
      ┊
 Baudry de Bosco = ?
 of Baudemont
                │
           Goel = Agnes Crispin
   ┌──────────────┬──────────────┐
 Baudry    Osbert de (1) = Heudeberge (2) Robert de Picquigny
           Cailly
   ┌──────────────┬──────────────┐         ┌──────────────┬──────────────┐
 Stephen (1) = Petronilla = (2) Geoffrey   Henry (1) = Matilda = (2) Reginald
 Longchamps          │         du Bois     de Vere       │         du Bois
                                                   
      Baudry de Longchamps                        Henry de Vere
```

III. The Lords of Gisors

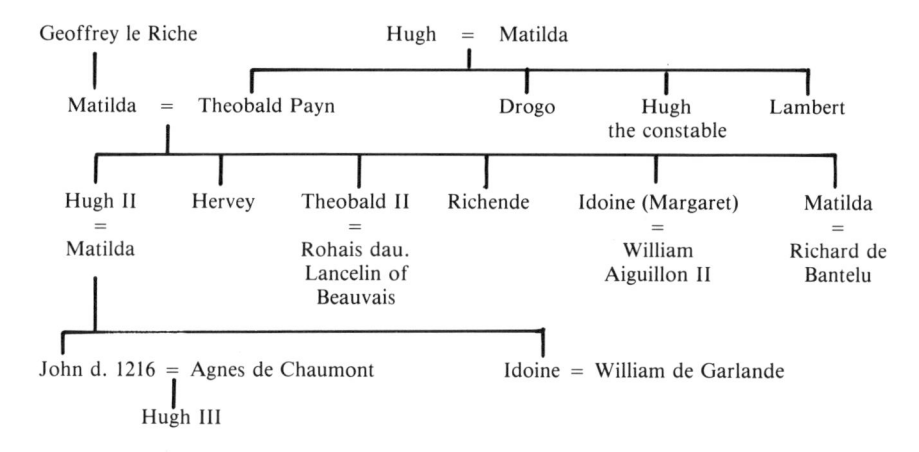

```
Geoffrey le Riche                    Hugh  =  Matilda
       |                    ┌───────────┬──────────┬──────────┐
Matilda  =  Theobald Payn  Drogo      Hugh       Lambert
            |                       the constable
  ┌─────┬──────┬──────────┬─────────┬──────────────┬──────────┐
Hugh II  Hervey  Theobald II  Richende  Idoine (Margaret)  Matilda
  =                =                         =                =
Matilda         Rohais dau.                William         Richard de
                Lancelin of                Aiguillon II    Bantelu
                Beauvais
  |
  ┌──────────────────────────────┐
John d. 1216 = Agnes de Chaumont    Idoine = William de Garlande
        |
     Hugh III
```

IV. The family of Chaumont, lords of Guitry

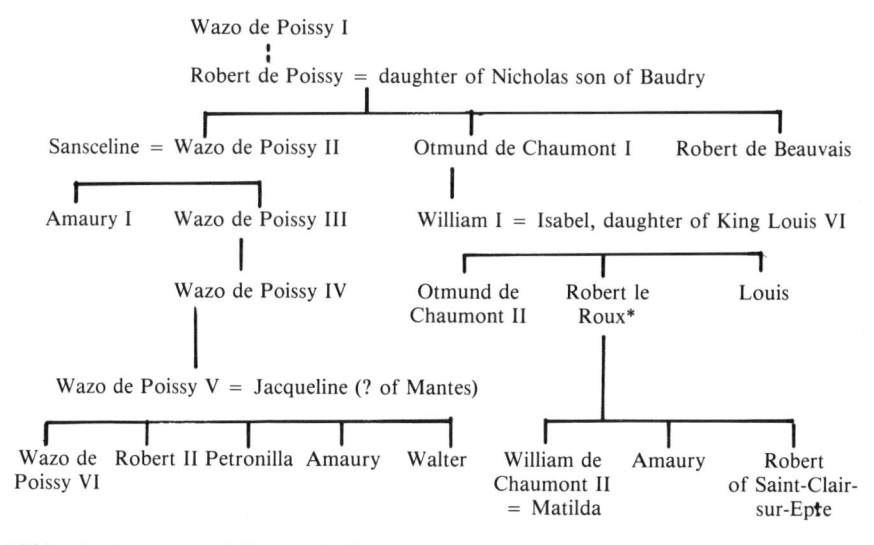

```
                  Wazo de Poissy I
                         ⋮
          Robert de Poissy = daughter of Nicholas son of Baudry
  ┌──────────────────────────┬──────────────────────┐
Sansceline = Wazo de Poissy II   Otmund de Chaumont I   Robert de Beauvais
  ┌──────────┬──────────┐              |
Amaury I   Wazo de Poissy III   William I = Isabel, daughter of King Louis VI
              |                  ┌──────────────┬────────────┐
          Wazo de Poissy IV    Otmund de     Robert le      Louis
              |                Chaumont II    Roux*
Wazo de Poissy V = Jacqueline (? of Mantes)
  ┌──────┬──────────┬────────┬──────┐    ┌──────────┬─────────┬────────────┐
Wazo de  Robert II Petronilla Amaury Walter  William de  Amaury   Robert
Poissy VI                                   Chaumont II         of Saint-Clair-
                                            = Matilda           sur-Epte
```

* Either brother or son of Otmunt de Chaumont II (wrongly styled Otmund III by Depoin, 373).

Note to genealogies

The genealogies of the lords of Gisors and Chaumont are based on the information in the appendices to the *Cartulaire de l'Abbaye de Saint-Martin de Pontoise*, J. Depoin, Publications de la Société Historique du Vexin, 1895. Early generations of the Crispin family are identified in the Crispin genealogy, 'Quo B. Maria subvenit Guillelmo Crispino Seniori', *Patrologiae cursus completus, series latina*, ed. J.-P. Migne, 221 vols., Paris 1844—55, cl, 735—43. The suggested reconstruction of the ancestry of Baudry de Bosco, earliest known lord of Baudemont, is based on Orderic, ii, 82—4. Evidence that Baudry was descended from Nicholas of Bacqueville is cited in the text above. The complicated history of the lordship in the late twelfth and early thirteenth century is usefully summarized by F.M. Powicke, *The Loss of Normandy*, Manchester 1913, 489—91.

STRONGBOW, HENRY II AND ANGLO-NORMAN INTERVENTION IN IRELAND

Marie Therese Flanagan

The involvement in Ireland of Richard Fitz Gilbert, popularly known as Strongbow, will here be considered against the background of his career and circumstances in England, Wales and Normandy. In 1166 Diarmait Mac Murchada, king of Leinster, was forced into exile and determined to seek military aid in Henry II's dominions to try and regain his kingdom.[1] Diarmait's action led to the first direct intervention of Anglo-Normans in Ireland. Of those Anglo-Normans whom he recruited to his service the most important was Richard Fitz Gilbert to whom Diarmait in the winter of 1166—67 made a proposal of marriage to his daughter Aoife and succession to the kingdom of Leinster after his death in return for military service. Strongbow took up that offer in 1170 by going to Ireland, marrying Aoife and fighting a series of successful military campaigns on Diarmait Mac Murchada's behalf which resulted in Diarmait's recovery of the kingdom of Leinster and Strongbow's succession to it after his death.

Before examining the consequences for Strongbow of involvement in Ireland it is necessary to consider his family origins and the extent of the estates which he held in England, Wales and Normandy. Strongbow was a descendant of Richard Fitz Gilbert, lord of Orbec and Bienfaite, who had crossed with William the Conqueror to England in 1066 and had been rewarded with the lordships of Clare in Suffolk and Tonbridge in Kent. When Richard died in 1090 his French possessions were inherited by his eldest son, Roger, while the English estates went to his younger son, Gilbert, founder of the de Clare line of the family in England. The family enjoyed the favour of King Henry I.[3] Walter, a younger brother of Gilbert, lord of Clare, was granted the district of Netherwent in Monmouthshire by Henry sometime before 1119; it came to be known as the lordship of Strigoil or Chepstow from the principal castle situated in it.[4] Henry also granted to Walter a number of estates which had been held by William of Eu (but had been confiscated in 1096 because of William's rebellion against William Rufus), notably the

---

1 For the Irish background see G.H. Orpen, *Ireland under the Normans*, i, London 1911; E. Curtis, *A history of medieval Ireland from 1086 to 1513*, 2nd edition, London 1938; F.X. Martin, *No hero in the house: Diarmait Mac Murchada and the coming of the Normans to Ireland*, Dublin 1975.
2 I.J. Sanders, *English baronies: a study of their origins and descent, 1086—1327*, London 1960, 34—5; M. Altschul, *A baronial family in medieval England: the Clares, 1217—1314*, Baltimore 1965, 17—28; GEC, iii, 242—4, vi, 498—501, x, 348—57.
3 Gilbert Fitz Richard and his brothers, Walter and Robert, were frequent witnesses to Henry I's charters: *Regesta*, ii, 420—1 *sub nomine* Clare.
4 Sanders, 110—1.

manor of Weston in Hertfordshire and Badgeworth in Gloucestershire.[5] In 1130 Roger, lord of Orbec and Bienfaite, died without heirs. Henry I then granted his estates to Gilbert, a younger son of Gilbert, lord of Clare. About 1137—38 Walter, who had been granted the lordship of Strigoil by Henry I, died without heirs and King Stephen bestowed his estates on Gilbert, who had received the lordship of Orbec and Bienfaite in 1130. Gilbert now held the estates of the senior branch of the family in Normandy, which had been held by his paternal uncle Roger, and the lordship of Strigoil, which his paternal uncle Walter, a younger son like himself, had received from Henry I. In addition, in 1138 King Stephen created Gilbert Earl of Pembroke.[6]

Such was the inheritance to which Gilbert's son, Richard, known as Richard Fitz Gilbert or Strongbow, succeeded on the death of his father in 1148. It was not, however, to remain intact.

During the civil disturbances of Stephen's reign Strongbow had remained loyal to King Stephen and that even after the Angevin party had taken possession of the city of Bristol, which was menacingly close to Strongbow's lordship of Strigoil. The first certain consequence of Strongbow's loyalty to Stephen was the loss of the lordship of Orbec and Bienfaite when the Angevin party gained control of Normandy: from 1153 onwards Orbec and Bienfaite was in the possession of Robert de Montfort, who must have been granted it by Henry as duke of Normandy.[7] More serious was to be Strongbow's forfeiture

5 The lordship of Strigoil had been granted by William the Conqueror to William Fitz Osbern, Earl of Hereford, who in turn enfeoffed Ralph de Limesi. In 1075 Roger, Earl of Hereford, who had succeeded his father in 1071, and Ralph de Limesi forfeited Strigoil and other lands on account of rebellion against the Conqueror. By 1086 when Domesday book was compiled Strigoil and the other holdings of Ralph de Limesi were held of the king by William of Eu: *Domesday Book*, i, 162a; A.S. Ellis, 'On the landholders of Gloucestershire named in Domesday book' in *Trans. of the Bristol and Gloucestershire Archaeological Society*, iv, 1879—80, 86—198 at 125—9. William of Eu in turn forfeited Strigoil and the former lands of Ralph de Limesi by rebelling against William Rufus in 1096 (but not apparently his patrimonial lands): E.A. Freeman, *The reign of William Rufus and the accession of Henry I*, ii, London 1882, 64—5, 68. By 1119 at the latest they had been granted to Walter Fitz Richard. The lands which Walter Fitz Richard acquired with Strigoil which had belonged formerly to William of Eu may be identified by isolating in Domesday book those holdings of William of Eu which had been held previously by Ralph de Limesi and/or Alestan of Buscombe whose estates Ralph de Limesi acquired after the conquest. In 1130 Walter Fitz Richard paid danegeld on land in Hertfordshire, Bedfordshire, Gloucestershire, Berkshire and Wiltshire: *Pipe roll 31 Henry I*, 1833, 23, 62, 80, 104. For William of Eu's holdings in these counties see *Domesday Book*, i, fol.61a, xii, 71b, xxxii, 162a, 166b, xxxi, 211b, xviii. Walter Fitz Richard also acquired the manor of Chesterford in Essex which almost certainly came from the royal demesne: below note 57.
6 Orderic, vi, 520.
7 In 1153 Orbec was in the hands of Robert de Montfort of Montfort-sur-Risle, son of Hugh de Montfort by Adeline, daughter of Robert de Beaumont, Count of Meulan and Earl of Leicester and sister of Isabella, mother of Strongbow: Robert of Torigny, *Chronicles, Stephen, Henry II and Richard I*; ed. R. Howlett, iv, RS 1890, 177—8. Orbec was still held by Robert de Montfort in 1172: *Magni rotuli scaccarii Normanniae*; ed. T. Stapleton, ii, London 1844, cxxxvii. After Robert's death in 1178 it was in the possession of his widow Clemence: *Cartulaires de Saint-Ymer-en-Auge et de Bricquebec*; ed. C. Bréard, Société de l'Histoire de Normandie, lxxi, 1908, no. xii. This charter, which has been dated by Bréard to 1194, should probably be assigned to a period after 1181—2, as Clemence's gift is not mentioned in the papal bull of 1182, as pointed out in GEC, x, 353 and before 1194. By 1194 Orbec was held by her son Hugh de Montfort: *Cartulaires*, no. xiii. It was recovered by William Marshal in right of his wife Isabella, daughter of Strongbow, at some point between 1194 and 1204—5. In 1204 in the division of estates resultant upon King John's forfeiture to the French crown Orbec was retained by William Marshal: F.M. Powicke, *The loss of Normandy*, 2nd edition, London 1961, 350.

of the earldom of Pembroke after Henry's accession as king of England in 1154. Henry must have had some negotiations with Strongbow, as he had with the majority of Stephen's supporters, but the full details are not known. Henry recognized Strongbow's inheritance of Strigoil and other estates in England and Normandy, but he was not prepared to restore to him the lordship of Orbec and Bienfaite nor to allow him the use of a comital title or possession of the earldom of Pembroke.[8] Pembroke appears to have been retained as a royal county throughout Henry's reign.[9]

Although Strongbow's father, Gilbert, had been granted the earldom of Pembroke in 1138 there is little evidence that he ever made much effort to take possession of the earldom as distinct from use of title. The closest Gilbert appears to have got to Pembroke was his fortification of the castle of Caermarthen on behalf of King Stephen in 1145.[10] The only tangible advantage which Gilbert seems to have derived from the earldom of Pembroke was the right to style himself *comes Gilbertus*. If a 15th century transcript of a charter granted by Gilbert to the Templars may be relied upon, he actually styled himself on occasion *comes de Weston* taking the name from his demesne manor in Hertfordshire.[11] In 1153 after Strongbow had succeeded to his father's inheritance he witnessed the treaty between King Stephen and Henry, duke of Normandy, as *comes de Pembroc*.[12] This is the last occasion, however, in any royal document in which Strongbow is so named, which suggests that Henry II after his accession in 1154 refused to acknowledge Strongbow as earl of Pembroke. Strongbow issued at least two charters in which he styled himself *comes de Pembroc*.[13] The charters, however, cannot be dated precisely: they may, or may not, have been issued during the period 1148—54 when Strongbow could have used the title legitimately. It is certain, however, that after 1154 Strongbow is not accorded a comital title in official sources, being termed merely Richard Fitz Gilbert, or at best Richard son of Earl Gilbert.[14]

8 In January 1156 Richard Fitz Gilbert without comital title was a witness to a charter issued by Henry II: *Sir Christopher Hatton's book of seals*; ed. L.C. Loyd and D.M. Stenton, Northamptonshire Record Society, xv, 1942—1950, no. 40; R.W. Eyton, *Court, household and itinerary of King Henry II*, London 1878, 16. Strongbow is not found again in the company of Henry II until late 1167, early 1168 when he accompanied Princess Mathilda to Germany: below note 28.
9 Returns from Pembroke are not recorded on the pipe rolls but Gerald of Wales mentions a sheriff of Pembroke, one William Carquit about 1174: *Giraldi Cambrensis opera*; ed. J.S. Brewer, i, RS, 1861, 25.
10 *Brut y Tywysogyon or the Chronicle of the Princes: Red Book of Hergest version*; ed. T. Jones, Cardiff 1955, 121; *Brut y Tywysogyon or the Chronicle of the Princes: Peniarth Ms 20 version*; ed. T. Jones, Cardiff 1952, 54.
11 *Records of the Templars in England in the twelfth century: the inquest of 1185*; ed. B.A. Lees, London 1935, 218.
12 *Foedera*, i, pars 1, 1816, 18; *Recueil des actes de Henri II*; ed. L. Delisle and E. Berger, i, Paris 1909, 64.
13 In favour of Tintern Abbey: *C Ch R*, ii, 72; in favour of Bertram son of Thierry relating to Barrow in Suffolk: *C Ch R*, iii, 96—7.
14 *Recueil*, i, 310, 467; ii, 376, 398. That Strongbow was earl of Pembroke only betweeen 1148 and 1154 has been overlooked by GEC, X, 352—60 and many other publications. Between 1154 and 1199, when the earldom of Pembroke was conferred on William Marshal by King John, Pembroke was retained in the king's hand and, insofar as the Welsh permitted it, was administered as a royal county. G.H. Orpen's interpretation of Strongbow's circumstances in his *Ireland under the Normans*, i, London 1911, 85—91 was substantially correct, but his remarks have been largely ignored by subsequent writers on the Normans in Ireland and Strongbow appears in numerous works as Earl of Pembroke without qualification.

From 1164 onwards Strongbow could claim that he was further deprived by Henry II of lands to which he had an inherited claim. In that year Walter, Earl Giffard, died without male heirs. Strongbow and his cousin, Roger Fitz Richard, lord of Clare, each had an entitlement to the estate as descendants of Rohesia Giffard, daughter of Walter Giffard, who had been married to Richard Fitz Gilbert the companion of the Conqueror.[15] Henry II however, retained the Giffard honour in his own hands until his death in 1189.[16]

According to Gerald of Wales when Strongbow entered into an agreement with Diarmait Mac Murchada about 1166—67 'he had a great name, rather than great prospects, ancestral prestige rather than ability; he had succeeded to a name rather than possessions'.[17] Gerald's statement is apt insofar as Strongbow had lost Orbec and Bienfaite and the earldom of Pembroke and had been withheld his entitlement from the honour of Giffard. William of Newburgh provides a similar assessment of Strongbow's circumstances: the reason why Strongbow was anxious to go to Ireland was because he had wasted most of his inheritance and wanted to get away from his creditors.[18] During the winter of 1166—67 when Diarmait Mac Murchada was actively recruiting Cambro-Normans for military service in Ireland[19] he was the guest of the Bristol merchant Robert Fitz Harding and it may have been Fitz Harding who first put Diarmait in touch with Strongbow. Fitz Harding had been an astute moneylender during Stephen's reign with a keen eye for impoverished landowners.[20] There is circumstantial evidence to suggest that Strongbow had financial dealings with Fitz Harding. Nicholas, second son of Robert Fitz Harding, and his heirs subsequently held the manor and advowson of Tickenham in Somerset, which was attached to the honour of Strigoil.[21] In Domesday book Tickenham was held in demesne by William of Eu,[22] whose

15 Altschul 24—5; S. Painter, *William Marshal*, Baltimore 1933, 74.
16 Pipe rolls 14—34 Henry II under Bucks = Pipe roll society, vols xii—xxxviii; Stapleton, i, 59.
17 Gerald of Wales, *Expugnatio Hibernica*; ed. A.B. Scott and F.X. Martin, Dublin 1978, 54—5.
18 William of Newburgh in *Chronicles, Stephen, Henry II and Richard I*; ed. R. Howlett, i, RS 1885, 167—8. From the pipe rolls it may be inferred that Strongbow was in debt to Aaron the Jew of Lincoln: Pipe roll 3 Richard I, 1191, reveals the *comes de Strigoil* owing 80 marks to Aaron the Jew of Lincoln mortgaged on Weston: *Pipe rolls 3 and 4 Richard I*, 290. This was the first year in which the exchequer recorded the debt. Aaron had died early in 1186 and his estate escheated to the crown. Debts formerly owing to him were then collected on behalf of the king: H.G. Richardson, *The English jewry under the Angevin kings*, London 1960, 247. The debt must have been incurred before Aaron's death in 1186; Strongbow was therefore the only *comes de Strigoil* who could have borrowed from Aaron. The debt is listed under Gloucestershire, a county under which Strigoil was occasionally entered on the pipe rolls, but Weston must refer to Strongbow's manor in Hertfordshire. From Pipe roll 3 Richard I, 1191 to Pipe roll 3 John, 1202, the debt is re-entered each year under Gloucestershire until in 1202 William Marshal, who had married Strongbow's daughter and heir in 1189, finally secured a pardon for it from King John: *Pipe roll 3 John*, 41. An entry on the *Pipe roll 16 Henry II*, 78 records that Josce, a Jew of Gloucester, owed 100 shillings as an amerciament for the money which he lent to those who went against the king's prohibition to Ireland. Strongbow may also have borrowed from Josce of Gloucester.
19 *Song of Dermot and the Earl*; ed. G.H. Orpen, London 1892, 11.230—5, 300—11.
20 As suggested to me by John Prestwich. Robert Fitz Harding purchased estates in Somerset from Robert, Earl of Gloucester, Richard de Morevill and Julian de Banton, in Gloucestershire from Richard Foliot and in Devon from William de Braose: John Smyth of Nibley, *The lives of the Berkeleys*; ed. J. Mc Clean, i, Gloucester 1883, 34—5. Fitz Harding also leased land from the Benedictine abbey of Gloucester for a term of five years in return for a loan of £80. See *VCH Gloucestershire*, ii, 54 and note 32.
21 John Smith of Nibley, i, 45—6.
22 *Domesday Book*, i, 96b.

estates including the lordship of Strigoil were subsequently granted to Walter Fitz Richard, Strongbow's grand-uncle.[23] It is therefore likely that Tickenham was a portion of the lordship of Strigoil which had been mortgaged or sold by Strongbow to Robert Fitz Harding whence it passed to Nicholas Fitz Harding.[24] It may have been Robert Fitz Harding who considered Strongbow just the man to take a gamble on recovering his fortunes in Ireland, and, if the venture succeeded, it might create more favourable conditions for an increase in the already existent trade between Bristol and Dublin[25] in which Fitz Harding would have had a vested interest.

According to Gerald of Wales Strongbow first sought and obtained permission from Henry II to go to the aid of Diarmait Mac Murchada in Ireland, although, says Gerald, Henry gave it more in jest than in earnest.[26] Gervase of Canterbury agrees with Gerald that Strongbow secured the king's permission to go to Ireland but that, nevertheless, Strongbow's relations with Henry remained strained.[27] Gervase dates Henry's displeasure with Strongbow to three years before the king's own expedition to Ireland. Henry went to Ireland in October 1171; this would assign the incident which Gervase had in mind to about 1168. In that year Strongbow was a member of the escort of Henry's daughter, Matilda, to Germany on the occasion of her marriage to the duke of Saxony.[28] Yet there is little evidence that Strongbow had enjoyed the favour of the king at any point between 1154 and 1168: he was not a regular member of Henry's household, nor frequently seen at court. Possibly, Strongbow had gone to the king to request permission to go to Ireland and Henry had delayed his departure deliberately by despatching him on the embassy to Germany. Henry may then have agreed, albeit reluctantly, to let Strongbow go to Ireland. According to William of Newburgh Strongbow was about to sail for Ireland when persons acting on behalf of Henry II tried to present his departure threatening him with sequestration of his estates.[29] Despite these threats Strongbow set out for Ireland about August 1170.

That Strongbow's lands in Wales and England were sequestrated is evidenced from the pipe rolls. Pipe roll 16 Henry II (19 December 1169—18 December 1170) records a payment of £10 by the king's writ for the fortification of the castle of Strigoil, thus indicating that it had been taken into the king's hand.[30] Strongbow's manor of Weston in Hertfordshire is listed on pipe rolls 16, 17 and 18 Henry II as in the king's hand.[31]

Strongbow's decision to go to Ireland in August 1170 was not his first positive response to Diarmait Mac Murchada's proposal of military service

---

23 See above note 5.
24 It continued to be held of the honour of Strigoil for the service of 40 days guard duty at the castle of Strigoil in time of war: A.S. Ellis, 'On the landholders of Gloucestershire named in Domesday Book' in *Trans. of the Bristol and Gloucestershire Archaeological Society*, iv, 1879—80, 86—198 at 125—9.
25 A. Gwynn, 'Medieval Bristol and Dublin' in *Irish historical studies*, v, 1946—7, 275—86.
26 Gerald of Wales, *Expug.hib.*, 54—7.
27 Gervase of Canterbury, *Opera historica*; ed. W. Stubbs, i, RS 1879, 234.
28 Ralph de Diceto, *Opera historica*; ed. W. Stubbs, i, RS 1876, 330.
29 William of Newburgh; 167—8.
30 *Pipe roll 16 Henry II*, 75.
31 *Pipe roll 16 Henry II*, 25, 105; *Pipe roll 17 Henry II*, 56, 119; *Pipe roll 18 Henry II*, 48; *Pipe roll 19 Henry II*, 70.

and reward in Ireland. The group of Cambro-Norman mercenaries led by Robert Fitz Stephen who went to Ireland in the autumn of 1169 had been accompanied by Strongbow's uncle, Hervey de Montmorency, and Raymond le Gros, who was a member of Strongbow's household, was acting on Strongbow's behalf when he captured the city of Waterford in the spring of 1170.[32] Despite Gerald of Wales's unfavourable portrayal of Strongbow and his poor opinion of him as a military leader compared with the greater achievements of Gerald's relatives as he presents them to us, the Cambro-Normans had no significant or permanent successes in Leinster until Strongbow arrived there in August 1170. Thereafter, there was a dramatic improvement in the strategic position of Diarmait Mac Murchada both within Leinster and beyond it. Even Gerald of Wales had to admit grudgingly that within a short time of his arrival Strongbow had 'overrun not only Leinster but many other places which did not belong to himself or his wife by any legal right'.[33]

Gerald recounts that news of these events spread rapidly and that in reaction Henry II closed the ports to Ireland and ordered that all persons from his dominions who had gone there without permission should either return before Easter 1171 or face seizure of their estates. The closing of the ports is corroborated by William of Newburgh and the pipe rolls furnish a number of fines paid by individuals who went to Ireland without the king's permission.[34]

Already by 1170, therefore, Henry II was disquieted by Strongbow's activities in Ireland. William of Newburgh relates that Henry II obliged Strongbow 'now nearly a king' to make peace with him.[35] Gerald of Wales describes Strongbow sending Raymond le Gros to speak on his behalf to Henry II and awaiting a reply from the procrastinating king when news of the murder of Thomas Becket (29 December 1170) reached the court.[36] Raymond apparently had to return to Ireland without a favourable response from Henry.

Diarmait Mac Murchada died in May 1171 having regained possession of the kingdom of Leinster and with his Cambro-Norman allies in control of the Hiberno-Norse towns of Dublin and Waterford. Immediately, Ruairi Ua Conchobuir, king of Connacht and high-king of Ireland, challenged Strongbow for possession of the city of Dublin. Strongbow resisted successfully, but nevertheless failed to win formal recognition of his Irish acquisitions from Ruairi Ua Conchobuir. In these circumstances Strongbow had little option but to continue to negotiate with Henry II. His estates in England, Wales and Normandy had been sequestrated and it was by no means clear in 1171 that his gains in Ireland would be sufficiently great or permanent to allow him to abandon his estates in Henry's dominions.

32 Gerald of Wales, *Expug.hib.*, 30—3, 57—65.
33 Gerald of Wales, *Expug.hib.*, 70—1.
34 William of Newburgh, 167—8; Wido Wallensis entered under Somersetshire, Geoffrey Cophin under Devon, Roger de Ulhela under Warwickshire and Leicestershire; *Pipe roll 17 Henry II*, 17, 29, 92; Peter Morell under Buckinghamshire and Bedfordshire: *Pipe roll 18 Henry II*, 49.
35 The death of Robert Fitz Harding in February 1170 may have been a contributory factor to Henry's disquiet, news of which may have caused Henry to try and prevent Strongbow's departure for Ireland. It is possible that Fitz Harding had indicated to Henry II that he would act as guarantor for Strongbow's conduct in Ireland.
36 Gerald of Wales, *Expub.hib.*, 72—3.

Accordingly, Strongbow despatched his uncle Hervey de Montmorency to resume negotiations with Henry II. Robert of Torigny writing in Normandy describes de Montmorency's arrival at the court of Argentan in July 1171.[37] On Strongbow's behalf Hervey offered the surrender of his nephew's Irish acquisitions to the king. Henry's response, however, was to persist in the sequestration of Strongbow's lands in England and Normandy and to order Strongbow to surrender to Henry the land which he had acquired in Ireland in right of his wife and that he should regard himself merely as a military commander acting on behalf of the English king in Ireland. On de Montmorency's return to Ireland Strongbow was persuaded both by his uncle's personal entreaty and by letters brought him from the king that it would be politic to go and visit Henry in person.[38]

Strongbow travelled to meet Henry at Newnham in Gloucestershire and after lengthy argument agreed to surrender the city of Dublin and its adjacent territory, the coastal towns and all castles to the king and to hold from Henry the remainder of the land which he had acquired in Ireland.[39] Strongbow might promise to do so; it was quite another matter to effect his compliance. Henry II appears to have decided that the only way in which he could ensure the agreement was to go to Ireland himself and demonstrate overlordship and possession of those areas which Strongbow had ceded to him. This Henry did during his expedition to Ireland in 1171—72. It is a tribute to Strongbow's military successes during 1170—71 in Ireland that Henry felt obliged to intervene personally in that country.

It was not just Strongbow's uncontrolled activities within Ireland which may have worried Henry II but even more importantly perhaps the potential resources which Strongbow's Irish acquisitions placed at his disposal for creating trouble within Henry's dominions and particularly in Pembroke. From 1153 onwards Strongbow had been harbouring a claim to the lordship of Orbec and Bienfaite, from 1155 to the lordship of Pembroke and from 1164 to a share of the Giffard honour, all of which Henry had refused to concede. Strongbow had most recently raised the issue of the 'lands which fell to him by right of inheritance' with the king when he sought his permission to go to Ireland about 1168.[40] In 1171 Henry II was faced with the possibility that Strongbow's geographically strategic acquisitions in Leinster would provide him with the means of forcibly taking Pembroke from the king. As Gerald of Wales remarked, on a clear day Ireland was visible from St David's Head and the sea crossing between Pembroke and the Irish coast was a short day's journey.[41] A significant number of the Cambro-Normans who had gone to fight in Ireland were drawn from the district of Pembroke. If Strongbow had not managed to gain *de jure* recognition as their lord in Pembroke from Henry II he was now *de facto* their lord in Ireland. The security of their newly won possessions in Ireland now depended on him. If Strongbow was to stage a revolt in Pembroke it was therefore possible that he might be able to raise a significant measure of support.

37 Robert of Torigny, 252.
38 Gerald of Wales, *Expug.hib.*, 88—9.
39 Gerald of Wales, *Expug.hib.*, 88—9.
40 Gerald of Wales, *Expug.hib.*, 54—5.
41 Gerald of Wales, *Opera*; ed. J.F. Dimock, vi, RS 1868, 109.

The negotiations that took place between Henry and Strongbow at Newnham in 1171 must indeed have been argued long and hard and not just about what land Strongbow might hold in Ireland, but also in relation to the lands which he held or claimed in England, Wales and Normandy. The first concession which Strongbow appears to have wrung from Henry was acknowledgement of a comital status. In the charter granted by Henry II to Hugh de Lacy before his departure from Waterford in 1172 Strongbow, who acted as a witness, was styled *comes Ricardus* for the first time in a royal document since Henry's accession in 1154.[42] Contemporary chroniclers, thereafter, refer to Strongbow as *comes de Strigoil*.

Henry put Strongbow's loyalty and obedience to the test at the earliest opportunity. In 1173, when the king was faced with the rebellion in Normandy of his son, he summoned Strongbow to fight on his behalf.[43] As Strongbow had shown himself to be in Ireland, so he proved himself again to be a competent military commander successfully defending Gisors for the king. His reward was to be allowed to return to Ireland in 1173 as *vices regis Anglie in Hibernia agens*, a position which he held until his premature death in 1176.[44] In 1173 Henry also ceded to Strongbow the town of Wexford and the castle of Wicklow which he had retained in his own hand in 1171.[45]

Strongbow's gamble to try and repair his fortunes by accepting Diarmait Mac Murchada's invitation to Ireland may be said to have yielded dividends. A man who had been unable to find favour with Henry II throughout the period 1154—71 died as Henry's representative in Ireland in 1176.[46] If he had not succeeded in getting possession of the earldom of Pembroke, he had managed to persuade the king to recognize him as *comes de Strigoil*. William of Newburgh recounts, furthermore, that as a result of his acquisitions in Ireland Strongbow, who had little fortune previously, became celebrated for his wealth and great prosperity in England and Ireland.[47]

The effect to which Strongbow's reconciliation with Henry II was effective may also be demonstrated by the fate of his estates in England, Wales, Normandy and Ireland after his death. In 1171 Henry had ordered Strongbow to surrender his Irish acquisitions to the king. Theoretically, Henry had taken them into his own hands and regranted them to Strongbow, who then held them neither in virtue of his marriage to Aoife, daughter of Diarmait Mac Murchada, nor by right of conquest, but as a grant from Henry II. Although Gerald of Wales and the *Song of Dermot and the Earl* agree that Henry's grant to Strongbow of his Irish lands was made in fee 'to him and his heirs',[48] Henry, nevertheless, might have taken the opportunity when Strongbow died in 1176 to grant the lordship of Leinster to another feudatory. Henry was quite

---

42 G.H. Orpen, *Normans*, i, 285—6.
43 *Gesta regis Henrici secundi Benedicti abbatis*; ed. W. Stubbs, i, RS 1867, 51; *Song of Dermot*, 11.2864—2945; Ralph de Diceto, i, 375.
44 Strongbow styles himself thus in a charter issued on behalf of Henry II to Thomas, abbot of Glendalough: *Crede mihi*; ed. J.T. Gilbert, Dublin 1897, 46—7.
45 Gerald of Wales, *Expug.hib.*, 120—1; *Song of Dermot*, 11.2902—2905.
46 *Comes Ricardus de Strigoil* was also to be found at the king's court in 1175 about the time when the Treaty of Windsor was being negotiated with Ruairi Ua Conchobuir: Eyton, 196; *Chartularies of St Mary's Abbey, Dublin*; ed. J.T. Gilbert, i, RS 1884, 79—80.
47 William of Newburgh, 169.
48 Gerald of Wales, *Expug.hib.*, 88—9; *Song of Dermot*, 11.2616—2622.

capable of ignoring the rights of inheritance of his subjects even where there was no ambiguity in their title[49] as it might be argued there was in the case of the lands which Strongbow had acquired in Ireland. There was no compulsion on Henry to honour the succession to the lordship of Leinster of Strongbow's heirs; yet he chose to recognize Strongbow's wife, Aoife, and her two children, Gilbert and Isabella, as the beneficiaries and heirs of Strongbow in respect of his lands in Leinster, Strigoil, England and Normandy.

When Strongbow died in 1176 his only son, Gilbert, was a minor and the responsibility of administering Strongbow's estates as a former tenant-in-chief fell to the crown. Gilbert died sometime after 1185 before coming of age whereupon Isabella became Strongbow's sole remaining heir. The crown retained responsibility for the wardship of Strongbow's widow, Aoife, and her children and for the administration of his estates from 1176 until they passed to William Marshal in 1189 in virtue of his marriage to Isabella.

Strongbow's wife, Aoife, is mentioned in royal records as a widow in the custody of the crown on a number of occasions between 1176 and Isabella's marriage in 1189. Aoife, Countess of Strigoil, received a payment of 60 shillings in 1176—77 and a payment of £4 in 1180—81 levied on Strongbow's demesne manor of Weston.[50] In 1183—84 the *comitissa Hibernie* was granted an advance of £20 from the king to support herself in the Welsh march.[51] In 1184—85 the *comitissa Hibernie* was granted 26 shillings out of the honour of Strigoil and 20 marks out of Strongbow's estates in Cambridgeshire.[52] In 1186—87 when the honour of Strigoil was assessed for the scutage of Galloway at 65½ knights' fees £10 of the sum due to the king was remitted to Aoife.[53]

In 1185 the *rotuli de dominabus* (which recorded details of widows in the wardship of the crown from a number but not all counties) shows Aoife in enjoyment of the manor of Weston in Hertfordshire and Chesterford in Essex in dower.[54] She may have held other lands of which no record has survived. Corroboration of the fact that Aoife enjoyed the use of estates in England comes from a charter which she granted to the nunnery of Ickleton in Cambridgeshire. In 1309 the prioress of Ickleton claimed an annual rent of 13 shillings from a mill which has been granted to her convent by Aoife, Countess of Ireland, and cited the following charter in support of her claim:[55]

> Eva comitissa Hibernensis uxor Richardi comitis omnibus hominibus et amicis suis presentibus et futuris salutem. Notum sit vobis quod ego pro salute anime mee et anime Ricardi comitis domini mei et anime Gilberti filii mei dedi et concessi et hac presenti carta mea confirmavi Deo et

---

49 In 1175, for example, Henry denied the inheritance of the estates of Reginald, Earl of Cornwall, to his daughters and to his brother William: J.E.A. Jolliffe, *Angevin kingship*, 2nd edn., London 1963, 128. Compare also Henry's treatment of the earldom of Gloucester: *Earldom of Gloucester charters*; ed. R.B. Patterson, London 1973, 5 and note 7.
50 *Pipe roll 23 Henry II*, 149; *Pipe roll 27 Henry II*, 106.
51 *Pipe roll 30 Henry II*, 154.
52 *Pipe roll 31 Henry II*, 8, 55.
53 *Pipe roll 33 Henry II*, 142; *Red Book of the Exchequer*, i, ed. R. Hall, RS 1897, 67.
54 *Rotuli de dominabus et pueris et puellis de xii comitatibus*, Pipe Roll Society, xxxv, 1913, 66, 76. The manors were estimated to yield a potential annual income of £40 and in 1185 yielded an actual income of £27.
55 London, PRO, E 159/82/m.62. I wish to thank Dr J.R.S. Phillips, Dept of Medieval History, University College, Dublin, for bringing this text to my notice.

ecclesie Sancte Marie Magdalene de Ikelington et eiusdem ecclesie monialibus unam marcam redditus in molendino meo de Sproteford in liberam et puram et perpetuam elemosinam scilicet unam dimidiam marcam ad luminare ecclesie. Et predicte moniales recipient supradictam redditus ad duos anni terminos scilicet unam dimidiam marcam ad pascham et aliam dimidiam marcam ad festum sancti Michaelis. Hiis testibus Willelmo capellano, Silvestro persona de ville de sancto Leg., Willelmo de La More, Waltero Le Balde, Petro le Botiler, Waltero Maltravers, Godefrido Butiler, Willelmo Venator, Radulpho de Bedeford, Henrico filio Willelmi de Dukesworth, Richardo scriptore.

It is impossible to date this charter precisely because of the obscurity of the witnesses. It may date from the period between Aoife's marriage to Strongbow and his death in 1176. Thereafter, since Aoife merely had a life interest in her dower lands she should not have granted away any portion without the consent of her husband's heir and the confirmation of the king. It has not proved possible to identify the mill of Sproteford from which the prioress of Ickleton claimed a mark originally granted to her convent by Aoife. It is noteworthy, however, that Ickleton priory held land in Chesterford[56] and that a portion of the lands attached to Strongbow's manor of Chesterford was located in Cambridgeshire.[57] This provides a satisfactory explanation of how Aoife might have come into contact with the Cambridgeshire nunnery of Ickleton and strongly supports the authenticity of the claim and the text of the charter recited by the prioress of Ickleton before the king in 1309. Although this is a 14th century transcript of a 12th century charter there is no reason to doubt the reliability of the text. The style *comitissa Hibernensis* apparently used by Aoife in the charter can be paralleled in contemporary references to Aoife on the pipe rolls and the *rotuli de dominabus*.[58] Although Henry had refused to acknowledge Strongbow as earl of Pembroke, Strongbow, did, as we have seen, win royal recognition after 1171 for his enjoyment of a comital title. After his death Aoife was variously styled *comitissa de Strigoil* and *comitissa Hibernie* in royal records and this charter suggests that the latter was the style which she herself preferred. It may be that she or her advisers were attempting to associate the comital title with the lordship of Leinster.

56 *Monasticon*, iv, 440; *VCH Cambridgeshire*, ii, 223—6.
57 In the Domesday survey of Essex the manor of Chesterford appears as royal demesne consisting of 10 hides in the custody of Picot the Sheriff. One and a half hides, however, are stated to have been in Cambridgeshire. These may be located at Histon for the Cambridgeshire domesday states that Picot had 1½ hides of the manor of Chesterford which were taxed in the hundred in which they were situated in Cambridgeshire but which had been appraised in Essex: *Domesday Book*, i, 189b, ii, 3. The Cambridgeshire lands of Chesterford manor explains the payment of 20 marks to Aoife on the pipe roll of 1184—5 which were accounted for by the sheriff of Cambridgeshire and Huntingdonshire: above note 52. The manor of Chesterford did not as Painter thought come to Strongbow's predecessors out of escheated estates of William of Eu: Painter, 77. It was almost certainly granted to Walter Fitz Richard by Henry I out of royal demesne possibly after 1130 and before Walter's death in 1138 for Walter does not appear to have paid danegeld on lands in Essex in 1130: above note 5.
58 *Pipe roll 27 Henry II*, 106; *Pipe roll 30 Henry II*, 154; *Pipe roll 31 Henry II*, 55 (note that she is styled *comitissa de Strigoil* on the same roll, 8); *Rotuli de dominabus*, 66, 76. Compare J.H. Round, 'The countess of Ireland' in *The Genealogist*, n.s., xviii, 1901, 166—7. A small point in favour of the authenticity of the charter is the witness William Dukesworth. William Marshal can be shown to have held £5 worth of land at Dukesworth: *Red Book*, ii, 331, 575.

Aoife's proven enjoyment of Strongbow's estates in England and Wales raises an interesting question about the negotiations which may have taken place between Strongbow and Diarmait Mac Murchada in 1166—67 or on the occasion of the marriage of Aoife and Strongbow in 1170. Irish historians have not been slow to suggest that Strongbow's inheritance of Leinster in right of his wife was invalid in Irish law, which did not recognize succession through the female line, but they have overlooked the fact that if Strongbow gained an inheritance in right of his wife in Ireland, so too did Aoife and her children gain an inheritance in right of Strongbow in England, Wales and Normandy. Was Diarmait Mac Murchada aware of this possibility when he offered his daughter in marriage to Strongbow? It has to be admitted that on the evidence of contemporaries neither Strongbow's wealth nor position was considered great in 1166—67. But it had potential. The lordship of Strigoil was conveniently situated to the port of Bristol which had important trading relations with the eastern Irish ports of Dublin, Waterford and Wexford in which Diarmait Mac Murchada had strong connections and interests. In addition, Strongbow had a claim to the lordship of Pembroke which, if realised, would indeed have been most appositely positioned across the Irish sea from Diarmait Mac Murchada's patrimonial lands of Uí Cheinnselaig,[59] which represented the area of Leinster over which he exercised the most effective lordship. It is not impossible that the issue, not merely of recovery of the kingdom of Leinster, but also of the lordship of Pembroke was discussed by Diarmait Mac Murchada and Strongbow. As Diarmait Mac Murchada would have been aware, Irish aid recruited in Leinster had restored a number of Welsh princes to their kingdoms in the 11th and early 12th centuries.[60] Diarmait Mac Murchada might have calculated another advantage from the alliance with Strongbow besides military aid to recover the lordship of Leinster. He may also have taken into account that according to feudal custom Aoife might enjoy certain revenues from Strongbow's estates in England, Wales and Normandy and that children from the marriage of Aoife and Strongbow would inherit the title to Strongbow's estates within the Angevin dominions. According to feudal custom a widow was entitled for the duration of her own life to the profits of one third of her husband's demesne estates.[61] The designation of dower lands was often determined before or on the occasion of marriage. It is therefore possible that Strongbow may have assigned dower lands to Aoife when they married in 1170. That this is not improbable is suggested by the surviving text of a dower charter which John de Courcy, the Norman conqueror of Ulaid, granted to Affrica, daughter of the king of the

---

59 Broadly Co. Wexford and a portion of south Co. Wicklow. Uí Cheinnselaig was coterminous with the medieval diocese of Ferns for the boundaries of which see the map in A. Gwynn and R.N. Hadcock, *Medieval religious houses: Ireland*, London 1972.
60 See M.T. Flanagan, *Gaelic society, Norman settlers and Angevin Kingship: a study in interactions in Ireland in the late twelfth century*, unpublished D.Phil. thesis, Oxford, 1980, chapter 1, 38—51.
61 *The treatise on the laws and customs of the realm of England commonly called Glanvill*; ed. G.D.G. Hall, London 1965, 58—69, 183—4. A demesne manor was one which the lord had retained in his own hands as an economic unit and which remained directly accountable to his officials. Only such a manor could be given in dower. The two manors known to have been held by Aoife in dower therefore provide no real indication of the extent of Strongbow's lands which were held by tenants in fee from him.

Isle of Man on the occasion of their marriage about 1180.[62] Indeed, de Courcy's marriage to the daughter of the king of the Isle of Man bears comparison with that of Strongbow and Aoife in its awareness of the potentialities of coordinated cooperation across the Irish sea, for a major advantage which John de Courcy's marriage to Affrica afforded him was access to his father-in-law's fleet.

There is no similar extant dower charter from Strongbow to Aoife which might have suggested that such matters as Aoife's enjoyment of Strongbow's estates in Henry's dominions had been raised when she married Strongbow in 1170. But, even if dower was not discussed then, Diarmait Mac Murchada may well have been content to gamble on the advantages of a marriage alliance which might provide him with grandchildren who would inherit the lordship of Strigoil and other estates in England and Normandy and a claim to the lordship of Pembroke.

Whether or not Strongbow made a formal settlement of dower on Aoife in 1170 she was still entitled in feudal law in the event of her husband's death to one third of those estates which Strongbow possessed in demesne at the time of his marriage. The king, who took custody of the entire estates of a tenant-in-chief at death if his heir was a minor, was in theory obliged to assign dower to his widow.[63] In practice, the king might, and often did, decide quite arbitrarily just how much or how little she would get. In the case of Aoife Henry did acknowledge her right to dower and the inheritance of Strongbow's children by Aoife of his estates within Henry's dominions.

Aoife received her first allowance, levied on Strongbow's demesne manor of Weston, from the king in 1176—77,[64] that is within a short space of Strongbow's death. In addition to the other subsequent payments which she received there is some evidence to suggest that she may also have enjoyed the lordship of Strigoil for a period. How the lordship of Strigoil was administered between Strongbow's death in 1176 and 1183—4, when it is first mentioned on the pipe rolls, is obscure. In 1183—4 Aoife is recorded to have received an advance of £20 from the king to support herself in the Welsh March.[65] The Welsh were attacking Glamorgan in 1184 and it is possible that it was thought that Strigoil was endangered.[66] The sum of £20 suggests that Aoife was in fact being assigned the responsibilities of a military commander in this region, for from 1184—5 onwards £20 was precisely the figure paid to Ralph Bloet for his custody of the honour and castle of Strigoil on behalf of the king.[67] The expenditure on repairs to the castle and on restocking and seed also recorded in 1184—5 suggests that the administration of Strigoil had been taken over by the crown for the first time in that year. There is also a separate entry on the pipe

---

62 E. Curtis, 'Two unpublished charters of John de Courcy *princeps Ulidiae*' in *Belfast Natural History Society Proceedings*, session 1928—29, 1930, 2—9.
63 Above note 61.
64 Above note 50.
65 Above note 51.
66 The seriousness of the threat in South Wales in the last decade of Henry's reign is reflected by the increased expenditure upon the castles of this area: R.A. Brown, 'Royal castle-building in England, 1154—1216' in *EHR*, lxx, 1955, 353—98 at 359—60.
67 *Pipe roll 31 Henry II*, 8; *Pipe roll 32 Henry II*, 203; *Pipe roll 33 Henry II*, 16, 29, 141, 142; *Pipe roll 34 Henry II*, 203.

roll of 1184—5 for Strongbow's castle of Usk.[68] Thereafter, Strigoil (there is no further separate mention of Usk) appears as farmed by the crown until the end of Henry's reign. There is a blank entry for Strigoil on the pipe roll of 1 Richard I;[69] presumably the exchequer had prepared the headings for the roll in advance and then ascertained that Strigoil had been taken over by William Marshal on the occasion of his marriage to Strongbow's daughter and heir, Isabella, in 1189.

There is therefore a possibility that Aoife retained control of Strigoil from 1176 until 1184 when Henry took over responsibility for its administration in response to the Welsh military threat. If Aoife did in fact enjoy the lordship of Strigoil between 1176 and 1184 she was being treated very favourably by Henry II. Alternatively, it may be that Henry had taken over Strigoil in 1176 and had the revenues paid directly into the chamber, so that the details were not recorded on the pipe rolls of the exchequer, although this seems less likely in view of the fact that Aoife appears to have been responsible for the defence of her portion of the Welsh March in 1183—4.[70]

There is little information about the administration of the estates held or claimed by Strongbow in Normandy during the minority of 1176—89. Although Orbec and Bienfaite had been lost by Strongbow in 1153 and were still in the possession of his cousin Robert de Montfort in 1172,[71] Strongbow held other estates in Normandy since Robert of Torigny mentions that at the meeting between Hervey de Montmorency and Henry II at Argentan in July 1171 the king had refused to reverse the sequestration of Strongbow's estates in England and Normandy.[72] Unfortunately, there are very few extant exchequer rolls from Normandy: complete rolls survive only for the years 1180, 1195 and 1198 and partial rolls from the years 1184 and 1203. The complete roll of 1180 does reveal that the *terra comitis Ricardi* situated in Saint Saens and the neighbouring Omonville was being farmed by ducal agents;[73] this must have been on behalf of Strongbow's heirs.

It is difficult to determine in detail Henry's intentions towards and treatment of Strongbow's lordship of Leinster in the period 1176—89 in the absence of early Angevin administrative documents from Ireland. In 1189 in virtue of his marriage to Isabella, daughter of Strongbow, William Marshal succeeded to the lordship of Leinster, and according to the *Histoire de Guillaume le Maréchal*, Richard I, in consenting to the marriage, was fulfilling the wishes of Henry II.[74] From the death of Strongbow in 1176 until the

68 *Pipe roll 31 Henry II*, 8, 10, 55.
69 *The great roll of the pipe for the first year of King Richard the First*, 1188—89; ed. J. Hunter, London 1844, 5.
70 It is possible that the change in 1184 may be associated with an illness or the death of Strongbow's son, Gilbert, around this time.
71 Above note 7.
72 Robert of Torigny, 252.
73 Stapleton, i, 59; ii, cxxxvii. Stapleton thought that these lands belonged to Richard Fitz Roger who had succeeded his father as lord of Clare and Earl of Hertford in 1173. As Powicke pointed out, however, there is no reason why Richard Fitz Roger's lands should have been in the hands of ducal agents in 1173. He suggested that the lands belonged to Strongbow and that they may have been confiscated during the civil war period: Powicke, 336. Confirmation of his suggestion comes from the fact that Isabella, widow of Earl Gilbert, that is Strongbow's mother, was a benefactor of the convent of Saint Saens: *Recueil*, ii, 161.
74 *Histoire de Guillaume le Maréchal*, ii, ed. P. Meyer, Paris 1894, 11.8303—8305.

assumption of the lordship of Ireland by Prince John in 1185 Leinster was administered by custodians appointed by Henry II.[75] There is no evidence of any new infeudations made by Henry in Leinster between 1176 and 1185. In 1177 at the Council of Oxford Henry had created his son John *dominus Hiberniae* and in 1185, when John formally took over the Angevin lordship of Ireland from his father, the administration of Leinster became the responsibility of his household. Such charters relating to Leinster as survive from John's visit to Ireland in 1185 and his administration of the lordship of Leinster between 1185 and 1189 indicate his acceptance of the hereditary succession of Strongbow's heirs in Leinster.[76]

Yet according to the *Histoire de Guillaume le Maréchal* William Marshal had to invoke the aid of King Richard against Prince John in order to obtain seisin of all his wife's lands in Leinster after their marriage in 1189. Upon Richard's intervention, John agreed to give seisin provided that the grants of land which he had made to his own men within Leinster should remain and be confirmed to them. King Richard is depicted as responding 'what would then remain to the Marshal seeing that you have given all to your people'? John then requested that the lands which he had granted to Theobald Walter within Leinster should be left to him and King Richard consented provided that Theobald held them of the Marshal and not John.[77] This suggests that John had encroached on the rights of the lord of Leinster.

There is, however, no evidence that John had enfeoffed Theobald Walter with land in Leinster before the marriage of William Marshal and Isabella in 1189. The text of a copy of a charter of John, Count of Mortain, in favour of Theobald survives which grants him the manor of Tullach in Leinster; it may be dated about 1192, that is four years after the accession of William Marshal to the lordship of Leinster.[78] The difficulties which developed between William Marshal and Prince John in Leinster appear to date from the period after the death of Henry II in 1189. By contrast with Richard I, Henry appears to have kept a vigilant eye on John's activities as lord of Ireland through the person of Ranulph de Glanville to whose tutelage John had been entrusted.[79] With the

---

75 *Gesta regis Henrici secundi*, i, 164; Roger of Howden, *Chronica*; ed. W. Stubbs, ii, RS 1869, 134.
76 In 1185 John confirmed to William son of Maurice Fitz Gerald the lands 'quam comes Ricardus dedit Moricio patri ipsius Willelmi tenendam de heredibus comitis Ricardi per servicium v militum pro omni servicio': *Calendar of the Gormanston Register*; ed. J. Mills and M.J. McEnery, Dublin 1916, 145, 193. Between 1185 and 1189 John confirmed to Walter de Ridlesford 'totam terram quam comes Ricardus filius comitis Gilberti dedit . . . tenenda de heredibus comitis Ricardi per servicium quatuor militum pro omni servitio comitis': National Library of Ireland, MS 1, fol. 19r; E. St. J. Brooks, 'The de Ridlesfords' in *Royal Society of Antiquaries of Ireland Journal*, lxxxi, 1951, 115—38; lxxxii, 1952, 45—61. A charter from Prince John to Gerald Fitz Maurice confirmed to him a half cantred in Uí Faeláin in Leinster as well as lands in Cork 'salvis serviciis dominorum suorum': *Red Book of the Earls of Kildare*; ed. G. Mac Niocaill, Dublin 1964, 14.
77 *Histoire de Guillaume le Maréchal*, ii; 11.9584—9624.
78 *Red book of Ormond*; ed. N.B. White, Dublin 1932, 9.
79 Ranulph de Glanville witnessed at least two of John's Irish charters between 1185 and 1189 granting land out of the royal demesne: *Calendar of Ormond deeds, 1172—1350*; ed. E. Curtis, Dublin 1932, nos. 17, 863 (no. 863 was granted by John as lord of Ireland and not, as the editor inadvertently stated, as king of England). It is probably also significant that William Marshal collected Strongbow's daughter Isabella, from Ranulph de Glanville's household when he married her in 1189: *Histoire de Guillaume le Maréchal*, 11.9513—4. cf. W.L. Warren, 'John in Ireland' in *Essays presented to Michael Roberts*; ed. J. Bossy and P. Jupp, Belfast 1976, 11—23 at 16—17.

accession of Richard in 1189, who had little time for Glanville, and with Glanville's death in 1190 there was much less constraint on John's actions in Ireland. Although the *Histoire de Guillaume le Maréchal* implies that the Marshal's dispute with John arose at the time of his assumption of the lordship of Leinster in 1189 as a result of actions which had been taken by John prior to that date, it is probable that the chronology is none too precise and that John's grants of land within Leinster were made after 1189.

From the death of Strongbow in 1176 until his own death in 1189 Henry II appears to have acknowledged the hereditary claims of Strongbow's heirs in Leinster. The only evidence of Aoife's presence in Leinster after Strongbow's death is a copy of a charter which she issued as *Eva comitissa heres regis Deremicii* in which she confirmed to John Comin, Archbishop of Dublin (1181—1212)

> omnes possessiones et elemosinas tam in ecclesiasticis quam in mundanis tenementis quas eis comes Johannes et alii boni viri de Lagenia pia largitione contulerunt.[80]

Prince John can have given neither grants nor confirmations to the archbishop of Dublin before 1185 when he took over the administration of the lordship of Ireland from Henry II. Aoife's charter ought, therefore to date from the period between 1185 and the accession of William Marshal to the lordship of Leinster in 1189. However, the reference to Prince John as *comes* implies a date after 1189, for he did not become Count of Mortain or Earl of Gloucester until that year.[81] It is possible that the scribe who transcribed Aoife's charter into the episcopal register has inadvertently substituted *comes Johannes* for *dominus Johannes*, the latter being the style by which John was known between 1185 and 1189. The only alternative explanation is that Aoife issued a confirmation charter to the archbishop of Dublin after 1189 in spite of the fact that William Marshal became lord of Leinster in that year. Since in fact the date of Aoife's death is unknown, it is conceivable that she could have issued this charter after 1189. Although there is no evidence for alienation by Prince John of lands from the lordship of Leinster before 1189 the *Histoire de Guillaume le Maréchal* may, nevertheless, be correct in implying that William Marshal did not gain immediate possession of Leinster in 1189 because John arrogated it to his own use. There may have been uncertainty in Ireland for a number of years after 1189 as to whether John or William Marshal was lord of Leinster. The issue was resolved in favour of William Marshal by 1193 at the latest when John's lands in England and Normandy together with the lordship of Ireland were taken into Richard I's hands pending John's trial for rebellion against Richard. It may have been in the years of uncertainty between 1189 and 1193 that the archbishop of Dublin, who had received a number of charters of grant and confirmation from Prince John,[82] took the precaution of securing a general confirmation of the lands which he held in Leinster from Aoife as the heir of Diarmait Mac Murchada. The tenor of Aoife's charter, which contains nothing other than a very general statement of confirmation,

---

80 *Crede mihi*, 50.
81 John seldom used the latter title: *Earldom of Gloucester charters*, 23.
82 G. Mac Niocaill, 'The charters of John, lord of Ireland, to the see of Dublin' in *Repertorium novum*, iii, 1963—64, 282—306.

as well as the style *Eva Comitissa heres regis Deremicii* supports such an interpretation.

As a result of his marriage to Isabella in 1189 William Marshal succeeded to Strongbow's estates in Wales, England and Normandy and to the lordship of Leinster. The Marshal asserted himself vigorously and successfully against attempts by Prince John to diminish his wife's inheritance in Leinster. Furthermore, William Marshal persuaded Richard I to allow him half the Giffard honour to which Strongbow and through him his wife had a claim as a descendant of Rohesia Giffard and which the crown had withheld since 1164.[83] William Marshal also managed to recover the lordship of Orbec and Bienfaite.[84] But undoubtedly his greatest achievement was to secure the earldom of Pembroke from King John in 1199 thereby effecting a full restoration of the estates which Strongbow had inherited from his father Gilbert in 1148.[85]

Although it fell to William Marshal to complete the restoration of Strongbow's inheritance, it was Strongbow's intervention in Ireland in 1170 which had paved the way for the recovery of his fortunes and eventually led to the full restoration of his patrimonial inheritance to his heirs. King John's grant of the earldom of Pembroke to William Marshal in 1199 was the final dividend resulting from the alliance which Strongbow had entered into with Diarmait Mac Murchada in 1166—67.

A more far reaching consequence of the successful alliance between Diarmait Mac Murchada and Strongbow was the reaction which it provoked from Henry II and his determination to intervene personally in Ireland in 1171—72, thus inaugurating English royal lordship in Ireland.

---

83 In 1189 William Marshal paid Richard I a fine of 2000 marks for half the Giffard honour, the other half going to the lord of Clare: *Pipe roll 2 Richard I*, 102, 144; *Cartae antiquae rolls, 11—20*, Pipe Roll Society, lxxi, 1957, 165—6.
84 See above note 7.
85 There is no evidence for William Marshal's recognition as earl of Pembroke before 1199 when he was girt by King John. Painter, *William Marshal*, 77 assumed that William Marshal became earl of Pembroke in 1189 when he married Isabella, but in his *The reign of King John*, Baltimore 1949, 14 he altered his opinion pointing out that Pembroke Castle was in the custody of the king in 1199: *Pipe roll 1 John*, 182. According to Gerald of Wales, *Opera*, i; 76 the lordship of Pembroke was granted by Henry II to his son John in 1185 at about the same time, therefore, as he was made lord of Ireland. It would certainly have made sense to do so because of the proximity of Pembroke to Leinster and the fact that there were many landholders in Pembroke who also held land in Ireland. But there is no evidence apart from Gerald's statement that John ever did exercise lordship in Pembroke. There are for example no extant charters issued by him relating to Pembroke in the period 1185—89. It is possible that it was Henry's intention to give John Pembroke, but that he changed his mind after John's disastrous expedition to Ireland in 1185 and that Pembroke continued to be administered by the crown although there is no evidence for this on the pipe rolls.

RICHARD I AND THE SCIENCE OF WAR
IN THE MIDDLE AGES[1]

John Gillingham

So far as most historians are concerned there was no such thing as a science of war in the Middle Ages.[2] This is a profoundly mistaken view, but for the purposes of this paper I propose to concentrate on one aspect of war only — strategy, the planning and conduct of campaigns, and in particular in the 12th and 13th centuries, though I shall try to draw out some of the wider implications for other periods.[3] My chief reason for this choice is the fact that strategy still remains the most neglected area of medieval military history. It is true that the days when a book on the history of war turned out to be little more than a history of battles are almost gone. Modern scholars have tended to investigate subjects like military obligation, organization, recruitment, pay, armament and the ethos of war — all of them important subjects. As a result most recent historians have been so busy getting their armies into the field that they have left themselves little room in which to consider what they did once they were there. Thus in a recent admirable survey of the whole subject Philippe Contamine devotes only nine out of four hundred pages of printed text to strategy — rather less, for example, than he gives to the subject of courage. Even so Contamine's conclusion is worth emphasising — that medieval generals were 'capables de concevoir et d'exécuter une "grande stratégie"'[4] — and much of what follows will be an elaboration of some of the points which

---

1 I am grateful to John Prestwich for his kindness in reading a draft of this essay. Needless to say he did not at the time know where I intended to publish it. Had he done so he might have been less helpful than usual. I first gave some shape to these ideas in a lecture delivered to an audience at the Tower of London in March 1980, so for the invitation and the original stimulus I owe a debt of thanks to Peter Hammond and his colleagues at the Tower.

2 See, for example, the powerfully expressed conclusion to Ferdinand Lot, *L'art militaire et les armées au Moyen Age*, Paris 1946, ii, 449. My choice of the term 'the science of war' is, of course, intended to provoke scepticism. But notice Jean de Bueil's opinion: 'Car je puis dire . . . que la conduite de la guerre est artifficieuse et subtille; par quoy s'i convient gouverner par art et par science' and his description of La Hire as 'ung bon docteur en ceste science', Jean de Bueil, *Le Jouvencel* ed. C. Favre and L. Lecestre, Paris 1887—9, i 15, ii 246. Also the phrase *in scientia et virtute bellandi* in the early 13th century *Genealogia comitum Flandrensium* MGH ix 333.

3 I shall deal with the purely military conduct of campaigns, not with 'grand strategy' in the sense of political and diplomatic alliance-building, nor with information-gathering (spying) — though both of these were, of course, parts of the normal preliminaries of war.

4 Philippe Contamine, *La Guerre au Moyen Age*, Paris 1980, 365—78, 406—18. Most of Contamine's examples are drawn from the 14th and 15th centuries whereas I shall be chiefly concerned with an earlier period. The chapter on strategy in J.F. Verbruggen, *The Art of Warfare in Western Europe during the Middle Ages*, Amsterdam 1977, 249—300, consists largely of a summary of a dozen or so late 13th and early 14th century projects, most of them schemes for a new crusade. Thus he deals mainly with 'grand designs' while I shall restrict myself to a discussion of the practice of war — though see Verbruggen 283—4, 288.

he makes.

As will become apparent it could equally well be said that I am doing no more than transferring to a wider stage many of the insights contained in R.C. Smail's *Crusading Warfare*.[5] Yet although this book was published as long ago as 1956 few historians, not even military historians, can be said to have come to terms with his findings. For example, in one recent, and rightly much praised book, John Keegan doubts whether 'generalship' and 'planning' are concepts which can usefully be applied to medieval warfare.[6] In the opinion of the Chichele Professor of the History of War it was in the sixteenth century that 'cautious professional competence took the place of the quest for glory in the planning and conduct of campaigns.'[7] Thus it is hardly surprising that if we turn to current encyclopaedias we find the view that 'strategy was notably absent' from medieval warfare and it was in 1453 (!) that 'a new military age dawned'.[8] If such opinions still hold the field then the fault is undoubtedly ours; as medieval historians we have clearly failed to puncture some of the more widely held misconceptions about the Middle Ages.

My own strategy will be twofold. First, to take Richard I's military career as a model of medieval generalship.[9] Second, to use vernacular sources wherever possible, in the belief that the vernacular brings us closer than Latin to the thoughts and actions of soldiers. In particular I have relied heavily on three chronicles: *L'Estoire de la Guerre Sainte* by Ambroise; Joinville's *Life of St Louis*; and Jordan Fantosme's *Chronicle*. Two of the three deal primarily with warfare in the Middle East and this is no accident. We know much more about crusading warfare than we do about contemporary warfare in the West and where we have more evidence it is easier to work out the logic behind military operations. Thus Richard's reputation as a general rests very largely on his conduct of the war against Saladin but in fact, of course, he fought many more campaigns than this. When he went on crusade he had eighteen years of warfare behind him. So far as we know his earliest firsthand experience of war came in 1173 when he was fifteen years old. In the summer of that year he joined in the great revolt against his father Henry II, and took part in an attack on eastern Normandy — an attack which was launched by Count Philip of Flanders.[10] Since Count Philip was well-known as one of the shrewdest soldiers of the day, it seems likely that Richard began his apprenticeship under a good master.[11] After 1173 Richard went to war in 1174, 1175, 1176, 1177, etc. etc. In

5 R.C. Smail, *Crusading Warfare 1097—1193*, Cambridge 1956.
6 John Keegan, *The Face of Battle*, Harmondsworth 1978, 336.
7 Michael Howard, *War in European History*, Oxford 1977, p. 27. In part these views rest on the assumption that medieval armies were 'mere crowds', Keegan 175—6 and compare Howard, 56: 'Feudal men-at-arms were totally, gloriously indisciplined.' But on the importance of discipline in the face of the enemy see Smail 124—30 and Verbruggen 76—94.
8 *The New Encyclopaedia Britannica*, 15th edn., Chicago 1974, vol. 19, 558—9, 576—7; *Encyclopaedia Americana*, New York 1977, vol. 25, 772—3. A remarkably similar view was expressed by Geoffrey Parker in his chapter 'Warfare' in *The New Cambridge Modern History*, Vol. XIII, *Companion Volume* ed. P. Burke, Cambridge 1979.
9 Richard's reputation for political negligence has never prevented military historians from recognising his competence in their field, e.g. Smail 203, Verbruggen 210—12. For a fine recent assessment of Richard's grasp of strategy see J.O. Prestwich, 'Richard Coeur de Lion: *Rex Bellicosus*', *Accademia Nazionale dei Lincei. Problemi attuali di scienza e di cultura* 253, 1981, 3—15.
10 Roger of Howden, *Gesta Regis Henrici Secundi* ed. W. Stubbs, RS 1867, i 49.
11 'Felipe de Flandres, li proz/Qui par son sens sormontot toz/Cels qui estoient a son tens'

the year 1180 we know nothing of Richard's movements, so we simply cannot say whether he went to war or not, but apart from this one gap, we know that he was on campaign in every year between 1173 and his crusade. He then missed a year when he was sitting in prison in Germany, but as soon as he was released he threw himself into the compelling military task of throwing Philip Augustus out of those lands which he had grabbed while Richard was in prison. So between 1173 and his death in 1199 Richard had something like 25 years at war and in these circumstances it is obviously misleading to concentrate on just one small part of his military career to the exclusion of the rest. Indeed if we can believe Ambroise one reason for Richard's successes in the Mediterranean, in Sicily, in Cyprus and in Palestine, was that his followers were full of confidence, conscious that they were men of 'tried renown' who knew more of the art of war than did many of their enemies.[12]

How then should we analyse these 25 years of campaigning? Much of it, of course, consists of laying siege to one or more strongpoints.[13] To this subject I shall return, but for the moment I want to look at warfare in the field. In his chapter on 'The Latin Field Army in Action' R.C. Smail divided armies' activities into three categories. (1) Campaigns without battle. (2) Fighting on the march. (3) Pitched battles.[14] If we accept these categories, as I think we should, and ask how many pitched battles Richard fought, then the answer is only two or three. It is arguable whether or not the famous action at Arsuf on 7 September 1191 should be counted as a battle. It was, in Smail's terms, simply a particularly heavy attack on an army on the march. The charge of the crusader knights forced Saladin to break off the engagement, but two days later he was once again harassing the march just as he had done throughout the fortnight since the army left Acre.[15] However since it seems that the bulk of the forces on both sides became involved in the fighting at Arsuf, I am prepared to count it as a battle. It is equally arguable whether or not the action outside Jaffa on 5 August 1192 should be termed a pitched battle. Richard drew up his troops in so solid a defensive formation that the Muslims never closed with them. Spearmen and crossbowmen, working together like the pikemen and musketeers of a later age, presented so formidable an array that Saladin's cavalry always veered away at the last moment. Eventually Richard himself went over to the attack but it looks as though Saladin's troops were thoroughly demoralized and in no mood to fight — so much so that the day was famous chiefly for Richard's individual prowess and a chivalrous gesture on the part

Histoire de Guillaume la Maréchal, 3 vols., ed. P. Meyer (Paris, 1891—1901) i, 11. 2715—7, cf. 11 3065—6. See also the description of him as 'Felipe le Pugnaire' and 'le noble guerreur' in ed. R.C. Johnston, *Jordan Fantosme's Chronicle*, Oxford 1981, 11. 28, 438 ff.
12 'Mais nos savions plus de guere' Ambroise, *L'Estoire de la Guerre Sainte* ed. G. Paris, Paris 1897, 1. 1512. I shall usually quote from the splendidly doggerel translation of M.J. Hubert and J. La Monte, *The Crusade of Richard Lionheart*, New York 1941,
13 As did both Richard's first campaign — the siege of Drincourt 1173, Howden, *Gesta*, i 49 — and his last. The campaign of 1199 involved the siege not just of Chalus-Chabrol but also of Nontron, Montagut and probably eleven other places in the Limousin, including Limoges itself. See John Gillingham, 'The Unromantic Death of Richard I' *Speculum* liv, 1979, 18—41, especially 29—31. Richard's first known independent action was an attempt on La Rochelle in 1174; see John Gillingham, *Richard the Lionheart*, London 1978, 67—8. His troops on crusade were characterised by Ambroise as men 'Qui mainte vile aveient prise' Ambroise 1. 742.
14 Smail 138—203.
15 Ambroise 11. 6915—6922; Smail 162-5.

of Saladin.[16] Obviously the line of demarcation between a pitched battle and other forms of combat is not always a clear one, but for the purposes of this paper, in order not to make things too easy for myself, I am also prepared to count Jaffa as a battle.

Yet although there may be some degree of uncertainty about the number of Richard's battles on crusade, what is certain is that he did not adopt a battle-seeking strategy. Not once did he go after Saladin's army and try to destroy it. This is not because the 'hot-headed Westerner' once out East became infected by the ultra-cautious strategy of the Franks of Outremer.[17] In all the wars which Richard fought in the West, he fought only one battle and this came fairly early in his military career in May 1176, when he defeated a force of Brabançons employed by a coalition of rebels from the Angoumois and Limousin.[18] Moreover if we compare Richard with his contemporaries then it is clear that there was nothing unusual about this apparent reluctance to fight battles. Henry II, for example, in his whole life never fought a single battle — though Jordan Fantosme described him as 'the greatest conqueror since Charlemagne'.[19] Philip Augustus fought only one — Bouvines in 1214 — and although that battle brought the victory which crowned his career, we should note that he had been trying to avoid battle and fought only when it became unavoidable.[20] These kings were successful rulers who regularly mustered troops and led them to war — but they did not fight battles. It was not just timid commanders like Philip Augustus who avoided battle. Even a man like Richard I who at times in skirmishes and on reconnaissance patrols seems to have been recklessly brave, did not seek battle. In this sense Richard's military career was an unremarkable one but it is surely worth noting that the most famous soldier of the day shared to the full the reluctance of less distinguished commanders.[21]

Battles then were rare events. This is an observation which has become a commonplace.[22] Yet historians seem to have been content to stop there. Very rarely have they gone on to ask what it was that armies were doing when they were not fighting battles. Thus books on the art of war in the middle ages still tend to focus on battles, and not on the army's typical activities; they concentrate on the exceptional rather than the routine, indeed they fail to make clear just what the routine was.[23] And it is with this neglected side of warfare, the

---

16 Ambroise 11. 11455—11652. The most recent account of these events from Saladin's point of view certainly makes it appear that no battle took place, M.C. Lyons and D.E.P. Jackson, *Saladin: The Politics of the Holy War*, Cambridge 1982, 358.
17 So lucidly demonstrated by Smail, 138—40.
18 Howden, *Gesta* i 120. And see below n. 25. His famous encounters with Philip Augustus, at Fréteval 4 July 1194 and near Gisors 28 September 1198, were pursuits not battles, since on both occasions Philip ran for cover and made no effort to fight.
19 Fantosme 11. 111—13.
20 Georges Duby, *Le Dimanche de Bouvines*, Paris 1973, 156.
21 Compare Fulk Rechin's summary account of the military career of his turbulent grandfather Fulk Nerra. In over fifty years as count of Anjou (987—1040) Fulk, described as a man of *probitas magna et admirabilis* fought just two pitched battles: *Chroniques des comtes d'Anjou et des seigneurs d'Amboise* ed. L. Halphen and R. Poupardin, Paris 1913, 233—4.
22 See, for example, Duby, 142 f; Verbruggen, 288; J.H. Beeler, *Warfare in Feudal Europe 780—1200*, Ithaca 1971, 45, 57, 116. H. Delbrück, *Geschichte der Kriegskunst im Rahmen der politischen Geschichte* Part 3, 2nd edn. Berlin 1923, 344—5.
23 One of the few authors to devote much attention to an army's 'typical activities' is H.J.

planning of a routine campaign, that I shall be concerned.

Most campaigns did not end in battle largely because both commanders were reluctant to risk battle. This was in accord with the advice given in what is perhaps the best book ever written on medieval warfare — and one read by many medieval commanders: the *De Re Militari* by Vegetius. This late Roman handbook on war remained popular thoughout the middle ages and was frequently translated into the vernacular.[24] Vegetius' advice on giving battle was quite simple: Don't. Well, you might occasionally, if you heavily outnumbered your enemy, if their morale was poor, their supplies short, if they were tired and poorly led, then in these circumstances you might, but otherwise, no. Normally battle was the last resort. 'Every plan therefore is to be considered, every expedient tried and every method taken before matters are brought to this last extremity'.[25] Some rulers indeed took this advice so much to heart that they actually issued formal prohibitions, ordering their commanders not to engage in battle: Charles V after Poitiers, Louis XI after Montlhéry, Charles VII during the greater part of his reign.[26] Why this hostility to battle both in the commonplace theory of Vegetius and in the normal practice of medieval generals? What were the potential advantages and disadvantages of battle?

If the aim of war was either to win or hold territory and this meant taking or keeping strongpoints — castles and fortified towns — then victory in battle might, in some circumstances, bring a decisive advantage.[27] It did, for example for Saladin in 1187 and probably would have done even if he had not captured Guy of Lusignan at the Battle of Hattin. Crucial here was the kingdom of Jerusalem's desperate shortage of garrison troops. In these circumstances a battle-seeking strategy made sense — and in these circumstances ravaging could be used in order to provoke or tempt the defender to battle.[28] It made sense, for example, for William of Normandy in 1066 since, given both the

---

Hewitt, *The Black Prince's expedition of 1355—1357*, Manchester 1958, 46—75; H.J. Hewitt, *The Organization of War under Edward III*, Manchester 1966, 99—118. See also Eric Christiansen, *The Northern Crusades: The Baltic and the Catholic Frontier 1100—1525*, London 1980, 160—69.
24 Walter Goffart, 'The date and purpose of Vegetius' *De Re Militari, Traditio* 33, 1977, 65—100; Alexander Murray, *Reason and Society in the Middle Ages*, Oxford 1978, 127—30; Diane Bornstein, 'Military Strategy in Malory and Vegetius' *De Re Militari, Comparative Literature Studies 9*, 1972, 123—129.
25 Vegetius, *Epitoma rei militaris*, ed. C. Lang, Leipzig 1885, 86—9 and, in particular p. 86 'Ideo omnia ante cogitanda sunt, ante temptanda, ante facienda sunt, quam ad ultimum veniatur abruptum.' It seems likely that Richard indeed held all the advantages when he fought his 1176 battle against the Brabançons. According to Howden 'magnum exercitum congrevagit de Pictavia, et magna militum multitudo de circumjacentibus regionibus ad eum confluebat, propter ipsius stipendia quae illis dabantur. Et cum omnes essent congregati, promovit exercitum suum . . ,' Howden, *Gesta* i 120. The contrast between medieval and modern attitudes to battle can be overdrawn. As Delbrück noted — though with some reluctance — 'Auch ein moderner Feldherr schlägt in der Regel nicht, ohne dass er auf den Sieg rechnet,' Delbrück, vol. 3, 345. It may well be the case that much of Vegetius' strategic advice consisted of no more than 'eternal common-sense principles' (Smail, 15 n.l.); but platitudes have their uses.
26 Contamine 379.
27 As was pointed out by the author of the *Chronica de gestis consulum Andegavorum*, a work closely linked with the Angevin court of the mid 12th century, Halphen and Poupardin 55—6.
28 R.C. Smail, 'The Predicaments of Guy of Lusignan 1183—1187', in *Outremer — Studies in the History of the Crusading Kingdom of Jerusalem. Presented to Joshua Prawer*, Jerusalem 1982, 159—176. cf. Guillaume de Poitiers, *Histoire de Guillaume le Conquéránt* ed. Raymond Foreville, Paris 1952, 180.

volatile nature of Northern French politics and the massive preparations which the 1066 expedition had required, it was highly improbable that he would ever again have so large an army at his disposal.[29] Guy of Lusignan, of course, was also faced by the dangerous temptation of having an exceptionally large army under his command and, in the end, he chose a battle-risking strategy.[30] (On the other hand it seems unlikely that this was Harold Godwineson's predicament in October 1066).

But the fact that some victories in battle brought decisive gains — and these, of course, are the famous battles — should not lead us into assuming that most victories did. If we take the example of Richard's three victories in battle then one was decisive but two were not. His defeat of the *routiers* in 1176 facilitated the rapid capture of all the major rebel strongholds, including both Limoges and Angoulême.[31] On the other hand neither Arsuf (1191) nor Jaffa (1192) resulted in a signficant shift of the strategic balance in his favour. From the attacker's point of view if the defender's strongpoints were still able to offer prolonged resistance, allowing the defender time to re-organise and raise fresh troops, then victory in battle would have achieved little. From the defender's point of view if he could force the enemy to withdraw without battle then he would have achieved his aim with relatively little risk. Battle was a desperately chancy business. A few minutes of confusion or panic and the patient work of months or years might be undone. Moreover although comparatively few knights were actually killed in battle, the king or prince who committed his cause to battle was also putting himself in jeopardy since it was always clear that the surest way to win a battle was to kill or capture the opposing commander.[32] As Smail pointed out in the course of a superb analysis of the defensive strategy of the Franks of Outremer, in a well-managed campaign 'the rewards of victory could be won by other means which did not involve the penalties of defeat.'[33]

What then were these 'other means'? What, in other words, were Richard's twenty five years of campaigning all about? I begin with some advice on how to make war, advice attributed to Count Philip of Flanders, and recorded in Jordan Fantosme's metrical *Chronicle*. In the course of a 'reasoned speech' the count envisages William, King of the Scots invading Northumbria as an ally of Louis VII of France.

> Let him aid you in war, swiftly and without delay
> Destroy your foes and lay waste their country
> By fire and burning let all be set alight
> That nothing be left for them, either in wood or meadow
> Of which in the morning they could have a meal.

---

29 R. Allen Brown, *The Normans and the Norman Conquest*, London 1969, 145—52.
30 On Guy's motives see Smail, 'The Predicaments' and Hans Eberhard Mayer, 'Henry II of England and the Holy Land' *EHR* xcvii, 1982, 721—39.
31 Howden, *Gesta* i 120—1.
32 On the eve of Agincourt 'eighteen esquires of the French army . . . bound themselves by oath that . . . they would with their united strength force themselves sufficiently near to the king of England to strike the crown from off his head, or that they would all die, which they did', Harris Nicholas, *The History of the Battle of Agincourt*, London 1833, 250.
33 Smail, *Crusading Warfare* 139. Cf. Vegetius, 91—2: 'Illa enim ante temptanda sunt, quae si male cesserint, minus noceant, si bene, plurimum prosint.'

> *Then* with his *united* force let him besiege their castles.
> ....
> Thus should war be begun: such is my advice.
> First lay waste the land.[34]

The aim, in other words, is to capture your opponents' strongpoints, but the first stage is to ravage the countryside in order to deprive them of supplies — 'so that nothing is left for them . . . of which they could have a meal'. *Then* besiege their castles. This was in fact the strategy adopted by King William during his invasion of the north in 1173. Eventually an English army moved up to confront him; William made a brave speech about standing and fighting, about never yielding a single foot of the land which rightfully belonged to him — all the proper sentiments — but in fact he withdrew. He left Northumbria, however, in ruin, devastated in extreme famine. As the poet said —

> King William knows well how to fight his foe
> How to grieve and damage them.[35]

If one looks at Richard's campaigns in Europe, whether against rebels in Aquitaine or against King Philip of France, this, it is soon clear, is the pattern to which they conform — a pattern of ravaging and besieging.[36]

In 12th and 13th century sources ravaging is frequently referred to but infrequently described. One source, however, the *Chanson des Lorrains* contains an unusually detailed description of an army advancing through enemy territory which is well worth quoting.

> The march begins. Out in front are the scouts and incendiaries. After them come the foragers whose job it is to collect the spoils and carry them in the great baggage train. Soon all is in tumult. The peasants, having just come out to the fields, turn back, uttering loud cries. The shepherds gather their flocks and drive them towards the neighbouring woods in the hope of saving them. The incendiaries set the villages on fire and the foragers visit and sack them. The terrified inhabitants are either burned or led away with their hands tied to be held for ransom. Everywhere bells ring the alarm; a surge of fear sweeps over the countryside. Wherever you look you can see helmets glinting in the sun, pennons waving in the breeze, the whole plain covered with horsemen. Money, cattle, mules and sheep are all seized. The smoke billows and spreads, flames crackle. Peasants and shepherds scatter in all directions.[37]

---

34 Fantosme ll. 439—50 (my italics). With minor alterations I preferred to retain the familiar lines of Howlett's translation, *Chronicles of the Reigns of Stephen, Henry II and Richard I*, ed. R. Howlett, vol. 3, RS 1886, 241—3. The sequence of first ravaging then besieging is well brought out in the 'Plantagenet' account (see n. 27) of Geoffrey Martel's attack on Tours, Halphen and Poupardin 55—6.

35 Fantosme ll. 657—8.

36 See, for example, the importance of devastation as a preliminary to the most famous of Richard's early deeds, the capture of Taillebourg in 1179, Ralph Diceto, *Opera Historica* ed. W. Stubbs, RS 1876, i 431—2. Time and again Geoffrey of Vigeois, a chronicler who had the misfortune to live in a war zone, emphasises the ravaging of the Limousin carried out by Richard, his subordinates and his enemies, especially in the years 1182—84, *Recueil des historiens des Gaules et de la France* 18, Paris 1879, 212—23.

37 Quoted in Achille Luchaire, *Social France at the time of Philip Augustus* trans. E.B. Krehbiel, London 1912, 261.

It is clear that there was nothing unusual about this. This is how Charlemagne operated: we might think of Einhard's description of Avar territory turned into desert by Charlemagne's armies and of the huge waggon loads of plunder.[38] This is how Edward III, the Black Prince, and Henry V operated: remember Henry V's dictum: war without fire is like sausages without mustard.[39] This indeed is the essence of war as perceived by Vegetius: 'the main and principal point in war is to secure plenty of provisions for oneself and to destroy the enemy by famine. Famine is more terrible than the sword.'[40] The point about ravaging was that it simultaneously achieved both these ends. Moreover as an efficient method of waging war it made sense not only from the point of view of the overall campaign strategy of the army commander; it made sense also from the point of view of the individual soldier who was fighting for private profit, for plunder.

In the face of this threat to his territory what strategy could the defender adopt? His main object would be to deprive the attacker of supplies either by preventing him from ravaging (or 'foraging' as it is frequently and euphemistically termed) or — in cases where the attacker was chiefly relying on his supply lines — by cutting those supply lines. In the first instance the defender's usual strategy was to assemble an army and move it up to confront the invader. If he approached too close then he might find himself compelled to fight a battle in unfavourable circumstances — as happened to Harold in October 1066 — but it was not necessary to come as close as this in order to achieve his aim. The mere presence of an opposing army somewhere in the vicinity was normally enough to force the invader to keep his own army together and thus prevent him from ravaging and plundering — since these were operations which involved the dispersal of troops over a wide area. As Count Philip advised, after the devastation 'Then with his *united* force let him besiege their castles.' The ravaging, in other words, was done by scattered forces.

Obviously any defender who could catch an invader while his troops were dispersed had won a great advantage.[41] Reconnaissance was vital for both sides. In 1173 King William was informed of the English advance and withdrew; in 1174 he was attacked at Alnwick while his troops were scattered and he himself was captured. Jordan Fantosme reports a discussion between the English commanders as they advanced towards Alnwick.

Said Ranulf de Glanville: Let us act wisely.
Let us send a scout to estimate their numbers.[42]

---

38 Éginhard, *Vie de Charlemagne* ed. and trans. L. Halphen, 3rd edn. Paris 1947, pp. 38—40.
39 The culinary opinion attributed to Henry V by Juvenal des Ursins, *Histoire de Charles VI* in ed. J.A. Buchon, *Choix des Chroniques*, Paris 1875, p. 565. 'il respondit que ce n'estoit que usance de guerre, et que guerre sans feu ne valoit rien, non plus que andouilles sans moustarde.'
40 'Saepius enim penuria quam pugna consumit exercitum et ferro saevior fames est . . . In omni expeditione unum est et maximum telum, ut tibi sufficiat victus, hostes frangat inopia.' Vegetius, 69.
41 See, for example, *Gesta Henrici Quinti* ed. and trans. F. Taylor and J.S. Roskell, Oxford 1975, 22. Vegetius pointed out that in these circumstances an able commander had an ideal opportunity to 'blood' his less experienced troops, Vegetius, 91.
42 Fantosme 11. 1738—9

They do this and on learning that most of the Scots were away plundering the countryside, they rode through the night and took William by surprise while he was guarded only by a small force. Normally, of course, commanders were not as careless as William had been, but it is clear from this example that the defender only had to keep his own army in being in order to achieve his objective of stopping the enemy from ravaging. From the point of view of the invading troops once they could no longer go out plundering, soldiering lost its appeal and they just wanted to go home. Unquestionably there were men who enjoyed going to war, but there were very few, if any, who enjoyed the imminent prospect of a pitched battle.

In the case where an invader was relying more on supply lines than ravaging then the defender's obvious course was to try to cut those lines. The most dramatic example of the successful use of this strategy is undoubtedly the Egyptian campaign of 1249—50. After the crusaders had captured Damietta (summer 1249) Louis IX held a council meeting:

> The king summoned all the barons of the army to decide in what direction he should go, whether to Alexandria or to Cairo. The good Comte Pierre Bretagne, as well as the majority of the barons, agreed in advising him to go and besiege Alexandria, because that city had a good harbour, where the ships bringing food for the army could land their supplies. But the Comte d'Artois was of a contrary opinion, maintaining that he would never agree to their going anywhere except to Cairo, because it was the chief city in the kingdom of Egypt, and if you wished to kill the serpent, you must first of all crush its head. The king rejected the barons' advice in favour of his brother's.[43]

So the crusaders advanced up the Nile. In February 1250 they won a battle at Mansourah. Joinville's setpiece description contains a splendid account of the chaos and confusion of the battle and, incidentally, makes clear the crucial role of the king's contingent of crossbowmen. But the victory brought no real advantage to the crusaders. Egyptian re-inforcements came up and both sides settled down — once again — to the round of trench warfare and mutual artillery bombardment that is so typical of medieval war.

> A fortnight later the Turks did something that came as a great shock to our people. In order to starve us they took several of their galleys lying upstream above our camp, and after dragging them overland put them back into the river, a good league below the place where our tents were pitched. These galleys caused a famine among us; for because they were there no one dared to come up the river from Damietta to bring us fresh supplies of food.[44]

The sickness in the crusader camp then reached such devastating proportions that total surrender became unavoidable. The whole army, king and nobles all included, either died or were made prisoner. Not even the battles of Hattin and Hastings had been as decisive as this. Vegetius, of course, had made the point

---

43 Joinville, *The Life of Saint Louis* in trans. M.R.B. Shaw, *Chronicles of the Crusades*, Harmondsworth 1963, 210.
44 Joinville 237.

explicit: 'Time and opportunity may help to retrieve other misfortunes, but where forage and provisions have not been carefully provided for, the evil is utterly without remedy.'[45] The Egyptian campaign of 1250 is certainly exceptional in the scale of its consequences but it serves to highlight the crucial — and perennial — problem of the relationship between supply and disease. In this context it is worth noting the Third Crusade casualty list preserved by Roger of Howden.[46] Of the 98 people on the list fourteen are picked out as being either drowned, captured or killed. Presumably at least most of the other eighty-four died of other causes of which the diseases of the army camp are by far the most likely.[47] Ambroise made the point:

> I dare say too with certainty,
> By famine and by malady
> More than 3,000 were struck down
> At the siege of Acre and in the town.

Though it should be said that in Ambroise's eyes an even bigger killer was self-imposed chastity.

> In pilgrims' hearing I declare
> A hundred thousand men died there
> Because from women they abstained.
> 'Twas for love they restrained
> Themselves. They had not perished thus
> Had they not been abstemious.[48]

The principal duty of a general then was to ensure that his troops were kept reasonably fit and well-fed and usually, of course, there were plenty of women with the army.[49] The point is an obvious one, but its implications are rarely brought out. What, for example, did an army camp look like? Ambroise describes one for us:

> As if it were a market town
> Oxen and cows and goats and swine
> Most vigorous and fair and fine
> And rams and sheep and lambs were there
> And many a goodly colt and mare
> And cock and hen and fat capon
> And full-fleshed mules —.[50]

---

45 'Deinde reliquis casibus potest in tempore subveniri, pabulatio et annona in necessitate remedium non habent, nisi ante condantur.' Vegetius, 69. See, for example, the fate of the German army in Asia Minor in 1190, Lyons and Jackson 315.
46 Howden, *Gesta* ii 147—50.
47 During the American-Mexican war of 1846—8, for example, 1100 U.S. soldiers died of disease and only 150 as a result of enemy action. See the table in Parker, *Warfare*, 216.
48 Ambroise 11. 12, 237 ff.
49 So many essential services did female camp followers perform that an army without women is hard to imagine; see, for example, the reference to their work of washing, cleaning and de-lousing the troops, — *E d'espucer valeient singes* Ambroise 11. 5696—99. In crusader armies, of course, women were always felt to be a problem and indeed in Muslim eyes their activities, whether military or sexual, sometimes took on legendary proportions. See the passage from Imad ad-Din quoted in F. Gabrieli, *Arab Historians of the Crusades*, London 1969, 204—7.
50 Ambroise 11. 1676—84. See Joinville, 233 for a reference to 'the butchers and . . . the women

Problems of disease and supply were doubtless more prominent in the Middle East but they were obviously in no sense confined to that theatre of war. No sooner had Henry II taken the cross than he wrote to Frederick Barbarossa, Bela of Hungary and Isaac Angelus to ensure that his army had an adequate market — *victualium copiosum mercatum* — as it passed through their territories.[51] When Richard I returned to Normandy in 1194 to find Philip Augustus laying siege to Verneuil his response was to send a force round to the east of Verneuil to cut the French king's supply lines. This compelled Philip to abandon the siege — in such haste indeed that he left behind rich pickings for the garrison of Verneuil.[52] In 1197 Philip invaded Flanders and Count Baldwin, instead of bringing the French to battle, concentrated on blocking roads and breaking down bridges. No supply wagons could get through and so the French troops were forced to try to live off the land i.e. they were forced to ravage when it was dangerous for them to do so. Dispersed in this manner they became hopelessly vulnerable to Count Baldwin's well-timed counter-attacks. According to the Coggeshall chronicler they even suffered the indignity of being beaten by bands of Flemish women. As a result Philip had to sue for peace and accept humiliating terms.[53]

What about the strategy of attack?

Richard, of course, is famous as an aggressive commander — leading the attempt to capture Jesusalem, and then, later in the 1190s, recovering the territory lost while he was in prison. A close look at these campaigns makes it clear that supply problems were decisive in the shaping of strategy. Turning first to the crusade, we find that, having captured Cyprus, Richard used it as a supply base. On his arrival at Acre he was given a rapturous welcome — and Ambroise explains why.

> The king, by taking Cyprus, had
> Made all the army to be glad
> For therefrom would they food derive
> To keep the mighty host alive.[54]

After the capture of Acre Richard then led the army south along the coast road to Jaffa, the nearest port to Jerusalem. The army was accompanied by supply ships and the waggon train, of course; even so Muslim observers noted there were not enough transport animals and so Richard ordered that each man

---

who sold provisions'. According to al-Maqrizi there were no less than 7,000 shops in Saladin's army market outside Acre. The opposing Frankish market may well have been smaller; on the other hand it seems to have outstripped the Muslim camp in terms of wine-shops and brothels, Lyons and Jackson 308, 329.

51 Diceto, ii 51—54.
52 'Tant fist li reis qui molt fu sages/Que trestoz toli les passages/Par unt la viande veneit/A rei qui le siege teneit/E par icest mesestance/S'en departi le reis de France.' *Histoire de Guillaume* 11. 10491—96. Rigord, *Gesta Philippi Augusti* ed. H.F. Delaborde, *Oeuvres de Rigord et de Guillaume le Breton*, Paris 1882—85, i 127.
53 Roger of Howden, *Chronica*, ed. W. Stubbs, RS 1868—71, iv 20; Ralph of Coggeshall, *Chronicon Anglicanum* ed. J. Stevenson, RS 1875, 77—8; William of Newburgh, *Historia Rerum Anglicarum* ed. R. Howlett in *Chronicles*, ii 495—6.
54 Ambroise 11. 2366—70; Cf. 11. 1896—1902; 2102—6. John Prestwich has adduced plausible grounds for believing that the conquest of Cyprus, far from being accidental, may have been in Richard's mind from the outside of his crusade, Prestwich, 8—9, 12.

should carry ten days supply of food. This meant that they advanced very slowly — covering the 81 miles to Jaffa in 19 days — but they got there in a classic demonstration of fighting on the march. It was a dogged march which won the admiration of Saladin's secretary, who was well aware that the slow pace was conditioned by the needs of the heavily burdened foot soldiers.[55] But even so this rate of four miles a day was lightning fast when compared with the speed of the advance from Jaffa towards Jerusalem.

The army began to leave Jaffa on 31 October 1191. On 22 November it camped at Ramleh, approximately ten miles inland. Why was the advance so slow? Because if they had simply marched inland Saladin would cut off their supplies. Therefore the road behind them had to be protected by castles and since Saladin had systematically been destroying all strongpoints (except Jerusalem itself), this meant that they had to be, equally methodically, rebuilt.[56] At Ramleh Richard waited six weeks, stockpiling supplies, while the winter weather got worse and worse.[57] What was Richard doing? Why the delay? Because essentially this was a war of skirmishing and attrition. The question was, who could hold their army together the longer, Richard or Saladin? Winter was traditionally the season when supplies ran out and armies were disbanded. Saladin's men were tired and hungry and wanted to go home. Eventually Saladin had to bow to this pressure; he himself withdrew behind the walls of Jerusalem while the bulk of his army dispersed. Now at last Richard could advance again. By early January he was at Beit Nuba, another ten miles inland and about twelve miles from Jerusalem. He had brought with him enough supplies to be able to lay siege to the city and then, having captured it, to stand siege himself.[58] But, as is well known, he never advanced those last twelve miles. On a second occasion, six months later in June 1192, he again advanced to Beit Nuba — and this time, having fortified the roads, was able to do so more quickly. This time the journey from the coast took only five days. But again at Beit Nuba he gave the order to withdraw. On both occasions it is clear that the question of supplies was uppermost in the mind of the army council. Despite all their efforts, that supply line to the coast just looked too vulnerable — and even if they did take Jerusalem and hold it while the crusaders were there, what would happen when they returned to Europe? The answer to this question was clear and there can be no doubt that, in terms of military strategy, Richard and his advisers took the right decision — though they were of course bitterly unpopular ones.[59] In purely military terms Jerusalem was not a sensible objective — and Richard indeed had been reluctant to go for it in the first place. His own strategy had been to march down the coast, capture Ascalon and Daran, cutting the caravan route between Egypt and Syria, and then go for an attack on Egypt itself — the standard 13th

---

55 Ambroise ll. 5549 ff. Verbruggen 212—15.
56 Ambroise ll. 7029 ff; 7181—3; 7209—14; 7447—60; 7614—5; Lyons and Jackson 341. More drastic than Saladin was Theobald IV of Champagne in 1229 when 'he set fire to all his towns himself before his enemies could reach them so that they would not find them full of supplies', Joinville, 184.
57 Ambroise ll. 7471—78, cf. 7635—42.
58 Ambroise ll. 7610—53.
59 Ambroise ll. 7,700—16; 10,161—70. Lyons and Jackson 345—6.

century strategy, and a sensible one.[60]

About Richard's campaigns in the West we possess much less detailed information than we do about the crusade, but I would like to call attention to one matter — the building of Château-Gaillard. We know that in the space of two years up to September 1198 he spent about £11,500 on this. This is a fantastically large sum. In the whole of his reign he spent £7,000 on *all* English castles. The nearest approach to the expenditure on Château-Gaillard is the sum of nearly £7,000 spent on Dover between 1180 and 1190.[61] So £11,500 in two years is phenomenal. What was it for? The conventional answer is that it was meant to defend Rouen, to plug a gap in the Norman defences. But in the years of its building Richard was not on the defensive. He was recovering those castles which had been lost while he was in prison in Germany, so a place has to be found for Château-Gaillard within a strategy of aggression. Château-Gaillard and the new town Andeli, associated with it, was to be the forward base from which the Vexin was conquered. Men and supplies could be sent up the Seine from the main arsenal at Rouen. Richard built river boats — long ships — for this purpose. Or they could travel by road, taking a more direct route which crossed the Seine twice — at Pont de l'Arche and Portjoie. Richard we know built bridges, residences and castles along this royal and military road between Rouen and Andeli. The pattern of Richard's advance into the Vexin is, in other words, a very similar one to the pattern of Richard's advance from Jaffa.[62]

By way of conclusion I would like to make two points, one particular and one general. First, that as an army commander Richard was very far from being the impetuous leader of romantic legend.[63] Rather, his usual approach was methodical and carefully prepared. His strategy was based on the systematic use of magazines, supply lines and ravaging, the 'strategy of manoeuvre' which is usually associated with a later period, but the strategy which was in fact adopted by all good medieval generals. This kind of war is largely a matter of effective administration and one of the most comic of modern misunderstandings of Richard I is the widely accepted view that he was a poor administrator.[64]

Secondly, developing further this view of medieval warfare, I would argue that victory in battle normally offered rewards sufficient to offset the risks involved only in those societies where the science of fortification was relatively poorly developed. But, as is well known, throughout most of the European

---

60 Gillingham, *Richard* 194, 300—1.
61 R.A. Brown, *English Castles* (2nd edn.) 1976, 160—61.
62 Gillingham, *Richard* 262—265. Delaborde, i 207—209. Undoubtedly Richard's intention was 'to recover territory not to gain it' (Prestwich 11), but within the Vexin, as elsewhere along the Angevin—Capetian frontier, this meant adopting an aggressive campaign strategy.
63 It remains true of course, that his prowess and recklessness made him a legend in his own lifetime. This was an image of the king which he himself took pains to cultivate — not surprisingly since it was politically valuable and helped to maintain the morale of his troops, Prestwich 4—5, 14; Gillingham, *Richard*, 284—5.
64 On the importance of administrative preparation, Keegan 296. According to the *Encyclopaedia Americana* 773, Montgomery's successes in World War II induced British military experts to add two 'new' ideas to their list of strategic maxims; thorough administrative preparation and careful provision for the maintenance of troop morale!

Middle Ages this science was a higly developed one. Fortification consumed a significant proportion of men's financial resources and, on the whole, the technology of defence was more than equal to the challenging technology of artillery. In these circumstances a Napoleonic or Clausewitzian *Niederwerfungsstrategie* made little sense.[65] It may well be that for much of its history England has been a special case in that relatively little was spent on fortification. This seems to have been so before 1066 and was certainly so from the 15th century onwards, when English patrons and their architects — unlike their continental counterparts — felt no compulsion to develop defence systems capable of resisting the revolutionary siege artillery of the late 14th century. In consequence warfare in England has been fairly battle-orientated, both in the Wars of the Roses and in civil wars of the 17th century.[66] But in this respect the military history of England has been a peculiar one. In European medieval history as a whole battles are rare and making war did not normally involve seeking battle.

The dominance of the fortified strongpoint meant that wars were mostly wars of attrition and that, in consequence, there was a demand for soldiers who were experts in this kind of war: garrison troops, artillerymen (engineers) and bowmen, incendiaries and foragers. The infantry arm, in other words, was vitally important. Cavalry, of course, was also important, particularly when out on reconnaissance patrol or escorting and guarding foraging parties. But it would be difficult to think of generalisations more misleading than such statements as in the Middle Ages 'the principal arm in any military force was the heavy cavalry' or that as a result of 'deeply significant' Renaissance innovations 'defence became superior to offence' and infantry 'more decisive'.[67] All such statements are based upon a view of medieval warfare which sees it as being largely composed of battles dominated by the charge of heavily armoured knights. But against this view, distorted by its reliance on evidence concerning exceptional and therefore news-worthy occasions we must bear in mind the routine reality of medieval warfare, and the army commander's constant effort 'to secure plenty of provisions for himself and to destroy the enemy by famine'. For the medieval reality of war was very like the medieval theory of war as outlined by Vegetius and it was in his cautious mastery of the logistics of Vegetian warfare that even a 'romantic hero' like Richard I showed his real competence as a general.

---

65 It is for this reason that some historians have concluded that in the Middle Ages strategy 'im höheren Sinne des Wortes' could not really have existed, Delbrück 3, 344.
66 There is the further point that in civil wars both sides, in order not to alienate the people whose support they are seeking, are usually under great pressure to avoid ravaging and to bring the war to a swift conclusion. They are thus more willing to seek and to risk battle — to act, as Defoe put it in commenting on the English Civil Wars 'as if they had been in haste to have their Brains knock'd out'. John Gillingham, *The Wars of the Roses*, London 1981, 15—50; John Gillingham, *Cromwell: Portrait of a Soldier*, London 1976, 23—28.
67 Parker, 201—3.

THE LOSS OF NORMANDY AND ROYAL FINANCES

J.C. Holt

The resources which the Capetians and Angevins could bring to bear in their struggle for Normandy have become a controversial matter. It is quite possible to argue, on the one hand, that French resources were superior enough to account for the Angevin collapse, and, on the other, that the accounts of known resources are misleading and that King John threw away what was still a good hand in failing to defend Normandy in 1203. Some important pieces in the exchange are missing. It is unlikely, for example, that the total yield of the Seventh levied on revenues in England in 1203 will ever come to light. Yet, on the whole, the participants in the debate are well provided with material: the continuous run of Pipe rolls of the English Exchequer, a considerable fragment of a Norman Pipe roll for 1203 and complete rolls for 1195 and 1198, and the first surviving account of Capetian finances of 1202—3. That ought to be sufficient to settle many matters and to define the terms of debate on the remainder. Indeed there would be little room and less proclivity for argument were the debate not part of the general assessment of King Richard and, even more, of King John. It is a chapter in an old story going back to within twenty years of John's death, when already the Barnwell writer believed that in abandoning Normandy the King had bowed to the inevitable, whilst Roger Wendover attributed the collapse to John's uxorious idleness.[1]

The chief materials have long been known. The Capetian account of 1202—3 was published by Nicolas Brussel in 1727, in an edition which became the sole source after the destruction of the original by fire in 1737.[2] The Norman Pipe rolls were edited by Thomas Stapleton between 1840 and 1844,[3] and the printed series of English Pipe rolls reached 1204 in 1940. Yet the argument only began to take shape in 1932 when Ferdinand Lot and Robert Fawtier published a comprehensive study of the French account of 1202—3.[4] Their calculations indicated that in this critical year Capetian resources were at least equal and perhaps superior to those which King John could bring to bear in the defence of Normandy.[5] They were followed to some degree in this in 1936 by Powicke,[6] although he had not used the account of 1202—3 in his earlier work, *The Loss of Normandy*,[7] and more emphatically in 1975 by the

---

1 *Memoriale Fratris Walteri de Coventria*, ed. W. Stubbs, RS 1872—3, ii, 197; Matthew Paris, *Chronica Majora*, ed. H.R. Luard, RS 1872—3, ii, 482.
2 N. Brussel, *Nouvel Examen de l'usage général des fiefs en France*, Paris 1727, ii, cxxxix—ccx.
3 T. Stapleton, *Magni Rotuli Scaccarii Normanniae sub regibus Angliae*, 2 vols, London 1840—1844.
4 F. Lot and R. Fawtier, *Le Premier Budget de la Monarchie Française*, Paris 1932. This contains a facsimile of Brussel's text following p. 298.
5 Lot and Fawtier, pp. 135—9.
6 *Cambridge Medieval History*, vi, 328.
7 Manchester, 1913. The work of Lot and Fawtier was noted, without comment, in the 2nd edn,

present writer.[8] In 1978 Mr Gillingham expressed serious doubt both about the handling of the figures and the conclusion to which they seemed to point. He argued that in the account of 1202—3 sums derived from the Temple, which served as the French royal treasury, should not be included in the 'revenue' or 'income' of the year, that it was 'absurd' to leave Anjou and the other southern dominions out of the count, and that English resources, especially the Seventh of 1203, should not be lightly underestimated. His conclusion returned to the difference apparent in the conflicting opinions of the Barnwell chronicler and Roger Wendover: 'If John was no match for Philip Augustus it was not because he had inherited inadequate financial resources; it was because he did not know how to rule'.[9] That would appear to leave some room for further examination of the problem.

What follows is not aimed solely at defining what ought to be counted and how, important though that is. It also casts the net of comparison somewhat wider, especially to include the important studies of Capetian finances published by Professor Baldwin in 1980 and 1981,[10] and by Professor Bisson in 1982.[11] Most important of all, it seeks to get the figures right, or more nearly so than heretofore. For one figure which has come to be embedded in the argument, £24,000 for the 'ordinary' revenue of England in 1203, is nothing other than a 'guesstimate'. Yet another assessment, that of Norman revenues for 1198, which has been put variously at 20,000 l.*ang.* or 98,000 l.*ang.* is seriously misleading; the true total was half as much again as the larger figure. No one, finally, has totalled the Norman Pipe rolls of 1195 and 1203. The calculation or recalculation of these accounts is an essential preliminary to a proper reassessment. The result is one which is more complicated than has been imagined hitherto. It brings new arguments into the discussion. It provides the strongest confirmation for the views of Lot and Fawtier.

It will be useful first to define some terms precisely. The argument is about *revenues*. Revenues embrace two items: first, *receipts* in the form of deposits into the Treasury or Chamber, and secondly *expenditure*, that is regular *allowances* of one kind or another, and specifically authorised *charges*. Revenues should not be confused with cash income. In 1203 English revenues, very roughly stated, amounted to 55% receipts and 45% expenditure. Such a proportion is by no means uncommon. Revenues sometimes included the expenditure of sums derived from the Treasury or Chamber. These were in fact *withdrawals* from deposit for current expenditure. Some withdrawals involved *transfers* of sums either between Treasury and Chamber or between one Angevin treasury and another. Transfers were also made between accounts, by the assignment of individual debts or between one official and another.

Manchester 1961, 249 n. All references below are to the 2nd edn.
8 J.C. Holt, 'The End of the Anglo-Norman Realm', *Proceedings of the British Academy*, lxi, 1975, 223—265.
9 John Gillingham, *Richard the Lionheart*, London 1978, 303—4.
10 Michel Nortier and John W. Baldwin, 'Contributions a l'étude des finances de Philippe Auguste', *Bibliothèque de l'École des Chartes*, cxxxviii, 1980, 5—33; John W. Baldwin, 'La décennie décisive: les années 1190—1203 dans le règne de Philippe Auguste', *Revue Historique*, cclxvi, 1981, 311—37.
11 Thomas N. Bisson, 'Les comptes des domaines au temps de Philippe Auguste. Essai comparatif' in *La France de Philippe Auguste: le temps des mutations*, ed. R-H. Bautier, Paris 1982, 521—38.

Transfers of this last kind were used very frequently in Normandy as a means of directing money to the chief spending agents.

All these terms will be used precisely and consistently in the following discussion. Other definitions are possible. These conform reasonably both to medieval practice and modern experience.

The records under consideration are all statements of account of the receipts and expenditure presented in particular years. In comparing them it is essential to use a method which is, as it were, the highest common factor, applicable to the French as much as to the Norman and English accounts. Hence the calculations are based on a very simple method. In each case the gross total is of receipts and expenditure recorded, whether derived from earlier or current years or from ordinary or extraordinary sources.[12] Only a few pardons, chiefly those where an error has clearly been made, are excluded.[13] Transfers between one accounting official and another are totalled under the final, not the preliminary, account, and the quittance given on the preliminary account is not included in the total expenditure. This method avoids duplication but it follows that where the final account for such transfers is not cleared on the current roll it is necessarily excluded from the total.[14] Assignment of individual debts has been treated in the same way. Net totals are reached by discounting certain items, transfers from Treasury to Chamber, for example, and receipts on the Norman accounts from the English Treasury. But these deductions are noted, as also are large receipts from earlier years, withdrawals and the major extraordinary measures.

The French account of 1202—3

No attempt has been made to recalculate the sums of Lot and Fawtier.[15] They followed a slightly different procedure from that outlined above in that they totalled notional receipts and then subtracted expenditure. In this they followed the pattern of the record, in which each account is divided into receipts and expenses. Their total, after allowing for *debets* and transfers was

---

12 I have ignored renders in kind except where commuted. This does not distort my comparisons. Such renders are scattered throughout the accounts and constitute *in toto* an insignificant portion of total revenues. On none of the accounts under consideration are statements of produce, whether in kind or in cash, as important as they are in the Flemish account of 1187. See A. Verhulst and M. Gysseling, *Le Compte Général de 1187, connu sous le nom de 'Gros Brief'*, Brussels 1962, 47—58; Bryce Lyon and A. Verhulst, *Medieval Finance: a comparison of financial institutions in Northwestern Europe*, Bruges 1967, 36—7; Baldwin (1981), 326—7.

13 Other pardons are included in the totals on the ground that they were probably matched by some kind of *quid pro quo*. But some of these, which seem quite exceptional, are noted as being deducted. However, in general pardons are not a major problem, certainly nowhere near so as in the Pipe Roll of 31 Henry I. See Judith A. Green, 'The last century of Danegeld', *EHR*, xciv, 1981, 245—51; 'Praeclarum et Magnificum Antiquitatis Monumentum: the Earliest Surviving Pipe Roll', *BIHR*, lv, 1982, 12.

14 See, as an example, the transfer from Henry de Gray to Richard Silvein in 1198, Stapleton, 315, 357.

15 It is disconcerting to discover that Lot and Fawtier made a number of errors in their elucidation of a sample account (4—5). Other items which I have pursued are entered and calculated accurately. I have not checked the arithmetic systematically.

196,327 l.*par.*[16] Of this 59,375 l.*par.* were withdrawn from the Temple[17] and 27,370 l.*par.* were a levy for the raising of paid troops, *servientes*.[18] The recorded expenditure to be set against the total, came to 95,445 l.*par.*[19] The unexpended balance, equivalent to the receipts on the Norman and English Pipe rolls, therefore came to 100,882 l.*par.*

The sum of this account, 196,327 l.*par.*, is the central point or baseline for the comparisons which follow. It was equivalent in 1202—3 to 286,310 l.*ang.*[20]

The Norman Pipe rolls

1203: Not surprisingly the Pipe roll for 1203 is incomplete. By Michaelmas the Norman defences were beset and Angevin control of Normandy was on the point of collapse. The account for the *bailliage* of Caux was rendered but is not now included in the roll.[21] Whether the other missing accounts were even rendered must be problematical. Quite apart from this the remaining accounts clearly reflect severely diminished resources. The revenues of the ten *bailliages* accounted is only 38% of their yield in 1198, 9,654 l.*ang.* as against 25,366 l.*ang.* The total of 9,654 l.*ang.* is made up of 3,735 l.*ang.* receipts and 5,919 l.*ang* expenditure.

1198: Lot and Fawtier advanced two sums for the revenues of Normandy in 1198: 20,000 l.*ang.* for the farm of the *prévôtés* and 93,193 l.*ang.* for total revenues.[22] The first figure was derived from Powicke, who used it simply to illustrate how inadequate the customary farms were to pay for the garrisoning of the Norman defences.[23] The source of the second figure was Sir James

---

16 Lot and Fawtier, 48; cp. 26, 51.
17 Lot and Fawtier, 25.
18 Baldwin (1981), 328. Cp. Lot and Fawtier, 20 and below, 99.
19 Lot and Fawtier, 131.
20 The conversion is usually expressed as 1:1.46, and sometimes as 1:1.43, i.e. 7:10. See Françoise Dumas, 'La Monnaie dans le royaume au temps de Philippe Auguste' in *La France de Philippe Auguste*, 547; and Françoise Dumas and Jean-Noël Barrandon, 'Le titre et le poids de fin des monnaies sous le règne de Philippe Auguste (1180—1223)' in *Cahiers Ernest-Babelon*, Paris 1982, i, 23. The rate cannot have been expressed in decimal terms. It seems to have been 350 *deniers angevin* to the *livre* i.e. 240 *deniers parisis*. This depends on three instances in the account of 1202—3: clxxiv, clxxxiv, cxcvi. There is a fourth instance (ccii) in which the conversion was 1:1.33 i.e. 320 *deniers angevins* to the *livre parisis* but this was an issue, and that to the Hospitaller, Brother Guérin, the King's Vice-Chancellor and household Treasurer, and not an account due. 1:1.46 is the conversion used in all the calculations which follow. It has also been assumed that the *livre tournois* and the *livre angevin* were at par. That this was so across the chronological divide of 1204 was demonstrated by Léopold Delisle, 'Des Revenus Publics en Normandie', *Bibliothèque de l'École des Chartes*, 2 ser., v, 1848—9, 187—9. The *tournois* was also equated by implication with the *angevin* in Philip Augustus's ordinance *De mutacione monete* of 1204 in which it is set at 4:1 of the sterling mark of silver. But there are two complications. First, the same ordinance discounted the *livre angevin* against the *livre tournois* at 180:192. Second, by 1221 the conversion of the *livre tournois* to the *livre parisis* was 5:4. See A. Dieudonné, 'L'Ordonnance de 1204 sur le change des monnaies en Normandie' in *Mélanges offerts à Gustave Schlumberger*, Paris 1924, ii, 328—337 and Baldwin (1980), 27.
21 Stapleton, 565.
22 Lot and Fawtier, 138.
23 Powicke, 234.

Ramsay's *Revenues of the Kings of England*.[24] Ramsay gave no indication of how the total was calculated; he may well have omitted revenues of earlier years and withdrawals from both Treasury and Chamber.[25] In fact the totals for 1198 were 75,654 l.*ang*. receipts and 100,267 l.*ang*. expenditure, a total of 175,922 l.*ang*. From this certain deductions have to be made. 4,500 l.*ang*. which passed through the account were simply transfers from the Treasury at Caen to the Chamber,[26] and the equivalent of 18,291 l.*ang*. were received from the English Treasury. The deduction of these items leaves a total of 153,131 l.*ang*.

Of this net total 39,224 l.*ang*. were withdrawals from the Treasuries of Caen and Rouen and from the Chamber. A forced loan contributed at least 15,864 l.*ang*. and a tallage 'for keeping sergeants in the Marches' at least 16,602 l.*ang*. A further tallage 'levied on the order of the King' totalled 11,270 l.*ang*. and sundry other tallages came to 3,615 l.*ang*. These extraordinary sources totalled 47,351 l.*ang*.

The contributions from earlier years is particularly important on this roll. Sewhal fitz Henry, Robert fitz Hermer and Matthew fitz Enard rendered account for two years, 1197 and 1198, for the construction and munitioning of Château-Gaillard and other works. Their expenditure totalled 50,223 l.*ang*. Château-Gaillard cost over 45,000 l.*ang*. Of this, 16,502 l.*ang*. from various sources and some portion of 5,700 l.*ang*. drawn from the Treasury of Caen were funded from the revenues of 1197.[27]

1195: The account for this year, which seems to be as complete as that of 1198, is more modest. Receipts totalled 40,766 l.*ang*. and expenditure 47,385 l.*ang*., a gross total of 88,151 l.*ang*. Of this, 7,008 l.*ang*. receipts and at least 16,414 l.*ang*. expenditure were concerned with the payment of King Richard's ransom and the release of hostages from Germany.[28] At least 579 l.*ang*. were written off as depredations of war.[29] Pardons were more prominent on this roll than on that of 1198 and sums totalling 3,221 l.*ang*. probably ought to be excluded.[30] Transfers from Treasury to Chamber amounted to 4,969 l.*ang*. The deduction of all these items leaves a net total of 28,795 l.*ang* receipts and 27,171 l.*ang*. expenditure: total 55,966 l.*ang*.

The withdrawals during the year came to 30,408 l.*ang*. but 16,000 l.*ang*. of these were used on the King's ransom. The withdrawals which contributed to the net total therefore amounted to 14,408 l.*ang*.

---

24 Sir James H. Ramsay, *A History of the Revenues of the Kings of England 1066—1399*, Oxford 1925, i, 227.
25 It is unfortunate that Ramsay did not explain his method. Where his method is obvious it can be shown that he counted accurately. For example, his total for Pipe Roll 31 Henry I, *mutatis mutandis*, is within £10 of Dr Green's. See Ramsay, i, 60 and Green (1982), 16.
26 Stapleton, 485.
27 Stapleton, 309—11.
28 Stapleton, 136, 137, 183, 253.
29 Stapleton, 211, 237.
30 Stapleton, 127, 133, 146, 167, 191, 262.

The English accounts of 1202—3

Lot and Fawtier compared English and French resources by using Pipe-roll totals.[31] They derived these from S.K. Mitchell who calculated a total of £26,000 ordinary revenue for both 1201 and 1205[32] and from Sir James Ramsay who estimated £24,000 for 1203. This last figure was nothing more than a rough and ready hazard; Ramsay abandoned the systematic calculation of each financial year after 1199.[33]

This procedure is seriously misleading. First, the Pipe roll account for 1203 was considerably larger, amounting to £20,830 receipts and £14,625 expenditure, a total of £35,455. Of the expenditure £828 was in effect the cancellation of a bad debt, being revenues due from Patrick Earl of Salisbury who was killed in 1168.[34] That reduces expenditure to £13,797 and the overall total to £34,627.

Secondly, that sum, impressive though it is, is very little indication of the English resources which could be deployed on the continent. Of the expenditure of £13,797 only one item, a later entry on the roll which belongs properly to the next financial year, £1,000 paid for the ransom of Roger de Lacy, the defender of Château-Gaillard, went directly to the war in Normandy.[35] The remainder comprised the varied outgoings necessary to maintain the royal establishment in England. Of the receipts a total of £588 paid or accounted *in camera* or to the King in person must certainly have been transferred to Normandy. It is also reasonable to add £2,732 received from the fourth scutage and ecclesiastical *dona* totalling £1,051.[36] So it is tolerably certain that £4,371 receipts and £1,000 expenditure, total only £5,731, were directed to the Norman war. Any further calculation based solely on the Pipe roll would be guesswork.

Fortunately there is another possible line of attack. Between 17 October 1202 and 8 October 1203, which coincides with the financial year, receipts were sent to the English Treasury for £15,153 which had been transferred to Normandy.[37] To this should be added £1,067 received from the Chief Forester, Hugh de Neville,[38] and £1,314 paid on the English Treasury to Laurence del Donjeon, who was responsible for the provisioning and fortification of some of the Norman defences.[39] If the £1,000 paid to Roger de Lacy is added to these sums they come to £16,220 receipts and £2,314 expenditure: total £18,534. That is equivalent to 74,136 l.*ang*.

---

31 Lot and Fawtier, 135—8.
32 S.K. Mitchell, *Studies in Taxation under John and Henry III*, New Haven 1914, 15—16.
33 Ramsay, i, vi, 228, 236—8.
34 *Pipe Roll 5 John*, 13.
35 *Pipe Roll 5 John*, 214. I exclude here alms and *terrae datae* to Norman religious houses and also the money fees, totalling £580, credited to Baldwin de Béthune, William Marshal, Geoffrey Luterel and William de Humez, since there is no certainty that these payments went abroad.
36 My total for the fourth scutage is lower than Mitchell's because he included payments made in 6 John. I have taken his total of the *dona*. See Mitchell, 54—5, 61—2.
37 Lady Stenton reached a slightly different total of £14,733 6s 8d. See *Pipe Roll 5 John*, i.
38 *Rot. Lit. Pat.*, 18b, 22.
39 *Rot. Lit.*, 40, 57.

Comparisons

The recorded net totals for 1202—3 in *livres angevins* are:—

	Receipts or unexpended balances	Expenditure	Total
France	146,960	139,350	286,310
Normandy	3,735	5,919	9,654
Transfers from England	64,879	9,257	74,136

On that evidence alone the Capetian resources were overwhelmingly preponderant. However, the comparison is unsatisfactory in two respects. First no *liberate* roll, from which to derive the receipts of English transfers, survives for 4 John covering the first half of the financial year from October 1202 to May 1203. To be sure, the gap falls largely in the winter, when the transport of treasure was more risky and the campaigning was less active. There are also reasons, discussed below, for thinking that the transfers after May 1203 were abnormally high. Nevertheless it is probable that the total of transfers from England was considerably more than the recorded figure. Secondly, the surviving Norman Pipe roll is only a fragment, although a considerable one. The *bailliages* which appear yield on average 38% of their yield in 1198. 38% of the total of 1198, after subtracting Évreux which was surrendered by John at Le Goulet in 1200,[40] would have amounted to 51,438 l.*ang.*,[41] if the extraordinary taxes of that year are included in the calculation, and 34,442 l.*ang.* if not. Even the larger figure would leave the total of Anglo-Norman resources at no more than 41% of the Capetian.

That still leaves room for the argument. It could well be that the Norman account of 1203, even when so extrapolated, stood far below a 'normal' year, that it reflects resources and financial administration at the point of breakdown. But even the most extreme correction possible, that of replacing the 1203 total by that of 1198, 136,629 l.*ang.* (153,131 l.*ang.* less 16,502 l.*ang.* derived from 1197) would still leave the Angevin total at no more than 70% of the Capetian. Put another way, it would have to be assumed that transfers from England came to well over double those recorded (another £21,200) to bring the two sides to par. That assumption would be hazardous. It is equally hazardous to take the 1198 account as 'normal'. It was a year of extreme financial pressure both in England and Normandy.[42] It is worth noting that the extrapolated figure of 51,438 l.*ang.* for 1203 comes close to the recorded total of 55,966 l.*ang.* for 1195. It the 1195 figure were considered the more suitable of the two it would raise the ratio of Angevin to Capetian resources from 41% to 42%.

There is another possible treatment of the figures, yet more hazardous, which yields roughly similar results. This is to use as the base-line, not the French account of 1202—3, but the Norman accounts of 1198 or 1195. This

---

40 A deduction of 1,270 l.*ang.* See Stapleton, 462—4.
41 This total excludes that part of the expenditure on Château-Gaillard which was derived from the revenues of 1197. It includes all the extraordinary revenue of 1198.
42 Powicke, 232—5. See also the comments of Roger of Howden on the exactions in England *Chronica Rogeri de Hovedene*, ed. W. Stubbs, RS 1868—71, iv, 46—7, 61—6.

involves a structure of guesswork of Byzantine complexity. The new base-line would be either 136,629 l.*ang.* (1198) or 55,966 l.*ang.* (1195). To that should be added 18,291 l.*ang.*, the known transfers from England in 1198. So the total to be matched on the French side would be roughly 155,000 l.*ang.* (1198) or 74,000 l.*ang.* (1195). It scarcely matters which. From the French account of 1202—3 it would be necessary to subtract the revenues of Évreux, which was transferred at Le Goulet in 1200 and Meulan which was confiscated from Count Robert in 1197. This would reduce the 1202—3 total to 282,146 l.*ang.* for 1198 and to 276,379 l.*ang.* for 1195. If the account of the *bailli* William Poucin who was active in the Vexin and the southern Évrecin, were also subtracted the totals would be 270,287 l.*ang.* for 1198 and 264,520 l.*ang.* for 1195. In short, on these calculations Angevin revenues would be roughly 57% of Capetian in 1198 or 28% in 1195. Even when stretched in this way the figures are quite intransigent. They leave room for all kinds of imaginary reductions in French revenues and increases in transfers from England before the scales are tipped in favour of the Angevins. Even if the transfers from England in 1203 were substituted for those of 1198 they would do no more than raise the ratio to 74% for 1198 and 45% for 1195.

If this conclusion seems surprising or unacceptable it may help to dwell on yet another more certain comparison. The levy for the raising of sergeants embodied in the Capetian account of 1202—3 has been totalled variously to 27,370 l.*par.* or to 41,077 l.*par.* The lower figure is much the more convincing.[43] The *prisia servientum* of 1194, of which the levy of 1202 was a direct continuation, was worth 36,911 l.*par.*[44] This does not necessarily mean that this important sources had diminished between 1194 and 1203; the ratio of service to commutation is likely to have varied with each occasion. But it does establish that in one respect which is very close to the heart of the argument the French crown was no worse off at the earlier than the later date.

There is no need to press the comparison further back in time. The state of affairs revealed in the account of 1202—3 arose directly from the reorganisation of royal financial administration initiated by Philip Augustus in 1190, from the consequent development of the office of *bailli* which contributed 82,459 l.*par.*, that is over 40%, to the receipts of 1202—3, and from the expansion of the royal demesne, first from the accession of the greater part of Artois and Vermandois between 1186 and 1191,[45] and secondarily from the contested and less secure absorption after 1194 of some of the Norman frontier fiefs and castles: Gisors, Évreux, Pacy and Nonancourt.[46] The 1190s, as Professor Baldwin has rightly said, were 'the decisive decade'.[47]

There is one other possible manipulation of the figures still to be considered, namely to distinguish between ordinary and extraordinary revenues. This is

---

43 Lot and Fawtier, 15—20; Baldwin (1981), 328.
44 E. Audouin, *Essai sur L'Armée Royale au temps de Philippe Auguste*, Paris 1913, 11, 129. I have converted the service of 1194 at the rates of 1194 and 1203, viz. 3 l. per sergeant and 13½ l. per cart. See Audouin, 21—4. See also Baldwin, (1981), 328—9 and Bisson, 526—7.
45 Borrelli de Serres, *La Réunion des Provinces Septentrionales à la Couronne par Philippe Auguste*, Paris 1899. See also Baldwin (1981), 324—5.
46 Powicke, 111—26. For further comment on the importance of the acquisition of these Norman castleries as well as the northern provinces see the important remarks in Bisson 527—8 which demonstrate that survey quickly followed on conquest and acquisition.
47 Baldwin (1981).

much easier done within a single accounting institution, and indeed it is an essential step in comparing French royal revenues in 1202—3 with the more fragmentary accounts of later years.[48] Comparisons between different financial institutions are more difficult, and, since the argument is essentially about war economies, it is not very clear what they are intended to achieve. Still, major items, whether in the form of withdrawals or extraordinary levies can easily be deducted. It makes little difference. For if, as Mr Gillingham suggests, 59,375 l.*par.* (86,687 l.*ang.*) are deducted on the Capetian side, 39,324 l.*ang.* must also be deducted from the Norman account of 1198 and 14,408 l.*ang.* from that of 1195. By the same token some proportion of the transfers from England would have to be discounted. Again, if the levy for sergeants of 27,370 l.*par.* (39,960 l.*ang.*) is deducted from the Capetian account then it would be necessary to deduct certainly the tallage for the sergeants in the Marches of 16,602 l.*ang.* and probably the forced loan of 15,864 l.*ang* from the Norman account of 1198. By the same token there would be no need to give any consideration to the English Seventh of 1203. None of this would alter the overall balance very much; none of these adjustments raises the ratio of Angevin to Capetian resources above 50%. The same holds if the ultimate reduction is made to the rock bottom of ordinary revenue. Powicke calculated the farms of the Norman *baillis* and *vicomtés* at 20,000 l.*ang.*[49] In 1202—3 the farms of the French *prévôtés* were more than twice that, 28,217 l.*par.* (41,196 l.*ang.*).[50] The equivalent figure for the farms of the English shires was approximately £13,000 (52,000 l.*ang.*), but only a small proportion of that could be brought to bear on the war in Normandy.[51]

The method used in all these comparisons may seem vulnerable. To compare the total revenues of the Capetian demesne and Normandy is fair enough. But to bring in from England, not the total revenue, but only the known transfers to Normandy, is to cease to compare like with like. This is true, but it should not be an objection. For the method acknowledges the proper political context. The war was not one between England and France for the possession of a French province, but one between a feudal monarch and an increasingly contumacious vassal who happened also to be a king. The comparison concerns the resources available in the confrontation on the Norman frontier, and English resources which were not transferred are quite irrelevant. In the crisis of 1203 John acknowledged the receipt of 400m of silver and 200 ounces of gold from Ireland,[52] yet no-one has argued that total Irish revenues should also be brought into the count. It could also be argued that any revenues not devoted to the war, whether English, Norman or Capetian, are equally irrelevant. But such expenditure, on alms or non-military building or the sustenance of the court, was a common factor. It has to be set against, or was allowed within, all the revenues under consideration, both Capetian and Anglo-Norman, including the transfers from England.

48 Baldwin (1980), 21—30.
49 Powicke, 234.
50 Lot and Fawtier, 11. I have deducted Évreux.
51 G.J. Turner, 'The sheriff's farm' *TRHS*, n.s. xii, 142. I have made an addition for increments on the shires. See Mabel H. Mills, 'Experiments in Exchequer procedure' *TRHS*, 4th ser., viii, 1925, 159—60.
52 *Rot. Lib.*, 70.

The Loss of Normandy and Royal Finance

Within these speculations there is something of considerable interest. The relationship of withdrawals to receipts or unspent balances and total revenues is surprisingly consistent:

	Withdrawals	% of unspent balance or receipts	% of total revenue
France 1202—3	59,375 l.*par.*	59	30
Normandy 1198	39,224 l.*ang.*	51	25
Normandy 1195	14,408 l.*ang.*	50	25

But the balance of the English accounts of 1203 is quite different. The total of £16,220 transported to Normandy during the financial year amounted to 77% of the receipts; and the total transfers of £18,534 came to 52% of the recorded revenue of the year. To all appearances England was being drained. Other sources demonstrate that the Crown was eroding its capital resources by selling royal forests. Indeed the transfers to Normandy in 1203 almost certainly included some of the proceeds of such sales in the sums received from the Chief Forester, Hugh de Neville.[53] It was still not enough.

Are the appearances to be accepted? Can the surviving accounts be taken roughly at their face-value? How much is missing?

The argument so far has involved a modicum of approximation, from estimation to guesswork. The surviving writs of receipt must sum up to less than the real total of the transfers from England to Normandy, for they survive for only half the year. This has been discussed above and allowance has been made where necessary; more will be said below.[54] Similar allowances have also been made for the disputed border castleries in the Vexin and southern Évrecin which Philip seized in 1193—4; except for Vernon these have been excluded from the count on the Capetian side.[55] On the Norman side a notional total for the fragmentary account of 1203 has been reconstructed.[56]

There are three other residual problems.

First, it is certain that none of the accounts is complete. They simply record the transactions which came before the Temple or the Norman and English Exchequers. Lot and Fawtier felt that most of the obvious *lacunae*, of *prévôtés* not included in the account of 1202—3, could be explained satisfactorily and hence they concluded that the account was indeed complete.[57] But both Professor Baldwin and Professor Bisson have expressed different degrees of doubt; the latter in particular has pointed out that the account included next to nothing of the profits of the mint.[58] Moreover, as Lot and Fawtier indicated, it says nothing of the expenses of the royal household, which they estimated;[59] equally, it cannot record any household receipts.

On the Angevin side the operations of the household are easier to follow. On

---

53 *Rot. Litt. Pat.*, 18b, 22, 31b. J.C. Holt, *Magna Carta*, Cambridge 1965, 52—3.
54 See above, 98—9.
55 See above, 99.
56 See above, 99.
57 Lot and Fawtier, 51—3.
58 Baldwin (1980), 24; Bisson, 524—5.
59 Lot and Fawtier, 131—3.

the Norman roll of 1198 the Chamber figures as a major source of cash; it contributed 18,261 l.*ang.* to the account for the building of Château-Gaillard over the two years 1197 and 1198.[60] Of the £16,220 for which receipts were sent to England in 1202—3 all but £2,200 was sent direct to the King; often the letters state that he or a Chamber official received the sums *in camera*. Of the apparently exceptional £2,200, £200 was received by John de Grey, bishop of Norwich;[61] £2,000 was received by the Exchequer of Caen in October 1202, and the Chamber drew an identical sum of English treasure from the Caen Exchequer in the following December.[62] For roughly half the financial year, therefore, it is possible to follow the receipts of the Chamber in some detail. The expenditure is more difficult. In 1198 Chamber disbursements appear on the Pipe roll; not so in 1203. A Chamber account survives covering 26 April 1202 to 6 July 1203, chiefly concerned with payments due to William Marshal and others for the defence of the castle of Arques.[63] It totals 4,672 l.*ang.*, none of which appears on the surviving portion of the Pipe roll.

It will now be apparent that the calculations made above embrace the financial activities of the Chamber. Transfers from England went to the Chamber either directly or ultimately. True, some allowance has to be made for the break in the series of receipts caused by the loss of the *Liberate* roll of 4 John, but there is no need to imagine that in addition there was some considerable Chamber operation of which the sources are totally silent. The calculations delineate, not the tip of the iceberg, but the iceberg itself.

There is one possible exception which lies submerged and may seem to wreck all calculations: the tax of a Seventh levied in England in 1203. The tax was not accounted on the Pipe Roll, which was common enough with such special measures. There are only four references to it in the royal records, only two of which belong to 1203.[64] This in itself is an argument for playing it down. Wendover referred to it, but misdated it to the end of 1203 and misinterpreted the occasion;[65] it was noted by the Bury annalist,[66] and it may have been the object of a more generalised story of financial exactions told by Ralph of Coggeshall;[67] otherwise it made no great splash in the chronicles. Certainly there is no reason to follow Sir James Ramsay, who concocted the enormous total of £110,000 by extrapolating from the known receipts of the Thirteenth of 1207.[68] The assessment of the Thirteenth led to considerable evasion and resistance, which left a trail of penalties in the records;[69] there is no such evidence for the Seventh. The Thirteenth was levied on revenues and chattels; the Seventh almost certainly on revenues alone.[70] The writ of assessment of the

---

60 Stapleton, 309.
61 *Rot. Lib.*, 58.
62 *Rot. Lib.*, 33; *Rot. Norm.*, 65.
63 *Miscellaneous Records of the Norman Exchequer*, ed. S.R. Packard, Smith College Studies in History xii, Northampton, Mass., 1926—7, 67—9.
64 *Rot. Lib.*, 43, 47—8; *Pipe Roll 6 John*, 256; *Pipe Roll 12 John*, 192.
65 *Chronica Majora*, ii, 483.
66 F. Liebermann, *Ungedruckte anglo-normannische Geschichtsquellen*, Strasbourg 1879, 142.
67 *Radulphi de Coggeshall Chronicon Anglicanum*, ed. J. Stevenson, RS 1875, 144.
68 Ramsay, 238.
69 *Pipe Roll 9 John*, xvii—xxi; *Rot. Litt. Pat.*, 72b; *Rot de Ob.et Fin.*, 372.
70 Among the contemporary sources Wendover is alone in stating that it was the tax on moveables. The Bury Annalist states very precisely that it was a seventh of revenues. In the records

Thirteenth laid down an exacting procedure for the levying of the tax;[71] for the Seventh no such writ survives. But there are two writs, dated 24 July and 13 August 1203, concerned with the levy of a Fifth on the Channel Isles. The first of these gave no rate of assessment but simply laid down that lords of fees were to make reasonable demands on their men.[72] The second ordered the levy of a Fifth on the revenues (not the chattels) of bishops, abbots, abbesses, clerks, knights and vavassors.[73] The two mandates seem to be complementary since the barons who are the subject of the first are not included in the second. The writs were addressed to Peter de Préaux, the lord of the Isles. The two writs sent to England were addressed to the Justiciar, Geoffrey fitz Peter.[74] Wendover states that Geoffrey taxed the laity, and the Archbishop, Hubert Walter, the clergy.[75] At all events the King was not on as strong ground in ordering the levy as he was in 1207, when his presence in England gave him the opportunity to deploy the 'common counsel and assent of our council at Oxford' as authority for the tax.[76] In 1203 the King was taxing at a distance and it is worth noting that the two surviving writs to the Justiciar are relaxations.

So the yield may not have been large. Whatever it was, it is possible that it enters the calculations in two ways. First, Mitchell pointed out long ago that the clergy could well have compounded the assessment by offering gifts.[77] *Dona* totalling £1,051 appear on the Pipe roll either as *dona prelatorum* or as *nova oblata*. Secondly the two writs addressed to Geoffrey fitz Peter were dated 18 June and 10 July. It is certain that the tax had been imposed by then and there is a strong presumption in the form of the first letter, that the Count of Aumale was 'to have the Seventh of pennies on his land', that, as far as the King knew, it was in process of assessment and collection. In short, such record evidence as survives suggests that money from the Seventh was becoming available by the summer of 1203. If that is so it is not at all unreasonable to assume that some of the transfers from England to Normandy were drawn from the proceeds of the Seventh. Of the receipts sent to the Treasurer from Normandy all but the first one of 17 October 1202, acknowledging receipt of 3000 m. at the Exchequer at Caen,[78] belong to the period between 27 May and 7 October 1203. The total received between May and October was 17,630 m. The receipt of 2,000 m. was acknowledged on 1 November and a further 3,000 m. on 3 November.[79] The grand total of the moneys transferred from the English Treasury to Normandy up to the King's return in December was 22,630 m. or £15,087.

The suggestion that this included some of the Seventh presupposes a straightforward system of administration: that the Justiciar was responsible

---

it is described as *de terra* or *de dominico* or *per assisam de dominico*. See *Rot. Lib.*, 43, 47—48, *Pipe Roll 6 John*, 256.
71 W. Stubbs, *Select Charters*, 9th edn. Oxford 1921, 278—9.
72 *Rot. Litt. Pat.*, 32b.
73 *Rot. Litt. Pat.*, 33b.
74 *Rot. Lib.*, 43, 47—8.
75 *Chronica Majora*, ii, 483.
76 Stubbs, *Select Charters*, 278.
77 Mitchell, 62.
78 *Rot. Lib.*, 33.
79 *Rot. Lib.*, 71, 74.

for assessment and collection from laymen; that the proceeds were deposited in the Treasury and that they were then transported to the King in Normandy whence receipts were sent to the Treasurer. That would explain why no receipts were sent to the collectors of the Seventh *eo nomine*, as they were to Hugh de Neville for the forest revenues. It would also explain why the transfers from England amount to such a high proportion of the deposits and total revenues recorded on the Pipe roll of 1203. In so far as they were drawn from the proceeds of the Seventh they were not included in the Pipe Roll. To risk a truly rash extrapolation, which assumes on the evidence of the Norman and French accounts that withdrawals could be expected to amount to roughly 50% of receipts and 25% of total revenues, the 'normal' withdrawals on the English account of 1203 would have been £8,800 to £10,400 say £4,800 between May and October. In fact transfers to Normandy in that period were more than double that: £11,750. The difference. roughly £7,000, provides some measure, within this financial year, of the contribution of the Seventh.

This extrapolation is obviously highly speculative. That the transfers included some contribution from the Seventh is more certain. That the receipts issued between May and October represent all the transfers from England seems inescapable.[80] And the lesson is that once attention is shifted from the totals of the English Pipe roll to the sums transferred to Normandy it necessarily comes to include operations which fell outside the immediate province of the Exchequer. Chamber finance and the Seventh then cease to be great unknowns lying beyond the evidence, undermining argument with awesome question-marks. The likelihood is that for the six months from May to October 1203 the evidence provides a very clear and apparently complete picture of the extent of the English contributions to Angevin fortunes in Normandy, embracing Chamber as well as Exchequer and both ordinary and extraordinary revenue.

This is important in yet one other direction. There is not the slightest indication throughout the records of any transfer to Normandy from Anjou or the other Plantagenet dominions in the south-west. Transfers were not made without receipts. In 1202—3 receipts were sent to England not only against transfers from the Treasury but also against the smaller sums derived from the forest revenues and from individual debtors.[81] Similar acknowledgements were issued against withdrawals from the Treasury at Caen.[82] The system demanded them. Yet not one receipt was issued against moneys from Anjou or Aquitaine. Indeed the flow of money was in the opposite direction from England and Normandy to Anjou and Poitou. That was so in 1195 and 1198,[83] and was still so in 1203 when Robert of Thornham Seneschal of Poitou, was instructed to take advice on the distribution of the money which the King had sent to him.[84] The evidence leaves no room for argument and the conclusion it

---

80 There is no way of proving this, but it was as true then as now that sums of money could only be transferred on the issue of a receipt. The general impression conveyed by the records is that procedures were meticulous. Receipts under the seal proceeded from the Chancery and it is these which were recorded on the *Liberate* Roll and the Patent Roll. No other system of receipting is apparent.
81 See above, 97.
82 *Rot. Norm.* 65, 69, 75.
83 Holt (1975), 23.
84 *Rot. Litt. Pat.*, 28b.

imposes, far from being absurd, is confirmed by the recently discovered French royal account for the term of All Saints 1221. This totalled 73,657 l.*par.* to which Anjou and Touraine contributed 2,284 l.*par.* In 1238 the contribution of Poitou was likewise miniscule: 1,302 l.*par.* out of a total of 101,279 l.*par.*[85] The Capetians found it no easier than the Angevins to exploit these south-western provinces. And the Angevin 'failure' is easily comprehensible. Seen from Anjou and the south, Normandy and England were simply acquisitions of the ruling house. The northern and transmaritime provinces were peripheral colonies. Chinon, Loches, Poitou, Fontevrault, Bordeaux and La Rochelle were the centres; Caen, Rouen, and even more London, the fringe. Why should these southern homelands be required to contribute to failure, especially since so few of their leading families, apart from the merchants of Bordeaux and La Rochelle, had gained so little from the earlier success? And by what authority or moral pressure were they to be taxed to defend the Norman frontier, especially when their own allegiance and their own defences were being probed by their ultimate feudal lord, the King of France?

This is not simply a question of rejecting a false Anglo-Norman centred view. It is a matter, ultimately, of the administrative coherence of Plantagenet government. This involves much more than the financial resources which have been the subject of this essay. But study of these resources leaves an impression which cannot be measured in arithmetic, of the compact nature of the Capetian base, from Arras in the north to Orléans in the south, and of the advantage which internal lines of communication gave them against the scattered lands of Henry of Anjou and his sons, severed by the Channel and diverse in their history and cultural associations. Angevin dominion was efficient here, ineffectual there, but always *in toto* cumbersome. It is now over fifty years since Lot and Fawtier first pointed to the financial consequences. It was from England, they wrote, 'that King John drew the greater part of his financial resources. But England . . . brought less to the Plantagenet than his little demesne did to the Capetian'.[86] For some reason English scholars have not found it easy to accept their view. But it was carefully argued, based though it was on information on the Anglo-Norman side which was far from satisfactory. The further investigation of that information has only strengthened their conclusion.

85 Baldwin, (1980), 26.
86 Lot and Fawtier, 139.

WHAT HAPPENED IN 1258?

D.A. Carpenter

Shortly after 7 April 1258 one of the most important parliaments of King Henry III's reign opened at Westminster. Its proceedings culminated in the king's oath, recorded on 2 May, accepting that the realm should be reformed by twenty-four men, twelve chosen by himself, and twelve by the magnates of the kingdom.[1] This concession opened the way for the ensuing period of baronial reform, rebellion and civil war. There was nothing new in 1258 about the demand for reform. It had been put at parliaments in 1244, 1248, 1249 and 1255.[2] Previously, the king had always refused to give way; not surprisingly because his control of policy, his choice of ministers, and his patronage of friends were thereby threatened. In 1258, however, Henry capitulated. Why? For R.F. Treharne the answer was clear. Henry surrendered in order to avoid papal excommunication and interdict. Treharne believed that these spiritual penalties were imminent because Henry had failed to find sufficient funds to fulfil an agreement with the pope concerning the throne of Sicily. In 1258 the only way to raise the money and escape the penalties was to secure an aid from parliament. When parliament refused to grant an aid unless there was reform of the realm, Henry had no alternative but to accept these terms. Aspects of this same interpretation are to be found in the work of Sir Maurice Powicke.[3] It is an interpretation which this paper will argue is misconceived. In reality, Henry was brought to surrender not by fear of the pope but by an armed demonstration of magnates. This use of force was largely overlooked by Treharne and Powicke. It grew out of events at the Westminster parliament, events which brought to a head the widespread hatred of the king's Lusignan half-brothers. Powicke believed that it was not until they resisted reform at the Oxford parliament in June 1258 that the brothers were 'marked down'.[4] In

---

[1] *Documents of the Baronial Movement of Reform and Rebellion*, ed. R.F. Treharne, I.J. Sanders, Oxford 1973, 73—7; R.F. Treharne, *The Baronial Plan of Reform 1258—63*, Manchester 1932, 65. The magnates were summoned to be in London for the parliament by 7 April; Treharne, Sanders, 73—4. However, the king's itinerary has him at Merton on 8 April and at Westminster only on 9 April; Treharne, 383. Probably the parliament opened on 9 April.

[2] W. Stubbs, *Select Charters and other Illustrations of English Constitutional History*, 9th edn. Oxford 1913, 326—9; Matthew Paris, *Chronica Majora*, ed. H.R. Luard, RS 1872—83, iv, 366—8. The specific demand at the parliaments mentioned was that the king should appoint a justiciar, chancellor and treasurer on the advice of his magnates. Also, in 1244, a general plan of reform was probably drawn up.

[3] Treharne, 62—6; Powicke, *Henry III and The Lord Edward*, Oxford 1947, 374—9.

[4] Powicke, *Henry III*, 384; F.M. Powicke, *The Thirteenth Century*, Oxford 1953, 140 n. 1. The Lusignans were the offspring of the marriage between Henry III's mother and her second husband, the great Poitevin noble, Hugh le Brun, lord of Lusignan and count of La Marche. The half-brothers came to England in 1247; see below p. 112, and H.S. Snellgrove, *The Lusignans in England*, Albuquerque, New Mexico 1950, which recognises the importance of the family in the crisis of 1258.

fact, the movement against them was central to the decision taken at the parliament of Westminster to force reform upon the king.

Henry III's Sicilian entanglement had begun in 1254. In that year he accepted a papal offer of the throne of Sicily for his second son, Edmund. In return, Henry was to pay the pope 135,000 marks, and send an army to conquer the kingdom from its Hohenstaufen rulers. All this was to be done within a stated time limit. If the conditions were not fulfilled Henry would find himself excommunicated, England would be placed under an interdict, and the pope would be free to withdraw the offer.[5] Henry quickly found the greatest difficulty in raising the 135,000 marks, and, although a commander was picked for a Sicilian army, there were no troops for him to lead.[6] In 1257, after pope Alexander IV had waived one time limit, strenuous diplomatic efforts were made to persuade him to further modify the conditions of the agreement.[7] Powicke believed that Alexander's 'reply cost Henry his independence'.[8] Treharne wrote that 'Alexander showed no consideration for Henry's difficulties . . . Thus, far from securing the alleviation which they desired, [Henry's]envoys returned to inform the King . . . that 5,500 marks must be despatched at once, and that unless Henry immediately gave an undertaking to pay the rest of the huge debt of 135,000 marks very soon, he would inevitably be excommunicated by the implacable Vicar of God . . . This was the situation, which, at the end of 1257, made it certain that the English political deadlock would soon be broken. Alexander's ultimatum would precipitate a crisis quite different from the barren encounters with which the English magnates had grown contemptuously familiar since 1244. Henry dared not face Papal excommunication, while the vastness of the sum required, and the narrowness of the time-limit allowed by the Pope would prevent him from evading the political issue between himself and the magnates by the irregular finance of recent years. He would have no alternative to an appeal to the Great Council for military and financial aid . . . The barons, having the King at their mercy, would thus be able to demand their own terms.'[9]

While features of Treharne's picture are correct, the whole is probably out of focus. Certainly Henry was not like his father John; he would have regarded the excommunication of himself, and an interdict placed on the kingdom as horrific disasters. What is not clear, however, is that Henry felt that these penalties were imminent in April 1258. Alexander's letters, written in December 1257, which the papal envoy, Master Arlot, brought to England the following March, were friendly and re-assuring. 'The strength of papal charity' was not to be 'vanquished by lengthy periods of hoping, nor is our proposal in respect of you to be withdrawn so long as there are indications that hope may be revived.' Probably Alexander had been concerned by the

---

5 *Foedera*, I, i, 316—8; Powicke, *Henry III*, 371.
6 *Foedera*, I, i, 359—60. For the financial side of the Sicilian affair see W.E. Lunt, *Financial Relations of England with the Papacy to 1327*, Cambridge Mass. 1939, 255—90.
7 *Foedera*, I, i. 359. The time limit of the original agreement expired at Michaelmas 1256; see *Foedera*, I, i, 350.
8 Powicke, *Henry III*, 376.
9 Treharne, 62. Alexander's specific demands can be seen from Henry's replies to them drawn up after 2 May. One of the demands was that Henry should seek a 'common subsidy', that is an aid from parliament; *Close Roll Supplement 1244—66*, 29—30.

possibility, raised by Henry's ambassadors, that the king would resign prematurely from the Sicilian enterprise, unless the terms were altered. The pope, therefore, sought to encourage the monarch. He wished the undertaking 'to arise in a state from which it might have a happy outcome'. More concretely, Alexander assured the king that he had not as yet incurred spiritual penalties, and he agreed to suspend them for another three months, that is until 1 June 1258.[10] According to Powicke, Alexander 'would go no farther'. This was not the case. In January 1258 the pope, 'wishing to help the affair forward, and so that it should not be destroyed for lack of time', gave Arlot the power, at his discretion, to extend the so-called deadline for another three months until 1 September. It is true that, after Arlot arrived in England, he probably delayed before conceding this extension, and he clearly made much noise about the prospect of excommunication and interdict. The Dunstable annals state that he 'threatened that he would excommunicate the king and all his magnates', while the annals of Tewkesbury record that Arlot brought papal bulls to place an interdict on the king's chapel and all the English church.[11] In a sense, however, this intimidation was aimed less at the king than at those from whom both king and pope hoped to extract money. Henry needed no coercion. He was the pope's greatest friend in England, and the chief enthusiast for the Sicilian project. Henry, as much as Arlot, must have hoped that the threat of penalties would induce parliament to grant money. Yet the king may well have appreciated that the threat was largely bluff and bluster.[12] Certainly this was shown to be the case when the time limit finally ran out in September. No spiritual thunderbolts hurtled down on England. The pope's response came in a letter dated 18 December. It was addressed to 'the illustrious king of England', a *rex Christianissimus*. The tone was more of sorrow than of anger. He could no longer hope that Henry would be able to fulfil his side of the bargain; he now held himself free to negotiate with other candidates. As for the penalties, 'with our accustomed kindness, and through our special grace, we suspend them during pleasure'.[13]

Even if, in April 1258, Henry was seriously concerned about the possibility

---

10 *Foedera*, I, i, 358, 366.
11 Powicke, *Henry III*, 376; *Foedera*, I, i, 369; *Annales Monastici*, ed. H.R. Luard, RS 1864—9, iii, 208; i, 163. That Arlot granted the extension is clear from *CR 1256—9*, 320, but there is no evidence as to precisely when he did this.
12 It is interesting to note that, according to Matthew Paris, the king 'greeted Arlot with rapture on his arrival, since he was invested with the greatest powers and authority'; Paris, v, 673.
13 *Foedera*, I, i, 379; Paris, vi, 416. When the king's clerk, Simon Passelewe, came to Waltham abbey in the middle of the Westminster parliament, he tried to persuade the monastery to stand surety for a loan to Henry from French merchants by lamenting that 'in three or four days his chapel will be placed under an interdict'. Simon went on to say much the same at the abbeys of St. Albans and Reading. It was largely bluff. The pope had warned Henry that his chapel would be placed under an interdict unless he allowed 5,500 marks, which the king's envoys to the pope in 1257 had obliged themselves to pay Siena merchants, to be given to the envoys from the clerical tenth then being collected in England. Henry was only too pleased to allow this. He also agreed, as the pope demanded, that another 4,500 marks should be raised for the same merchants from the tenth. Another threat to Henry's chapel could have arisen from an agreement which he made with Florentine merchants in June 1257, but it seems that this agreement was never completed; Paris, v, 682—8; *Flores Historiarum*, ed. H.R. Luard, RS 1890, iii, 349—52; *CLR 1251—60*, 434—5; *Foedera*, I, i, 368, 371; *Close Roll Supplement 1244—66*, no. 282; *CPR 1247—58*, 562, 625; Lunt, 279—80, 279, n. 1.

of excommunication and interdict, it is difficult to see why this should have forced him into the concession recorded on 2 May. By agreeing to reform of the realm, Henry lost his independence, and obtained no real prospect of financial aid. The king's concession, therefore, hindered rather than helped the Sicilian project, and, in that respect, made the penalties more, not less likely. The promise of financial aid made by the magnates needs careful inspection. The royal letter issued on 2 May, containing the terms of the agreement, states, that the king had negotiated with the great men of the realm about the furtherance of the Sicilian business, and 'they have replied to us that, if we should be pleased to reform the state of our realm by the counsel of our loyal subjects, and provided the lord pope would ameliorate the conditions which he had stated for the Sicilian affair in such a way that we might be able to take the matter up effectively, they would loyally use their influence with the community of the realm so that a common aid should be granted to us for that purpose.'[14] The magnates, therefore, did not say that they would grant an aid. They merely said that, on certain conditions, they would 'use their influence with the community of the realm' that one might be granted. This was no idle form of words. The day was passing when the barons could answer for the rest of the kingdom in the granting of taxation. Already in 1254 two knights from each county had been summoned before the king's council in order to say what aid 'all and each' in the shires were prepared to grant.[15] Perhaps some similar arrangement would have been necessary in 1258. There was thus no guarantee that the magnates would be able to obtain an aid from the community of the realm. Moreover, before they would even bring their advocacy to bear on the matter, they required the pope to alter the conditions of the agreement so that the king could prosecute the Sicilian project successfully. This stipulation made it virtually certain that no aid would ever be granted. It was for the magnates to judge on what terms the scheme might be practical, and since the Sicilian adventure was universally regarded in England as a monumental folly, they were almost certain to deem any papal concessions insufficient.[16] Alexander appreciated this. He simply ignored the magnates' offer to negotiate for an aid, and concluded that Henry was incapable of prosecuting the Sicilian venture any further.[17]

It seems unlikely, therefore, that Henry, in 1258, would have agreed to the reform of the realm because of papal threats which he probably suspected were empty, and in return for concessions which he must have feared were worthless.[18] But, if this is right, why did he capitulate? The answer is that he was forced to by his magnates. There are only two chronicle accounts of any length for the parliament at Westminster in April and May 1258; Mathew Paris's

---

14 Treharne, Sanders, 73—4.
15 Stubbs, 365—6; but see J.C. Holt, 'The Prehistory of Parliament', *The English Parliament in the Middle Ages*, ed. R.G. Davies, J.H. Denton, Manchester, 1981, 27.
16 For the unpopularity of the Sicilian enterprise, see Paris, v. 680—1; *Ann. Mon.*, i, 386—8.
17 *Foedera*, I, i, 379, Paris, vi, 416.
18 After 2 May the king drew up proposals for the pope as to how the the terms might be modified, and the Provisions of Oxford named twenty-four men to 'negotiate an aid for the king'; *Close Roll Supplement 1244—66*, 29—30; Treharne, Sanders, 104—7. This does not mean, however, that Henry actually thought an aid would be granted. (There is no evidence the twenty-four ever met.) The 'firm belief', expressed in a royal letter to the pope in August 1258, that assistance would be forthcoming if the terms were modified was probably a pretence to retain papal favour; *CR 1256—9*, 326.

Chronica Majora and the annals of Tewkesbury abbey. Paris's version of the king's surrender is as follows. After numerous criticisms had been made of the king, Henry 'on reflection acknowledged the truth of the accusations, although late, and humbled himself, declaring that he had too often been beguiled by evil counsel, and he promised and made a solemn oath at the altar of the shrine of St Edward, that he would fully and properly amend his old errors, and show favour and kindness to his native-born subjects.'[19] Paris, then, provides no evidence of coercion, but equally he says nothing about a promise of an aid for Sicily. He seems, indeed, to be ill-informed about certain aspects of the parliament. His account of the king's oath is vague and inaccurate. Paris knows nothing about its most vital feature: the agreement to abide by the work of the twenty-four reformers. Indeed he nowhere mentions the twenty-four. The account in the Tewkesbury annals, on the other hand, is far more detailed.[20] Around the feast of St Vitalis (28 April) the demand was put for an aid for Sicily. It was agreed that the magnates should give their reply in three days time. The bishops, having obtained licence, departed lest they incurred the king's anger. Then 'on the third day, as the third hour approached, noble and vigorous men, earls, barons, and knights went to the court at Westminster, armed in excellent fashion, and girded with swords. However, they placed their swords at the entrance to the king's hall, and, appearing before the king, saluted him as their lord king in devoted manner with fitting honour. The king was immediately disturbed in mind, and uncertain why they had come armed. He said, "what is this my lords, am I, wretched fellow, your captive?"'. To this Roger Bigod, earl of Norfolk replied, 'No, my lord, no! But let the wretched and intolerable Poitevins and all aliens flee from your face and ours as from the face of a lion, and there will be "glory to God in the heavens, and in your land peace to men of goodwill"'. Bigod then went on to reveal the general demand that Henry should swear to adhere to 'our counsels'. When Henry asked what such adherence would involve, 'the baronage replied: "together with your son and heir Edward, swear on the gospels that, without the consent of twenty-four prudent men of England to be chosen, namely bishops, earls and barons, you will impose no . . . unaccustomed yoke [e.g. tax] . . . and that you will not delay handing your royal seal, through the counsel of the foresaid [twenty-four], to a discreet man whom they will provide". The king, therefore, seeing that he was not able to put the matter off any further, along with Edward his son and heir, although the latter was unwilling, swore on the gospels on 30 April 1258, and commended everything to their counsel [presumably the counsel of the twenty-four], and conceded and approved all things which they wished to be done'.

The Tewkesbury annals, therefore, make it plain that an armed demonstration forced the king to accept reform in 1258. There seems no reason for rejecting the substance of the account.[21] On the contrary, it has a special claim to belief not hitherto appreciated, namely the likelihood that it was written up

---

19 Paris, v, 689.
20 *Ann. Mon.*, i, 163—5.
21 In his list of grievances drawn up in March—April 1261 Henry did not complain of pressure brought on him in 1258; see Treharne, Sanders, 236—7, no. 26. However, when this list was drawn up, Henry was in a delicate political situation and had not formally rejected his oath of 2 May and the Provisions of Oxford.

from a news-letter received from an eyewitness of the parliament. This would explain why it has a wealth of detail, and a use of direct speech which is found nowhere else in the Tewkesbury chronicle.[22] Clearly the circumstantial nature of the detail — the third hour of the day, the leaving of the swords at the entrance to the hall — suggests the testimony of an eyewitness. Other elements of the account also carry conviction. Roger Bigod's emphasis in his speech on the Poitevins, that is the Lusignans, is not surprising given previous events at the Westminster parliament.[23] The swearing of the king's oath on 30 April is consistent with the date, 2 May, given to the royal letter which recorded it, by which time Henry had chosen his panel of twelve reformers.[24] Admittedly, the chronicle says nothing about the promise concerning the Sicilian aid which Henry must have obtained before swearing his oath, but this merely reflects how insignificant the promise was felt to be. The demand that the king should impose no tax without the counsel of the twenty-four, and hand his seal to someone decided by them was not embodied in the king's concession as recorded on 2 May, yet these matters may well have been raised on 30 April. The Tewkesbury narrative grasps the vital point, namely the demand for the

---

22 The Tewkesbury annals are in BL Cotton MS Cleopatra A VII, fos. 1—67v. They were edited for the Rolls Series by H.R. Luard in *Annales Monastici*, i, 1890, 43—180. The annals contain, in fact, two distinct chronicles: Tewkesbury I, the main chronicle of the abbey which commences before 1066 (the year in which Luard's printed text begins) and continues into 1263 after which it is lost; and Tewkesbury II which begins in 1258 with Tewkesbury I's account of events between the arrival of Master Arlot and the expulsion of the Lusignans, and then gives an independent history down to 1264 after which it too is lost; *Ann. Mon.*, i, 162 n. 5; A. Gransden, *Historical Writing in England*, London 1974, 405, n. 13, 416. The appearance of the manuscript of Tewkesbury I strongly suggests that by 1258 it was being written soon after the news of the events which it records came in. (I hope to discuss this point in more detail in a forthcoming paper.) Tewkesbury II, by contrast, is unlikely to have been written before 1264, and its version of 1258 was thus copied from Tewkesbury I and not vice versa. Although roughly contemporaneous with the events which it describes, however, the Tewkesbury I account of the Westminster and Oxford parliaments in 1258, taken as a whole, is somewhat muddled. It is clear that before the account of the Westminster parliament begins with 'Circa festum Sancti Vitalis' (*Ann. Mon.*, i, 163) the chronicler had been writing about the parliament at Oxford in June. This confused the writer of Tewkesbury II, and he altered 'Oxford' to 'London'; *Ann. Mon.*, i, 163 n. 2. However, the reference to the bishops being at Merton makes it plain that Oxford is meant; see *Ann. Mon.*, i, 412. The author of Tewkesbury I may have tried to fit together his accounts of the Oxford and Westminster parliaments. Into the sentence, probably copied from the news-letter, about the bishops at the Westminster parliament excusing themselves and retiring there is a 'ut supradictum est'. This appears to refer to the earlier statement that the bishops were absent from the parliament at Oxford, and was perhaps inserted by the chronicler as a clumsy attempt to reconcile the two accounts. The nature of the chronicle around this time shows that its author had little practice at writing a connected narrative, and he also admits that he is wholly ignorant of the names of two of the Lusignans (Geoffrey and Guy); *Ann. Mon.*, i, 165. All this makes the coherent report of events between 28—30 April — 'Circa festum Sancti Vitalis . . . concessit et approbavit' — which it is suggested comes from the news-letter, stand out the more sharply; *Ann. Mon.*, i, 163—4. (In Luard's text this section begins and ends a paragraph, but in the MS there are no breaks of this kind.)

23 See below p. 114. Whether, however, Bigod denounced all aliens, as opposed to merely the Lusignans, may be questioned since he was at this time in alliance with Peter of Savoy; see below p. 116. (He was, nonetheless, engaged in 1258 in a private dispute with Peter.) The Tewkesbury annals alone give the information that the aid demanded was a thirtieth on moveables and immoveables. The church was probably exempted from this demand since it was already making heavy financial contributions for Sicily. Hence it was possible for the bishops to obtain licence to withdraw.

24 Treharne, Sanders, 74—5.

twenty-four reformers, and its statement that the king 'commended himself and everything to their counsel, and conceded and approved all things which they wished to be done' is not dissimilar from the passage in the oath, as recorded on 2 May, where Henry swore 'to observe inviolably whatever shall be ordained by the twenty-four' in the reform of the realm.[25] If the chronicler's information did indeed come from a news-letter, it is possible that the writer was the Tewkesbury monk, William de Bekeford. The Tewkesbury chronicle notes that in June 1258 Bekeford accompanied the eldest daughter of Richard de Clare, earl of Gloucester, to Lyons for her marriage to the marquis of Montferrat. Perhaps Bekeford was also present in the earl's retinue at the Westminster parliament, where details of the marriage were settled. If that was the case, he may well have sent back an account of procedings there to his brothers at Tewkesbury.[26]

If it is agreed that it was a menacing démarche by the barons, not any threats from the pope, which made Henry III accept reform, the question arises as to why in 1258 the king's critics took action, whereas previously they had demanded changes but done nothing to compel them. By 1258 there were, of course, several reasons for what the barons called the *statum imbecillem* of the country. Throughout the counties of England there was discontent with the financial burden of the general eyre, the oppressions of the sheriffs, and the policies of the exchequer by which the latter were aggravated. All these matters were subject to reform in the Provisions of Oxford, and Westminster, in 1258—9.[27] By themselves, however, such grievances would not have caused the revolution of 1258. Although doubtless made aware by their followers and supporters of the feelings in the counties, the great magnates who led the revolution were amongst the least vulnerable to the abuses of the sheriffs, and the financial exactions of the justices in eyre. For events to come to a head in 1258 additional incitement was needed. In part this was clearly provided by the farcical state of the Sicilian enterprise, underlining as it did both the king's incompetence and insolvency. These weaknesses were also exhibited in Henry's inability to meet the challenge of Llywelyn in Wales and the Marches. But perhaps the most important of the immediate spurs to action was the issue of the Lusignans. The king's Poitevin half-brothers had come to England in 1247. In that year, the second youngest, William de Valence, married one of the heiresses of the Marshal earls, and obtained with her the county of Pembroke. The king also granted him Hertford castle and, over the ensuing years, a large number of manors. In 1250 the youngest brother, Aymer, became bishop-elect of Winchester. The more senior brothers, Guy and Geoffrey de Lusignan, did not settle in England, but they made frequent visits, and were granted money fees and wardships by the king.[28] Henry III had also planted in England his wife's uncles, Peter of Savoy, who was granted the honour of Richmond in 1240, and Boniface who, in the next year, became archbishop of

---

25 Treharne, Sanders, 74—5.
26 At the Westminster parliament on 2 May the king stood surety for money which the earl of Gloucester owed the marquis for the marriage; *CPR 1247—58*, 662. For Tewkesbury abbey and the earls of Gloucester, see *Ann. Mon.*, i, xvii, 159, 167; for Bekeford, *ibid*, 162.
27 *Ann. Mon.*, i, 457; D.A. Carpenter, 'The Decline of the Curial Sheriff in England', *EHR*, xci, 1976, 22—3, 28 n. 3, 29; Treharne, Sanders, 108—9, 118—23, 140—3, 146—7.
28 For the Lusignans, see Snellgrove.

Canterbury.[29] The king, however, was far from being surrounded by a cohesive and exclusive party of foreign relatives. There were bitter quarrels between Lusignans and Savoyards. There were also many native barons prominent at court. In 1258 it was essentially a group of *curiales*, comprising native barons, Simon de Montfort, and Peter of Savoy, which turned on the Lusignans and their allies, and imposed reform on the king. In that sense the revolution of 1258 was very much a revolution within the court of Henry III.

One reason for the unpopularity of the Lusignans was the extent to which they monopolised the fruits of royal patronage.[30] Another was that their conduct was frequently arrogant and violent. The king's protection, moreover, seemed to place the brothers above the law. If, as seems the case, the Savoyards were far less unpopular in England than the Lusignans, it was because they behaved in a more circumspect and responsible fashion. When, for example, Archbishop Boniface came to St Albans in 1253 the monks were impressed by his moderation and civility. By contrast, the year before they had been outraged by Geoffrey de Lusignan's pride and contempt for others — his marshal had expelled all the horses from the abbey's stables to make way for Geoffrey's, although there was plenty of room.[31] The landed possessions in England which the king gave the Lusignans meant that many lesser men were exposed to the brutality and ruthlessness of their local agents. The unfortunate characteristics of the brothers could also be displayed in numerous disputes with great men over lands and rights. Aymer bishop-elect of Winchester came into conflict with Boniface of Savoy, archbishop of Canterbury, Roger Bigod earl of Norfolk, and the king's steward, Robert Walerand; William de Valence clashed with the earls of Leicester, Gloucester, and Hereford, with Humphrey de Bohun, Hereford's eldest son, and again with Archbishop Boniface. Meanwhile, Guy and Geoffrey de Lusignan offended Henry de Hastings and Geoffrey de Lucy.[32] A notorious example of the violence of the half-brothers occurred in a dispute between the bishop-elect of Winchester and Archbishop Boniface in 1252. 'A multitude of armed Poitevins from the *familia* of . . . the elect of Winchester, William de Valence and their brothers', as a jury of presentment put it, broke into the archbishop's palace at Lambeth, stole his money, jewels and silver plate, and dragged his servants off to the elect's castle at Farnham. Aymer appears to have escaped punishment for this incident. It was settled out of court on the strength of his oath disclaiming knowledge of the attack, and not all the archbishop's property was returned. In and after

---

29 For the Savoyards, see E.L. Cox, *The Eagles of Savoy*, Princeton, 1974.
30 See below p. 118.
31 Paris, v, 344—5, 413—4; see also iv, 177; Cox, 172—9, 233—6.
32 Relations between the Lusignans and Richard de Clare, earl of Gloucester, were sometimes cordial, but there seems to have been a dispute between Richard and William de Valence over Roxhill manor in Bedfordshire, which ended with Richard ejecting William from the manor; M.R. Altschul, *A Baronial Family in Medieval England: the Clares*, Baltimore 1965, 66—7, 83; PRO E/163/2/30 (henceforth all manuscript references, unless otherwise stated, are to documents in the PRO); Just/1/9, m.39d; E/101/505/9. For the earl of Hereford and William de Valence, see R. Vaughan, 'The Chronicle of John of Wallingford', *EHR*, lxxiii, 1958, 76; see Paris, v, 442. For conflicts between the earl's son and William over their rights as respectively lords of Haverford and Pembroke, see KB/26/159, mm.1d,6; E/368/32, m.2d. For Guy and Geoffrey de Lusignan, see *CR 1256—9*, 20; Just/1/873, m.6d. The other cases are mentioned below in the text and in note 44.

1258 the complaint was frequently voiced that the king's protection had made it impossible to secure legal redress against the Lusignans and their followers. This belief was one reason why Henry III was accused of breaking the clause in *Magna Carta* which forbad the denial and delay of justice. In 1259 a Kentish knight alleged that he had been unable to obtain justice in the king's court against Roger of Leybourne because of the 'favour' which Roger had then enjoyed as one who 'stood' with William de Valence.[33] The king's protection of his half-brothers can be suspected in other cases. Perhaps it was why Archbishop Boniface, although disseized by William de Valence of the custody of a fee in Preston (Kent) around 1255, obtained redress only from the council of fifteen imposed on the king by the Provisions of Oxford in 1258.[34] Perhaps too it was why Robert Walerand abandoned a case of novel disseisin he brought against the elect of Winchester on the Hampshire eyre of 1256. Here, after the jury had given its verdict, plainly in Walerand's favour, Robert withdrew from his writ, and the elect went without day.[35] In another case on this eyre Roger Bigod earl of Norfolk accused the elect of deforcing him of the wardship of Richard son and heir of Richard de Bere. After the earl and Aymer had pleaded their cases, the earl sought judgement, and it is difficult to see, on the evidence of the pleadings, how this could have been other than in his favour. The judges, however, postponed their sentence for over two months until a later stage of their eyre. Unfortunately records of the case are then lost, but the whole episode may have left a legacy of ill feeling which influenced Bigod's actions in the crisis of 1258.[36]

By 1258, therefore, there was a great deal of pent up resentment against the Lusignans. Events at the Westminster parliament served to bring this to an explosive climax. An account of the parliament should begin with an episode which both Treharne and Powicke overlooked. At Shere in Surrey on 1 April 1258, little more than a week before the parliament opened, an armed band, allegedly on the orders of the bishop-elect of Winchester, attacked some servants of John fitz Geoffrey, the lord of the manor, and took them to the elect's castle of Farnham where one died of his wounds. All this was occasioned by a dispute between Aymer and John fitz Geoffrey over the advowson of Shere. When the parliament at Westminster opened John complained to the king about Aymer's attack, and sought redress. But Henry III, as the legal record made three months later stated, 'did not wish to hear him and wholly denied him justice'.[37] Fitz Geoffrey was a dangerous man to offend in this

---

33 Just/1/873, mm.8,18d; Paris, v, 348—54, 359, 738—9; *Ann. Mon.*, i, 458—9. The point about *Magna Carta* comes from a schedule of complaints against Henry III's government drawn up in 1263; Treharne, Sanders, 270—1.

34 *CR 1256—9*, 276. The most numerous sufferers from the corruption of the judicial system were, of course, the lesser men who had no remedy against the abuses of the local officials of the Lusignans; see Treharne, Sanders, 270—3.

35 Just/1/778, m.17; see *Cal. Inq. Post Mortem*, ii, no. 626. There is no sign that Aymer and Robert came to an agreement. For Walerand, see also *CPR 1247—58*, 537.

36 Just/1/778, mm.10,13. Later in 1256 Aymer is found owing Bigod 100 marks and perhaps this was in settlement of the dispute. Aymer, however, did not give the money to the earl but arranged with the king to have it deducted from the payments Bigod was supposed to make towards his debts at the exchequer; *CLR 1251—60*, 292. Whether Bigod welcomed this form of settlement may be questioned.

37 Just/1/1187, m.1; Paris, v, 708.

way. The son of King John's justiciar, Geoffrey fitz Peter, he was a great baron who had risen high in the king's service. In 1237, in return for a grant of taxation, the magnates had insisted that John join the royal council. Subsequently he had served a long term as justiciar of Ireland; he was still a prominent figure at court.[38] Not surprisingly, therefore, John's experiences in April 1258 caused fury at the Westminster parliament. As a letter which the baronage wrote to the pope, complaining of Aymer's conduct put it, 'lately to John fitz Geoffrey, a noble and powerful man amongst us, we know that [Aymer] has committed the most atrocious injuries, so that the *majores* of the kingdom *vehementer scandalizati sunt contra eum*, recalling to their minds his earlier deeds'.[39] The incident at Shere, with its obvious echoes of the attack on Lambeth palace in 1252, seemed to typify the violence of the half-brothers.[40] The king's reaction illustrated in the most blatant fashion the way his protection placed them above the law, and supported the statement, made by the baronage in another letter to the pope, that, 'if anyone brought a complaint and sought judgement against [the Lusignans] . . . the king turned against the complainant in a most extraordinary manner, and he who should have been a propitious judge . . . became a terrible enemy'.[41] The king's failure as an impartial judge was one reason why the Provisions of Oxford in June 1258 re-established the office of justiciar. The first case the justiciar heard was that of John fitz Geoffrey.[42]

At the Westminster parliament this scandal concerning Aymer de Lusignan was quickly followed by angry scenes involving William de Valence. William, because of his possession of Pembroke, was especially interested in the debate about the situation in Wales where Llywelyn was spreading destruction, and he accused certain English nobles of treacherous connivance with the Welsh prince. These remarks infuriated both the earls of Gloucester and Leicester, and the latter would have come to blows with William had not the king intervened.[43] Later in the parliament de Montfort demanded justice against William. The issue here may well have been the claim which Simon's wife had to Pembroke.[44] According to Matthew Paris, one of the barons' final charges

---

38 Paris, iii, 383; GEC, v, 433.
39 Paris, vi, 409.
40 For the Lambeth incident being recalled in 1258, see Paris, vi, 405—6.
41 *Ann. Mon.*, i, 459.
42 Just/1/1187, m.1; Treharne, Sanders, 260—1, 270—3.
43 Paris, v, 676—7; Powicke, *Henry III*, 381.
44 Paris, v, 689. In 1256 Simon and his wife Eleanor, the sister of Henry III, brought a case against the heirs of the Marshal earls of Pembroke for Eleanor's dower as the widow of William Marshal, earl of Pembroke, who had died in 1230. No details of the case survive, but the Montforts' claim may well have been for Pembroke (and thus one directed in the first instance against William de Valence) since Simon and Eleanor had maintained in an earlier case that it was with Pembroke that Eleanor had been dowered. No judgement was given in the 1256 case, although, in 1260, Simon implied that one should have been; C. Bémont, *Simon de Montfort*, Paris 1884, 335; see, KB/26/159, mm.2d,3,3d. Eleanor was also in dispute with the Lusignans over their respective shares of their mother's inheritance in France; BN Clairambault 1188, fos. 18—18v. It is interesting to note that the chronicle known as the Merton *Flores Historiarum* (for which see Gransden, 456—63) says that Simon de Montfort and John fitz Geoffrey were the leaders of the faction opposed to the king in 1258, stimulated by a 'common contention against the elect of Winchester and William de Valence'. It also implies that they resented their recall from respectively the seneschalship of Gascony and the justiciarship of Ireland; *Flores Historiarum*, iii, ed. H.R. Luard, RS 1890, 252.

against the king also centred on the Lusignans. Henry had 'exalted his uterine brothers in a most intolerable fashion, as if they had been native born, contrary to the right and law of the kingdom, nor would he allow any writ to go out from the chancery against them'.[45]

It is against this rising tide of complaint against the half-brothers that the famous confederation formed at the Westminster parliament should be placed. In this, on 12 April 1258, the earls of Gloucester, Norfolk, and Leicester, Peter of Savoy, Hugh Bigod, John fitz Geoffrey, and Peter de Montfort, all save the earl of Norfolk *curiales*, swore to 'help each other, both ourselves and those belonging to us, against all people, doing right and taking nothing that we cannot take without doing wrong, saving faith to our lord the king of England and to the crown'.[46] The purpose of this alliance, therefore, was for the participants to provide each other with mutual aid.[47] Although that aid was to be against 'all people', it is likely that the pact was aimed chiefly at the Lusignans. Of the seven confederates, the earls of Leicester, Norfolk, and Gloucester had all quarrelled with them, as, of course, had John fitz Geoffrey. Hugh Bigod was the earl of Norfolk's brother; Peter de Montfort, though no relation, a close ally of the earl of Leicester.[48] Peter of Savoy doubtless shared the feelings of the archbishop of Canterbury and the queen about the half-brothers.[49] Probably the seven were already agreed on a reform of the realm, which would contain the reduction of the Lusignans as a major ingredient. The alliance was designed to meet the possibility that the brothers would defend themselves by force. Significantly, Matthew Paris records an alliance made precisely for 'safety' against, by implication, the 'snares' of the Lusignans. Concluding his account of the Westminster parliament, he noted that, 'the nobles of England, for instance the earls of Gloucester, Leicester, Hereford, the earl Marshal [Roger Bigod earl of Norfolk], and other men of distinction, took precautions and provided for their safety by forming a confederation, and as they greatly feared the traps and snares of the aliens and had exceeding respect for the king's nets, they turned up at the Oxford parliament with horses and arms and the protection of an ample escort'.[50] Although Paris erroneously included the earl of Hereford among its members, it may be that

---

45 Paris, v, 689. The point about the writs was a reference to the way the king had obstructed legal actions against the Lusignans; see Treharne, Sanders, 270—3; Paris, v, 594.
46 Bémont, 327. The translation is from, *English Historical Documents*, iii, ed. H. Rothwell, London 1975, 361.
47 Powicke thought that the agreement was one 'to give each other aid . . . in the cause of right . . . and well doing'; Powicke, *Henry III*, 377; see *The Thirteenth Century*, 130. However, the 'doing right and taking nothing that we cannot take without doing wrong' were merely conventional phrases, designed to give a gloss of respectability to the nature of the help to be provided. I discuss the phraseology of agreements to provide mutual aid in 1258—9 in a forthcoming note in *BIHR* which prints the Lord Edward's oath of October 1259 to aid Simon de Montfort.
48 For Peter and Simon, see D.A. Carpenter, 'St Thomas Cantilupe: his political career', *St. Thomas Cantilupe Essays in his Honour*, ed. M. Jancey (Hereford, 1982), 61—2. It is also worth noting that John fitz Geoffrey was the brother-in-law of Roger and Hugh Bigod.
49 For the queen's relations with Aymer de Lusignan, see *CR 1259—61*, 265; the Waverley annalist says that she welcomed the changes of 1258 because they rid England of the Lusignans; *Ann. Mon.*, ii, 355; see also Paris, v, 703. It is significant that in 1258 the earl of Gloucester became connected to the house of Savoy through the marriage of his daughter to the marquis of Montferrat; see above p. 112; Cox, 275—6, 462.
50 Paris, v, 689—90.

he was here referring to the alliance of 12 April. Whether the half-brothers planned armed resistance may be doubted, but it was not difficult to suspect them. They had young and warlike allies in John de Warenne, earl of Surrey, Henry son of Richard of Cornwall, and, above all, the king's eldest son, the Lord Edward.[51] William de Valence's and Edward's preparations against Llywelyn could easily cover mobilization for civil war. On 17 April the king ordered the constable of St Briavels to deliver 2,000 cross-bow bolts to William. Around the same time William himself augmented Edward's means to raise troops by giving him a large sum of money in return for the lease of some manors.[52]

The Westminster parliament, then, opened with John fitz Geoffrey's complaint against Aymer bishop-elect of Winchester, and continued with angry exchanges between William de Valence and the earls of Gloucester and Leicester. On 12 April an alliance was formed, directed chiefly against the Lusignans. Meanwhile Arlot threatened the kingdom with an interdict, and the king, having refused justice to John fitz Geoffrey, begged for money to pursue his Sicilian dreams. The bishops, wanting no part of the extreme measures which they knew were afoot, withdrew from the parliament. The climax on 30 April seems hardly surprising. The occasion for the march on the king's hall was to reply to the request for the Sicilian tax; but the first demand that Roger Bigod put to Henry was: 'Let the wretched and intolerable Poitevins and all aliens flee from your face'.[53]

It is difficult to agree with Powicke, that after the concession of 2 May, the parliament ended with 'the king, his son, and his half-brothers . . . in agreement with the confederated barons', and that it was only at the Oxford parliament that the 'family party . . . broke asunder'.[54] In reality, between the two parliaments the magnates prepared at best for a show of force, at worst for civil war. Both the Burton abbey annalist and Matthew Paris state that the barons came to the Oxford parliament, which opened around 11 June, in arms, their excuse being that they were going on from Oxford to campaign in Wales. The truth, as Paris reported, was that 'they were in no slight fear that, in consequence of the disagreement of parties, civil war would break out between them, and that the king and his Poitevin brothers would call in aliens to aid him against his native born subjects'. The king was indeed bringing foreign knights into England, ostensibly for the campaign against Llywelyn. On 25 May he instructed eleven of them to be paid and sent on to the forthcoming parliament at Oxford.[55] At the parliament, having created Hugh Bigod justiciar, the reformers moved to appoint new castellans to the royal castles, thus depriving the king of the means of resistance.[56] That done, they turned their attention to the Lusignans. A letter which the barons wrote to the pope, explaining their actions, indicated that the offence of the brothers was to resist the programmes of reform at Oxford, and to try to get the king to renege on

---

51 Treharne, Sanders, 92—3; Paris, v, 697.
52 *CR 1256—9*, 210; Paris, v, 679.
53 *Ann. Mon.*, i, 164.
54 Powicke, *Henry III*, 378, 381.
55 *Ann. Mon.*, i, 438; Paris, v, 695—6; *CR 1256—9*, 223—4.
56 Treharne, Sanders, 90—1, 258—9; Treharne, 74.

his oath of 2 May.[57] The brothers' conduct was scarcely unprovoked. Apart from the threat implicit in the justiciarship, another part of the reform programme was aimed directly at them — an act of resumption of 'all lands, tenements and castles alienated by the king from the crown'.[58] This measure could be presented as a public spirited attempt to restore the king's financial position. In reality, it was a partisan attack upon the Lusignans. The half-brothers, of course, were not the only potential victims of an act of resumption, but they knew that it would be enforced against themselves far more rigorously than against anyone else — in fact, once the proposed act had been used to intimidate the brothers it appears to have been quietly abandoned. William de Valence, moreover, was particularly vulnerable to schemes for resumption. Since coming to England in 1247 he had received far more land from the king than anyone else. Indeed, Henry had formally promised to give escheats to no one save his brother, Richard of Cornwall, until William's £500 annual pension was converted into land held in fee. An act of resumption would leave William with his wife's lands in Wales; but he would lose his chief base in England, Hertford castle, the royal demesne manors of Essendon, Bayford and Bampton, and, if the act extended to escheats, at least six other manors. His power in England would have been ended.[59] At the Oxford parliament, therefore, according to Matthew Paris, the brothers swore by the death and wounds of Christ that they would not surrender the castles, lands and wardships given them by the king. Simon de Montfort's riposte to William de Valence was 'either you give up your castles or you lose your head'. It was in this atmosphere, having refused to agree to the act of resumption, that the brothers fled from Oxford to Winchester; perhaps, as their enemies claimed, to make a stand at the elect's castle and call in foreign mercenaries, perhaps in pure desperation. The barons immediately broke up the Oxford parliament and followed them. They demanded that Guy and Geoffrey de Lusignan leave England *finaliter*, and that William and Aymer remain in custody until the reform of the realm was complete. Alternatively all the brothers were to leave England while reform was in progress. The Lusignans chose to depart together and crossed the channel on 14 July.[60] Fear and suspicion of them was now so great that when, later in the month, the deaths occurred of the abbot of Westminster and William de Clare, and the latter's brother, the earl of Gloucester, fell dangerously ill, it was widely believed that they were victims of a Lusignan poison plot.[61]

57 *Ann. Mon.*, i, 458.
58 Treharne, Sanders, 92—3.
59 *CChR 1226—57*, 339, 351; *CLR 1251—60*, 202, 396; *CR 1253—4*, 214—5. See Powicke, *Henry III*, 383—4. The only description of the proposed act of resumption is in a letter from an eye-witness of the parliament: 'it was provided that all lands, tenements and castles alienated by the king from the crown should be restored to him'; this is the passage quoted in the text above; Treharne, Sanders, 92—3. Paris (see below in text) adds the story of the oath of the half-brothers, and states that Simon de Montfort returned to the king *gratis* the castles of Kenilworth and Odiham (granted to him for life), although he had recently done much to improve them; Paris, v, 697. The lack of information about the act strongly suggests that it was never implemented. There is no evidence that the king ever took possession of Kenilworth and Odiham.
60 Paris, v, 697—8; Treharne, Sanders, 92—5. Reluctance to stand trial against John fitz Geoffrey and other complainants may have been a factor in the decision to depart; see *Ann. Mon.*, i, 459.
61 Paris, v, 700, 702—5, 707—9, 747; *Ann. Mon.*, i, 165, 167, 460.

There was, of course, much more to the revolution of 1258 than the expulsion of the Lusignans. Whether, however, the movement would have begun without the hatred of the half-brothers, and the particular incidents which fanned this into flames at the Westminster parliament may be questioned. After April 1258 the king's opponents could never escape from the fact that their enterprise had commenced with the coercion of the king and an attack on his closest friends. They were bound to anticipate a royalist attempt to recover power. To prevent this it was imperative to make their movement as popular and as widely supported as possible. This need for support helps to explain perhaps the most striking feature of the reforms of 1258—9 — the way they encompassed the courts and officials of the great magnates as well as those of the king.

THE LORD EDWARD'S CRUSADE, 1270—2: ITS SETTING AND SIGNIFICANCE

Simon Lloyd

There can be no doubt that the Lord Edward's crusade of 1270—2 possesses only marginal significance for the history of the crusades.[1] His force originally constituted but one division of the much larger expedition carefully prepared by Louis IX between 1267 and 1270, but the diversion to Tunis and Louis' death in August 1270 began a process of disintegration which culminated in the general postponement of the passage to the Holy Land. Edward, however, refused to set aside his vow. When he landed at Acre in May 1271 he was, therefore, the leader of the pitifully small remnant of the crusade, and this circumstance dogged him from the first. He tried, with some success, to alleviate the problem of manpower by raising mercenaries, allying with the Mongols, and mobilising the bickering forces of the Latin East, but he was nevertheless capable only of mounting a few insignificant raids. Following the attempt to assassinate him in June 1272, Edward accepted the truce which King Hugh III had realistically concluded with Sultan Baibars and in September he sailed away from Acre.[2] In no sense can his crusade be considered a practical success.

The significance of Edward's crusade lies apart from its limited impact upon the Latin East at the time. Simply by fulfilling his vow Edward won an enviable reputation of international proportions, and for the rest of his life he was widely regarded as the potential leader of a new crusade, for the time being supplanting the Capetians as the expected saviour of the Holy Land. It was an image which he did something to foster but little, ultimately, to justify, for he never returned to the East. As far as his career as King of England is concerned, Powicke considered that Edward learned a great deal from the crusade through his direct experience of the factionalism rampant in the Latin East; he came to reflect upon the possible consequences of political disintegration within his own inherited dominions.[3] Morris, with an eye to Edward's military achievements at home, suggested that he was taught something by exposure to Eastern methods of fighting.[4] For M. Prestwich the establishment of

---

1 J.R. Strayer, 'The Crusades of Louis IX', in *A History of the Crusades*, ii, ed. R.L. Wolff and H.W. Hazard, Philadelphia 1962, 518, comments scathingly that 'as a military expedition his crusade had been useless . . .' F.M. Powicke, *King Henry III and the Lord Edward*, Oxford 1947, ii, 600, observed more soberly that 'Edward has a very modest place in the history of the crusades', but all modern historians are agreed that the crusade was a minor expedition with limited results.
2 The fullest account of the events of Edward's crusade in the East remains R. Röhricht, 'Études sur les derniers temps du royaume de Jérusalem. A. La croisade du Prince Édouard d'Angleterre (1270—1274)', *Archives de l'Orient latin*, i, 1881, esp. 622—30.
3 Powicke, ii, 604—5.
4 J.E. Morris, *The Welsh Wars of Edward I*, Oxford 1901, 111.

'firm and lasting friendships with a select group of companions' was perhaps the foremost result of the crusade; many of those who accompanied him came to play vital roles in the events of his reign.[5] But it may be argued that Edward gained as much from the attempts which he and Louis made to overcome the immense logistical and organisational problems involved in mounting the crusade. In particular, the measures which Edward took to recruit and organise his force, especially his use of contracts, have some significance for his later campaigns as king.

Edward took the Cross in June 1268, but the formal origins of his expedition lie in the measures taken by Urban IV in 1263 to mobilise the West for a new crusade. On or before 12 July 1263 Walter Cantilupe, bishop of Worcester, was appointed to preach the Cross in England, but it is doubtful if anything came of this at the time.[6] The realm was already sliding into civil war and active promotion of the crusade seems to have been suspended until the slow, painful restoration of order following the battle of Evesham.[7] Clement IV's legate, Cardinal Ottobuono, then emerged as chief executor of the Cross. In October 1266 the pope urged him to promote the crusade *ferventius*, which suggests that he had already taken up the cause again and lends credence to Clement's report to the Patriarch of Jerusalem in August 1266 that the Cross was then being preached in England.[8]

It was probably in response to this mandate that Ottobuono presented the matter of the crusade for deliberation at the parliament and ecclesiastical council held at Bury St. Edmunds in February 1267.[9] Neither assembly was enthusiastic and he met with a decidely negative response.[10] Ottobuono pressed ahead nevertheless: he instructed the friars to preach the crusade and sent his own letters of exhortation to be published throughout the realm.[11] He

---

5 M. Prestwich, *The Three Edwards*, London 1980, 7—8.

6 *Les Registres d'Urbain IV*, ed. L. Dorez and J. Guiraud, Paris 1899—1958, no. 397, instructing the English prelates to assist Walter and his *cooperatores* in preaching the Cross. For his commission, dated 4 October 1263, see no. 466. Bishop Walter was granted wide executive powers over all aspects of the crusade. See also nos. 392, 467, 468, 472.

7 I cannot accept the argument of B. Beebe, 'The English Baronage and the Crusade of 1270', *BIHR*, xlviii, 1975, 128—30, that the crusade to the Holy Land was promoted in an attempt to create domestic peace in the years 1263—4. The available evidence makes it clear that both Urban IV and Clement IV authorised their respective legates to preach the crusade *against* the rebels as part of papal policy to aid the beleaguered Henry III. Far from the rebels being the object of a crusade recruitment campaign to entice them from England, they were in fact the declared object of a 'political' crusade within England. Only when peace was restored was the Holy Land crusade again promoted with vigour. See *Registres d'Urbain IV*, nos. 596—9, 608—12; *Les Registres de Clément IV*, ed. E. Jordan, Paris 1893—1945, nos. 56—9, 62, 76—7; E. Martène and U. Durand, *Thesaurus novus anecdotorum*, Paris 1717, ii, no. 148. I hope to publish a more detailed study of this matter, and Beebe's overall thesis, in the near future.

8 *Registres de Clément IV*, nos. 1110, 1146. Ottobuono had already been promoting the crusade in Ireland, perhaps as early as January 1266 and certainly by June. For his role in general, see A. Lewis, 'The English Activities of Cardinal Ottobuono, Legate of the Holy See' (Manchester MA thesis 1938), esp. 140—3.

9 At some point before this Ottobuono wrote to Rome declaring his intention of laying the business of the crusade before the prelates. See R. Graham, 'Letters of Cardinal Ottoboni', *EHR*, xv, 1900, no. 12.

10 *Willelmi Rishanger . . . Chronica et Annales, regnantibus Henrico tertio et Edwardo primo*, ed. H.T. Riley, RS 1865, 52; *The Chronicle of William de Rishanger of the Barons' War*, ed. J.O. Halliwell, Camden Society, os xv, 1840, 60—2.

11 *Continuation* of William of Newburgh, in *Chronicles of the Reigns of Stephen, Henry II, and*

preached in person as well, and on three occasions he can be observed in action: at St. Paul's, London, during Gilbert de Clare's occupation of the city in 1267; at Lincoln, and then at Barlings, in October.[12] He may also have preached at the parliament of Northampton in 1268 when, on 24 June, the Lords Edward and Edmund, Henry of Almain, Gilbert de Clare, John de Warenne, William de Valence, and others took their crusade vows.[13] This was the crucial breakthrough, for those who took the Cross on that day were to provide the nucleus of the crusade which left England in 1270—1.[14]

That Edward took the Cross and was allowed to fulfil his vow is, *prima facie*, surprising. By June 1268 scarcely a year had passed since Gilbert de Clare's occupation of London and the surrender of the Isle of Ely, the last major rebel stronghold. The political situation remained tense and uncertain, peace still a novelty. Edward's departure on crusade betokened the absence of the foremost royal commander accompanied by many of the realm's most doughty warriors and efficient administrators, so leaving the ageing Henry III with a depleted command to confront any further disturbances in the far-flung Angevin territories. The danger was exacerbated by the wretched state of royal finances after the civil war, and these would inevitably be strained even further by the demands of so costly an enterprise as a crusade.[15] And Edward, of course, was heir to the throne; what if he should die in God's service?

Henry, not surprisingly, seems to have been initially opposed to Edward's crusade plans, first apparent from a paper letter of January 1268.[16] Certainly it was not the simple matter, as Runciman and Beebe suggest, of Henry urging Edward to act as his substitute in the tardy fulfilment of his 1250 vow, still binding upon him after his disastrous flirtation with the Sicilian business.[17]

Richard I, ed. R. Howlett, RS 1885, ii, 552; *Annales Monastici*, ed. H.R. Luard, RS 1864—9, iv, 217; Graham, 'Letters', no. 29.

12 *Willelmi Rishanger . . . Chronica*, 57; *Flores Historiarum*, ed. H.R. Luard, RS 1890, iii, 14; *Annales sex regum Angliae, 1135—1307*, ed. T. Hog, English Historical Society, 1845, 271; 'Extracts from the Barlings Chronicle', in *Chronicles of the Reigns of Edward I and Edward II*, ed. W. Stubbs, RS 1883, ii, cxv—vi. Beebe, 'English Baronage', 129—30, considers that his preaching at this time was a political act.

13 Among other sources reporting the event, *Annales Monastici*, iv, 217—8; *De Antiquis Legibus Liber*, ed. T. Stapleton, Camden Society, os xxxiv, 107; *Continuation* of Florence of Worcester, in *Chronicon ex Chronicis*, ed. B. Thorpe, English Historical Society, 1848—9, ii, 201, which reports that Ottobuono personally gave the Cross to Edward, Gilbert de Clare, and other nobles. No account states that Ottobuono preached to the assembly, but considering the importance of the occasion it would be surprising if he had not.

14 Gilbert de Clare and John de Warenne did not ultimately depart on crusade. John seems to have put aside or redeemed his vow at an early date, and nothing further is heard of his proposed crusade. Gilbert de Clare, however, as late at November 1270, seems still to have intended to fulfil his vow. See below, 129.

15 For a survey of the circumstances of this period, see Powicke, ii, chs. xii, xiii. For the Crown's finances, see E.F. Jacob, *Studies in the Period of Baronial Reform and Rebellion*, Oxford 1925, 222—75; M.H. Mills, 'Adventus Vicecomitum', *EHR*, xxxvi, 1921, and xxxviii, 1923. Henry needed money so desperately that he was forced even to pledge the precious Westminster and Crown jewels in 1267, and he so impressed Clement IV by his plight that the pope granted him a triennial tenth from the English clergy. See W.E. Lunt, *Financial Relations of the Papacy with England to 1327*, Cambridge, Massachusetts 1939, 292—310; Powicke, ii, 558—9, 563—8. Powicke, ii, 569, considered that the crusade was 'a great waste of money, squandered when money was needed most'.

16 *Registres de Clément IV*, no. 1288; Martène and Durand, no. 583.

17 S. Runciman, *A History of the Crusades*, Cambridge 1951—4, iii, 335; Beebe, 'English

Edward ultimately bore Henry's Cross, it is true, but it seems very unlikely that this was the original intention because Clement IV authorised Ottobuono in April 1268 to release Henry from his vow if he sent the Lord Edmund in his place.[18] Although direct evidence is lacking, this was probably Clement's response to Henry's own petition; thereby his votive obligations would be met but Edward retained in England against possible future developments.

Papal policy also militated against Edward's wishes. In January 1268 Clement informed Louis IX that Edward had recently sought papal counsel concerning his crusade plans and petitioned for financial support. Clement strongly advised Edward to desist, arguing that the political situation in England was still a cause for concern and that it would be *minime tutum* to leave his father in such straits. He therefore rejected Edward's request for aid, which was tantamount to cold-shouldering the whole project, although he reluctantly accepted that Edward might nevertheless proceed to join Louis' crusade.[19] Henry and Clement were agreed that the settlement of England should take precedence over Edward's personal wishes.

The obstinate Edward remained unmoved and by June 1268 had presumably brought Henry and the pope around to his point of view. We know that he had succeeded with Ottobuono because the legate recommended Edward to Clement as a worthy champion who should be afforded financial aid.[20] It was probably Ottobuono's pleading which persuaded his master and Henry to acquiesce in Edward's plans.[21]

Edward's evident determination to take the Cross, and complete his crusade, is probably explained by his circumstances as the heir apparent, his love of martial exploits, and perhaps the influence of Louis IX. Studd has recently shown that Edward was never so free an agent as has been thought. He had been granted a very extensive appanage in 1254 but his control over it was severely restricted by conditions attached to the grant, and Henry constantly interfered in his son's administration and uses of its revenues.[22] Edward clearly found the situation to be galling, head-strong youth that he was. Moreover, he had played a major part in the affairs of the realm, particularly since 1263, but by 1268 his openings for action were circumscribed with the end of the clearing-up operations following Evesham. There was little prospect of large-scale campaigning in England, and the settlement with Llywelyn ap Gruffydd in 1267 closed for the time being any opportunities for military glory

---

Baronage', 130, who misdates Henry's vow. See, in particular, on Henry's crusade vows, A.J. Forey, 'The Crusading Vows of the English King Henry III', *Durham University Journal*, lxv, 1973, 229—47, who establishes beyond doubt that Henry's vow remained to be fulfilled in the 1260s.

18 *Registres de Clément IV*, no. 609.

19 *Registres de Clément IV*, no. 1288; Martène and Durand, no. 583. The significance of Clement's decision is emphasised by his active support for Louis' expedition, and by his agreement, only three months later, to the transfer of crusade monies to the Lord Edmund should he bear Henry's Cross to the Holy Land. See *Registres de Clément IV*, no. 609.

20 Graham, 'Letters', no. 26.

21 Chronology almost certainly rules out the guess of Runciman, iii, 335, that the fall of Antioch, 18 May 1268, acted as the stimulant to Edward's assumption of the Cross. It is hard to believe that the news would have reached him only five weeks later. *Flores Historiarum*, iii, 451—2, reports, in terms which suggest that this was something of a record, that in 1260 a Templar messenger took 13 weeks to reach London from the Holy Land.

22 J.R. Studd, 'The Lord Edward and King Henry III', *BIHR*, l, 1977, 4—19.

against the Marchers' traditional foe.[23] The series of tournaments which began in late 1267, after years of official prohibition, were but a poor substitute.[24]

Restless, and chafing under restraints, Edward may have regarded the prospect of the crusade with relish, a splendid opportunity to act in an unfettered capacity in charge of his own expedition.[25] Louis IX may also have encouraged him to consider the crusade. The Capetian had urged Henry III to fulfil his vow on a number of occasions in the 1260s, and he probably promoted the cause ever more ardently among his Angevin kin after taking the Cross for the second time in March 1267.[26] That Edward and Louis had already been in contact over the matter by late 1267 is clear from Clement IV's letter of January 1268, in which he anticipated that Edward might join Louis' crusade, and this may be interpreted as evidence that Louis had been making overtures to Edward.[27] Whatever the case, Edward's crusade was soon to be integrated with Louis' expedition.

Louis naturally turned chiefly to his own kinsmen and great vassals to support his crusade. On taking the Cross, he proceeded to cajole and persuade his surviving brothers, Alphonse of Poitiers and Charles of Anjou, his nephew, Robert II of Artois, and the other great men of France to follow the example of himself and his three sons.[28] Edward, too, was a kinsman of Louis, and following the Treaty of Paris Edward's Gascony was a direct fief of the French King, so, as far as the crusade was concerned, Louis probably regarded Edward in the same light as the other great lords of France. In August 1269 Edward journeyed to Paris to attend a council of the various crusade leaders. Its primary purpose seems to have been to strengthen the cohesion and organisation of the crusade force as a whole, setting departure dates and musters, and laying down the principles governing transport and provisioning.[29] On 27 and 28 August Edward and Louis sealed the documents which formally bound Edward to the French King's expedition. Louis would loan 70,000 *l. tournois* to Edward. Of this total, 25,000 *l.* were to be reserved for Gaston de Béarn, his contingent of Gascons, and their passage overseas, while the remainder went to Edward *pur chevaus, pur viandes, pur nefs, e pur passage de celi Edward*... In return, Edward agreed to arrive at Aigues

---

23 T.F. Tout, *Collected Papers*, ii, 88—97, in explaining why English forces were not turned against Llywelyn at the time, argued that Edward had decided upon the crusade as early as February 1267, but he produced no evidence to this effect. It seems more likely that the decision to make a settlement with Llywelyn, and to use the cash resulting from it, encouraged Edward and the Marchers, many of whom went on the crusade, to look to an entirely different theatre of war: the Holy Land.
24 N. Denholm-Young, 'The Tournament in the Thirteenth Century', in *Studies in Medieval History presented to Frederick Maurice Powicke*, ed. R.W. Hunt, W.A. Pantin, R.W. Southern, Oxford 1948, esp. 257—60. The leading role taken by Edward, Edmund, Gilbert de Clare, and William de Valence, who all took the Cross, is significant.
25 This is not to say that other motives were absent. Edward may already have held the cause of the Holy Land close to his heart, and he had strong dynastic reasons for responding to the crusade call.
26 See Forey, 'Crusading Vows', 245—6, and references cited.
27 *Registres de Clément IV*, no. 1288; Martène and Durand, no. 583. Clement sought assurances that if Edward went with Louis then the French king would aid the Angevin house should war be resumed in England.
28 See Strayer, 'Crusades', 509ff.
29 Strayer, 'Crusades', 510—12.

Mortes for embarkation not later than 15 August 1270, to accompany Louis wherever he might go, and to obey him in good faith *cum un de nos Barunes de nostre reaume pour faire le service nostre Seniur.*[30] Strayer suggests that the primary purpose of the loan was to secure the participation on crusade of Gaston de Béarn and other Gascons, but the terms of the agreement make it plain that the chief intention was to provide Edward with sufficient ready-cash to cover transport, victuals, and horses for himself and Gaston.[31] The money was to be paid over to those whom Edward should appoint to make purveyances in France against his passage, and any outstanding sums were to be delivered to Edward when he joined Louis overseas.[32]

The agreement is best treated not just as a loan but as a binding contract which formalised relations between Louis and Edward by laying reciprocal obligations upon the two parties, parallel to agreements made by Louis with other crusade leaders around this time. The intention was clearly to encourage recruitment and to create a unified command structure through the use of instruments which would reinforce the prior tendencies towards unity and discipline inherent in lordship and kinship bonds. As far as Edward's force was concerned, the Paris agreement was fundamental since Edward now had to ensure that he could meet his obligations. The agreement does not specify the number of bannerets, simple knights, and other ranks whom Edward was to lead, but it is difficult to see how the firm figure of 70,000 *l.* was arrived at without reference to actual numbers.

The terms of the agreement envisaged two distinct groups under Edward's command. The first comprised Edward's Gascon vassals, most of whom, it seems, would serve with Gaston de Béarn, . . . *le quel Gaston nous retenoms lui e ses genz, en nostre* [Edward's] *compaignie.*[33] Whether Edward and Gaston then came to a more precise agreement regarding their relationship on crusade and the numbers who should accompany Gaston, is unknown, but it is certain that Edward was eager to ensure that the troublesome viscount went on crusade. Indeed, to bind him more closely, Edward took a leading part in the negotiations that resulted in the marriage of his friend and cousin, Henry of Almain, to Gaston's daughter, Constance, in June 1270.[34] Gaston, however, never joined the crusade; he remained behind in Gascony, although it seems that as late as October 1270 he had every intention of departing. Perhaps, as Ellis suggests, he preferred to wait upon events following Louis' death at Tunis, or considered transferring his services to his other overlord James I of

---

30 *Diplomatic Documents, I (1101—1272)*, ed. P. Chaplais, London 1964, no. 419; *Foedera*, I, i, 481; *De Antiquis Legibus*, 111—4. For the repayment of the loan see J-P. Trabut-Cussac, 'Le financement de la croisade anglaise de 1270', *Bibliothèque de l'École des Chartes*, cxix, 1961, esp., 114—24. Henry III ratified the terms of the agreement in September 1269. Trabut-Cussac prints the copy contained in the miscellaneous books of the Exchequer of Receipt: PRO E 36/275, f. 33v. (not f. 64v. as stated by Trabut-Cussac).
31 Strayer, 'Crusades', 510.
32 For the payments to Edward, see Trabut-Cussac, 'Financement', 115. In April 1270 Alphonse of Poitiers ordered the seneschals of the Venaissin, and Toulouse and Albi, to permit Edward's men to take away victuals and other necessaries to the value of 1,000 *l.* in each bailiwick. See *Correspondance administrative d'Alfonse de Poitiers*, ed. A. Molinier, Paris 1894—1900, ii, nos. 1419, 1824. In 1270 John de Grilly and John Hardel made purveyances in France against Edward's arrival. See *CLR 1267—72*, 123, 126; *CPR 1272—81*, 102.
33 *Foedera*, I, i, 481. Gaston was present in Paris and put his seal to the documents.
34 *CPR 1266—72*, 323.

Aragon, who was then preparing his own expedition.[35]

Ebles IV of Ventadour was another Southern lord who enlisted in Edward's force, but he left the crusade at Tunis and in 1277 found himself pressed by the papal legate in France to fulfil or redeem his vow. Edward then petitioned John XXI on Ebles' behalf, informing him that Ebles had been *de familia nostra* when he set out on crusade but, stricken by illness at Tunis, he had left for home with Edward's licence.[36] In April 1271 Ebles acknowledged that he was bound in 500 *l. tournois* to Edward for this release, a sum which probably represents the fee for which he had been retained in Edward's force.[37]

If it is questionable whether Edward used contracts to mould the Gascon forces to his service, it is certain that the written contract was to provide the backbone of the English crusade. On the Pipe Roll of 1 Edward I is entered the account, up to 20 October 1272, of the three initial receivers of the twentieth, which was granted for the crusade in 1269—70.[38] The section of the account recording expenditure contains a list of payments made to 18 crusaders who contracted to accompany Edward with a fixed quota of knights each. Altogether 22,500m. were paid out from the receipts for this purpose, and as the rate was set at 100m. per knight Edward therefore raised 225 knights for his crusade service by this means.[39] Most of the original contracts to which the Pipe Roll entries refer have vanished, but the one between Edward and Adam de Gesemue (Jesmond) survives and has been printed by Richardson and Sayles.[40] Fortunately another has since come to light whereby Payn de Chaworth and Robert Tiptoft contracted to accompany Edward with 10 knights, 5 apiece according to the Pipe Roll, and remain in his service for one year to begin *al procheyn passage de septembre*, presumably when Edward should embark at Aigues Mortes.[41] In return they were granted 1,200m., 'e

---

35 J. Ellis, 'Gaston de Béarn, A Study in Anglo-Gascon Relations 1229—90' (Oxford D.Phil thesis 1952), esp. 278—83.
36 *List of Ancient Correspondence of the Chancery and Exchequer*, PRO Lists and Indexes, xv, new edn., New York 1968, 13.154, 154a; *Foedera*, I, ii, 542.
37 *Gascon Register A*, ed. G.P. Cuttino and J-P. Trabut-Cussac, London 1975—6, i, no. 157. The sum was to be paid to Guy de la Marche on Edward's behalf. Ebles was released from this sum in November 1275. See *CPR 1272—81*, 113. After his return Ebles was appointed seneschal of Périgord. See J-P. Trabut-Cussac, *L'Administration anglaise en Gascogne*, Paris, Geneva 1972, 181—2, 382.
38 PRO, Pipe Roll 1 Edward I, m.6. The receivers were Giles de Audenarde, clerk of the Wardrobe, and the Treasurers of the New Temple, London, and the Hospital, Clerkenwell. J.A.C. Vincent, *Lancashire Lay Subsidies*, I, Lancashire and Cheshire Record Society 1893, 100—5, printed part of the account. On the twentieth, see in particular S.K. Mitchell, *Taxation in Medieval England*, New Haven 1951, *passim*; Powicke, ii, 563—9. The list of contractors was first printed by T.H. Turner, 'Unpublished Notices of the Time of Edward I', *Archaeological Journal*, viii, 1851, 46. Beebe, 'English Baronage', 142, omits Gilbert de Clare from the list, presumably on the grounds that he remained at home. *Adam* de Monte Alto (Monthaut) should be read for *Alan*.
39 This figure postulates 99 knights serving with Edmund, 11 with Hamo L'Estrange, and 9 with Gilbert de Clare. The account records only the payments to these men and not their respective quotas.
40 H.G. Richardson and G.O. Sayles, *The Governance of Mediaeval England from the Conquest to Magna Carta*, Edinburgh 1963, Appendix VI, 463—5 (from BL, Cotton Charter xxix, 65). They comment that the contract 'does not look in the least like a novelty but, on the contrary, it has every appearance of being in common form, and we can hardly doubt that other troops of knights who accompanied Edward entered into similar contracts.'
41 BL, Additional Charter 19829; seals attached. According to the Paris agreement of 1269, Edward was to arrive at Aigues Mortes by 15 August 1270. His passage from England had been set

passage ce est a dire, luage de la nef e ewe a taunt de persones, e de chevaus cum il afert de chevalers'. Should they be prevented from serving then substitutes were to be provided or the money repaid in proportion to the service owing. If Edward died they were bound to serve whomsoever he should appoint in his place.[42]

Comparison between the two contracts reveals that the terms were identical and we may conclude, with the additional evidence from the Pipe Roll, that general terms of service were offered for participation in the crusade.[43] As both contracts are dated 20 July 1270, at Westminster, it is also probable that the remainder were drawn up at this time, and from the Pipe Roll we find that, with the exception of Gilbert de Clare, all the contractors were paid at the New Temple on 26 July.[44] Nevertheless, the terms are lamentably vague and rudimentary in comparison with contracts of a later age. No attempt is made to specify the number of other ranks or the number or type of horses to accompany each knight. Nothing is said about the means of payment to the knights in each contractor's squadron. There is no reference to compensation for horses lost in service, nor to bouch of court, nor whether Edward had full rights over spoils of war and if he was expected to provide arms and mounts. Nevertheless, it is of considerable interest that Edward should make systematic use of contracts to organise his crusade force and in some sense to expand his household for the expedition.

For the most part the contractors were men whom he had come to know and trust over the years, some of them his followers, others his friends and kinsmen. He had campaigned with most in the turbulent days of the 1263—7

---

originally at 24 June, but it was put back for a variety of reasons. According to *The Chronicle of Walter of Guisborough*, ed. H. Rothwell, Camden Society, ns lxxxix, 1957, 205, Edward did not reach Aigues Mortes until around 29 September.

42 It is interesting that Payn and Robert should contract together. The two were close friends and are often found in each other's company, both before and after the crusade. Shortly before the crusade Robert married Eve, possibly Payn's daughter but more probably his sister. See GEC XII, ii, 93 and note. Their respective careers are well-known and do not require extensive treatment here, but it should be noted that both were closely associated with Edward throughout the 1260s and served him loyally as King. Perhaps the single best illustration of the ties between the three before the crusade is the famous attempt, in which Payn and Robert participated, to rescue Edward from captivity in Wallingford in 1264. See Powicke, ii, 486. Both men appear among the executors of Edward's will drawn up at Acre in 1272. See *Foedera*, I, i, 495.

43 For those setting out with Edmund in 1271 a different period of service was presumably stipulated.

44 Edward sailed within the month. The late date for the drawing-up of the contracts probably has something to do with the raising of the twentieth, which was still being assessed in the spring and summer of 1270. The earliest surviving orders for its collection are dated 2 April 1270, and it was only on 10 July that Henry III instructed the three receivers to lay up the proceeds at the New Temple against future orders for disbursement. See Mitchell, esp. 47—8; *CPR 1266—72*, 439. Almost certainly, too, the delay was related to differences over terms and conditions for the crusade. The Annals of Winchester, in *Annales Monastici*, ii, 108, report that at the Hoketide parliament of 1270 the magnates met to treat *de vicesima et itinere crucesignatorum*, but after long discussion it was agreed to refer the business to Richard of Cornwall. Gilbert de Clare, and others, did not agree to this and the matter was prolonged until after Midsummer. Since a further parliament met at Westminster in late July, when the contracts were drawn up, it is probable that Earl Richard only arrived at his decisions at this time. This is further suggested by the burst of Chancery activity in the weeks following 10 July when the bulk of letters of protection and attorney, and licences to alienate, were issued to crusaders. Doubtless Edward had already come to verbal agreements with the contractors, however.

period and acted in affairs of state with others. Three were great lords in their own right and kinsmen of Edward; it was not perhaps intended that Lord Edmund, William de Valence, and Henry of Almain should enter into close household service with Edward. Walter de Percy was one of Edmund's knights, and had been in Henry III's household. Adam de Monte Alto, Hamo L'Estrange, Brian de Brampton and William de Huntercumbe were prominent royal servants. Robert de Munteny had been a knight of Gilbert de Clare. Of the rest, Robert Tiptoft, Richard de la Rochelle, Thomas de Clare and Roger de Leyburn definitely appear as being in Edward's close circle before the crusade, while Payn de Chaworth, Adam de Gesemue, William fitzWarin, and Roger de Clifford were closely associated with both Henry III and his son.[45] It was entirely natural that Edward should turn to such men for support.

In expanding his household forces Edward was following normal practice. The nucleus of most of Henry III's armies, at home or abroad, was provided by his household knights and Walker has shown how the needs of campaign led to a contraction or expansion of the number of knights in his service.[46] As King, of course, Edward was to pursue a similar policy.[47] Furthermore, Louis IX himself sought to create a nucleus of knights in his immediate service for the crusade by use of contracts. Typical was the agreement with Erard de Valéry, who later joined Edward's force in Sicily.[48] Erard was to serve Louis with 30 knights for one year in return for 8,000 *l. tournois*, transport, and *restor de chevaux*, but he was not to receive bouch of court. Payment of the 30 knights was his responsibility: they were to receive a moiety of their fees at the beginning of the year of service, and the other moiety after six months. Erard was also to ensure that each banneret had two horses and each simple knight one horse, a groom to every mount.[49] Altogether around 400 knights made up Louis' extended household for the crusade.[50] By comparison Edward's contracts are vague indeed, but their very use may in part have been suggested by Louis' practice.

By means of these contracts Edward could show Louis at muster that he was accompanied by a given number of knights bound to his service. Furthermore,

---

45 Space forbids detailed references, but their connections and careers can be traced in the various Chancery and Exchequer records of the period.
46 R.F. Walker, 'The Anglo-Welsh wars, 1217—67' (Oxford D. Phil. thesis 1954), esp. 67—81.
47 See in particular, Morris, *passim*; M. Prestwich, *War, Politics and Finance under Edward I*, London 1972, chs. ii, iii; J.O. Prestwich, 'The military household of the Norman kings', *EHR*, xcvi, 1981, esp. 1—6.
48 Röhricht, 'Etudes', 622. Erard had for long been associated with Henry III and Edward. See Powicke, ii, 497, 607; *CPR 1258—66*, 158, 163, 272, 391; *CR 1259—61*, 487; *CR 1264—8*,106; *CLR 1260—7*, 44, 90, 115. He was also committed to the cause of the Latin East. See J.S.C. Riley-Smith, *What were the Crusades?*, London 1977, 67—8. His transference to Edward's expedition following Louis IX's death is therefore explained.
49 *Recueil des Historiens des Gaules et de la France*, ed. M. Bouquet *et al.*, Paris 1738—1904, xx, 305. Other contracts were essentially of this type, but there were variations according to whether the knights concerned were to receive bouch of court. See *Recueil*, xx, 305—8; xxiii, 732—4. Louis was only following his earlier practice for the crusade of 1248—54.
50 This helps to explain why the Dover Chronicle, in *The Historical Works of Gervase of Canterbury*, ed. W. Stubbs, RS 1879—80, ii, 249, should refer to Edward as promising in 1269 to accompany Louis *quasi unus baronum et de familia sua*. See also the statements of Wykes, *Annales Monastici*, iv, 230; *Continuation* of Florence of Worcester, 203—4. It is revealing that they should think of Edward's participation in terms of quasi-membership of Louis's household.

they placed men such as the Lord Edmund and William de Valence under his command, and thus acted to prevent what Louis and Edward clearly feared: the disintegration of the crusade into a number of loosely cohesive forces. In this context the terms of the other agreement known to use are revealing. According to the award made by Richard of Cornwall on 27 May 1270, Gilbert de Clare was bound to join the crusade in the passage next following Edward's departure, presumably in the watchful company of the Lord Edmund. Should he wish to lead an independent force on reaching the Holy Land he was to be granted 2,000m. by Henry III, but if 'il soit atendaunt e eydaunt a syre Edward en servise nostre Seynur, dunk luy dora le roy de Engletere viij^m mars e une nef covenable luy fra aver a son passage'.[51] The extra inducements make it plain that unity of the English force under the direction and command of Edward was a priority.

The network of contracts can be taken one stage further. By agreeing to serve Edward with a stipulated number of knights the contractors had in turn to meet their obligations. Just as Edward looked first to those of his immediate connection, so they sought the aid of their own knights, friends, kin, or acquaintances. Many agreements were probably never committed to writing, but traces of the process of sub-contracting survive. In 1269, for example, an agreement between William de Valence and his brother-in-law William de Munchensi was enrolled in Chancery. Munchensi was under a bond to pay 1,000m. to de Valence, *si forte non transfretaret cum ipso ad Terram Sanctam*, and he does indeed seem to have forfeited and withdrawn from de Valence's crusade *mesnie*, for by this instrument de Valence remitted 500m. and terms were agreed for the payment of the remainder.[52] The most interesting cases concern those men who were drawn into new or changed relationships stimulated by the demands of the crusade. The Lord Edmund was accompanied by Robert de Turberville, a Marcher knight already in his service, for

51 The award is printed in *Historical Papers and Letters from the Northern Registers*, ed. J. Raine, RS 1873, no. XX; *The Register of Walter Giffard, Lord Archbishop of York*, ed. W. Brown, Surtees Society, cix, London 1904, no. dccxliii. Another copy is to be found in PRO E 36/274 f. 297v.—298v. It is reported in some detail by Wykes, in *Annales Monastici*, iv, 231—3, who also states that Gilbert wanted clarification on certain points, duly provided by Richard at Reading on 17 June. Gilbert remained in England but it seems that as late as 1 November he still intended to join Edward, although in an independent capacity. In accordance with the award he was then paid 1,000m. from the receipts of the twentieth as a moiety of the agreed sum of 2,000m. However, an interlineation on the Pipe Roll states that the 1,000m. was *de prestito*, and a later hand has added *de quibus idem Comes respondet in Glouc' in R.nono*. Edward's anxiety to ensure Gilbert's departure on crusade is well illustrated by their journey together to consult Louis in February 1270. See *CPR 1266—72*, 410, 412. According to the Dover Chronicle, ii, 249—50, Edward strongly hinted that Gilbert's departure might be a *sine qua non* for his own, but Gilbert refused to heed Louis' exhortations. Gilbert's failure to fulfil his vow almost certainly has much to do with his struggle with Llywelyn over Caerphilly castle at this time. See J.E. Lloyd, *A History of Wales from the earliest Times to the Edwardian Conquest*, London 1912, ii, 752—4; M. Altschul, *A Baronial Family in Medieval England: the Clares, 1217—1314*, Baltimore 1965, 128—31.
52 *CR 1268—72*, 241. Munchensi, a former Montfortian, was captured at Kenilworth and his lands granted to de Valence in accordance with the Dictum of Kenilworth. Was his intended crusade service perhaps one of the terms of the redemption agreement between the two? See *CPR 1258—66*, 532, 667; *CPR 1266—72*, 32, 161, 181; *CR 1264—8*, 506—7, 512. De Munchensi may have thought again of participating, but this time with Gilbert de Clare, since he was granted a protection in February 1270 to go with the earl and Edward to consult with Louis over the crusade. See *CPR 1266—72*, 410, 412. He seems to have been in Gilbert's household since 1267. See Altschul, 113, 118.

which he had been granted 20 *l.* per annum from the issues of the manor of Minsterworth at some point prior to the crusade. In February 1271, 'because he is about to cross the sea with him', Edmund granted the manor to Robert for a three-year term, after which he was to receive his 20 *l.* as before.[53] Shortly before, in January 1271, Edmund granted to Geoffrey de Langley junior, another of his knights, the manor of Kingshaugh and the mills of Hungerford for the service of ½ knight's fee, provided that if Edmund should assign him 20 *l.* of land he should resume seisin of both. Almost certainly Geoffrey's prospective service to Edmund on crusade lay behind this enfeoffment. One month later Geoffrey took out a crusader's protection.[54]

The most significant case of all, however, concerns Thomas de Clare who contracted to serve Edward with nine knights. In 1269—70 he entered into a complex agreement with Nicholas de Sifrewast, a knight of Oxfordshire and Berkshire and former sheriff. First, by chirograph dated 11 May 1269, Nicholas enfeoffed Thomas for life with his manor of Hampstead Norris, ½ knight's fee held of him in Bensington, one knight's fee in Pebworth, and the services of William de Mackele, William de Huntercumbe, and the Abbot of Eynsham. In return, William agreed to provide Nicholas for life with land of equivalent value to Hampstead Norris, along with 10 *l.* of arable land, and a payment of 100 m. when Thomas should take seisin of the manor. It was also agreed that 'Esi durra lavantdit sire Thomas a celui sire Nicole, se il veet od lui en la Tere Sente a la primere monte ke serra ansi cum a un de ses bacheliers ke od lui irunt.'[55] Hampstead Norris formed part of Nicholas' inheritance from his father William, along with the manors of Aldworth and Purley.[56] These, too, Nicholas made over to Thomas in 1270, but this time in perpetuity, receiving Aldworth back from Thomas, with rights which he possessed in Purley, for term of life.[57] In addition, on 11 January 1270, Thomas acknowledged before the King that he was bound in 60s. per annum to Nicholas for life, to be paid every Michaelmas at the New Temple, London, and he further granted Nicholas, again for life, his lands in Cottesmore, Belaugh, Playford, Withersdale, and Weybread.[58]

Although certain features of their agreement remain obscure, it may be argued that Thomas had retained Nicholas for life, his service to include crusading with Thomas as one of his bachelors.[59] If so, then this is of

---

53 *CPR 1266—72*, 515; and see comments of J.M.W. Bean, *The Decline of English Feudalism 1215—1540*, Manchester 1968, 308—9. Robert is found frequently in Edmund's circle. See, for example, *CPR 1266—72*, 502, 515; *CR 1268—72*, 265. He was granted a crusader's protection in July 1270, and again in January 1271. See *CPR 1266—72*, 479, 588.

54 *CChR 1257—1300*, 162; *CPR 1266—72*, 588. Geoffrey was the son of a notable Angevin servant. Initially, he seems to have been attached to Robert de Ferrers, but on the earl's downfall he transferred his services to Edmund. He first appears as a witness to one of Edmund's charters in November 1268. See P.R. Coss, 'The Langley Cartulary' (Birmingham Ph.D. thesis 1971), i, 73—4. Thereafter he was closely connected with Edmund.

55 *CR 1268—72*, 143—4; *CPR 1266—72*, 474—5. Nicholas and Thomas both received a crusader's protection in July 1270. See *CPR 1266—72*, 440, 479.

56 *Book of Fees*, ii, 843, 845, 851, 857.

57 *CR 1268—72*, 249—50.

58 *CPR 1266—72*, 474. This was perhaps in accordance with his promise to provide Nicholas with land to the equivalent value of Hampstead Norris, along with 10 *l.* of arable land.

59 In 1273 and 1274 Nicholas appears as making attorneys for Thomas and acting in a suit on his behalf. See *CCR 1272—9*, 56, 125, 131. But the connection seems to have ended soon after. By

exceptional interest as a very early example of a life retainer, and the fact that the relationship seems to have been initially stimulated by the needs of Thomas as a contracting crusader lends it greater significance. Comparison with later indentures shows it to be a primitive agreement, tantalisingly vague in its terms. There is little indication of what the retainer envisaged nor, unfortunately, of the precise terms offered to Nicholas as one of Thomas' bachelors on crusade. We do not know whether Nicholas was to serve in peace and war with a stipulated number of men-at-arms, or if he was to receive bouch of court, harness and equipment, and compensation for horses lost in service. Nor do we know if he was to wear Thomas' livery, attend him at time of parliament, or support his lord in those other ways familiar to us from later indentures.[60] Nevertheless, the very existence of the relationship lends support to recent suggestions that magnate use of indentures was already well-established by the early fourteenth century, if not earlier.[61]

At the centre of the English crusade of 1270—2, then, lay a group of important lords intimately connected to the Angevin house, tied to Edward through contracts, and serving with their own squadrons of knights raised for the crusade. They were accompanied by the single largest group of crusaders, men who were in the service of Henry III, his sons, and their respective wives, either as household members or in administrative and military positions. A number of reasonably well-defined circles can be identified. One was formed of men in Edward's own household at the time of the crusade, ranging in status and position from his groom Fowin, his balister Richard de Saundon, and the chaplain Stephen de London, through an important group of clerics which included Anthony Bek, William de Blyburgh and Philip de Willoughby, to *valetti* such as John Hardel, and knights of the stature of Richard de la Rochelle, Edward's former justiciar in Ireland, and Hugh fitzOtto, probably his steward on crusade. Another group accompanied Eleanor of Castile, men such as John le Espeynol, her *valettus*, her knight and steward John de Weston, and her tailor Richard de la Garderobe. A third household group went with Edmund: knights such as Richard de Wykes, his steward, and *valetti* like Roger de Coyners. Yet others appear to have been seconded to the crusade by Henry III and Eleanor of Provence, perhaps in response to requests from Edward or the other crusade leaders, although some were probably already linked to Edward, Edmund, William de Valence, and Henry of Almain, since it seems to have been common practice to switch men from the King's immediate service to his

---

November 1275 Nicholas appears as an attorney of Roger de Clifford. See *CCR 1272—9*, 79, 256; and also *CPR 1272—81*, 163. The lands granted to him for life then reverted to Thomas. In 1276 Thomas surrendered the manors of Hampstead Norris, Aldworth, Cumpton, and Alvescote, along with rents in Cottesmore, to Robert de Mucegros in return for certain interests in Ireland. See *CFR 1272—1307*, 66; *CCh.R 1257—1300*, 198. On Robert's death in 1281 they were used for his wife's dower. See *CCR 1279—88*, 82; *CIPM*, II, 233.

60 Compare, for example, with the earliest permanent retainer thus far printed: that of Roger Bigod and John de Segrave in 1297. See N. Denholm-Young, *Seignorial Administration in England*, Oxford 1937, 167. Compare also with those of Aymer de Valence and Thomas de Berkeley, 1297, and Thomas of Lancaster and William Latimer, 1319. See *Calendar of Documents Relating to Scotland*, ed. J. Bain, Edinburgh 1881—8, ii, no. 905; J.R.S. Phillips, *Aymer de Valence, Earl of Pembroke 1307—24*, Oxford 1972, ch. 9, Appendix 2; G.A. Holmes, *Estates of the Higher Nobility in Fourteenth-Century England*, Cambridge 1957, 71, 122—3.

61 Phillips, 255; Holmes, 80; M. Prestwich, *War*, 61—2.

close kin on occasion. They included men of all ranks: knights such as Geoffrey Gacelyn, William Belet, and William le Latimer; sergeants such as William Peche and William le Marechal; the Queen's knight and steward Guy Ferre, and her *valettus* Ralph Barry; the surgeon Hugh Sauvage, and the King's merchant Henry le Waleys.[62]

If Edward's crusade was indeed an extended household operation in its essentials, then certain features of the expedition are more easily explained. It has been pointed out that the crusade was extremely costly and placed a tremendous strain upon royal finances. Resort was had to virtually every expedient open to the Crown to raise the required cash: the tax of the twentieth in 1269—70, the fifteenth of 1275, tallages of the royal demesne and the Jews, the profits of justice, regalian right to ecclesiastical vacancies, the income of wardships and escheats, and a series of loans contracted in the Holy Land.[63] If Edward was personally responsible for most of the provisioning, transport, and possibly maintenance of a very large number of those accompanying him, then the burden of expense would be his.

To help defray the cost the Church contributed with the grant of a biennial tenth in 1272.[64] Furthermore, the evidence relating to the preaching of the crusade in England reveals that the raising of monies through the redemption of vows of the *plebeia multitudo*, as Wykes puts it, was a prime objective.[65] Along with monies derived from obventions and legacies for the Holy Land these sums were then paid to Edward and other crusaders.[66] This was entirely in line with the general evolution of papal crusade policy in the thirteenth century, which had come to prefer limited crusade forces composed of well-equipped knights to the more indiscriminate recruitment of earlier times. Edward's expedition was of the type so envisaged: militarily powerful, well-organised, and supported by the monies derived from vow redemptions and other sources.

Finally, it may be suggested that Edward's experience on the crusade helped to determine some of the features of his later campaigns as King. Morris considered that Edward's reign was crucial in the development of a paid army as an alternative to the traditional feudal host, but it is now clear that he overstated his case.[67] Nevertheless, Edward's tendency to prefer cavalry forces raised through contracts and sub-contracts is quite apparent, and his initial use of the system for his crusade almost certainly recommended further

---

62 The circumstances and careers of these royal servants suggest that if their services were required they had little choice but to go on crusade. Committed to Angevin service and dependent upon the benevolence of their royal masters, if not for survival then at least for advancement, their freedom of choice was somewhat limited, especially in the lower grades.
63 See in particular, Powicke, ii, 568—9; M. Prestwich, *War*, 169—70.
64 Lunt, 230—8.
65 Wykes, in *Annales Monastici*, iv, 217—8; *Continuation* of Florence of Worcester, 552; Lunt, 446—8. The surviving episcopal registers for this period point to the same conclusion. For example, over 200 vows were redeemed in the diocese of York alone in 1274—5. See *Register of Walter Giffard*, 277—86.
66 Payn de Chaworth and Robert Tiptoft were each granted 600m. from this source by Clement IV although they were claiming by 1273 that they had received nothing. Roger de Leyburn was granted, and received, 2,000m. See *Les Registres de Grégoire X*, ed. L. Auvray, Paris 1899—1955, nos. 171, 232.
67 Morris, esp. 68. His classic view is modified in important respects by M. Prestwich, *War*, ch. iii.

experimentation on his return. He had already learned the maxim that 'Pay produces discipline, and naturally leads to a subordination of command'.[68] Further, if Tout was broadly right in saying that the Lord Edward's household became the household of Edward I, and if he was largely correct in suggesting that the armies of the King were composed essentially of 'the household in arms', then the extended household crusade was evidently of great importance in suggesting the nucleus of Edward's later campaigns.[69] The crusade, too, must have strengthened his confidence and trust in many of those who accompanied him, and brought to his attention potential commanders and administrators for the future. The significance of the crusade for so many of Edward I's servants after his return should not be overlooked. Edward's crusade, then, was not merely a relatively minor expedition to the Latin East, during which the heir to the throne marked time: it has long-term implications of some considerable importance.

68 Morris, 68.
69 T.F. Tout, *Chapters in the Administrative History of Mediaeval England*, Manchester 1937, ii, 133, 138.

THE GASCON NOBILITY AND THE ANGLO-FRENCH WAR, 1294—98

M.G.A. Vale

'Si l'on cherche à pénétrer au fond des choses, il faut des faits précis, notés par des gens d'administration'.[1] (Charles Bémont)

Bémont's words serve to remind students of war and government in the Middle Ages that they must turn to the records of administrative and financial offices in order to ascertain verifiable facts. Although chroniclers' accounts can never be disregarded, analysis and generalisation must rest ultimately upon the evidence presented by these 'gens d'administration'. The context in which Bémont declared his belief was a study of the Anglo-French war of 1294—98.[2] This conflict had not been explored in detail until his editorial work upon the Gascon Rolls led him to other classes of record preserved in the Public Record Office.[3] Since that time, there has been little attempt to reopen his discussion of the war, or to bring further evidence to bear upon its origins, course and aftermath. My purpose in this brief essay is to explore one aspect of this phase of an Anglo-French confrontation which has recently been dismissed as a minor and inconclusive[4] episode which had little effect upon the course of Anglo-French relations.[5]

Yet the alleged insignificance of the war, in political and diplomatic terms, is far outweighed by its effects upon the financial and constitutional development of both England and France. The crises of 1296—7 in both kingdoms can be directly attributed to the strains imposed by the war, compounded by the outbreak of hostilities in Flanders.[6] Edward I's government spent about £400,000 to save the duchy of Aquitaine from complete annexation by Philip IV;[7] Philip in turn incurred costs of at least 673,000 *livres tournois*;[8] the extent of Edward I's debts to the merchants of Bayonne alone totalled almost

---

1 R[ôles] G[ascons] iii, ed. C. Bémont, Paris 1906, clxxxii.
2 *RG* iii, pp. cxxiv—clxxxii.
3 For a discussion of the sources see *RG* iii, pp. cxxiv—cxxv.
4 M.W. Labarge, *Gascony: England's first colony*, London 1980, 75—6.
5 J.R. Strayer, *Philip the Fair*, Princeton 1980, 325, where the military operations of 1294—97 are summed up as 'not a bloody war, no major battles and relatively few skirmishes' (p. 319).
6 Strayer 319—20, 325—6; cf. F.M. Powicke, *The Thirteenth Century* 2nd edn. Oxford 1954, 644—50; also *Documents [illustrating the crisis] of 1297—98 [in England]*, ed. Michael Prestwich, Camden Soc., 4th ser., xxiv, London 1980, 3—4, 25—37.
7 Michael Prestwich, *War, Politics and Finance under Edward I*, London 1972, 172. See the itemised totals from the account of John de Sandale and Thomas of Cambridge, king's clerks, enrolled on the Pipe Roll for 8 Edward II (PRO E.372/160, m.41 r—v) and *RG*, iii, pp. clxvii—clxix. These were estimated at £359,288 0s. 5d. Total receipts were £300,148 19s 1½d.
8 Strayer, 165—66; and J.R. Strayer, 'The Costs and Profits of War' in *The Medieval City*, ed. H. Miskimin *et al.*, New Haven 1977, 269—91.

£51,700;[9] and the so-called 'constitutional' crises which accompanied the conflict furthered the development of national taxation in France and representative government in England. Seen in this light, the skirmishes and sieges of 1294—98 assume a crucial, if indirect, importance. The war certainly absorbed English manpower and money to provide expeditionary forces for the defence of the duchy,[10] but Gascon troops accounted for the greater part of Edward I's expenditure on soldiers' wages and the *restaur* of horses lost during the conflict.[11] The defence of the duchy was therefore largely undertaken by its own inhabitants;[11a] much has rightly been made of the loans and advances offered by the citizens of Bayonne. But the rôle of the Gascon nobility — who provided the fighting forces which held back the French — in the retention of Edward's inheritance against a predatory Capetian régime has not been properly examined. Many of them preserved their allegiance to a tottering English administration, undermined by debts, so that the French were effectively prevented from over-running the whole of the duchy. The reasons for this demonstration of loyalty are the main concern of this essay.

One reason was put forward by a contemporay observer. Pope Boniface VIII, experienced as none other in dealing with the French, told Pierre Flote and other French envoys in 1298 that:

> 'les Gascoigns ne voudroient mie estre du tut sanz meen [seig]nurie le Roi Dengleterre [soutz] la sovereinete du Roi de France. Ben poet estre par aventure qe ascunes persones le voudraient par ascune singulere afeccioun, mais je vous parle du [co]mun. Car tele est la manere de soutzmes qi voillent einsi avoir plusors seignurs qil ne puissent mie moult estre greveez par un.'[12]

Boniface's view that the majority of the duchy's inhabitants would not tolerate the direct rule of a sovereign crown of France without an intermediate lord had much to commend it. A multiplicity of obligations to many lords made tenurial conditions in the South-West very complex, and the nobility of the region were renowned for their independence.[13] Some were clearly ungovernable by any superior power — the counts of Foix-Béarn led the way along which others followed.[14] Professor Jean Favier has recently commented that 'unir le duché [d'Aquitaine] au domaine royal eût sans doute procuré des

---

9 Prestwich, *War* 213.
10 Prestwich, *War* 171.
11 *RG* iii, pp. clxviii—clxix; E.372/160, m.41ʳ. The wages bill for Gascon knights, men-at-arms and foot serjeants exceeded that for English troops by over £100,000.
11a cf. Strayer, *Philip the Fair* 325: Aquitaine was 'not particularly wealthy and not very conscious of its identity; it could not defend itself through its own resources.' This statement is hardly borne out by the sums raised by Bayonne and other towns.
12 Printed from PRO, Diplomatic Documents, Chancery, P.63 by J.G. Black, 'Edward I and Gascony in 1300', *EHR* xvii, 1902, 523. It was on this occasion that Boniface made his famous remark that 'he who has dealings with the French has dealings with the devil'.
13 See Powicke 296—7; P. Wolff 'The Armagnacs of Southern France (14th—15th centuries)', *BIHR* xx, 1945, 186—91, esp. 187.
14 See Devic and Vaissette, *Histoire générale de Languedoc*, ix, Toulouse 1885, 193—5, 205; x, cc. 265—91, 328—34, 335—8, 340—43; J. Gardelles, *Les Châteaux du Moyen Age dans la France du Sud-Ouest (1216—1327)*, Geneva—Paris 1972, 32—3, 44—5, 80, for the extent to which this tendency was reflected in the proliferation of castles.

Key to Map   *Gascon lordships in English allegiance*
June-July 1294

Compiled from:
(1) Letters of Edward I to the *magnatibus* of Gascony, dated at Portsmouth, 29 June 1294 (*RG*, iii, nos 3374-5, 3382-94).
(2) Letter of Edward I to Amanieu VII, lord of Albret, dated 19 Oct. 1295 (*RG*, iii, nos. 4056-7).
(3) Letter of Edward I to certain Gascon nobles in French allegiance, 19 Oct. 1295 (*RG*, iii, nos 4059-60).

Bordelais and Bazadais:
1. Arnaud de Blanquefort
2. Olivier de Lignan
2a. Ebles (*Ebulus*) de Lignan
3. Eymeric de Bourg
4. Lord of Marestanh
4a. Bernard Amanieu d'Arrameste
5. Géraud de St-Genès
6. Raymond de Cantemerle
7. Pierre de Lamote of Ludon
8. Gaillard d'Agassac
9. Pierre-Guillaume de Mateplane
10. Pierre d'Arsac
11. Bernard de Blanquefort
12. Arnaud d'Espagne
13. Géraud de Lamote of Latresne
14. Lord of Blaye
15. Lord of Rions
16. Bertrand de Podensac
17. Bernard d'Escoussans
18. Amaubin (Amalbinus) de Ambarès
19. Raymond de Bouglon, captau of Latresne
20. Guillaume Fort d'Ornon
21. Gaillard de Lalande
22. Bertrand de Noaillan
23. Lord of Bénauges
24. Arnaud-Garsie de Got
25. Pierre de Montpezat
26. Bertrand de Caumont
27. Pierre de (Les) Cazes
28. Guillaume-Raymond de Gensac
29. Alexandre de la Pebrée, lord of Bergerac and Gensac
30. Pierre de Gavarret, co-seigneur of Langon
31. Gaillard de Lamotte, lord of Castelnau and Landiras
32. Amanieu de Lamotte
33. Guillaume-Sanche de Pommiers
34. Arnaud, lord of Gironde, knight
35. Anessant de Caumont
36. Gerard de Lamotte
37. Bertrand de Mesmes (= Castelnau-de-Mesmes?)
38. Pierre de Pompéjac, knight
39. Raymond-Guillaume de Sauviac, knight
40. Gaillard de Fargues, lord of Arbanats

Landes and 'curia Sancti Severi':
41. Roger-Bernard, count of Foix and *vicomte* of Béarn
42. *Vicomte* of Tartas
43. Augier de Mauléon
44. Fortaner, lord of Lescun
45. Assieu de Navailles, knight
46. Otton de Doazit, knight
47. Raymond-Bernard de Castelnau
48. Sansaner de Poudeux
49. Arnaud de Marsan
50. Arnaud de Monein
51. Aspanus d'Arance (?Araux)
52. Seguin, lord of Estang
53. *Vicomte* of Orte
54. Arnaud d'Estibeaux
55. Gaillard de Tilh
56. *Vicomte* of Furens (= Hours?)
57. Arnaud-Guillaume de Pulibalt (Poyloaut)
58. Lord of Montaulieu
59. Tenton, lord of Carcarès-Ste-Croix
60. Guillaume de Soa
61. Sanche-Loup de Castandet
62. Fravanet de Campet-et-Lamolère
63. Arnaud-Guillaume de Mauvezin
64. Lord of Domezain
65. Sanche-Arnaud de Mauléon
66. Guillaume-Arnaud de Morlanne
66a. Garsie Arnaud, lord of Navailles and Sault

Agenais:
67. Amanieu du Fossat
68. Gautier du Fossat
69. Rainfroi de Montpezat, co-seigneur of Aiguillon
70. Amanieu, lord of Cancon
71. Arnaud de Marmande, lord of Taillecavat
72. Etienne Ferréol, lord of Tonneins
73. Hugues de Pujols
74. Grimoard de Valence
75. Otto de Cazenove
76. Rudel de Seyches
77. Guillaume-Raymond de Lort(?) (Lorcat), co-seigneur of Tonneins
78. Arnaud-Garsie du Fossat
79. Otto de Lomagne
80. Bertrand de L'Isle
81. Assivus d'Agualayt
82. Barthelémy de Pins
83. Augier de Podio Bardaco
84. Raymond-Bernard de Goulens
85. Rainfroi de Durfort
86. Lord of Podenas
87. Gaston de Gontand
88. Vital de Gontaud

Béarn(?)
89. Bets de Cazenove
90. Constance, *vicomtesse* of Marsan
91. Marguerite, *comtesse* of Foix and *vicomtesse* of Béarn
92. Arnaud-Guillaume, count of Andoins
93. Otto de Sadirac
94. Raymond-Arnaud de Dauns (= Diusse?)
95. Arnaud d'Engyne, lord of Jasses
96. Raymonde-Arnaud, lord of Gerderest
97. Arnaud-Guillaume de Mauléon
98. Assivus de Castetpugon
99. Gaillard de Castetpugon
100. Raymond de Morlanne
101. Raymond-Garsie, lord of Coarraze
102. Knights *et al.* of Labourt
103. Knights *et al.* of Mauléon
104. Bertram de Montlieu
105. Geoffroi de Mortagne
106. Elie de Chalais
107. Aimar d'Archiac, knight
108. Robert de Matha
109. Bernard de Beauville, lord of Limeuil
110. Gaston de Gontaud, lord of Badefols
111. Amanieu VII, lord of Albret
112. Bernard VI, count of Armagnac

Note: Nos. 4a, 81, 83 and 89 have not yet been identified, and therefore do not appear on the map.

+ Lordship in English allegiance 1294 (June-July)

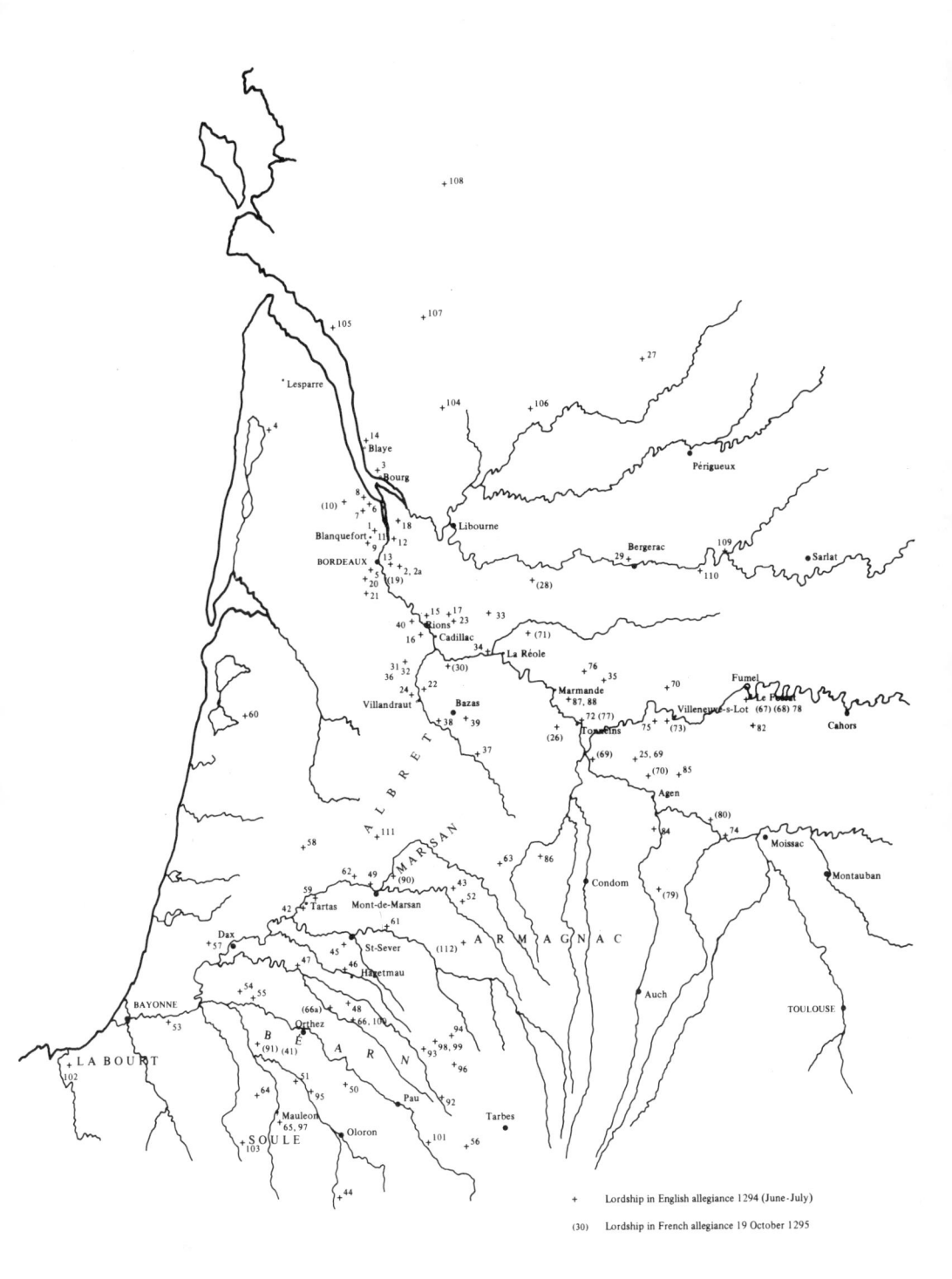

(30) Lordship in French allegiance 19 October 1295

vassaux aussi dificiles à gouverner pour le Capétien qu'ils l'avaient été pour le Plantagenet'.[15] Both sides in the Anglo-French conflict of 1294—7 were to a considerable extent dependent upon the degree of regional support they could command, attract or buy within the duchy or on its frontiers. The means whereby such loyalty was secured and sustained deserves further examination.

On 29 June 1294, Edward I addressed a circular letter to the magnates of Gascony.[16] He called upon their loyalty in the recovery and defence of his duchy, snatched from him by the malicious behaviour of the French.[17] These Gascons were reminded that their ancestors had served the English king-dukes of Aquitaine and their own services were now required. A list of about 100 nobles, not including the 'militibus et aliis gentibus' of Labourd and Mauléon, or potential allies on the frontiers, was drawn up.[18] These were Edward's 'men', bound by their homage and fealty to serve him against Philip IV.[19] Edward saw the recovery and defence of Aquitaine as a matter concerning his personal honour: Walter of Guisborough reported that he told the Parliament of 1294 that 'si majorem non haberet sequelam, cum uno puero et uno equo jus suum prosequi velle usque ad mortem'.[20] On 16 October 1297, he wrote of his debts to the men of Bayonne as the most pressing call upon his revenues, telling the treasurer and barons of the exchequer that:

> 'nous voloms totes voies qe vous eez tieu regard as busoignes de Gascoigne, qe nos gentz qui la sount seient sauvez et aidez en ce qe homme peut en bonne maniere . . . Car en ceste busoigne gist nostre honneur ou nostre deshonour e de toutz ceaux qui nous aiment e nomement de ceaux qui de nos busoignes se entremettent en les parties ou vous estes . . .'[21]

Edward's determination to uphold his just rights in Aquitaine inevitably led him into heavy expenditure. By 19 October 1295, the effects of the French occupation and its associated bribery and coercion had led to the defection of a minority of Gascon nobles (at least 20) from the English cause.[22] They were concentrated in the Agenais (see map) and were reminded of their former loyalty by Edward when, he wrote, they had revered him 'as a natural lord'.[23] To retain a hold upon the allegiance of Gascon vassals tempted by French pensions and grants, however, or conquered by force of French arms, necessitated

15 J. Favier, *Philippe le Bel*, Paris 1980, 233.
16 *RG* iii, nos. 3374, 3382—3. A further letter to loyal Gascons was dated 19 Oct. 1295 (*RG* iii, nos. 4056—7).
17 *RG* iii, no. 3374: 'idem rex [Francie] de . . . terra nostra Vasconie nos maliciose decepit'.
18 *RG* iii, nos. 3382—3 (pp. 231—36).
19 See map and the accompanying list. Many of them (or their forbears) had acknowledged their obligations to Edward I in the tenurial enquiry of 1274—5. See *Recogniciones Feodorum in Aquitania*, ed. C. Bémont, Paris 1914, *passim*.
20 *The Chronicle of Walter of Guisborough*, ed. H. Rothwell, Camden 3rd ser. lxxxix, London 1957, 243.
21 *Documents . . . of 1297—98*, 163. The letter was written at Ghent, under the privy seal.
22 *RG* iii, nos. 4059—60. The recipients included the counts of both Foix and Armagnac, the *vicomtesse* of Marsan and the lords of Caumont, Montpezat and l'Isle-Jourdain. A draft of the letter (PRO, S.C.1/13, no. 23) is headed: 'Baronibus de Agenesio et aliis de Vascon.' qui stant cum Rege Francie'.
23 *RG* iii, no. 4059. The letter is couched through in terms of an appeal to the recipient's honour.

more than a display of moral exhortation. In a petition heard at Plympton after Easter 1297, the Béarnais Arnaud de Gabaston (the father of Edward II's favourite) told the king that if he were able to persuade any of his relations or friends to return to Edward's service, they should be provided for 'juxta decenciam personarum et sicut moris est aliis providere'.[24] Edward replied on 6 May that they were to be paid wages and rewards according to their status.[25] The material incentives offered to these nobles can be discussed under six main headings: wages for military service; *restaur* of horses lost during that service; pensions and fees; prests for military equipment; plunder, booty, and compensation for the loss of lands, lordships and goods. These concrete and tangible means of securing allegiance must be seen against such issues as the structure of noble families, the geographical position of their lands, and their traditional relationship to the English administration.

Walter of Guisborough gives the impression that paid military service by members of the Gascon nobility began with the arrival of an English expeditionary force under John of Brittany and John St. John in October 1294.[26] This was not the case. Since the winter of 1293, payments for garrison and other duties had been made to a number of nobles of the Agenais, Gers and Soule for military service 'cum equis et armis' at Bonnegarde, Puyguilhem, Castelnau-de-Rivière, Mauléon and Lectoure.[27] The duchy had therefore been put on a war footing well before its confiscation for default by Philip IV on 19 May 1294.[28] Indeed, the exchequer accounts for wartime expenses ran from Michaelmas 1293 until 24th March 1298.[29] From December 1294 onwards, further prests and advances of wages were made to Gascon nobles and their retinues for war service.[30] The earliest of these reflected both the geographical origins of those loyal to Edward I and the balance of forces within the duchy. With the exception of the Anglo-Gascon strongpoints at Blaye, Bourg and Rions, the basis of the English administration had shifted southwards after the seizure of Bordeaux and its hinterland by the French.[31] Bayonne was a centre of pro-English sentiment, crucial to the régime's survival, but it was not the only point on the Pyrenean frontier and in the southern part of the duchy which held out. At St. Sever, Hagetmau and Roquefort-de-Marsan the nobility of the ancient duchy of Gascony mustered and contracted with the English administration.[32] They came to Bayonne to join John St. John's force

---

24 *RG* iii, p. clxxxiv. Gabaston had been a hostage at the court of France for almost three years (Feb. 1294—?Jan. 1297).
25 *RG* iii, no. 4476, where Henry de Lacy, earl of Lincoln was instructed to receive them 'benigne'.
26 Guisborough 245: 'remanseruntque in eodem loco [Rions] ut populum terre sibi attraherent dominus Johannes de Britannia et dominus Willelmus Latimer.'
27 PRO, E.101/152/6. nos. 1—4, 8 (Mar. 1294) and E.372/160, m. 41^r for payments to certain Gascon nobles 'ante guerram predictam'. See also E.101/208/1A, no. 8, 1B, nos. 1, 8.
28 See P. Chaplais, 'Le duché-pairie de Guyenne: l'hommage et les services féodaux de 1259—1303', *Annales du Midi* lxix, 1957, 24; *RG* iii, pp. cxxviii—cxxix.
29 PRO, E.372/160, m.41^r; Powicke 650.
30 E.101/152/8, nos. 50—53, 55—69; 152/14/3, all dating from 1—29 Dec. 1294.
31 *RG* iii, cxlvii. Bayonne was described by Guisborough (p. 245) as 'civitas fortissima et quasi inexpugnabilis'.
32 E.101/152/8, nos. 50—53, 55—69. They included Devot de Peyre, Arnaud de Campet of Brassenx, Gaillard de Morlanne, Sanche-Loup de Poyloaut, Arnaud-Guillaume de Mauvezin, and Guillaume de Soa, *domicelli*; Arnaud-Guillaume de Marsan, Augier de Douzon and Raymond-

because, Guisborough tells us, he had treated the Gascons well during his previous service as king's lieutenant there.[33] At least 18 nobles from the Landes, Chalosse, Marsan, Béarn, Sault and Labourd mustered at Hagetmau and Roquefort in December 1294.[34] The support of the house of Albret for Edward I was reflected by the appearance of Guillaume de Garland, knight, at the Albret stronghold of Labrit to receive a prest to prepare himself for war.[35] Amanieu VII d'Albret was a household knight of Edward who, with his retinue, was to serve the king in Scotland as well as in Gascony.[36]

Between March 1297 and March 1298, when Bayonne had been the effective centre of the English war effort for almost three years, no fewer than 90 Gascon nobles received prests, wages and *restaur* of horses from the king's clerks responsible for war finance there.[37] Many of these were simply promises to pay, but to pay only at the Westminster exchequer.[38] There is plentiful evidence for reimbursement in England, both to the creditor in person and to his representatives. Gascon nobles were not unfamiliar figures at the doors of the exchequer, and some who served Edward in his Scots campaigns thus had additional incentives to advance the king's cause in that kingdom.[39] Guillaume-Arnaud and Arnaud-Bernard de La Dos, Guillaume-Arnaud de Sault, Arnaud de Meurin, knight, Arnaud-Guillaume de Mauvezin, Fortaner de Lescun, Arnaud de Caupenne, knight, Vital de Poudenx and Arnaud de Castetpugon appeared personally at York and Westminster to receive what was due to them and to other nobles.[40] In June 1302 a cart laden with £1,000

Arnaud de Lobier, knights. For the notion of a separate, allodial duchy of Gascony see P. Chaplais, 'Le traité de Paris de 1259 et l'inféodation de la Gascogne allodiale', *Le Moyen Age*, 1955, 121—37.

33 Guisborough 245. For his previous service in Gascony see J.P. Trabut-Cussac, *L'Administration Anglaise en Gascogne sous Henry III et Edward I de 1254 à 1307*, Paris—Geneva 1972, 107—8, 371 (12 July 1293—1 July 1294).

34 E.101/152/8, nos. 50—53, 55—69. They were to serve with a total of 54 men-at-arms, not including themselves.

35 E.101/152/8, no. 69 (1 Dec. 1294). He was compensated for his dispossession by the French with a grant of 200 l. *chipotenses* in Aug. 1299 (*RG* iii, no. 4529 [175]).

36 He was mentioned in the heraldic poem on the *Siege of Caerlaverock (1300): The Roll of Arms of the princes, barons and knights who attended King Edward I to the siege of Caerlaverock, in 1300*, ed. T. Wright, London 1864, 11.

37 E.101/152/8, nos. 5—12, 16; 152/9, nos. 25, 34; 153/1, nos. 11, 23; 153/2, no. 2; 153/4, no. 18; 153/7 nos. 17, 18; 154/11, nos. 1, 2, 5—31; 154/12, nos. 2, 5, 7, 9—28, 32—40; 154/15, nos. 1, 2, 5, 7—11, 18, 20—29, 32, 37, 38, 40, 41. These are sealed quittances; receipts and recognisances of debt.

38 See e.g. E101/154/11, no. 1 for a recognisance of £200 debt by Henry de Lacy, earl of Lincoln, to Gaillard de St. Martin, esquire, 'por gages e restor de chevaux de lui et de sa compaignie du tens que il est demorez en vostre [Edward I's] service ... et nous lui avons promis en bone foi que il serra paiez en Engleterre a vostre eschequier' (at Bayonne, 3 April 1297).

39 For a list of Gascons 'volentes ire in excercitu Scocie' see E.101/14/10, m.2ᵛ. Among them were Amanieu de Marmande, esquire, Elie Scarlet, esquire, Arnaud de Gabaston, knight, the lord of Castillon, Arnaud d'Eyquem, knight, Odo de La Dos and Vital de Seguin, esquires. The latter was owed £87 11s. 1d. in wages for service in Gascony (E.101/155/15, no. 1,—12 Nov. 1299). Elie Scarlet was owed £38 18s. 5d. (E.101/155/15, no. 7,—1 Dec. 1299).

40 See E.101/153/1, no. 11 (Guillaume-Arnaud de Sault); 154/11, no. 16 (Arnaud Bernard de La Dos, at London); 17 (Arnaud de Meurin, at London); 18 (Arnaud-Guillaume de Mauvezin, at York); 23 (Fortaner de Lescun, acting for Sansaner de Poudenx, esquire, at London); 24, 25 (Arnaud de Caupenne, at York and London); 154/12, no. 19 (Arnaud de Meurin, acting for Bernard de Sensiard, knight, at Westminster); 24 (Vital de Poudenx, at York and London); 35 (Arnaud de Castetpugon at York, Westminster and London).

was brought from York to Westminster in order to pay Amanieu d'Albret and many other Gascon creditors still not fully satisfied of their wages.[41] Finally, Edward's government took the normal escape route of an embarrassed crown and assigned all outstanding debts to Gascons upon the revenues of the duchy.[42]

If payment of wages was generally partial, fitful and dilatory, there must have been other factors which bound so many Gascon nobles to the service of Edward I.[43] Many of them had lost all their lands and goods as a result of the French occupation of the duchy. In August 1299, Edward was to set about the arduous task of compensating them until their possessions were restored, and granted them sums ranging from 40s. to 1,500 *livres chipotenses* drawn on confiscated alien property in England.[44] Some enjoyed the additional income of a fee or pension as members of the king-duke's household. In June 1286, there were 40 Gascons in the household, including 4 knights banneret, 3 knights bachelor, and 21 king's esquires.[45] Some of them, such as Arnaud and Elie de Caupenne, Auger Mote, Pierre de Campagne, Eble de Puyguilhem, Amanieu d'Albret and Bertrand de Podensac were to demonstrate conspicuous loyalty to Edward's cause against Philip IV and his officers between 1293 and 1298.[46] Bertrand de Podensac, king's esquire, was captured by the French early in the war and thereby lost his lordship at Podensac.[47] As he lay dying at Bayonne on 15th May 1296, he ordered his executors to build a burial church at a distance of just over a crossbow's shot from the castle at Podensac. As this could not be done until 'our lord the king of England has recovered the

---

41 E.101/155/15, no. 2. (11 June 1302). Albret was owed £689 19s 7d for himself and his company during the truce of 1298—99 (1 Dec. 1299).

42 Most of the unpaid residue of debts in E.101/154/11, 12 and 15 was assigned on Gascon revenues. The total sum to be paid by the constable of Bordeaux was £13,522 4s. 1d. because only £2,903 11s. 9d. had actually been paid out to these creditors by 24 Mar. 1298 (E.101/154/15, no. 43).

43 See P. Capra, 'Les bases sociales du pouvoir anglo-gascon au milieu du xive siècle', *Le Moyen Age* lxxxi, 1975, 273—99, 447—73, esp. 292—99 for a similar conclusion based upon later evidence. A list of principal supporters of the English régime in the mid-fourteenth century (pp. 294—5) contains the names of many families loyal to Edward I between 1294 and 1298. See also N. de Peña, 'Vassaux Gascons au service du roi d'Angleterre dans la première moitié du xive siècle: fidelité ou ésprit de profit?', *Annales du Midi* lxxxviii, 1976, 5—21 for a study of the Durfort family which concludes that 'il conviendrait donc de chercher ailleurs que dans les avantages pécuniaires et le bon ordre administratif les raisons de l'attachement gascon au duc-roi' (p. 21).

44 *RG* iii, nos. 4528—31 (25 Aug. 1299). The grants were based on a valuation of their lands and tenements in C.47/27/6,7 headed 'Hec sunt nomina Vasconum de paragio et aliorum qui amiserunt terras suas in Vasconia pro Rege' (m. 1^r). Also S.C. 1/48, no. 173 for compensation for disinheritance in the Landes.

45 Trabut-Cussac 79, n. 21, citing E.101/351/25 and 26 (2 June 1286).

46 Arnaud de Caupenne served with 10 men-at-arms in 1297—98 (E.101/152/8, no. 5; 154/11, nos. 24, 25) and was appointed seneschal of Périgord-Quercy by Henry de Lacy and Odo de Grandson in Oct. 1303 (Trabut-Cussac 382). His brother Elie was a prisoner in French hands in Dec. 1294 (E.101/152/4, no. 3), and received 300 *l. ch.* as compensation for his lost lands in Aug. 1299 (*RG* iii, no. 4529 [192]). For an objection to a grant of high justice to him, raised by neighbouring nobles, see *RG* iii, no. 4744 (30 Mar. 1305). The letters patent reserving jurisdiction over the disputed places to the court of St. Sever had allegedly been destroyed by fire 'in guerra proximo preterita'. For Auger Mote, Eble de Puyguilhem, and Bertrand de Podensac see below nn. 51—54, 47, 48, 86, 87. For Amanieu d'Albret, above nn. 36, 41.

47 See *Le Trésor des Chartes d'Albret*, ed. B. Marquette, Paris 1973, no. 49 (? Sept. 1295), 50 (letter dated at Péronne, ? Sept. 1295).

duchy of Guyenne' his body was to be buried meanwhile in the Franciscan house at Bayonne.[48] His loyalty to Edward was unwavering. The supposed 'changeability of Gascon nobles' clearly did not operate in his case, nor, as we shall see, did it in others.[49]

From an early stage in the events which led to the Anglo-French war, members of the local nobility had displayed a distinctly unenthusiastic attitude towards Philip IV and his officers. In the winter of 1293, when the French seneschal of Périgord, advised by Pierre Flote, was taking copies of Philip's citation of Edward I before the Parlement of Paris to the major towns of the duchy, this attitude was clearly demonstrated.[50] At St. Emilion, on 12th December 1293, Eble de Puyguilhem, who was captain of the place, not only refused to accept a copy of the offensive document but, according to the seneschal's report, gathered a force of foot serjeants armed with crossbows, shields and lances just inside the main gate.[51] The seneschal feared violence and was forced to proclaim the summons outside the town. A notary, who had been ordered to fix a copy to the gate, was prevented from doing so by Eble's armed men.[52] There could be little doubt of the views of Eble de Puyguilhem. He was paid wages and *restaur* for military service at Bayonne on 18th March 1298,[53] and received 150 *l. ch.* as compensation for his dispossession by the French on 25 August 1299.[54] Men such as Eble de Puyguilhem and Bertrand de Podensac were as dependent upon Edward I's position as duke of Aquitaine as he was dependent on them. They were bound together by mutual self-interest.

A further material incentive offered to a prolific and often impoverished nobility by Edward's war was the lure of plunder and booty. A well-established tradition of private war in South-West France had accustomed noble families to seek profit in *cavalcante* or raids against their neighbours and their ancestral enemies.[55] The greatest of these private quarrels was the feud between the houses of Foix and Armagnac,[56] but there were constant eruptions of feuding among the Albret, Caumont and L'Isle-Jourdain, to name only the

---

48 *Le Trésor* i, no. 52, pp. 79—81. The church was to be built 'sus lo caming, en loc que de quere gleisa ne pusqua portar la balesta lo quairot entroce au castet' (pp. 79—80). He appointed Amanieu d'Albret as guardian of his heiress until she was 14 years old.
49 See M.W. Labarge, *Gascony*, 18.
50 See *Foedera* I, ii, London 1816, 793 for the citation; also *Olim* ii, ed. A Beugnot, Paris 1839, 5—8.
51 *Olim* ii, 21; also pp. 16—18. Also see *Actes du Parlement de Paris*, ed. E. Boutaric, i, 1254—99, Paris 1863, nos. 2858—9 (10 and 20 Dec. 1293).
52 *Olim* ii, 18. The seneschal, Jean d'Arabloy, had proceeded throughout the operation 'juxta consilium . . . domini P. Flote' (p. 21). For Flote's alleged views on the status of Aquitaine see Black, 523 and above n. 12.
53 E.101/154/12, no. 37. He was owed £177 18s. 9d. He was a member of Edward I's household (Trabut-Cussac 79, n. 211).
54 *RG* iii, nos. 4529 [66], 4923 [162] (6 Apr. 1305); 4934 [60] (4 Apr. 1305); 4970 (6 Apr. 1305, for wages and *restaur* of himself and his retinue 'de tempore quo steterunt in obsequio regis tempore guerre' — £110 13s. 1d.).
55 See, for example, the will of Géraud de Casaubon, knight (made in Feb. 1295), for 'quadam cavalcata quam fecit . . . in qua cavalcata depredavi plura animalia bovina.' (Archives Municipales de Bordeaux, MS 207, no. 15). He had participated in seven such raids.
56 Wolff 187—88; C. Samaran, *La maison d'Armagnac au xve siècle*, Paris 1908, 325—6; *Documents pontificaux sur la Gascogne . . . Pontificat de Jean XXII* (1316—34), ed. L. Guérard, Paris—Auch 1896, lxviii, lxxi—lxxii.

most significant.[57] A declaration of war by the king of France against his contumacious vassal, the duke of Aquitaine, broadened the horizons of a nobility in search of income with which to offset declining rents and high costs.[58] For the nobility of English Gascony, raids into territory occupied by the French were legitimised by the conflict, and attacks upon those who claimed to support Philip IV's cause given additional justification. Guisborough reports that a major activity of the Anglo-Gascon forces quartered at Bayonne during 1296—7 was the mounting of plundering raids into the Toulousain.[59] They returned to Bayonne at the outset of winter in 1296 'cum preda magna'. In the autumn of 1297 they raised the siege of 'Ste Kiterni' (? Ste-Quitterie) and returned laden with booty.[60] For both English and Gascons these raids must have compensated at least in part for the non-payment of their wages. The techniques of raiding and plundering applied during the Hundred Years War were not new, and the Gascon war of Edward I might be taken as one of the origins of the English *chevauchée*.

However, there were sources of plunder for Gascon nobles nearer home. In the spring of 1296, an expeditionary force under Edmund, earl of Lancaster and Henry de Lacy, earl of Lincoln, recovered Langon and St. Macaire from the French.[61] The army, which included many Gascons who had joined it at Bourg and Blaye, failed to take Bordeaux but entered the town of St. Macaire in April 1296.[62] Their arrival in the town was marked by pillage and the seizure of victuals. The inhabitants later petitioned that Pierre-Amanieu, captal de Buch, had taken wine, oats, hay and corn; Eble de Puyguilhem and his retinue had seized a consignment of bread; while an unfortunate burgess named Gaillard Ayquem listed the extent of damage to his property in detail.[63] One

57 See Trabut-Cussac 127—8; *RG* iii, pp. clxxvii, cxcv; *Recog. Feodorum*, 202—4, war between the lords of Beaumont and Caumont (May 1270). For the l'Isle-Jourdain see A[rchives Départementales de] T[arn et-]G[aronne], *Inventaire Sommaire*, ed. A Maisonobe and C. Samaran, Montauban 1910, A.297, fos. 587—92, 931.
58 For the penury of nobles in this region see M.G.A. Vale, 'Warfare and the life of the nobility in France and the Burgundian lands', *Adelige Sachkultur des Spätmittelalters*, Vienna 1982, 175—6, especially the valuations of war-horses in Table II.
59 Guisborough 262: 'exierunt quidam ex nostris versus partes Tholosanas et multas villas et urbes incendio concremarunt, reversique sunt contra hyemem cum preda magna.'
60 Guisborough 264: 'in sequenti estate moverunt se versus partes Tholosanas incendentes urbes et villas quas poterant et sevientes igne et gladio perimentes . . . Removeruntque obsidionem sancti Kiterni quam Tholosenses fecerant et reversi sunt cum preda magna usque Bayan.' Exemptions from certain war taxes were granted by Philip IV's officers to some inhabitants of Languedoc 'multipliciter et intolerabiliter fore gravatos occasione ipsius guerre' (8 Oct. 1297). The men of Ste Quitterie (Le-Mas-d'Aire, dép. Gers) were said to be 'en mult povre estat' in Apr. 1297 (E.101/152/9, no. 39), although one inhabitant was able to lend £7 7s. 7d. to Henry de Lacy on 23 Mar. (154/15, no. 15).
61 Guisborough 261. Bordeaux could not be taken from the French in 1296 because, according to Guisborough, the Anglo-Gascon force lacked siege engines and equipment. This defect had been remedied by 1297. See E.101/154/15, nos. 23, 42 for payments to Master Thomas de la Réole 'fossator' and Master Bernard 'carpentarius bridarum' (23 Mar. 1298). Also the references to siege engines (including 'belfries') in E.372/160, m. 41^r.
62 Guisborough 261: 'et congregati sunt ad eius Wasconienses multi et ceteri naciones' to an estimated number of 2,000 men; *RG* iii, pp. clii—cliii.
63 C.47/25/1, no. 19: petition of the inhabitants of St. Macaire to Thomas of Cambridge, king's clerk, as Edward I's commissioner, for compensation of damages suffered by them 'per gentes Regis'. The will of Pierre-Amanieu, captal de Buch, contains a clause in which he ordered his executors to make amends for all damages and excesses committed by him during the war (A[rchives Départementales des] P[yrénées —], A[tlantiques], E.20, no. 6: 19 May 1300).

Pierre d'Espagne of Bazas, in the retinue of Pons de Castillon, broke four coffers in Gaillard's house, from which he extracted 22s. st; 6 feather pillows worth 60s. *bordelais*, 8 sheets worth 4 *l. bord*; 2 cloaks worth 4 *l. bord*; and many bedcovers and hangings worth 100s. *bord*. Guillaume-Seguin, lord of Rions, had removed a quantity of grain from his storehouse, and his servant (*nuncius*) had been set upon, stripped of his shirt, and held prisoner for 3 or 4 days.[64] At the time, Gaillard Ayquem was a hostage in the hands of the French at Agen. Episodes such as this cannot have been exceptional in the disturbed conditions of wartime, and there were many among the fighting nobles of Gascony who turned the disruption of war to their advantage.[65]

War between sovereigns, however, was an aberration in this area of warring families, eager to prosecute quarrels theoretically put into abeyance by the greater conflict. During the Anglo-French conflict, for instance, private wars were prohibited by Philip IV. With the onset of a period of truce in 1297, the ban was thought to be in abeyance and Roger-Bernard, count of Foix, immediately attacked Bernard, count of Armagnac.[66] On 12th January 1298, an alliance between Roger-Bernard and his son, on the one side, and Bernard-Jourdain de l'Isle and his son, on the other, was concluded.[67] Bernard-Jourdain was to lend aid to Foix against Armagnac with arms and counsel, and promised not to make peace without the count's express licence. L'Isle-Jourdain had already lent Foix 700 *l.t.*[68] It is striking that in Charles of Valois' and Raoul de Nesle's appointment of the count of Foix as 'rector, gubernator ac . . . preceptor' in Aquitaine for the French (29 July 1295), the lands of Armagnac and Fezensac were excluded from his jurisdiction.[69] The military force which he was to raise on the king's behalf was not to be directed into war against his traditional enemy. Philip IV was in fact as powerless as Edward I in his attempts to win Roger-Bernard's effective and lasting aid.[70] Edward had tried in 1293—4 to enlist the rival support of Bernard, count of Armagnac. John of Havering, Edward's seneschal, ordered a payment of 200 *l. bord* without delay on 11th January 1294 to Odo de Casenave, knight, as Armagnac's proctor.[71] The urgency of the transaction was emphasised by Havering's order to Robert de Lesseth, constable of Bordeaux, to release the

---

64 C.47/25/1, no. 19.
65 For usurpations of authority and other excesses committed during the war by nobles see *Gascon Register A. Series of 1318—19*, ed. G.P. Cuttino, Oxford 1975, i, 262—3, 256, 251, 247.
66 Devic and Vaissette ix, 203—4; cf. ATG, A. 297, fos. 931^r—932^v for letters of Robert, count of Artois, Philip IV's lieutenant in Gascony and Aquitaine, at Dax, signifying the king's ordinance forbidding private war to the counts of Comminges, Armagnac, Foix and l'Isle-Jourdain (15 May 1297). The problems of enforcing such edicts are discussed in R. Cazelles, 'La réglementation royale de la guerre privée de St. Louis à Charles V et la précarité des ordonnances', *Revue historique de droit français et étranger* xxxviii, 1960, 530—48, esp. 539—48.
67 ATG, A. 297, fos. 223^v—224^v; Devic and Vaissette ix, 204.
68 ATG, A. 297, fo. 222^{r-v} (10 Jan. 1298).
69 Devic and Vaissette x, cc. 334—35. Roger-Bernard had served in person in the French army in Gascony in 1295 (x, cc. 289—91) and received extensive powers and payments from Raoul de Nesle. Foix claimed that he was owed at least 50,000 *l.t.* by Philip IV 'pro stipendiis Vasconie' (APA, E.371).
70 See, for example, the protests of Foix's proctors against Philip's officers, and the count's refusal to obey a summons from the seneschal of Carcassonne (Devic and Vaissette x, cc. 328—34, 335—38, 340—43).
71 E.101/152/6, no. 5 (11 Jan. 1294).

money 'as you respect the king's honour'.[72] The self-interest of the greater magnates of the South-West had to be indulged by both Plantagenets and Capetians if they were to retain even a tenuous hold upon their loyalties.

The structure of noble families in the South-West, as well as the ancient custom of private war, may have made their members readier to engage in warfare than was the case in some other parts of France. In areas of impartible inheritance — such as Béarn, Labourd, Soule and Chalosse — one 'universal heir' enjoyed the patrimony, often leaving the cadets unendowed with lands and forcing them to seek their own living.[73] Some vegetated in their father's or elder brother's households; others sought income and status in the profession of war.[74] In areas of partible inheritance — such as the Landes, Bazadais and Marsan — there was often insufficient land and revenue to support all the sons of a noble house adequately and to enable them to 'live nobly'.[75] Among the lists of nobles mustering for the English between 1294 and 1298 there are many instances of recurrent patronyms. In two undated horse-valuations (?1297), a number of brothers and other relations bearing the same name proliferate: three Semonjacs, three Jonquières, three Sescars, four Cassalis, three Navailles, two Caupennes.[76] An identical pattern emerges from an inquiry into the value of lands held before the war by dispossessed Gascons.[77] In some cases the words 'et fratres eius' are added to a name; in others the clerks spell out all their names. Arnaud-Eyquem, Thibaud and Garsie de Potensac; Gaillard and Guillaume-Amanieu de Breuil, and four members of the Sescars family were compensated. Two men — Bernard de Semens and Arnaud Elie — were listed with their 'nepotes'.[78] A tenurial structure in which co-seigneurie and *paréage* was extremely common would obviously be reflected in such records.[79] Consciousness of ancestry, dynasty and family ties was strong. Arnaud-Guillaume de Marsan, for example, in his petitions to Edward I, referred to his 'progenitor' Arnaud de Gabaston on every possible occasion, and was clearly dependent upon him for favour with the king.[80] Arnaud de Caupenne reminded Edward of his brother Elie's capture by the French and received money to pay Elie's expenses on 18th December 1294.[81] It was by such means that loyalties were kept fresh.

---

72 E.101/152/6, no. 5: the constable was to act immediately 'sicut honorem . . . Regis diligeretis'. For a further warrant ordering payment to Odo de Casenave see *ibid.*, no. 7. The pension had been confirmed when Edward was at Condom in Apr. 1289 (*RG* ii, nos. 1269, 1296).
73 See J. Poumarède, *Les successions dans le sud-ouest de la France au Moyen Age*, Toulouse 1972, 305—7. Many of those nobles who served the English administration between 1294 and 1298 came from these areas.
74 See J. Lartigaut, *Les campagnes du Quercy après la Guerre de Cent Ans*, Toulouse 1978, 471—2 and Vale, 'Warfare and the way of life of the nobility . . .', 180, 192—3.
75 Poumarède 238—40.
76 E.101/13/30, m.1ᵛ (Semonjac), 1ʳ (Jonquières); 14/4, m.1ʳ (Sescas) 1ᵛ (Cassalis, Navailles, Caupenne). See Table.
77 *RG* iii, nos. 2529—31; cf. C.47/26/6, 7. The inquiry appears to date from August 1299.
78 *RG* iii, no. 4529, [13], [16], [17], [22], [27], [130], [303], [242], [189], [165].
79 See Gardelles 18—19 for the sharing of castles and *maisons-fortes* by the Gascon nobility, especially in the Agenais.
80 *RG* iii, no. 4248 (18 May 1296). He had acquitted himself honourably at St. Sever in Apr. 1295. See also S.C.1/19/103: for Arnaud-Guillaume's surrender of his castle at Roquefort-de-Marsan to John St. John and Amanieu d'Albret, on the king's order, so that it could be garrisoned by the king's troops. In this petition Arnaud-Guillaume emphasised that Edward was his 'natural lord'.
81 E.101/152/14, no. 3 (at Roquefort-de-Marsan, 18 Dec. 1294).

Personal knowledge also played some part in the relationships established between Edward I and his Gascon vassals. The king had, after all, spent some time in the duchy and, during his visit of 1286—9, had granted rights and privileges, created *bastides*, and enacted a series of administrative ordinances.[82] His presence symbolised his concern for his inheritance, and many of those who served him in 1294—98 must have seen him at that time.[83] Most of them had never seen Philip IV of France. The splendour of Edward's entourage in 1286 was celebrated by the French poet Guillaume Guiart:

> 'Ne mena mie o lui gaillofres
> Mez granz destriers, sommiers et coffres
> Plains desterlins, tant que ieit rage . . .'[84]

Edward's international renown was high, and his cultivation of a chivalric aura and reputation for effective justice may have made some impression upon the Gascon nobility.[85] Few outside the Agenais, which had only been returned to him in 1279, felt compelled to appeal to the Parlement of Paris against his officers' judgements.[85a] The less tangible, non-material incentives to serve him must not be forgotten. The examples set by Arnaud de Gabaston or Arnaud and Elie de Caupenne, as members of a great royal household, held up the promise and expectation of a similar place in the sun to their contemporaries. On Easter Day 1287, Edward knighted Auger, son of Auger Mote, knight, lord of Meilhan, at Bordeaux.[86] Auger served him as castellan of Mauléon and sub-seneschal of the Agenais, and was admitted as a household knight on 20 April 1289 at Bonnegarde.[87] Others enjoyed Edward's liberality during his Gascon residence: on 7th January 1287, he gave two pieces of cloth of gold for the funeral of Guitard de Bourg, lord of Vertheuil, at Bordeaux;[87a] a minstrel

---

82 See Trabut-Cussac 81—102.
83 J.P. Trabut-Cussac, 'Itinéraire d'Edouard Ier en France, 1286—1289', *BIHR* xxv, 1952, 170—200; also Trabut-Cussac, *L'Administration anglaise* 95—100 for the assembly at Libourne attended by most of the duchy's nobility (May—June 1289).
84 Guillaume Guiart, *Branche des royaux lignages*, ed. J.A. Buchon, Paris 1828, II, 3735—37. Edward also took part of his menagerie with him to Gascony in 1287: see E.36/201, p. 61 for compensation to an inhabitant of Oloron (dép. Pyrénées-Atlantiques) whose horse had been killed by one of the king's lions.
85 For his acts as a mediator in Gascony see, e.g. Trabut-Cussac, *L'Administration anglaise* 84. For his chivalric reputation see Juliet Vale, *Edward III and Chivalry. Chivalric Society and its Context 1270—1350*, Woodbridge 1982, 15—22.
85a An exception was the case of the troublesome Gombaud de Tiran, *damoiseau*, lord of St. Médard-en-Jalle (*Recog. Feodorum*, no. 35). But the fault appears to have lain more with Edward's officers and with other nobles of the region (including Elie de Caupenne) than with the king-duke himself. See *RG* ii, no. 1537; iii, no. 2028. Also *Olim* ii, 5; *Actes du Parlement* i, nos. 2421, 2519, 2738. The affair lasted from 1282 until 1293 and was still reverberating in 1311 (*Actes du Parlement* i, no. 3892). For a similar case from the Agenais, see *RG* ii, 975, 979, 1166, 1201, 4828 (Bernard de Ravignan, co-seigneur of Buzet).
86 Trabut-Cussac, 'Itinéraire' 198, cit. E.36/201, p.79. Arnaud de Gabaston had been received as a king's banneret 'ad feodum regis et robas, sicut alii milites vasconici' at St. Sever on 17 Oct. 1287 (E.36/201, p. 78), while Gaillard de Tilh, knight, was similarly retained on 29 Sept. (E.36/201, p. 29).
87 *RG* ii, nos. 78, 772, 813, 826, 878, 920; E.36/201, p. 79.
87a E.36/201: 'per preceptum regis' p. 93. The Englishman John de Vaux, knight, who died at Dax, had 3 pieces 'per speciale preceptum regis' on 10 Sept. 1287 (p. 93). On 15 Sept. Edward gave cloth of gold for the tomb of Jean, late *vicomte* of Tartas, who had died while serving in Edward's Welsh wars (p. 94).

(*taburarius*) of Arnaud-Sanche, lord of Tardetz, received a gift of 8s. from him on 13 August 1287;[88] and the Gascon Rolls for the period suggest that Edward may have been rather more successful as duke of Aquitaine than as king of England at this time. Finally, in his reply to a petition from Bertrand de Panissau, a Périgordin knight, Edward seems to reveal personal acquaintance, declaring himself 'well content' with services performed for over thirty years.[89] He waived the need for supporting evidence to substantiate Panissau's claims. This 'minor and rather pathetic figure'[90] had held three *bailliages* — all of newly-created *bastide* towns — and claimed to have had 4,000 serjeants in the king-duke's service at Roquepine, Molières, Lalinde and Montpazier.[91] With others of his class, he had come to England as an exile during the French occupation of the duchy.[92] Edward had every reason to know and to reward him.

Throughout the three-hundred-year history of English Gascony, the loyalty of the Gascon nobility to the king-dukes of Aquitaine was often tenuous. Yet in periods of crisis, such as the Anglo-French war of 1294—98, a far from perfect administration successfully rallied the support of a majority of the duchy's nobles. Self-interest no doubt played an important part in their calculations, but other motives cannot be discounted. Their obligations towards an immediate and 'natural' lord — the duke of Aquitaine — clearly took precedence over any sentiment of loyalty towards the Capetian monarchy. The war of 1294—98 demonstrated to Philip IV that an accommodation with Edward I over French claims to sovereignty in Aquitaine was politically expedient and desirable, especially in view of Philip's conflict with the papacy. It had proved impossible to overcome active resistance to attempts to enforce French royal authority between the Garonne and the Pyrenees. For Edward I, the Anglo-French war produced significant gains as well as financial losses: the marriage alliance with France, which effectively allowed him to pursue his ambitions in Scotland without serious risk of French intervention; and an assurance that, when put to the test, the fidelity of some of his more turbulent vassals in what remained of the Angevin Empire was not in doubt.

---

88 E.36/201, p. 62. Arnaud-Sanche's heir, Brasc de Tardets, *damoiseau*, was said by Henry de Lacy to be Edward's 'ancien serjant darmes qui bien et loialment vous a servi grant tens a nomeement en ceste guerre' and was to be paid wages and *restaur* 'solonc la forme de vostre promesse . . . en maniere quil se puisse loer de vostre bone seignerie' (E.101/154/11, no. 2; 24 Apr. 1297). But he was paid only £59 0s. 8d. of the £249 15s. 4d. owed to him from the wardrobe. The residue was assigned on Gascon revenues. See also *RG* iii, nos. 4923, 4928, 4954.

89 *RG* iii, pp. clxxxv—clxxxvi: 'bene constat regi de servicio suo et inde bene est contentus, propter quod non est necesse quod habeantur littere testimoniales'. For Panissaus' career in Edward's service, see Trabut-Cussac, *L'Administration anglaise* 335, 361—2. See *RG* iii, no. 4475 for the grant which followed his petition (6 May 1297).

90 M. Beresford, *New Towns of the Middle Ages*, London 1967, 96—97. He was lieutenant for Jean de Grilly, seneschal of Aquitaine, in Périgord, and negotiated an important agreement between the abbey of Cadouin and the men of Molières (*RG* ii, no. 1688, 2 June 1289). He was appointed by Edward to arbitrate (with Bernard Faure, canon of St. Seurin at Bordeaux) a dispute between Alexandre de la Pebrée, lord of Bergerac and Gensac, and his wife (*RG* ii, no. 1239, 30 July 1289). Without such men, the English administration could scarcely have functioned.

91 *RG* iii, pp. clxxxv—clxxxvi. He had two sons, both unbeneficed clerks, and petitioned Edward for the writing-office of the *prévôté* of Ste. Foy-la-Grande in the Agenais to be granted for life to one of them (*RG* iii, p. cxcii; May 1297).

92 Trabut-Cussac, *L'Administration anglaise* 170; *RG* iii, no. 4529 [306] for 100 *l. ch.* compensation for his losses (25 Aug. 1299).

The Gascons had no innate liking for the English as English: their support for Edward perhaps stemmed partly from the fact that, unlike Philip IV, he was not a Northern Frenchman. In Aquitaine, where dynastic aims were not uppermost in Edward's mind, there was something to be gained from gifts and concessions. However fitful and unsatisfactory his rewards, it is clear that he was far from unaware of the political advantages that would accrue from the exercise of largesse.[93]

---

93 For another view of Edward's behaviour, based upon English evidence, see K.B. McFarlane, 'Had Edward I a "policy" towards the earls?', *History* 1, 1965, 159: 'the truth is that he showed no great belief in the virtues of largesse'.

CAVALRY SERVICE IN EARLY FOURTEENTH CENTURY ENGLAND

Michael Prestwich

The record of what had been the invincible elite of medieval armies, the heavily armed cavalry, was not a good one in the early fourteenth century. On the continent there was the shattering defeat of the French host at Courtrai in 1302, at the hands of urban levies, while English armies in Scotland conspicuously failed to follow up the successes achieved at Dunbar in 1296 and at Falkirk two years later. The disastrous humiliation at Bannockburn in 1314 was epitomized by the futile and suicidal charge by the earl of Gloucester into the ranks of the Scottish foot. It was a force largely composed of infantry that was responsible for the collapse of baronial resistance to Edward II at Boroughbridge in 1322, when the earl of Hereford, 'the floure of solace and of comfort, and also of curtesye', was unchivalrously and ignominiously slain by a footsoldier.[1] By 1327 English knights were being asked to give up their traditional mounted role, and to be ready to fight on foot.[2]

In such a situation changes in military organization were to be expected. The conventional view is that already under Edward I the old-fashioned feudal levies were increasingly irrelevant to the realities of military service, and that new methods of service were being developed, with pay according to the terms of contracts or indentures becoming increasingly important.[3] The evidence relating to cavalry service in the first quarter of the fourteenth century does not all tally with such established views. If feudal service was anachronistic and unsuitable, then it is necessary to explain why old-fashioned feudal summonses were issued in fourteen of the first twenty-seven years of the fourteenth century. It is surprising to find that the feudal contingent on the 1322 campaign in Scotland was larger than any since 1277. If armies were largely paid, then it is curious that the earl of Lancaster with his immense following features nowhere in the pay records for the army of 1319, nor indeed for any other expedition. It is also strange, if indentures were the answer to the problems of recruiting cavalry, that the crown did not make use of them in the experiments that were made in the 1320s in an attempt to create a new system of military obligation.

The army that Edward I took to Scotland in 1300 provides the best starting point, for it has left the fullest documentation of any expedition in this period.[4] There was a straightforward request for feudal service, and a roll

---

1 *Brut*, ed. F.W.D. Brie, Early English Text Society, 1906, i, 218.
2 *Rotuli Scotiae*, ed. D. Macpherson and others, London 1814, i, 203.
3 See for example M. Powicke, *Military Obligation in Medieval England*, Oxford 1962, 96—7.
4 The composition of the 1300 expedition is analysed more fully in my *War, Politics and Finance under Edward I*, London 1972, 69—70, 79—82, 88.

recording the muster shows that the tenants-in-chief provided a total of 40 knights and 366 sergeants, performing unpaid service for forty days. The wardrobe account book shows that there were about 850 cavalry men performing paid service; 23 of these held the rank of banneret. A unique source, the heraldic *Song of Caerlaverock*, names no less than 87 bannerets in the army, however, and claims that even this is not a full total.[5] Only three of these are listed as doing feudal service in person, and therefore it appears that over sixty bannerets, with their retinues, were serving voluntarily at their own expense. They were presumably responding to the second half of the writs of summons, which had asked men to provide as many men-at-arms as they could in addition to the formal feudal quotas. One further method was used to recruit cavalry for this campaign: the king asked all those with at least £40 worth of land to serve at royal wages. The response to this appeal was probably very limited. Contracts were not used by the crown in 1300, but many men must have been present in their lord's retinue because they were bound to serve under the terms of indentured agreements, such as the well-known one dating from 1297 between the earl of Norfolk and John de Segrave.[6] The total cavalry strength of the 1300 host was probably about 2,000, divided into four main battalions, one of which was almost exclusively composed of men from the royal household.

How did these various elements, feudal, voluntary and paid, feature in the armies raised between 1300 and 1327? The first problem is that of the feudal quotas. Neither the frequency of summons, nor the scale of the responses, implies the decline in their importance that is often suggested. Feudal musters took place in 1300, 1303, 1306, 1310, 1314, 1322 and 1327, while there were further summonses under Edward II for campaigns which were subsequently abandoned. Records are unfortunately not complete for all the musters: those for 1303 are probably incomplete, and those for 1306 little more than fragmentary. The rolls for 1314 and 1327 are missing.[7] In addition, magnates did not always trouble to have their quotas enrolled: in 1310 the earls of Surrey, Arundel and Gloucester, along with a few other important figures, came into this category.[8]

Why was this apparently outdated method of summons still used, and used so often, in this period? The numbers of troops that answered the call to a feudal muster were not remarkable. Just over 400 heavily armed cavalry in 1300, three-quarters of that total in 1303, but almost 440 in 1310 and about 500 in 1322 are recorded on the muster rolls. An analysis of the fullest of these rolls, those for 1300, 1310 and 1322 provides some details of how the service was actually performed.[9] It was rare for tenants-in-chief to perform service in

5 *The Siege of Carlaverock*, ed. N.H. Nicolas, London 1828.
6 N. Denholm-Young, *Seignorial Administration in England*, Oxford 1937, 167—8.
7 G.W.S. Barrow, *Robert Bruce and the Community of the Realm of Scotland*, 2nd ed., Edinburgh 1976, 294, suggests, following J.E. Morris, that there was no marshal's roll in 1314 because the summons was issued without parliamentary consent, but this seems unlikely. It is more probable that the records were lost in the course of the battle of Bannockburn.
8 *Calendar of Various Chancery Rolls, 1277—1326*, London 1912, 393—6.
9 *Documents and Records illustrating the History of Scotland*, ed. F. Palgrave, London 1837, i, 209—231; *Parliamentary Writs*, ed. F. Palgrave, London, 1827—34, II, i, 401—8; PRO C47/5/10. My thanks are due to the Travel and Research Fund of the University of Durham for facilitating consultation of manuscripts for this article.

person, even if they were present on the campaign. Out of 200 tenants in 1300, only a dozen, three of them admittedly earls, were recorded as serving themselves. Nor did many knights serve: it was usual to employ squires or sergeants, two of whom were equivalent to one knight. The number of barded, or armoured, horses was the same in either case, as a knight would come with two such horses, a sergeant with one. There were in addition sergeanty services. Few were as ridiculous as Hugo FitzHeyr who came in 1300 with a bow and one arrow, which he fired when the Scots were first sighted, and then left for home; the majority of sergeanties simply provided lightly armed horsemen.

Tenants-in-chief used various methods to provide men for feudal service. Sometimes other members of the family were sent: in 1300 one of those serving on behalf of the king's treasurer Walter Langton was his brother Robert Peverel, and in 1322 Ralph de Grey represented his father, John de Grey. Magnates might detach members of their retinue to perform feudal service: three of the knights who answered for the earl of Lancaster in 1310 were certainly his retainers.[10] Another technique was to engage a military contractor to provide the service that was due. Thus in 1314 William de Fauconberg promised to serve on behalf of John de Beauchamp, and to pay sixty marks to him if he failed in his task.[11] This method was particularly favoured by ecclesiastical tenants-in-chief. In 1306 Ralph de Gorges agreed to serve for the abbot of Abbotsbury, although in the event he failed to muster on time.[12] In 1322 the bishop of Salisbury initially intended to pay a fine in lieu of service, but instead he made an agreement with Robert de Sapy, a royal household knight who had served for him in 1300. Sapy agreed to provide five knights, or the equivalent, for £100. This works out at ten shillings a day for a knight, a very high figure when compared with royal wage rates of two shillings a day, but one which possibly reflected real costs more accurately.[13] Robert Constable of Flamborough obviously specialized in providing service, answering for the fees of the bishop of Ely in 1322, and making an agreement with the archbishop of York in 1327 at the same rates as those agreed five years earlier by Sapy with the bishop of Salisbury.[14] In only one case was it clearly difficult to raise men: in 1322 the abbot of St. Albans was short of knights for two fees, and obtained special authorization to send twelve hobelars, lightly armed horsemen, instead.

There was surprisingly little continuity in the body of tenants-in-chief who responded to the feudal summonses by sending troops. Up to 200 were represented in 1300, 1310 and 1322, but only about forty of these provided troops in all three years. About eighty tenancies sent men in both 1300 and 1310, and about ninety in both 1310 and 1322. The actual quotas for service

10 J.R. Maddicott, *Thomas of Lancaster 1307—1322*, Oxford 1970, 114.
11 *Parliamentary Writs*, II, ii, 427.
12 H.M. Chew, *The English Ecclesiastical Tenants-in-Chief and Knight Service*, Oxford 1932, 87.
13 *The Registers of Roger Martival 1315—30*, ed. K. Edwards, C.R. Elrington, S. Reynolds, D.M. Owen, Canterbury and York Soc., 1959—65, iii, 97—8.
14 PRO C47/5/10; N.B. Lewis, 'The Summons of the English Feudal Host, 5 April 1327', in *Essays in Medieval History presented to Bertie Wilkinson*, ed. T.A. Sandquist and M. Powicke, Toronto 1969, 242—9. For an abortive campaign in 1318 Melton had been able to strike a better bargain, for then Roger de Somerville had agreed to provide his service for only 100 marks: *Historical Letters and Papers from Northern Registers*, ed. J. Raine, RS 1873, 278—9.

were not as static as would be expected from an anachronistic system. In some cases changes in circumstances explain the alterations. The earl of Warwick provided the equivalent of eight and a half knights in 1310, but he claimed that only five were due from his own earldom, and that two and a half were due as a result of his custody of the Tony lands. In fact, however, the earldom had provided the equivalent of six knights in 1282, and of six and a half in 1277: there had been a slow erosion of this quota.[15] Royal favour is the obvious explanation for the dramatic decline in the obligation of the earldom of Cornwall from fifteen in 1300 to a mere three in 1310, for in the latter year the earl was the king's favourite Piers Gaveston. The fall in John of Clavering's quota from a surprisingly high eight in 1310 to five in 1322 is a clear reflection of his failure to retain his family lands in face of financial problems.[16]

Some changes are not so easy to understand, particularly in the case of religious houses whose landed fortunes are unlikely to have undergone major transformations. Miss Chew noted that, having sent the equivalent of two knights in 1300, Sherborne abbey sent only half that service in 1310.[17] Malmesbury, strangely, offered two knights in 1300 and 1322, but three in 1310, and the nunnery of Wilton displayed a similar pattern, with one in 1300 and 1322, and two in 1310. Some of these vagaries are in part to be explained by the fact that the crown's records of the obligations of its tenants-in-chief were inadequate. Sources such as the Book of Fees detailed the old large quotas which dated back to the twelfth century and before, but were uninformative on the new, radically reduced levels of service which had emerged in the thirteenth century. A note in the exchequer ordinances of 1326 commented wryly on the problems that arose because 'there is no certain remembrance that has been found at the exchequer of the king's fees.'[18] It was possible, of course, to look up earlier muster rolls, but it seems that in practice it was often left to the tenants-in-chief themselves to provide what they thought was the correct level of service. They might be in some doubt over this, as entries such as that for Edmund Stafford in 1300 show, where it was stated that his proffer of one and a half knights should not prejudice him in the future, should it be found that his obligation was in fact different. There might even be uncertainty as to whether a man was indeed a tenant-in-chief. In 1300 and 1303 William de Mountchesney performed service, although it was later found that he did not hold his lands directly from the crown.[19]

The forces provided directly as a result of a feudal summons were clearly not particularly impressive. Their numbers were not large, and save for very short campaigns such as that of 1322 the limitation of service to forty days must have been a disadvantage. It is not clear how the feudal quotas fitted into the

15 J.E. Morris, *The Welsh Wars of Edward I*, Oxford 1901, 60. For an actual request for a change in quota, dating from the mid-thirteenth century, see *Royal and other Historical Letters*, ed. J.S. Shirley, RS 1866, ii, 210—11.
16 GEC iii. 275.
17 Chew, 33.
18 *The Red Book of the Exchequer*, ed. H. Hall, RS 1897, iii, 960. For a discussion of the new quotas which had mostly emerged by 1245, see I.J. Sanders, *Feudal Military Service in England*, Oxford 1956, 59—90.
19 *Parliamentary Writs*, II, ii, 450. Two other cases of men who served although not obliged to do so are given by T. Madox, *The History and Antiquities of the Exchequer*, London 1769, i, 652. Sanders, 72—3, gives examples of 'uncertainty and ignorance' about quotas of service.

organisation of the army in the field; whether they served as a body or were integrated into the rest of the cavalry force. The latter seems more likely: at all events, it does not appear that armies recruited by means of a feudal summons were any larger or any more effective than those mustered by other means. Why then were so many feudal summonses issued in this period?

One possible reason for the continued use of what in many ways was an archaic system was financial. The fines paid by tenants-in-chief in lieu of service were of some value to the crown, amounting to some £2,000 in 1300. By 1327, however, the yield from this source was only £778.[20] One reason why this income was not higher was that it was clearly cheaper, if not easier, to provide service: in 1322 the bishop of Salisbury would have paid £200 as a fine, had he not paid Sapy £100 to do service. In one case, that of the abbot of Peterborough in 1310, the crown rejected the proffered service and demanded a fine instead, but this is a solitary example.[21] The other financial concomitant of feudal service was scutage. This was not charged like the fines on the actual service owed, but on the old twelfth century assessments of knights' fees. According to the theory doggedly maintained by the exchequer, even those who had done service were still liable to pay scutage, for they had not provided the massive quotas of the old assessments. The inevitable arguments over this meant that the crown was able to raise very little income from scutages. Its lack of interest in scutage as a source of revenue is strongly suggested by the delays in authorizing collection: it was not until 1314 that the levy for the 1306 campaign was set in motion, while only in 1319 was the machinery set up for collecting scutage on the 1310 expedition. The process caused much trouble, with those appointed as collectors 'much vexed that they are often made to come to court to present their accounts, which cannot then be despatched.'[22]

The tenants-in-chief themselves probably benefited much more from scutage than did the crown, for they were entitled, once authorized by royal writs, to collect the levy from their own tenants. The magnates demonstrated their dual concern over scutage in parliament in 1318, for in one petition they protested that the exchequer was demanding payment from men who had served on campaign, and in another requested that the king should allow them to collect scutages from their own tenants for the armies of 1310 and 1314.[23] The level of profit from this latter activity is suggested by the fact that the earl of Lincoln obtained £125 in 1305 from the honour of Pontefract as scutage for the 1300 campaign.[24]

For the crown, the traditional feudal summons had political advantages. It was very hard to raise objections to such a time-honoured method of recruitment, and although the actual quotas of service were small, it appears that many magnates were prepared to treat such a summons as a general invitation to go on campaign. It is likely that it was because of the hostility aroused by

---

20 Prestwich, *War, Politics and Finance under Edward I*, 82; Lewis, 'Summons of the English Feudal Levy', 240.
21 Chew, 88, where the date is wrongly given as 1311.
22 H.M. Chew, 'Scutage in the Fourteenth Century', *EHR* xxxviii, 1923, 19—41; *Red Book of the Exchequer*, iii, 960.
23 *Documents Illustrative of English History in the 13th and 14th Centuries*, ed. H. Cole, London 1844, 7.
24 Prestwich, 82.

novel methods of summons in 1297 that Edward I resorted increasingly to older, tried techniques in his final years. For Edward II it made good sense when his political position was difficult to use the most unexceptional forms of recruitment. In 1310 and 1314 there was considerable opposition to his planned campaigns, but it was not possible for even the earl of Lancaster to refuse to send his quotas of men to the musters, even though he would not attend in person. In the aftermath of Lancaster's defeat in 1322 it must have seemed wise to use as uncontroversial a means as possible for summoning an army, and the same consideration probably applied after Edward II's own fall in 1327.

The preference of the magnates for a feudal summons had been shown perhaps most clearly in 1282. J.E. Morris rightly suggested that it was baronial pressure that compelled Edward I to abandon a plan to employ a wholly paid army in Wales, and to summon the feudal host instead. 'They refused to descend to the level of stipendiaries, stood on their rights by insisting on the performance of their exact feudal obligations.'[25] As already shown, however, it was certainly possible in Edward I's later years for men to serve without pay, and so without compromising principles, simply in response to a polite request expressed in terms of fealty, with no mention of homage or feudal service. M.R. Powicke indeed suggested that in 1310 baronial hostility to the crown may have caused 'the change from the summons for *servicium debitum* to a request for as powerful a force as possible.'[26] In fact, this argument has no warrant, for what happened is that a supplementary non-feudal summons was issued after the initial request for the feudal quotas, to which it was an addition not a replacement.[27] In 1316 the magnates' preference for a feudal summons was clearly shown when in the Lincoln parliament they advised the king to use this means to recruit an army to march against the Scots.[28]

Whatever the financial and political attractions of a feudal summons for both king and magnates, the practical value of the quotas that mustered before the constable on campaign was very limited. It was accordingly normal to supplement such a summons with a polite request for service with as many men as possible, expressed in terms of fealty rather than of homage. This might be done in a clause added to the feudal summons, as in 1300, or be the subject of separate writs as in 1310 and 1322.[29] It was presumably this type of summons that yielded the voluntary unpaid service that is revealed by an analysis of the host of 1300. How normal was it in this period for many magnates to serve at their own expense? There is good evidence in the form of lists of those campaigning in 1304, which can be compared with the pay records, and which reveal that this was certainly the case then,[30] but for Edward II's reign the sources do not exist that would illuminate the position with the same clarity.

There are certainly hints of unpaid, non-feudal service under Edward II. There is no record of the payment of wages to the earl of Gloucester, and a

---

25 Morris, 158.
26 Powicke, 139.
27 *Parliamentary Writs* II. ii. 394—5, 399.
28 *RP*, London 1783—1832, i.
29 *Parliamentary Writs* I, 327; II. ii. 399, 568—9.
30 *Documents and Records Illustrating the History of Scotland*, i, 262—77; BL Add. MS 8835, fos. 55v—68v.

grant made to him in 1311 of 5,000 marks in wardships and marriages 'in consideration of the earl's great expenses in the king's service in Scotland and elsewhere' is unlikely to have been made to a man who served for pay.[31] There is, more surprisingly, an equal lack of evidence for the payment of wages to Piers Gaveston, earl of Cornwall. Admittedly the records are incomplete, but in view of the king's favourite's wealth, it seems very likely that his service was unpaid. The earl of Lancaster certainly never appears to have accepted wages from the crown, not even in his youth when he accompanied Edward I to Flanders in 1297. Obviously in his case political considerations made it hard for him to take the king's pay, but the traditional hostility of the great magnates to paid service may have played its part. Yet the costs of campaigning were not easily borne, even by one so wealthy: in 1322 he negotiated a grant from the northern clergy of 2,000 marks so that he could defend the northern borders against the Scots.[32] A rather different kind of unpaid service was proposed in 1312 in the course of the tedious negotiations in the aftermath of Gaveston's death, in the form of a baronial grant of four hundred men-at-arms to serve at their own expense for six months. This idea was dropped, however, and did not feature in the final agreement.[33] In 1315 the king went so far as to request unpaid service from a limited number of northern magnates: they were asked to provide defence against the Scots at their own expense with decent contingents. Other orders for the defence of the north, such as those in 1318 for Lancaster, Richmond and others to array both horse and foot may imply unpaid service.[34]

The situation under Edward II was not, however, identical to that of his father's reign. The war against the Scots became increasingly defensive, with few chances of profit and some danger of capture by the enemy, as the earl of Hereford among many others discovered in 1314. There was no longer the same sense of a united common enterprise against the Scots, and it is not surprising to find that under Edward II the great majority of earls were ready to accept royal pay. Pembroke, Richmond, Arundel, Winchester, Warenne, Hereford, Norfolk and Kent were all at some point in receipt of the king's wages. By 1322 it seems unlikely that there were substantial unpaid voluntary contingents on the campaign in Scotland.

In the difficult circumstances of Edward II's reign it was not sufficient to rely solely on traditional techniques for recruiting troops, and there were several attempts to introduce innovations. One approach was to try to make more use of the feudal obligation. Under Edward I homage was only mentioned in military summonses when the traditional *servitia debita* were requested, but in 1311 a small group of northern magnates were asked to provide specific numbers of men — bearing no relationship to the feudal *servitia* — to serve for wages in accordance with the fealty and homage that they owed to the king. It is tempting to suppose that this formula was simply the result of careless drafting, but again in 1315 some northerners were asked *in fide et*

---

31 M. Altschul, *A Baronial Family in Medieval England: The Clares*, Baltimore 1965, 161.
32 *Parliamentary Writs* II, i, 566.
33 'Annales Londonienses', in *Chronicles of the Reigns of Edward I and Edward II*, ed. W. Stubbs, RS 1882, i, 210—11.
34 *Parliamentary Writs* II, ii, 139, 511.

homagio to defend the march with all the forces that they could raise.[35] No objections seem to have been raised to these summonses, and it may be that it was acceptable to appeal to homage in this way when local forces were being mustered for defensive purposes. The use of an appeal to fealty and homage in 1316 was a very different matter, however. In February of that year an orthodox summons for feudal service was issued. Now it was quite usual, as already shown, to supplement such a summons with a polite request in terms of fealty and allegiance, but not of homage, for the magnates to bring as many troops as they felt they could, but this time the supplementary summons explicitly appealed to homage. Not only that, but the writs made unprecedented threats of confiscation of lands in cases of non-compliance.[36] It looks as if the crown was trying to extend feudal obligation in a very startling way, and it seems very likely that the form of this summons, at least as much as that of the accompanying request for the service of £50 landholders, contributed to the renewed hostility between the king and the earl of Lancaster in the summer of 1316.[37] The campaign never in fact took place, and the summonses for 1317 reverted to orthodox form. It was only in 1322 that Edward II again began to use the terminology of homage in requests for as many troops as could be provided.[38]

It was not only by summoning the magnates that the crown could hope to recruit cavalry forces. Although Edward I had been forced to abandon his attempts to impose an obligation to perform service on all those in possession of lands of a specific value — the request to the £40 landholders in 1300 was the last such summons of his reign — it was obviously tempting for Edward II to try to develop similar schemes of recruitment. The threat of civil war in the aftermath of Gaveston's death in 1312 prompted the first moves in this direction. In July the sheriffs were asked to draw up lists of all available men-at-arms and infantry, and this was followed by an order that all £40 landholders should take up knighthood. This was a well-tried technique, but in 1316 Edward II went much further, attempting the kind of levy that had proved so unpopular in 1297. On that occasion Edward I had tried to exact service from all £20 landholders: his son now ordered all £50 men to serve in the north, under threat of confiscation of their lands. The precise form of obligation was not mentioned, nor was pay specified. Inevitably, nothing came of such a move, which was bound to be widely resented.[39]

Continued difficulties against the Scots prompted some further experiments, but these did not extend to the knightly class until 1322.[40] The totality of the royalist triumph at Boroughbridge made it possible for the king and his

35 *Parliamentary Writs* II, ii, 416, 139, 435—6.
36 *Parliamentary Writs* II, ii, 461—2, 476.
37 Maddicott 187, suggests that the summons of £50 landholders may have been the cause of dissension between the king and the earl, but he also points out that the earl continued to prepare for the campaign after the summonses were issued.
38 *Parliamentary Writs* II, ii, 545, 549. A feudal character to the army which mustered at Coventry early in 1322 is suggested by letters patent issued by the earl of Athol, acting as constable, permitting John de Pyppelton to return home after serving the king satisfactorily: *Calendar of Documents Relating to Scotland*, Edinburgh 1887, iii, no. 748.
39 *Parliamentary Writs* II, ii, 418, 478.
40 *Parliamentary Writs* II, ii, 527 details arrangements for men in the north to have military equipment appropriate to their wealth, a revision of the Statute of Winchester necessitated by the defeat at Myton in 1319.

advisers to make demands for military service that would have been quite unacceptable earlier in the reign. The civil war of 1322 itself prompted some innovation, for prior to Boroughbridge the earls and a number of magnates were asked *in fide et homagio* to provide both men-at-arms and infantry.[41] For the Scottish campaign of 1322, in addition to the normal forms of summons, orders went out to the sheriffs asking them to proclaim that all cavalrymen, from bannerets to men-at-arms, who were not retained by others, were to muster at Newcastle. As many as possible were to be sent individual summonses, and the sheriffs had to return lists of all requested to appear in this way. A few of these returns survive. They display remarkable variation, from Essex with a list of 56 bannerets and knights, and 81 men-at-arms, to Huntingdonshire with only two knights and seven squires.[42] This attempt to obtain the military service of all capable of serving as cavalrymen was not particularly successful: the wardrobe account book shows that roughly 1,250 cavalry received wages on the campaign; not a very large force.[43]

For the projected campaign in Gascony in 1324 the crown again attempted a combination of feudal summonses with an ambitious attempt to compel all knights and men-at-arms to serve when required. A very intriguing summons was issued on 9 May 1324, which asked all knights to come to Westminster to meet with the king and magnates to discuss matters of state. On the next day a distraint of knighthood was ordered, and all who wanted to be knighted by the king in person were asked to come to London by 3 June. As part of the scheme of recruitment that was being planned, the sheriffs drew up lists of all the knights and men-at-arms in their counties. Regrettably these are not complete, while their value is further diminished by the way in which different criteria were adopted in different parts of the country. In Lancashire those with £15 worth of land were counted as men-at-arms, but in Cornwall the level was set at £40. The sheriff of Lincolnshire refused to give the names of those retained by magnates. The inaccuracy of the documents is shown by the fact that only thirteen men-at-arms are listed for all Yorkshire, whereas the sheriff of Northumberland provided 95 names. Nevertheless, the returns do give some impression of the total available cavalry resources: about 1,150 knights and 950 men-at-arms were listed. The number of knights was certainly not far short of what might be expected, and is consistent with other sources.[44]

In ordering the preparation of these lists in 1324, it seems clear that the crown must have been planning a reorganization of the structure of cavalry service. Arrangements made in November and December of the same year for recruiting an expedition to go to Gascony show what was envisaged. Initially commissioners were appointed with orders to array all knights, squires and men-at-arms for service in the duchy. Returns were to be made to the wardrobe, listing those prepared to serve, and specifying the names of those in magnate retinues. Then further orders set out specific numbers of men-at-arms, hobelars, or light cavalry, and infantry to be recruited. The numbers of

---

41 *Parliamentary Writs* II, ii, 545.
42 *Parliamentary Writs* II, ii, 586—96. For a discussion of the returns for one county, and the similar list for 1324, see N. Saul, *Knights and Esquires: the Gloucestershire Gentry in the Fourteenth Century*, Oxford 1981, 31—3.
43 N.M. Fryde, *The Tyranny and Fall of Edward II 1321—1326*, Cambridge 1979, 128.
44 *Parliamentary Writs* II, ii, 316, 636—58.

heavy cavalry were reasonable: 40 from Lincolnshire, and a mere five from Rutland, for example, with the total amounting to about 650 men.[45] These measures were not carried through, for as so often under Edward II the planned campaign was abandoned, but the concept that all knights and men-at-arms were to be ready to serve when required was not given up. In July 1325 the sheriffs were ordered to make proclamations announcing that all men were to be prepared to serve when needed. In December distraint of knighthood was repeated. The use of commissions of array, previously used to recruit infantry, was extended at the end of Edward II's reign to those of knightly status as well. In 1326 and 1327 arrayers were to check up on knights and men-at-arms as well as on those of lower rank.[46] Such measures were not, of course, successful when Queen Isabella's invasion eventually took place, for no effective opposition was offered to her.[47] Yet these attempts to transform the military obligations and recruiting methods of the heavy cavalry forces were not without significance.

Although the steps taken to raise troops in the last five years of Edward II's reign may not have been very effective, they were certainly disliked. They formed an important element in the tyrannical rule of Edward II and the Despensers, and were the subject of inevitable protests in Edward III's first parliament. The crown was traditionally reluctant to make major concessions with regard to military service, as was shown in the crises of 1215 and 1297, but the petition protesting at the way in which men had been compelled to provide service contrary to their rights and wishes, and contrary to the statute of Winchester of 1285, was largely conceded by the new government. The concessions made in 1327 did not, of course, mark the end of experiment, but it became very difficult for the crown to continue to develop a general obligation to service, applicable to all social classes including knights and esquires, implemented by means of commissions of array. When Edward III attempted similar experiments to those of his father, in the mid 1340s, they met with renewed hostility.[48]

The future was, of course, to lie increasingly with the system of contracts with magnates for them to bring their indentured retinues on campaign. How far was there development in this area under Edward II? For major royal campaigns, the cavalry were simply paid wages, calculated on a daily basis, by the clerks of the wardrobe, just as under Edward I. Contracts had, however, been used under Edward I to provide troops when the king himself was not present on campaign, as in Scotland in the winter of 1297—8. Edward II's disinclination to go to war in person inevitably resulted in an increase in the use of contracts. Thus in 1310 Roger Mortimer agreed to serve with 30 men-at-arms for a year in return for £1,000. In 1315 Pembroke contracted to provide 100 men-at-

---

45 *Parliamentary Writs* II, ii, 681, 687.
46 *Parliamentary Writs* II, ii, 723, 735.
47 Fryde, 189. In addition to the forces mentioned there, it should be noted that PRO E101/17/10 shows that £200 was paid at Chepstow to John de Kingston for the wages of men-at-arms and foot recruited in Gloucestershire to serve the king, while £100 was paid to Donald of Mar for the wages of those in his following.
48 *RP* ii, 8, 11. G.L. Harriss, *King, Parliament and Public Finance in Medieval England to 1369*, Oxford 1975, 93—5, 392—4.

arms, and Badlesmere, Mohaut, Grey and Botetourt lesser numbers.[49] Very interestingly, in the autumn of 1316 Edward II appears to have embarked on a deliberate policy of retaining magnates in his service by means of indentures, much as the magnates hired their own followers. The arrangements made with a number of men were clearly quite different from the normal recruitment of household knights who received the king's fees and robes. John de Cromwell, John Giffard and William de Montague all served both as household bannerets in receipt of fees and robes, and under the terms of separate indentures. The king's motives were probably both political and military, and these agreements, recently analysed by Dr Phillips, were an obvious response to the threat posed by Thomas of Lancaster's powerful retinue.[50] The indentures suggest that the structure of the military household, inherited from Edward I, was no longer considered adequate to meet the demands of the day. The case of the household knight Gilbert de Middleton and his notorious attack on the cardinals in 1317 is but one of several examples which show that Edward II could not rely on his household knights in the way that his father had done. The use of contracts did not, however, develop very greatly under Edward II: it was not until 1337 that an entire army, though admittedly only a small one, was to be raised by this means.[51] What was most significant with regard to pay in this period was the fact that by the time of the 1327 campaign virtually the whole cavalry force, save for the feudal contingents who were making their last appearance in an English army, were paid. The situation had been transformed since 1300.

In spite of the apparent conservatism shown with the frequent use of the antiquated feudal summonses, the first quarter of the fourteenth century witnessed several attempts to transform the system of military obligation. Had it not been for the political revolution of 1327, the attempts at change might have been more influential. Their significance was greater in political than in military terms. For all the experiments in methods of summons, there were no attempts to develop new methods of fighting on any scale until 1327, when for the first time in this period a whole English army was drawn up with knights and men-at-arms arrayed ready to fight on foot. On that occasion the Scots wisely chose not to fight, but Edward III's armies were soon to prove the efficacy of the new techniques. Although the innovations in recruiting methods did not transform the nature of the armies sent north to Scotland in this period, they did have major political repercussions. The experiments of 1316 probably did much to breach the fragile unity achieved at the Lincoln parliament, and the attempts to extend the nature of military obligation in Edward II's final years on the throne undoubtedly contributed to his downfall.

For many knights and squires this must have been a period of sad disenchantment. William Marmion, commanded by his lady to make the golden helm she gave him famous in a place of peril, rode out bravely against the Scots besieging Norham castle, but had to be rescued by the constable with a

---

49 Bodleian Library, MS Tanner 197, fo. 28; J.R.S. Phillips, *Aymer de Valence, earl of Pembroke 1307—1324*, Oxford 1972, 88—9.
50 Phillips, 148—50, 312—5.
51 N.B. Lewis, 'The Recruitment and Organization of a Contract Army, May to November 1337', *BIHR* xxxvii, 1964, 1—19; M.C. Prestwich, 'English Armies in the early stages of the Hundred Years War: a scheme in 1341', *BIHR* LVI, 1983, 102—13.

degree of ignominy.⁵² It seems symbolic of the fate of English knighthood that Giles of Argentein, crowned King of the Greenwood for his tournament triumphs, and reputed to be the third best knight in all Christendom, should have been cut down by Scottish axemen at Bannockburn.⁵³ Not surprisingly, one cynical commentator saw the English barons and knights as 'lions in the hall, and hares in the field'.⁵⁴ Edward II's attempts to find new methods of compelling knights to fight were ineffective, and the traditional ones he employed clearly outmoded. Yet under his son a different style of leadership and a new cause were to see attitudes transformed, and great victories at last achieved.

52 *Scalacronica by Sir Thomas Grey of Heton knight*, ed. J. Stevenson, Maitland Club 1836, 145—6.
53 'Annales Londonienses', 157; Barrow, 295—6.
54 *The Political Songs of England*, ed. T. Wright, Camden Soc. 1839, 334.

THE JURISDICTION AND ORIGINS OF
THE CONSTABLE'S COURT

M.H. Keen

In the later middle ages, the Court presided over by the Constable of England and the Earl Marshal, commonly known as the Court of Chivalry, enjoyed a wide and important jurisdiction. It dealt with cases arising out of acts of war, including disputes over rights in prisoners and their ransoms, in which substantial financial interests were often involved. It dealt with cases that concerned the right to armorial bearings, and the celebrated dispute between Sir Richard Scrope and Sir Robert Grosvenor over the right to the arms *azur a bend or* was commenced before it in consequence.[1] It took cognisance of appeals, principally of treason, in which battle was offered by the appellor: for this reason, the celebrated duel of Sir John Annesley and Sir Thomas Caterton was fought out before it in 1380.[2] Traitors taken in arms in open rebellion were brought to judgement before it — though its jurisdiction here was limited, for since it administered the civil law it could only levy execution upon the body and goods of a convicted traitor, and could not distrain upon his lands (only a common law court could do that).[3]

Because the procedures of the Constable's Court did not follow common law, it was suspected from time to time of being the instrument of would-be royal tyranny. It was one of the articles alleged against Richard II after his deposition that he had caused appeals to be brought in the Constable's Court against persons alleged to have spoken in disparagement of the King.[4] Later, in the time of the Yorkists, chroniclers viewed critically the summary judgements upon traitors taken in the field that were pronounced by John Tiptoft when he was Constable, by 'lawe padowe'. So he came, we are told, to be hated by the people, for the 'dysordinate dethe that he used'.[5] Even outside such violent times as Richard II's last year and the Wars of the Roses there were complaints about the Court of Chivalry, allegations (no doubt true) that it was seeking to extend the range of its view and was encroaching on matters that ought to go to common law. In 1379 the commons petitioned against appeals of treason being brought by bill before the Constable and Marshal, against the form of

---

[1] See N.H. Nicolas, *The Controversy between Sir Richard Scrope and Sir Robert Grosvenor*, 2 vols, London 1832.
[2] J. Bellamy, 'Sir John de Annesley and the Chandos inheritance' *Nottingham Medieval Studies* X, 1966, 94—105; Morley v. Montagu (PRO SP9/10, fo. 32 vo); Scrope v. Kighlee (CPR 1399—1401, 401); Inglose v. Tiptoft (BL MS Cotton, Titus C I, fo. 192); the Prior of Kilmain v. Ormond (PPC VI, 57—9); Lyalton v. Norres (PPC VI, 129).
[3] M. Keen, 'Treason trials under the Law of Arms' *TRHS*, 5th series, 12, 1962, 85—103.
[4] RP III, 420.
[5] J. Warkworth, *A Chronicle of the reign of King Edward the Fourth* ed. J.O. Halliwell (Camden Society, 1839) 5, 9.

the Great Charter.[6] In 1384 it was provided, in response to a petition of the commons, that the Court of Chivalry should not hold pleas touching the common law.[7] The inhibition seems to have been ineffective, for the commons continued to petition on the subject, and that in spite of a statute of 13 Richard II that defined within clear limits the jurisdiction of the court (once again in response to a commons petition). 'To the Constable it pertaineth' this statute declared

> to have cognisance of contracts touching deeds of arms and of war out of the realm, and also of things that touch arms and war within the realm which cannot be determined nor discussed by common law.[8]

This definition is expanded thus in a note in the *Black Book of the Admiralty*.

> The conestable and mareschall hath knowleche upon all maner crymes, contracts, pleets, quarell, trespas, injuries and offenses done beyonde the see in tyme of werre betwene souldeour and souldeour, betwene merchaunts, vytelers, leches, barbours, launders, corvesers [i.e. cobblers], laborers, and artificers necessary to the oost, and if any of the personnes be oone [of our own subjects], and the other personne be a straunger, the conestable and mareschalle shall have knowleche in the said matere done in the werre beyond the see: and of all maner dedes of armes here within the londe doone he hath cognoissance, and of the offenses doon beyonde the see he hath knowleche of here in the londe.[9]

This note gives a vivid impression of just how wide a compass there was to the jurisdiction of the Constable's Court, and of the importance of his power to consider matters arising out of acts done beyond the sea in which aliens might be parties. One can also see how easily conflicts of jurisdiction could arise between the Court of Chivalry and the common law courts — for instance in a case of debt which was related to a martial contract, such as an indenture of war.[10]

Given the wide range of its authority and the notoriety of some of the cases that were brought before it, it is perhaps initially surprising that the Court of Chivalry has not received more attention than it has from historians. The principal reason for this neglect is that the medieval records of the court have for the most part disappeared, in contrast with those of other and better studied prerogative courts, although it is clear that they were once fully registered. This is also the reason why the only full-scale modern study of the Court, G.D. Squibb's *The High Court of Chivalry*, published in 1959, is largely concerned

---

6 RP III, 65.
7 Statutes, 8 Ric II c. 5; RP III, 202.
8 Statutes, 13 Ric II st. 1, c.2; RP III, 265.
9 *Black Book of the Admiralty* ed. T. Twiss (RS 1872—6) I, 281.
10 This was the matter in issue in Pounteney v. Borney (YB 13 Hen IV, Mich, pl. 10). The case was commenced in the Court of Chivalry; the defendant obtained a writ of privy seal to stay proceedings there on the ground that it was triable at common law; the Council granted a *procedendo* allowing the Constable's Court to proceed, but this was successfully challenged: it was finally sent to the Exchequer Chamber. Comparable cases include Salisbury v. Montagu (CPR 1385—9, 67) and Tottenas v. Mareshal (*ibid*, 85).

with the activities of the Court in the seventeenth century, for which period quite extensive records have survived.[11] Even these for a long time lay forgotten in the College of Arms, until their significance was recognised by Sir Anthony Wagner, and Squibb's is the first study based on them.

The High Court of Chivalry is a fascinating book, which casts much light into interesting and obscure corners of the legal and social history of the seventeenth century. Very properly, it also includes a brief survey of the 'origins and medieval jurisdiction of the Court.'[12] Since my main excuse for putting together this paper is that I do not agree with a number of points made in this part of a work that has come to be justly considered as authoritative, I must stress that in Squibb's book they belong to an essentially introductory section, and that my criticisms of them in no way invalidate the very interesting and valuable discussion of the later activities of the court, which are his main theme. Indeed it is because his book has come to be authoritative that it is worth pursuing the matter further. Another reason for pursuing it is that, since Squibb wrote, a large part of the *dossier* of an important medieval Court of Chivalry case, the dispute concerning the ransom of the Count of Denia (captured at Najera in 1367) has been discovered among the Westminster Abbey muniments by Dr. A. Rogers,[13] and published. In addition, Professor R.I. Jack has focussed attention on another Court of Chivalry case, that of Grey v. Hastings (*temp*: Henry IV), which was known to Squibb but had not, when he wrote, been studied in any detail.[14] It has, in fact, become apparent since 1959 that there is rather more interest about the fragmentary records of the medieval Court than was once supposed.

Two central points in Squibb's account of the early history of the Court of Chivalry seem to me to be open to challenge. The first is the assumption that its jurisdiction was exclusive in cases triable by the 'law of arms' (those concerning ransoms, for instance, and disputes over armorial bearings) and that this jurisdiction was quite different and distinct from that exercised by the officers of royal hosts, in accordance with the Ordinances of War proclaimed in the host in question.[15] The idea that they were similar has arisen, he believes, because the officers appointed to preside in the courts of the host were usually referred to as the constable and marshal (as they are, for instance, in Richard II's Durham Ordinances of 1385, and in Henry V's Ordinances of 1419):[16] but their temporary jurisdictions, limited to matters (principally of discipline) that were mentioned in ordinances issued for a single campaign, were really quite different from the 'formal and settled' jurisdiction of the Court of Chivalry, he argues.[17] That they were different in degree I accept, but I believe the

---

11 G.D. Squibb, *The High Court of Chivalry*, Oxford 1959.
12 Squibb, chapter 1, 1—28.
13 A. Rogers, 'Hoton *versus* Shakell: a ransom case in the Court of Chivalry, 1390—5' *Nottingham Medieval Studies* VI, 1962, 74—108; VII, 1963, 53—78.
14 R.I. Jack 'Entail and Descent: the Hastings inheritance, 1370—1436', BIHR XXXVIII, 1965, 1—19. See also C.G. Young, *An Account of the Controversy between Reginald Lord Grey of Ruthyn and Sir Edward Hastings* (privately printed, 1841).
15 Squibb, 3—12.
16 *Black Book of the Admiralry* I, 453—8, 459—72. Squibb sees that often the Constable and Marshal of a host would in fact also be the Constable and Marshal of England, but still maintains that the court in the host would be different from the Court of Chivalry.
17 Squibb, 6, 12.

difference to be much less significant than Squibb suggests, and in particular in its relation to another point in his argument. For he goes on to suggest that we should not seek for the origins of the Court of Chivalry (as most historians have done) in a gradual extension of the jurisdiction which the Constable and Marshal of England had exercised from a quite early period in the King's hosts, and which is clearly comparable to that later exercised by constables and marshals in accordance with Ordinances of War. The Court of Chivalry originated, Squibb believes, as a result of the delegation by the King's Council to the Constable and Marshal of certain aspects of its general jurisdiction over matters which could not be tried by common law. The formal act of delegation can, he thinks, be pin-pointed fairly precisely to the years 1347—48.[18] This is the second point on which his view seems to me to be questionable.

Underlying Squibb's emphasis on the difference between the Court of Chivalry and the courts of the hosts over which their constables and marshals presided is the assumption that I have mentioned, that the former exercised a constant and more or less exclusive jurisdiction in certain kinds of cases, for instance heraldic disputes and disputes over rights in ransoms, and that this can be contrasted with that exercised by courts in the hosts which were principally concerned with matters of discipline. This assumption is demonstrably open to challenge.

It is true that all the half dozen medieval cases that originated in the Court of Chivalry and of which full records survive were concerned with the kind of matters that Squibb refers to its exclusive jurisdiction. The Denia case and the case of Gerard v. Chamberlayn concern rights in prisoners and their ransoms: that of Hawley v. des Roches a breach of safe-conduct 'done beyond the sea'. Those of Scrope v. Grosvenor, Lovell v. Morley and Grey v. Hastings all concern disputed rights to armorial bearings.[19] It is quite clear, however, that the Court of Chivalry had no exclusive jurisdiction in any of these matters. The Ordinances of War have a great deal to say about the taking of prisoners and about rights in their ransoms, and make it clear that it was the business of the constables and marshals of the hosts to enforce the regulations that they laid down.[20] Even disputes over bearings were regarded as within their jurisdiction: to quote from a fifteenth century set of Ordinances

> '*Item* that no man debate for *armes* prisoners nor for none other thyng so that none ryotte contest nor debate be ynne the hosts . . . but yff so be that any man felt hym grevyd shewe his grevaunce to the constabyll and marshall and right shall be done.'[21]

---

18 Squibb, 12—15.
19 For Scrope v. Grosvenor and the Denia case, see ante notes 1 and 13. Of the unedited causes, the records of three are among the Chancery Miscellanea; Lovell v. Morley is PRO C47/6/1; Hawley v. des Rochas PRO C47/6/4; Gerard v. Chamberlain C47/6/5. Grey v. Hastings survives in a seventeenth transcript, Coll. of Arms MS, *Processus in Curia Marescalli* i and ii (ii also contains a transcripit of Lovell v. Morley).
20 Durham Ordinances, cl. 12, 13, 19, 21; Henry V's Ordinances, cl. 14, 15, 16, 20, 27, 35 (*Black Book of the Admiralty* I, *cit. sup.* n. 16).
21 B.L. Add MS 33191, cl. 18: compare Durham Ordinances, cl. 8; Henry V's Ordinances, cl. 9.

This should not surprise us. Arms, as the means of recognition in the field, were directly relevant to good order in a host: besides, we know that commanders on occasion awarded armorial bearings to deserving soldiers, and if they could grant them, it was natural that they should also be able to judge disputes concerning them.[22]

Concrete examples show, moreover, that constables and captains, and summary courts assembled on their authority, did try cases involving all the matters mentioned above. A few examples among very many should suffice. In 1356 the Black Prince, as commander of the Poitiers host, took judicial cognisance of the dispute between Denis de Morbek and Bernard de Troye as to which of them had captured King John of France in that great battle.[22a] In 1427, when the English captured Le Mans, so many quarrels arose over rights in prisoners and ransoms that a special court had to be set up in the host under the presidency of Lord Scales, in order to deal with them.[23] In 1417 Thomas Duke of Clarence, as constable of the army, judged in a *curia militaris* (the same title which the Court of Chivalry was given in Latin texts) the charge against Walter Sydenham and William Broke that they had plundered persons travelling under the King's safe-conduct.[24] There are examples also of the trial of armorial cases in the courts of hosts. John of Gaunt told the Court of Chivalry in the Scrope v. Grosvenor case of how, when a dispute arose over armorial bearings in 1373 in the host that he was commanding, between Richard Scrope and Carminow of Cornwall, he had assembled a court of seven senior knights and submitted the matter to their judgement.[25] No one suggested that he had acted *ultra vires*.

The reason why we know about the case of Scrope v. Carminow is that it was referred to in a Court of Chivalry case. The dispute between Denis de Morbek and Bernard de Troye as to which had captured John the Good at Poitiers, which I have also mentioned, also seems to have come before the Court of the Constable and Marshal — presumably because it had not been finally settled when the Black Prince's host disbanded.[26] These facts are significant, for they show, and clearly, that far from being concerned with cases different in their nature from those judged by officers in the hosts, the Court of Chivalry was often concerned with the same kind of cases, sometimes even with the same cases. The relation between all these martial courts was indeed close, and necessarily so. The orders that a commander had given could be directly relevant to a Court of Chivalry case. Thus in the case of Gerard v. Chamberlain, heard in 1403 before commissioners on appeal from the Court of Chivalry, we find the marshal of Despenser's host of 1383 being called to testify that, under the terms of an ordinance that he had made, Gerard had

---

22 N. Upton *De Studio Militari* ed. E. Bysshe, London 1654, 154, 200, (accounts of grants of arms made to soldiers by the Earl of Salisbury in the 1420s).
22a J. Froissart. *Oeuvres* ed. Kervyn de Lettenhove, V, Brussels 1868, 468.
23 Arch Nat X'a 4795, fo 324 vo — 5.
24 *Foedera* IV, iii, 38: compare *Rotuli Normannie*, ed. T.D. Hardy, London 1835, I, 378. These cases show that *Curia Militaris* was not a title confined to the Court of Chivalry, as suggested by Squibb, 2–3.
25 Nicolas, I, 49–50.
26 *Foedera*, III, i, 193: and see further BL Cotton MS Cal D III, 102 (Bernard de Troye's testament).

had no right to take prisoner Hannequin Lower, whose standing as a prisoner of war was in dispute between him and Chamberlain.[27] The judgements of lesser captains could also be matter for the Court of Chivalry to consider: the case of Hawley v. des Roches came before it in consequence of a sentence of the Earl of Arundel as Captain of Brest.[28] Another case that arose, like that of Gerard v. Chamberlain, out of the 1383 expedition was that of Louis de Sancerre, (the famous French captain) against Matthew Gournay and others. Sancerre was seeking payment from various of Despenser's subordinate captains, presumably owing to him under the terms of their treaties of surrender to the French, and could not apply to the commander of the host in question, which had been disbanded. He had to sue somewhere else, and tried first in the court of the Captain of Calais: subsequently the case was revoked before the Court of Chivalry.[29]

Indeed, if a campaign had ended, and the powers of the commander of a host had lapsed when the host was disbanded, to whom was a complainant who, like Sancerre, believed himself to have been injured in rights acquired during the course of the campaign, to turn, if not to the Constable and Marshal as the standing lieutenants in war of the prince, against whose soldiers he wished to complain? It was here, as I see it, that the real difference between the Court of Chivalry and the courts in the hosts lay, that the one exercised a constant, the others a temporary jurisdiction, not that they were concerned with different kinds of cases. In the nature of things it was likely that routine issues of discipline would mostly be dealt with on the spot by the host's officers: and equally that claims which were knotty and which might involve large sums (as that which Sancerre was pursuing presumably did) often had to be referred to a higher tribunal. But neither kind of court had an exclusive jurisdiction over either kind of case. That is why the text in the Black Book of the Admiralty that outlines the *Office of the Conestable and Mareschall*, and that was quoted earlier in this paper, not only explains and expands the definition of the Court of Chivalry's jurisdiction given in the statute of 13 Richard II, but also notes that it is their business 'to punysh all manner of men that breken the statutes and ordonnaunce by the kynge made to be kepyd in the oost in the said tyme, and to punysh the same accordyng to the peynes provided in the said statutes'.[30] As the author of this text realised, the Constable and Marshal, especially if they were in the King's company in the King's host, might have to deal with matters of ordinary discipline, as well as with more exalted affairs.

If it is accepted that the jurisdictions exercised respectively by the Court of Chivalry and by officers of the hosts were not radically distinct but interrelated, then the suggestion, rejected by Squibb, that the former owed its origin to a gradual extension of the authority that the Constable and Marshal

---

27 PRO C47/6/5. Faringdon, the marshal, said he had published an order to the effect that Flemings who came into the obedience of the King should be free, and that any already taken prisoners of war should be delivered free of ransom. Gerard claimed Lower was his prisoner: Faringdon's evidence suggested he had no right to a ransom from him.
28 PRO C47/6/4 (Roll No. 5).
29 *Foedera* III, iv, 19: and see CPR (1388—92), 242.
30 *Black Book of the Admiralty* I, 281.

of England had traditionally exercised in royal hosts, becomes hard to resist. Vernon Harcourt, who held this view, instanced as early examples of the judicial authority of the Constable and Marshal the roll of the *placita exercitus* that survives for the Scottish campaign of 1294—5, and the trial in 1322 of Roger Damory (also described as one of the *placita exercitus*).[31] The former certainly shows a military court to have been in existence in 1294—5, though there is no hint of any body of usage that it followed, distinct from the common law. The latter is more interesting and needs a little more attention.

Damory in 1322 was sentenced for treason, for having been in arms against his liege lord King Edward II, by a tribunal whose members were Fulk Fitzwarin, constable of the King's host, John de Weston, Marshal of the Household, and the Justice Geoffrey Le Scrope. Squibb, in support of his view that this trial has no relevance to the history of the Court of Chivalry, points out that neither Fitzwarin nor Weston were officers of state — that they were not the Constable and Marshal of England.[32] Fitzwarin, however, was the constable of the royal army (Bohun of Hereford, the hereditary constable, was among the rebels), and Weston was the official deputy of the Marshal, Thomas Brotherton, Earl of Norfolk.[33] Squibb also points out that the proceedings were not specifically by 'law of arms': nevertheless, the manner of proceeding was very similar to that followed by later Constables who summarily sentenced to death traitors taken in arms in the field. To Squibb, this similarity is irrelevant, for his view is that the drumhead courts-martial presided over by Tiptoft and other Constables during the Wars of the Roses were distinct from the Court of Chivalry.[34] But, as I have shown elsewhere, they followed the same kind of procedure as was followed in 1405 when Henry Boynton was summarily condemned by the Constable John of Lancaster, and the record of his sentence is explicitly stated to have been extracted from the registers of the Court of Chivalry, and to have been in accordance with the 'law of arms'.[35] In the light of this record, and of other instances from the reigns of Henry IV and Henry VII when traitors were arraigned before the Court of Chivalry, the stated objection to allowing the trial of Damory any relevance to the history of that Court loses its force.

The *placita* of 1294—5 and the record of the judgement on Damory are not the only early references to the martial jurisdiction of the Constable. Matthew Paris, for instance, mentions it in connection with an incident during the Gascon campaign of 1254. Spoil had been taken by the King's Welsh troops,

---

31 L.W. Vernon Harcourt, *His Grace the Steward and Trial of Peers*, London 1907, 362—3. The *Placita* of 1294—5 are among the Exchequer Accounts Various, PRO E39/93/15: the record of Damory's trial is given in full by Vernon Harcourt 399—400: see also Parl. Writs II ii, Appx, 261.
32 Squibb, 11.
33 CCR 1318—23, 581.
34 Squibb, 26—8: 'in so far as such proceedings had any legal validity at all, they derived it from the direct grant of the Crown' i.e. from the terms of the patents appointing the Constables to their office. The most relevant patent is that appointing Lord Rivers Constable in 1467, printed by Vernon Harcourt, 407—12.
35 BL MS Add 9021, fos. 8—9 (transcript, made for Anstis of an exemplification of the sentence, from the registers of the Court of Chivalry, by letters patent of John of Lancaster, 26 May 1408). And see Keen, 85—103.
36 E.g. cases of Northumberland and Bardolph, commenced in the Court of Chivalry, RP III, 604: of Ralph Hastings, condemned by Fulthorpe, the Constable's lieutenant, RP III, 633: and the trial of Lord Audeley in 1497, Vernon Harcourt, 414—5.

and some of them were severely punished for this by the King's unpopular Poitevin relations. This caused an outcry, and Henry III had to take the quarrel into his own hands and patch it up. The whole affair should, however, says Matthew, have been referred in the first place to the Earl of Hereford, in accordance with custom and his hereditary right.[37] Hereford was constable of the host, but his hereditary right must refer to his office as Constable of England. So apparently as early as 1254 the Constable could claim jurisdiction over a case involving spoliation in war. Robert of Reading, in a similar vein, complains of Edward II's commission of the *regimen exercitus* (? the disciplining of the army) to Gilbert of Clare, because this office belonged to the Earl of Hereford by hereditary right.[38] There is also to be considered a record of the right claimed as pertaining to his office by Edward II's Earl Marshal, Thomas of Brotherton, and which states that jurisdiction in the King's host is the exclusive province of his Constable and Marshal. This text may not be authentic — it cannot be traced back further than the reign of Richard II, though its contents suggest an earlier date (for instance in their concern with the Marshal's duty of certifying the feudal service in the host of those holding by military tenure).[39] Even it if is not authentic, it does at least show that in Richard's reign the jurisdiction of the Constable and Marshal was considered to be closely associated with the offices that they discharged in royal hosts, and to have an old pedigree.

At this point it clearly becomes necessary to look more closely at Squibb's suggestion that the origin of the Court of Chivalry derived from a delegation by the royal Council of part of its power to try cases which could not be dealt with at common law. Part of the reasoning behind this suggestion is an analogy with what Marsden believed to have been the origin of the powers of the Court of the Admiral[40] — whose jurisdiction over 'deeds of war' done on the high seas was in many ways similar to that of the Constable and Marshal. Marsden traced the rise of this Court to the period 1340—57, but his account of the precise manner of its institution was not very definite, and, as he himself pointed out, left to be accounted for an enigmatic Year Book reference to the jurisdiction of the Admiral in 1297.[41] The other part of the reasoning behind Squibb's account of the origin of the Court of Chivalry is his assumption that, once it was in being, it had an exclusive jurisdiction in certain kinds of cases. There is a reference in a copy of a letter patent of 19 July 1347 to the appointment, in the host before Calais, of a commission to try disputes that had arisen in the army over rights to certain armorial bearings and war-crests.[42] This was a kind of matter that would have come into the purview of the Court of Chivalry, says Squibb: *ergo*, there was no Court of Chivalry in July 1347. But

37 Matthew Paris, *Chronica Majora* ed. H.R. Luard (RS 1872—83) V, 442.
38 *Flores Historiarum* ed. H.R. Luard (RS 1890) III 158.
39 BL MS Cotton Nero D VI, fo 85 vo. The MS appears to date from Richard II's reign (its list, fo. 76 ff, of the Kings of England *a Noe usque in hunc diem*, ends with Richard), and to have been written after 1385 (since it includes a text of the Durham Ordinances, fo. 89). The reference on fo. 65 vo to the claim of Margaret Brotherton to appoint a Marshal at Richard II's coronation perhaps suggests that the 'customs' claimed for Brotherton as Marshal were brought forward in that connection.
40 R.G. Marsden (ed.) *Select Pleas in the Court of the Admiralty* (Seldon Soc., 1894) I, xiv ff.
41 Marsden, xvii—xviii.
42 Squibb, 14, quoting Bodl. MS Ashmole 1137, fo 144.

in August 1348 there is a clear reference to the Court, when two serjeants of arms were ordered to arrest in Jersey William le Counte, claimed as a defaulting prisoner of war by William de Wynchelez, and to bring him before the Constable and Marshal to there answer the points to be put forward against him.[43] So, between July 1347 and August 1348 we have the date of the institution of the Court of Chivalry pin-pointed — and at a point in time which fits neatly into the same bracket of years to which Marsden traced the origins of the Admiral's Court.

There are two objections to the arguments outlined here. The first has already been stated, that the assumption that the Court of Chivalry ever had an exclusive right to try such matters as disputes over prisoners or armorial bearings is unsafe. John of Gaunt, as we have seen, could appoint an *adhoc* tribunal to hear an armorial dispute in 1373, when the Court of Chivalry was certainly in existence: *a fortiori* Edward III could do the same in 1347, whether or not there was such a Court then. The second derives from a reference in the record of the proceedings in the case of Lovell v. Morley, commenced in the Court of Chivalry in Richard II's time. John Molham esquire, aged seventy years, in this case testified that, on the Crecy expedition, he had been in the service of William de Bohun, Constable of England, and had filled the office of clerk to the Court of Chivalry. After Crecy — well before July 1347, it is implied — Nicholas Burnell had challenged the arms of Lord Morley and demanded that his claim be heard in the Court.[44] And so it was heard, later, during the siege of Calais, by the Constable and Marshal. This testimony shows that there was a Court of Chivalry in existence before either of the cases in Squibb's bracket of July 1347 to August 1348, so the bracket will not hold. Nothing Molham said, it should be noted, suggests that he thought that the post that he had held was a new one, associated with a novel jurisdiction. It is worth noting the glimpse that he gives us of the Court of Chivalry sitting *tribunalement* in the army, on campaign, in the same way that any court attached to the army might do.

If the pedigree of the Court of Chivalry has to be traced further back than the time of the Crecy expedition, then it becomes hard indeed not to accept the thesis that it developed as a result of a gradual extension of the lieutenancies that the Constable and Marshal traditionally exercised in the King's armies. It is especially so now that we have been shown the Court sitting in the host, on campaign, with a clerk in attendance, who was in the retinue of the Constable.

That is not, however, to say that the 1340s were not a key period in the rise of the Constable's court to the new prominence that it enjoyed in the later fourteenth century and in the fifteenth. The fact that the references to the authority of the Constable before that time are so few and enigmatic, and afterwards become so comparatively plentiful, tells its own story. In regarding the middle years of the fourteenth century as crucial to his story Squibb is absolutely right, I believe, even if he can be faulted on points of detail. For the outbreak of the Hundred Years War undoubtedly did give a new prominence to legal problems arising out of state of war. The taking of spoil and prisoners

---

43 CPR 1348—50, 174.
44 Coll. of Arms MS, *Processus in Curia Marescalli*, ii, 98. Molham states that he himself wrote out Burnell's bill.

began to be big business for English lords and gentlemen, and the division of shares in spoil became for them the subject of carefully drawn contractual arrangements in indentures of war. The observance of safe-conducts became more than a matter of discipline now that huge sums by way of ransom might be obtained by taking the bearer a prisoner, if only a technical legal fault could be found in the terms of his protection. The cult of chivalry, which Edward III encouraged for propaganda purposes, at the same time was sharpening sensitivities about such matters as the right to particular bearings with a particular history, and more people too, esquires as well as knights, were beginning to adopt heraldic arms. From the 1340s on, moreover, most of the acts of war in which Englishmen were involved and in which they could hope to win reputation and riches, were 'done beyond the sea', where the common law did not run. These new circumstances gave a new importance to the jurisdiction that all captains and constable of hosts exercised, and also created a new need for legal recourse to officers whose position and jurisdiction were not dependent on temporary posts of command. This gave a new importance to the offices of the Constable and Marshal of England, who had long been regarded as the King's standing lieutenants in martial matters.

Significantly, it did the same thing in France for the offices of the Constable and Marshals of France, and for the same reasons. Indeed, the picture is the same elsewhere too: everywhere in Europe, in this age, we come across Constables and Marshals — or officers with equivalent titles — judging on behalf of their princely masters disputes arising out of war. And we find at the same time advocates, trained in Roman law, beginning to bring their legal expertise to bear to elucidate and rationalise the issues arising in such cases, to give the ill defined military customs that constituted the 'law of arms' a respectable and coherent legal footing. Thus, at the same time that the Constable and Marshal achieved in England — as elsewhere — a new prominence in their judicial role, the law that they administered in their Court became more clearly distinguishable from the common law administered by the King's other judges.

It remains of course possible that, sometime in the 1340s, the advice of the King's counsellors (a group not well-defined) may have given the kind of legal business that was then raising new problems a push in the direction of the Constable and Marshal. If so, it was probably continental example that prompted them, and in any case it only needed a little push. A lieutenancy in an army, even at a humble level, cannot be exercised without some sort of jurisdiction being accepted as inherent in it, as any modern company commander or adjutant can tell you, and the Constable and Marshal of England were lieutenants at a far from humble level. 'Pleas of the army', as we have seen from Damory's case, had already come to include potentially such weighty matters as the judgement of traitors taken in arms. Besides, it should be remembered that well before the outbreak of the Hundred Years War the offices of the Constable and Marshal had grown in importance, because the size of the royal hosts in which they exercised their lieutenancies had grown, and the business of imposing order in them had become a larger business. Texts such as the *Tract on the Steward's Office* and the *Modus Tenendi Parliamentum* remind us that in the period when, under the first two Edwards, the organisation of war was imposing new strains, the sensitivity of the great hereditary officers of state, the Steward, the Constable and the Marshal had become sharper with regard to their rights, privileges and jurisdiction.[45] The parts played by Edward I's Constable and Marshal in the famous events of 1297 underscore the same point, that these great noblemen were beginning to establish their offices as offices of state rather than of the King's military household. It was as officers of the military household, however, that they had first achieved prominence: that was the context in which, way back in Henry I's time, the Constable Walter de Pitres was hailed as *princeps militiae domus regis*.[46] The first origins of the later authority and pre-eminence of the Constable and Marshal are, in short, to be sought in the position that they held in that institution whose importance in early times John Prestwich, before all others, has taught us to appreciate, the military household of the Kings of England.[47] As he has shown, it was a good training ground for officers whose role was at once military and judicial.

---

45 Vernon Harcourt, 164—69.
46 J.H. Round, *The King's Serjeants and Officers of State*, London, 1911, 79.
47 J.O. Prestwich, 'The military household of the Norman kings' *EHR*, xcvi, 1981.

SED NIHIL FECIT? THE LAST CAPETIANS AND THE RECOVERY OF THE HOLY LAND

C.J. Tyerman

Looking back on attempts of the previous fifteen years to recover the Holy Land, an anonymous historian writing in 1328 for Philip VI of France commented: 'the pope had the money . . . and the king and the others who had taken the cross did not set out, and the saracens are still there in peace and I think they may sleep on undisturbed'.[1] In similar vein the author of the *Vita Edwardi Secundi* remarked that the council of Vienne, which in 1312 had proclaimed a new crusade and ordered the collection of a new crusade tithe, 'profited the Holy Land nothing at all'.[2] A source close to the French court was even more brusque. Philip IV may have declared this crusading purpose 'sed nihil fecit'.[3]

How true was this? From 1305 when Philip IV offered to exchange his throne for that of Jerusalem, the French had made most of the running for a new *passagium*, in public at least.[4] Yet the period of highest-blown theory coincided with the period of least action, under Philip IV. Practical planning flourished only in a more prosaic setting. Philip IV's court had attracted ideas for the recovery of the Holy Land which bristled with solutions to the great issues of world history, the total defeat of Islam, the re-ordering of Christendom, the reformation of the church and the apotheosis of the line of St. Louis.[5] The extravagant and extreme ideas of Ramon Lull, Pierre Dubois and Guillaume de Nogaret were suited to a government which pitched its rhetoric and ambition high and loud. The years after the council of Vienne imposed more sober thoughts. Royal power was successfully challenged in 1314—15. After 1316, papal priorities centred on the anti-Ghibelline alliance in Italy and the restoration of curial finances. Any plans to help Cyprus and Armenia or recover the Holy Land had to be less comprehensive but more comprehensible. Planners began to confront the problems of logistics, men, money and ships. Advice was more expert. Whereas Dubois had had no experience of the east, increasingly sources which had, such as the citizens of Marseilles or the Venetian merchant Marino Sanudo, were consulted.[6]

---

1 J.N. Hillgarth, *Ramon Lull and Lullism in Fourteenth Century France*, Oxford 1971, 83 and note 136.
2 *Vita Edwardi Secundi*, trans. N. Denholm Young, London 1957, 46.
3 Guillaume de Nangis, *Chronique latine de 1113 à 1300 avec les continuations de 1300 à 1368*, ed. H. Géraud, Paris 1843, i, 392.
4 H. Finke, *Papsttum und Untergang des Templerordens*, Münster 1907, ii, 118.
5 Hillgarth, 46—134; A.S. Atiya, *The Crusade in the Later Middle Ages*, London 1938, 47—94.
6 C.J. Tyerman, 'Marino Sanudo Torsello and the Lost Crusade', *TRHS*, 5th ser. xxxii, 1982, 57—73; A. de Boislisle, 'Projet de croisade du premier duc de Bourbon', *Extrait de l'Annuaire Bulletin de la Société de l'Histoire de France*, xiv, 1872, 248—55.

But whatever their personal interest in crusading, the last Capetians pursued the recovery of the Holy Land for a variety of other political motives. The crusade was deliberately refracted into areas of the greatest political sensitivity and importance. Boniface VIII was accused of hindering the crusade.[7] The suppression of the Templars was clearly staked out in relation to the needs of the Holy Land, Philip IV's suggestions for a new military order and a new crusade. For example, the bulls for the Hospitaller crusade in 1308 were issued the day before the bulls against the Temple and the summoning of the council of Vienne.[8] The Hospitaller expedition itself, for which Philip IV promised but did not deliver funds, was seen as preparing the way for a French crusade.[9] In secular politics, Philip of Poitiers' candidacy for the Empire in 1312 was urged on the pope ostensibly because of the crusade opportunities his election would provide.[10] Disputes with Edward II of England over Gascon jurisdiction were settled in 1313 on the pretext that Edward and Philip IV were fellow *crucesignati*.[11] Frequently, the turbid and acrimonious Franco-Flemish negotiations were hitched to the fate of the crusade. In 1313 Cardinal Fréauville was both papal mediator between France and Flanders and chief preacher of the crusade. One of the French terms in the negotiations of 1316 was that Count Robert should join the next *passagium* as a punishment for failing to honour earlier treaties. In 1318, another papal envoy, Pierre de la Palud, publically hinted that a crusade might be launched against the contumacious Flemings as 'impeditores negotii Terrae Sanctae', an idea still current during the discussions on the final settlement of 1319—1320.[12] Even the planned restoration of the Frankish position in Greece, to be led by Philip of Taranto, was presented firmly as preparatory to the French crusade to Outremer.[13]

Nearer home, the crusade harnessed support to the Capetian regime. Men from Gascony and Languedoc, as well as the more traditional areas of Capetian influence, trooped to Paris in 1313 to take the cross, the ceremony providing both a symbol and a practical bond of community, obligation and mutual self-interest.[14] Money was invested in Mediterranean ports. Galleys were built and hired at Narbonne, Montpellier, Marseilles and other ports along the coast in 1319 and 1323. Marseilles was consulted about the crusade by Louis de Clermont and a consul of Narbonne discussed the crusade in Paris

---

7 C.V. Langlois, *Les derniers capétiens directs 1226—1328*, Paris 1911, 159.
8 *Regestum Clementis Papae V*, Rome 1885—92, nos. 2986, 2988 and 3626.
9 *Regestum Clementis V*, nos. 2986 and 7893.
10 J. Schwalm, 'Beiträge zur Reichsgeschichte', *Neues Archiv der Gesellschaft für altere deutsche Geschichtskunde* xxv, 1899—1900, 564—5.
11 R. Fawtier, *Registres du trésor des chartes, Inventaire analytique*, i, Paris 1958, nos. 1970—2, 1975, 2002, 2005—6, 2009, 2011, 2018, 2020, 2024, 2026—32 and 2174.
12 *Regestum Clementis V*, nos. 9941—62; Archives nationales MS J 560, nos. 3 and 5 and MS J 561a no. 24; E. Baluze, *Miscellaneorum* i, Paris 1678, 166—7 and 173; Nangis ii, 11.
13 Archives nationales MS J 411, no. 42; *Regestum Clementis V*, nos. 1604, 1605 and 7759; P. Topping, 'The Morea 1311—64', *History of the Crusades*, general ed. K. Setton, iii, Wisconsin 1975, 104—116.
14 F. Ehrle, 'Process über den Nachlass Clemens V', *Archiv für Literatur und Kirchengeschichte des Mittelalters* v, 1889, 7; J.P. Ludewig, *Reliquae manuscriptorum omnis aevi diplomatum ac monumentorum ineditorum adhuc* xii, Frankfort 1741, 48—60; Geoffroi de Paris, Chronique rimée, *Recueil des historiens des Gaules et de la France*, ed. M. Bouquet etc., Paris 1738—1876, xxii, 135—7.

late in 1319.[15] Ship owners and port authorities stood to gain from this royal interest. On each occasion the recovery of the Holy Land was proclaimed the objective, yet involving the nobility of the south in the crusade and filling the pockets of influential southern merchants and bankers had their own rewards for rulers based on the geographically and culturally distant Ile de France.

The last Capetians saw the recovery of the Holy Land as their and their subjects' God-given duty. The crusade 'communiter omnes tangit', 'specialiter illis de regno Francie quod pro defensione fidei catholice peculiari sibi Dominus per sui gratiam noscitur elegisse . . .'[16] At the council of Vienne, Philip IV promised to lead a general *passagium* to the east and this decision was confirmed a year later when he took the cross.[17] Throughout all crusade discussions, with Clement V, the Hospitallers, Philip of Taranto, John XXII, Robert of Naples, the ports of Marseilles or Narbonne, the Cypriots or the Armenians, one feature was constant. As the crusade was peculiarly a French obligation, the recovery was to be overwhelmingly a French campaign. Some theorists could argue for alliances with Aragon, Naples or Venice, but the Capetians insisted on prime and overall control of plans, strategy, tactics, ships, men and money, a proprietary attitude harmful to crusading prospects because it was so fiercely opposed by other rulers, notably James of Aragon and John XXII.

A crusader king could hope for ecclesiastical tithes to subsidise his efforts. But such revenue was not merely a bonus to swell the Capetian war-chest. By 1314, and especially after the cancellation of the Flemish war tax, clerical tithes saved the Capetian monarchy from financial collapse. A half-yearly account of 1316 records total royal receipts of 169,579*l*. 0*s*. 6*d*. *parisis* of which 112,086*l*. 6*s*. *tournois* (or just under fifty per cent) came from church taxes.[18] Clerical tenths continued to provide the largest single contribution to the revenue of the last Capetians. But the French clergy were as reluctant as the laity to agree to royal fiscal demands.[19] Royal coercion needed the assistance of papal approval so pressure on the pope could never flag. The crusade was one of the chief pretexts for securing the desperately important tithes. Small wonder that Franco-papal crusade finance at times brought the business of the curia to a halt.[20]

The entanglement of the crusade with other secular policies provides an obvious explanation for crusading inactivity. But it is not a wholly convincing one. Philip III, Philip IV and the papacy found adequate money, men and morale to fight crusades in Spain and Italy. Philip IV was able to wage an extended and expensive war with England in the 1290s. Financial and military assistance was available for Frankish Greece. It is evident that the financial, political and administrative effort expended on the recovery of the Holy Land

---

15 C. de la Roncière, 'Une escadre franco-papale', *Mélanges d'archéologie et d'histoire* xiii, 1893, 397—418; Boislisle, 'Projet', 248—55; Archives nationales MS JJ 58, no. 397.
16 J. Roucaute and M. Saché, eds. *Actes de Philippe le Bel relatifs au pays de Gévaudan*, Mende 1896, 141; BN MS Doat 16, fol 123 recto—125 recto.
17 Finke, *Papsttum* ii, 292—4; Nangis, i, 396.
18 R. Fawtier, *Comptes du trésor, Recueil des historiens de France, Documents financiers* ii, Paris 1930, nos. 543—551 and p. lviii.
19 A. Artonne, *Le mouvement de 1314*, Paris 1912, 79—89.
20 H. Finke, *Acta Aragonensia*, Berlin and Leipzig 1908—66, i, 489.

did not compare with the labours of the Capetians over Flanders, Gascony, the Templars, the papacy, extending their frontiers or asserting royal power over their subjects. Resources did exist, but were either not applied or applied inefficiently.

Nevertheless, the administrative investment in the crusade for its own sake was not entirely negligible nor measurable solely in livres, sous and deniers. As a barometer of international magnanimity, responsiblity and respectability, the crusade occupied a political position not dissimilar to modern programmes for overseas aid. But the crusade was also more than that. It provided a justification for French assertiveness and a moral safety-valve as the expression of the self-image of the ruling elite, public policy combining with personal obligation.

Was the chronicler right in saying that nothing was achieved for the Holy Land? In one sense he was. No French crusading expedition embarked. But this begs more questions. Why did the French kings continue to protest their devotion to the cause of recovering the Holy Land despite the acknowledged possibility and reality of public and political obloquy?[21] Was it simply a device to raise clerical funds? If so, it was hardly successful as none of Philip IV's sons received fresh grants of tithes specifically for the crusade. If crusade inertia is identified, what caused it and was it constant? To answer such questions it is necessary to look away from the rhetoric of high policy and examine secondary administrative activity, of diplomats, agents and officials.

The last Capetians usually allocated the crusade a subsidiary role in discussions with the papacy. At Vienne it was overshadowed by the fate of the Templars and the case of Boniface VIII. When Philip of Poitiers visited John XXII in September 1316 the crusade provided only the context for earnest discussions of the diversion of large amounts of the Vienne tithe to pay off royal debts. Fifteen months later the agenda of the embassy to Avignon led by Henri de Sully found the crusade jostling for attention with attempts to solve the Flemish problem. In 1321, despite the extraction of a conditional papal offer of crusade tithes, the central issues were Italy and Charles de la Marche's annulment.[22] This dispersal of concentration on the crusade and the continual admission by the French of other problems into debates on crusade planning and funding suited the pope whose sights were focussed on Italy and not beyond. It allowed the pope more easily to identify all the internal divisions and intractable problems in Christendom which precluded any immediate general crusade to the east and, hence, any immediate grant of general crusade tithes.[23]

But the autumn of 1319 saw the beginnings of a new French approach when, as he had often promised, Philip V started to concentrate on the crusade after the draft treaty with the Flemings had been agreed. Louis de Clermont's plans were encouraged and over a period of six months experts and crusade veterans were consulted.[24] Charles IV adopted an even more positive approach. For

21 Archives nationales MS JJ 60, no. 100 for French fears of 'la honte du monde'.
22 On Philip V and the crusade, C.J. Tyerman, 'Philip V of France, the Assemblies of 1319—20 and the Crusade', *BIHR* forthcoming; John XXII, *Lettres secrètes et curiales relatives à la France*, ed. A Coulon and S. Clémencet, Paris 1906—72, nos. 23, 471, 473, 479, 491, 505, 511—13, 1005 and 1262; Finke, *Acta*, i, 475—6.
23 John XXII, *Lettres secrètes*, nos. 53—6, 67, 74—6, 491, 1227, 1262, 1445 and 1710.
24 Tyerman, 'Philip V', *passim*.

years John XXII had complained of the vagueness of French proposals. In 1323 French ambassadors presented detailed ideas for a *primum passagium* in 1323 and a *passagium particulare* in 1324 or 1325.[25] As a result the debate shifted from consideration whether the moment was auspicious to mount a crusade to wrangles over the measure of French authority over any papal grant. This, in itself, was a step towards realising a *passagium*. During these discussions, Charles IV relied on regular spokesmen, Bishop Pierre Mortemart of Viviers, the designated leader of the crusade vanguard, Louis de Clermont and Mathieu de Varennes, who had organised a crusade fleet in conjunction with papal officials in 1319.[26] They were not going to be side-tracked. Their briefs were narrow and the crusade was no longer seen as part of an elaborate scheme of *quid pro quo*. To John XXII's disquiet, Charles IV treated the crusade as an issue apart.

There was a broad consensus on crusading strategy. The supply by Christian, mainly Italian, merchants of food, arms, ships and other raw materials used for war had been seen by an eye-witness, Thaddeo of Naples, as one cause for the loss of Acre in 1291.[27] Plans for an embargo on Egyptian exports and imports had subsequently won general acceptance. Many also saw that a general *passagium* needed at least one preliminary campaign to establish a base on the mainland of the Levant whence the main crusade could operate. Preliminary *passagia* were advocated by experienced campaigners such as Foulques de Villaret and the Armenian Hayton and accepted by organisers such as Clement V.[28] The French need not have been under any illusions about the complexities of logistics and finance either. The financial records of Louis IX's first crusade and crusading bulls of the thirteenth century were available in the royal archives.[29] Any commander could refer to Joinville's memoires, completed in 1309, for details of equipment, supplies, ships and tactics. Expert advice abounded, from ambassadors, travellers, Hospitallers and writers, Villaret, Hayton, Guillaume d'Adam, the bishop of Angers and Sanudo.[30] Nogaret filed advice from the king of Cyprus and both he and Guillaume Durand, bishop of Mende, wrote crusade tracts of their own.[31] Anthologies of crusade plans were compiled.[32]

But the complicated structure of multiple *passagia* confused two different objectives, practical and professional help for Armenia, Cyprus and Rhodes and the infinitely more ambitious and less practical recovery of the Holy Land

---

25 For the diplomatic exchanges, N.J. Housley, 'The Franco-papal crusade negotiations in 1322—3', *Papers of the British School at Rome* xlviii, 1980, 166—185.
26 J. Viard, *Les journaux du trésor de Charles IV le Bel*, Paris 1917, lv—lvii; Roncière, 'Escadre', *passim*.
27 Thaddeo of Naples, *Historia de desolacione et conculcacione Acconensis*, ed. Comte Riant, Geneva 1873, 37—8.
28 *Regestum Clementis V*, no. 2986; Atiya, 56—7 and 62—4.
29 *Recueil des historiens de France* xxi, 403—5 and 512—15; Archives nationales MS J 453—6. Two bulls of Clement IV, dating from 1268, one of them detailing crusader privileges, were copied and witnessed on 14 October 1305, Archives nationales MS J 442, nos. 13—14.
30 Atiya, 29—127; Tyerman, 'Sanudo', 57—9.
31 C.V. Langlois, 'Les papiers de Nogaret et de Plaisians', *Notices et Extraits des MSS de la Bibliothèque Nationale* xxxix, 1909, 224 no. 85; Archives nationales MS J 456 no. 36² and no. 36² bis; BN MS Latin 7470 fols 117 recto—123 recto.
32 BN MS Latin 7470, probably compiled during the reign of Charles IV.

itself. Successive theorists had assisted this confusion, especially those with interests in the Levant, Henry II of Cyprus, Hayton, Villaret, the Hospitallers of Rhodes and Sanudo. By associating local relief with the general crusade they could hope to convince nostalgic western leaders of the importance of their limited objectives. But even these, as the calculations of French officials demonstrated in 1323, were almost prohibitively expensive.

The response of French leaders was not always straightforward. There was no shortage of willing commanders, Charles de Valois, Louis de Clermont, Gaucher de Châtillon, Robert de Boulogne or Philip de Valois. Eager *crucesignati* were everywhere. In 1323 Amaury de Narbonne was even plucked from a prison cell to lead a *primum passagium*.[33] But crusade leadership, as any other position of influence, was open to faction. Philip IV's will had indicated the precedence of Charles de Valois as leader of the crusade after the king's sons.[34] But Charles opposed Philip de Poitiers' coup of 1316 and Louis de Clermont, a more distant relative but closer friend of Philip, superseded Charles as leader of the proposed crusade vanguard.[35] After Charles IV's accession, Charles de Valois returned to favour. In March 1323, Louis de Clermont, still officially the leader of the *particulare passagium*, presented the pope with a plan for a campaign of 1,000 knights to be led by himself and Gaucher de Châtillon in 1324.[36] But in May this plan was contradicted by one devised by Charles de Valois for a larger force to embark in 1325 under Charles' command.[37] The French appeared to be speaking with two voices and the curia needed little encouragement to become suspicious. Such rivalry was damaging to the crusade, but at the same time indicates that the court factions took the matter seriously.

The crusade also provoked tensions between enthusiasts and financial officials. In 1313 Philip IV 'et quasi omnes consiliarii' had enthusiastically agreed to Clement's request for money to pay for galleys to police the eastern Mediterranean. But later, in private, Enguerrand de Marigny, single-handed, reversed the decision complaining that 'ipse solus haberet onus expensarum faciendarum et de hoc alii consiliarii non curarent'.[38] It was not simply a matter of retrenchment versus profligacy, but a question of priorities. For Marigny, as for Philip V, Flanders and the royal debts preceded the crusade.

Nevertheless, some officials and royal advisers treated the crusade as more than a diplomatic expedient. In January 1313 an assembly gathered in Paris to discuss the crusade. It had a wide attendance and a record of its proceedings was kept by Nogaret who, with Guillaume de Plaisians, collected practical information and advice on crusade preparation and organisation.[39] However, activity faded with the deaths of Philip IV and Clement V, the long papal vacancy, the hostile reaction to Philip IV's policies in 1314—15 and the

---

33 Archives nationales MS JJ 61, no. 456.
34 Archives nationales MS J 403, no. 18.
35 Tyerman, 'Sanudo', 65—66.
36 John XXII, *Lettres secrètes*, nos. 1683—5.
37 John XXII, *Lettres secrètes*, nos. 1686—9 and 1710—11.
38 Schwalm, 'Beiträge', 562—66.
39 Roucaute and Saché, 141; P.H. Morice, *Mémoires pour servir de preuves à l'histoire de Bretagne* i, Paris 1742, col. 1243; Langlois, 'Papiers', 224 nos. 33—7, 240 no. 448, 242 nos. 491 and 510 and 243 no. 617.

succession crisis of 1316—17. The collection of the crusade tithe was left to the church authorities and plans for the crusade were, until 1319, only the parttime concern of a few councillors, notably Bishop Guillaume Durand and Louis de Clermont. It was characteristic of this lack of administrative commitment that, when the pope agreed to set aside 100,000 florins of the 1312 tithe in 1318 to build a Franco-papal fleet to guard the seas of the Levant, although the construction and collection of the fleet was to be conducted by a French admiral, Mathieu de Varennes, all his actions required papal authority, presumably as he was using clerical money. But that money had come *via* the royal *trésor*. The accounts of the venture are in the papal archives. Mathieu's original French colleague was replaced by a papal official and even the fate of the fleet and its diversion to the siege of Genoa was decided by the pope and the king of Naples, not the French.[40]

At almost the precise moment that Mathieu was gathering his fleet at Marseilles in 1319, Louis de Clermont was completing an entirely independent set of proposals for clerical funding for his *particulare passagium*.[41] In spite of some historians' easy assumptions, there is no discernible, let alone precise connection between Mathieu's fleet, Louis' plans and the advice Louis received from Marseilles.[42] There is no mention in either set of evidence of the other operation. But they had one thing in common. Philip V was not prepared to move towards the crusade without clerical funding and peace with Flanders. The latter he achieved in 1319—20, but the former only weeks before he was struck down with mortal illness.[43] Philip V's policy in 1316—19 echoed his father's response to the Hospitaller crusade of 1308—11 and the proposed flotilla of 1313. But, also like his father's policy, this was dictated by prudence rather than hypocrisy.

Charles IV was less cautious and detailed scrutiny of his actions reveals his departure from precedent. Although negotiations with the papacy remained incomplete, if not bogged-down, in the spring and summer of 1323, Charles began to prepare a small *passagium* for 1323, organised by Bishop Durand and led by Amaury de Narbonne and the admiral, Berengar Blanchi.[44] At least twenty galleys, two three-decked *naves* and four *galioti* were to be equipped for one year. The total complement of crew was 4,800 as well as 3,000 infantry and thirty cavalry who were to be landed in Armenia. After a year the fleet was to return to Marseilles to be available for future campaigns. Amaury was to receive 30,000 *l. tournois* (20,000 *l. parisis*) immediately, the balance of the 200,000 *l. parisis* set aside for the campaign being payable one month before embarkation for Cyprus. The king extended his protection to those who accompanied Amaury and their property. Volunteers were welcome. If the *passagium* never sailed, any expenses incurred by Amaury above the amount

---

40 John XXII, *Lettres secrètes*, nos. 511, 515, 531, 672—3, 705, 780, 784—5, 846—8, 852—3, 865, 885—8, 925—7, 983, 1032 and 1147; Archives nationales MSS K 40, no. 30, JJ 56, no. 334, JJ 59, no. 74; A Muratori, *Antiquitates Italicae Medii Aevi* vi, Milan 1742, cols. 131a and b; Roncière, 'Escadre' *passim*; N.J. Housley, *The Italian Crusades*, Oxford 1982, 100—101.
41 Archives nationales, MSS JJ 59, no. 76 and JJ 60, no. 100.
42 Roncière, 'Escadre', 399—400; Housley, *Italian Crusades*, 100.
43 John XXII, *Lettres secrètes*, no. 1262; Nangis ii, 37—8.
44 Housley, 'Crusade negotiations', 171—180; John XXII, *Lettres secrètes*, nos. 1683 and 1685; Archives nationales MS KK 1, fol. 298; Viard, *Journaux*, no. 2897.

Sed Nihil Fecit? 177

given by the king would be reimbursed.[45]

Since Vienne, all money for crusading purposes, excepting Greece, had come from the church. Even when large sums of the Vienne tithe were illegitimately misappropriated by Louis X and his brothers, it remained possible to keep account of what the crusade tithe had raised.[46] Royal accounts itemised tithes separately and distinguished between them. When Philip V's treasurer, Giraud Gayte, received crusade money, it could be traced to a particular collection in the diocese of Rheims.[47] When Charles IV's treasurer, Pierre Rémi, was paid a sum of 37*l*. 4*s*. 16*d*. *parisis* the journal of the royal *trésor* carefully distinguished between the 28*l*. 16*s*. *parisis* from the crusade tithe and the rest which came from other tithes.[48] Although gathered by clerics, the 1312 tithe found its way more or less directly into the royal *trésor*, yet it would have been possible over a decade later to estimate how much it alone had raised. There was no attempt at concealment even though none of it, except in 1318—19, was spent on the crusade.

In 1323, unlike 1313, the planned *passagium* of Louis de Clermont or the 1319 fleet, crusade money was not to come exclusively from ecclesiastical sources. Charles IV may have hoped for retrospective church funding, but he also authorised a lay subsidy for Amaury de Narbonne's *passagium* and a purchase tax for subsequent campaigns.[49] Meanwhile, for Amaury's expedition, Charles was prepared to borrow money. In April he secured 24,000*l*. *tournois* from the Scali and 12,000*l*. *tournois* from the Peruzzi.[50] Amaury began to borrow from Florentine bankers and Blanchi, acting as Amaury's agent, twice approached Avignonese bankers.[51]

Hiring ships was not so easy. Blanchi made a deal at Marseilles with one Pierre Medici of Toulon for the provision of 'certa ligna, usserios scilicet et galeas et navem quamdam', all fully equipped. Medici, a man of some local eminence, was a less than scrupulous businessman. On 23 July, Medici was arraigned by Blanchi before a Marseilles judge for breach of contract. Medici had delayed fulfilling his side of the contract and the day before, Blanchi claimed, Medici had despatched out of Marseilles harbour two of the *huissiers* already sold to Blanchi. On being confronted with this, Medici blustered, denying that these boats were those he had promised to Blanchi. The judge was suspicious. He postponed his judgement until the following Monday (the case was heard on a Saturday) but had Medici arrested, only releasing him on bail of 1,000 marks and a promise not to leave Marseilles until the suit had been decided.[52] Unfortunately, no record of the outcome appears to have survived, but Medici suffered no permanent damage to his position. In 1334 he was engaged by the pope to supply a galley for the fleet being raised to fight the

---

45 For these and other details, BN Nouvelles acquisitions françaises MS 7600, fols. 130 recto—130 verso; BN MS Doat l6, fols. 141 recto—146 recto; Archives nationales MS J 456, no. 37.
46 C. Samaran and G. Mollat, *La fiscalité pontificale en France au xive siècle*, Paris 1905, 14—15; John XXII, *Lettres secrètes*, no. 23.
47 Archives nationales MS JJ 60, no. 66.
48 Viard, *Journaux*, no. 4701.
49 John XXII, *Lettres secrètes*, nos. 1683 and 1685.
50 Viard, *Journaux*, nos. 2755—6 and 2897.
51 C. de la Roncière, *Histoire de la marine française* i, Paris 1889, 226.
52 BN Nouvelles acquisitions françaises MS 7373, fols. 15 recto—17 verso; Roncière, *Histoire de marine* i, 226 note 6.

Turks in the Aegean.[53] His was a world of ruthless entrepreneurs and profiteers. The king knew what he was doing when he inserted in the agreement with Amaury a clause directed against those who hindered the organisation of the *passagium*.[54]

In spite of the problems, at least six vessels were gathered from Narbonne and Montpellier as well as Marseilles; two large transports, the *San Nicolau* and the *Coquebaille*, four horse-carriers, the *San Jalicador*, the *San Peyre et son Aloy*, another *San Nicolau* and the *San Geneys*, and two galleys, the *Santa Victoria* and the *Santa Martha*. Of the stipulated numbers, the transports and small galleys had been acquired, but only two of the proposed twenty troop-carriers had been obtained.[55] Perhaps at this late season the plan was being modified to a less ambitious, solely maritime expedition as advocated earlier in the year by Sanudo and Cardinal Stefaneschi.[56] But when the final accounts were presented it was noticed that the ships had been cheap and that Blanchi, who died sometime between July and December 1323, had not spent all the crusade money.[57] The loss of the admiral was a severe blow, but the collapse of Anglo-French relations after the St. Sardos incident in October was fatal. By the end of the year, the *passagium* was abandoned.[58]

The fate of Amaury's flotilla vindicated the views of the Cypriot and Armenian ambassadors who never believed that Amaury would be ready in time and of those, such as Cardinal Stefaneschi, who thought that the expedition had been conceived on too grand a scale, the constant mistake of western crusaders.[59] Unfortunately, Amaury was bound to his agreement with the king which prevented him from embarking with less than the specified number of ships. This added to the delay caused by the difficulties of hiring ships, the suspicious attitude of the papacy and the deterioration of Anglo-French relations.

This was not the end of the business from an administrative point of view. Having repaid the Scali in December 1323, Charles IV wanted his money back.[60] In November 1324, Charles recorded that he had ordered Amaury to account for 30,000*l. tournois* outstanding. As Amaury 'n'a voulu fayre', the seneschal of Carcassonne commanded Amaury to appear in Paris before the following Candlemas to deliver his account to the *chambre des comptes*. If he refused, his lands would be confiscated 'sans rendre et sans recours'. The threat worked. Amaury paid 4,770*l. tournois* to the seneschal of Carcassonne. Another 2,000*l. tournois* went to Charles de Valois on the king's orders, presumably to assist the Gascon campaign. In 1325 Amaury's final accounts were challenged by Blanchi's heir and successor as 'patronus et rector' of the crusade fleet, Jean Fouquin of Narbonne. Fouquin's objections were over-

---

53 John XXII, *Lettres secrètes*, no. 5418.
54 BN Nouvelles acquisitions françaises MS 7600, fol. 134 recto.
55 BN Nouvelles acquisitions françaises MS 7373, fols. 10 recto, 12 verso, i48 recto—verso; Roncière, *Histoire de marine* i, 228 note 1; C. de Vic and J. Vaissete, *Histoire général de Languedoc*, ed. A. Molinier etc., Toulouse 1872—1904, ix, 420.
56 Tyerman, 'Sanudo', 63 and note 45.
57 BN Nouvelles acquisitions françaises MS 7373, fol. 11 verso; Archives nationales MS JJ 62, no. 355.
58 BN Nouvelles acquisitions françaises MS 7373, fols. 10 recto and 15 recto.
59 John XXII, *Lettres secrètes*, nos. 1690—1.
60 Viard, *Journaux*, no. 4436.

ruled and he appears to have fled the country, but the matter dragged on into the reign of Philip VI.[61]

Amaury's accounts illustrate how much had been done. To support them, Amaury presented to the *chambre des comptes* documents concerning the administration of the crusade finances and the acquisition of ships. They were accepted by officials as solid evidence of Amaury's and Blanchi's honesty in accordance with their instructions and may be accepted by historians as evidence of the earnestness and industry of the French endeavour, even if it was only for a small-scale *passagium*.[62]

The continuing importance of finance was further emphasised by the destiny of Blanchi's ships themselves. They became an exploitable asset of the French crown. The *San Nicolau*, probably the larger one, was given to Mathieu de Varennes in settlement of a royal debt and the remaining *huissiers* were converted into cargo ships available for charter by merchants from Narbonne and Montpellier, with the king retaining a stake in the business. When, in 1325, one of these ships was captured by the Aragonese off Sardinia and its cargo sold to help pay for their war against Pisa, Charles IV received compensation and damages from James II. It was significant that a ship hired to clear the Mediterranean of Moslem shipping and transport the vanguard of a crusade was captured, laden with merchandise, off Sardinia in one of the interminable feuds which precluded any effective response by Christendom to the victories of Islam.[63]

The plans of 1323 were a major concern of the French government. In his *Informacio Brevis*, probably dating from 1320, Bishop Durand had urged the king to appoint 'certos et approbatos viros per quas haberetur iam cura de navigio, de victualibus, equis et armis necessariis pro passagio'.[64] To some extent the 1323 *passagium* was served by such a group. There were the collectors of the French subsidy led by Durand and Abbot Courpalay of St. Germain des Prés.[65] Preparations were conducted by Durand, Amaury and Blanchi. Their work drew in others. From the *chambre des comptes* came Pierre de Condet and from the *trésor des chartes* came its guardian, Pierre d'Etampes.[66] Louis X's keeper of the Seals, Etienne de Mornay was involved in the financial transactions and negotiations with the papacy.[67] Bishop Mortemart led three crusade embassies to Avignon within a year.[68] Further down the hierarchy, a notary, Etienne de Gien was paid 'pro pluribus factis per eum super passagium transmarinum'.[69] Louis de Clermont wrote letters to

---

61 E. Martin-Chabot, *Les archives de la cour des comptes, aides et finances de Montpellier*, Paris 1907, 199, note 1 and no. 606; Viard, *Journaux*, no. 6585; BN Nouvelles acquisitions françaises MS 7373 fols. 9 recto—13 verso; Archives nationales MS JJ 62, no. 355.
62 BN Nouvelles acquisitions françaises MS 7373, fols. 12 verso—13 verso, exhibits A, B, C, D and P.
63 Archives nationales MS KK 1, fol. 447; Roncière, *Histoire de marine* i, 228, note 1; BN Nouvelles acquisitions françaises MS 7373, fols. 147 recto—152 verso; L. d'Achéry, *Spicilegium*, Paris 1723, iii, 712—13.
64 G. Dürrholder, *Die Kreuzzugspolitik unter Papst Johann XXII*, Strassburg 1913, 108.
65 John XXII, *Lettres secrètes*, no. 1683.
66 Archives nationales MS J 456, no. 37; Viard, *Journaux*, no. 2688.
67 Viard, *Journaux*, lv—lvi and no. 6907.
68 Viard, *Journaux*, lv—lvii.
69 Viard, *Journaux*, no. 5534.

'pluribus militibus regni Francie propter viagium transmarinum'.[70] Maps were purchased.[71] It is possible that Durand commissioned a collection of useful crusade tracts, his own included, to instruct those about to go on crusade.[72] At every stage the king consulted his councillors and assorted experts and, at the pope's insistence, was able to produce a detailed budget of crusade expenses right down to the costs of espionage.[73] But as little of the scheme eventuated, the administrative organisation remained amorphous. The chroniclers largely ignored the plans of 1323, a reflection that despite the papal grant of crusade privileges in December 1322 no widespread preaching, or even tax-raising, campaigns were conducted.[74] Charles IV himself was contradictory in his estimates of the popularity of the *passagia* and uncertain in his negotiating tactics, whether to say too little or to promise too much, whether to bully or flatter, whether to support Clermont or Valois.

In spite of the failure in 1323, Charles IV maintained an interest in the Holy Land. In 1326 there were rumours of a relief expedition to Armenia led by Louis de Clermont and the master of the Hospital, a rapprochement with Byzantium was attempted and Charles even tried to negotiate a peaceful return of Christian rights and possibly territory from the Mamluk sultan in 1327, although this attempt was expertly sabotaged by Aragonese agents.[75] The context for the 1323 plans was not a never-never dream-land. For Charles IV and his courtiers, help for Armenia and the crusade appeared as a serious political option for which they were prepared to expend effort and cash. As one cardinal observed, it was Charles' 'first great policy'.[76]

However, when confronted by Cypriots and Armenians speaking for themselves, instead of theorists speaking on their behalf, the French, perhaps to their surprise, discovered considerable disagreement. The French ultimately wanted a general crusade. The pope, more in touch, perhaps, with local feeling and, anyway, more concerned with Italian crusades, saw immediate aid to Armenia as the priority. The Cypriots were concerned lest the Mamluks overran the sea-lanes between Cyprus, Asia Minor and Syria. Armenia, on the other hand, wanted military or financial assistance for defence against the regular invasions by the Mamluks. French plans were distorted by the emotional charge of the crusade, although this was vital for recruitment. The theorists Durand and Sanudo, tried to hold the ring. In the end the French tinkered with the plans of the experts and ignored the views of the locals and their obsession with large *passagia*, in which neither the pope nor the Levantines were much interested, caused fatal delay. But any suggestion that Charles tagged onto a genuine relief plan for Armenia an extragavant and insincere plan for larger *passagia* in order more easily to be granted tithes cannot, given

70 Viard, *Journaux*, no. 1710.
71 Fawtier, *Comptes royaux*, no. 13902; Tyerman, 'Sanudo', 68.
72 BN MS Latin 7470.
73 John XXII, *Lettres secrètes*, nos. 1562, 1685 and 1848; Archives nationals MS J 1026, nos. 43 and 34 bis.
74 John XXII, *Lettres secrètes*, nos. 1571—2.
75 Finke, *Acta*, ii, 742; A. Laiou, *Constantinople and the Latins*, Cambridge, Mass. 1972, 324—8; H. Lot, 'Projets de croisade sous Charles le Bel', *Bibliothèque de l'Ecole des Chartes* xix, 1859, 503—9 and 'Essai d'intervention de Charles le Bel en faveur des chrétiens d'Orient', *Bibliothèque de l'Ecole des Chartes* xxxvi, 1875, 588—600.
76 John XXII, *Lettres secrètes*, no. 1704.

the administrative and political efforts, be credited. Charles IV's blunder was to try to prepare Amaury's fleet with inadequate resources. It was to this that Sanudo, who was closely involved in the planning, attributed Amaury's failure.[77]

The difficulties of 1323 left their mark. In the 1330s Philip VI deliberately kept plans for the defence of Romania against Turkish pirates separate from his plan for a general *passagium*..[78] Although the conversion of the French commitment into practical help for beleaguered Outremer had been hesitant and slightly incompetent, the preparations of 1323 did provide a model for a crusading future which lay with small forces not huge military leviathans. For the first time since 1270, large practical problems of strategy, tactics, diplomacy and finance were tackled. Charles and Amaury's failure illustrated to those who came after that the crusade in the fourteenth century, as in earlier centuries, needed to be simple in conception, direct in appeal and loaded with money. Yet the events of 1323 also demonstrated that in spite of dissensions within Christendom it was possible to order priorities so as to organise at least a small campaign against the Infidel, a lesson remembered in 1334 and 1343—44. Charles IV's methods and experience helped to dispel contemporary crusade myopia and reintroduce an element of realism into schemes to recover the Holy Land.

For diplomatic and personal reasons the last Capetians could not abandon or ignore the Holy Land. Their devotion was sincere. Their attempts to re-ignite the glorious tradition of St. Louis failed partly because of the distracting clash of political priorities, but more fundamentally because of the financial crisis after 1314, consistent and serious disagreements over the crusade with the papacy especially as regards finance, Italy and leadership, and muddled strategic thinking on the crusade itself. Simply, the crusade was much more difficult to realise than had been imagined. Charles IV's exertions served to illustrate that problems identified are not problems solved. *Sed nihil fecit*? The remarks of Cardinal du Four provide a clue. Writing in 1323, he commented that anyone who criticised crusade inactivity and followed the 'via obloquendi . . . nescit negotii veritatem et difficultatem'.[79]

---

77 J. Bongars, *Gesta Dei Per Francos*, Hanover 1611, ii, 297.
78 L. de Mas Latrie, 'Commerce et expéditions militaires de la France et de Venise au moyen âge', *Mélanges historiques, Choix de documents,* Paris 1873—86, iii, 101—2.
79 John XXII, *Lettres secrètes*, no. 1693.

THE FINANCIAL POSITION OF RICHARD, DUKE OF YORK

J.M.W. Bean

When Richard, duke of York, in the parliament which reassembled in February 1454 stated the conditions for his acceptance of the Captaincy of Calais, he complained that 'for somuch as of tymes here tofore I have been desired to doo our said Soveraine Lord service, as well in his Reaume of Fraunce and Duchie of Normandie, as in his lande of Irlond, whereunto at the plaisyr of his good grace I alweye applied me, to my grete and outrageous charge and coste, which drowe and compelled me lak of paiement of my wages, to celle a grete substance of my lyvelood, to leye in plege all my grete Jowellys, and the most partie of my Plate not yit raquited, and therefor like to be Frendes, by chevisance of good of thaire love, for their accomplishement of the service and charge, whiche at the seid desire I toke upon me in the said Reaume of France, Duchie and Lond of Irlond, not saisible without notable good, for the which divers sommes of moneye bee to me due; for paiement whereof, many promisses have to me made, not parfourmed . . .'[1]

Historians of the events that led to the seizure of the throne by York's son and heir, Edward IV, have long been aware of his financial difficulties. One authority has claimed that, 'This burden of debt goes far to explain why in the years following 1450 York made increasingly desperate attempts to storm his way into the king's council. The bankruptcy of Lancaster drove York to rebellion'[2]; and another[3] has suggested that a decline in the revenues of his estates in Wales and the Marches must have aggravated the consequences of the failure to secure his financial due from the Crown. But there has so far been no investigation of the extent of the Crown's indebtedness to York during the period of his service in France and Ireland.[4] Nor have the effects on his fortunes that York depicted — the selling of lands and the pawning of plate and jewels — received examination. There is the possibility that a study of these complaints might throw light on York's motives in the events that led to the outbreak of the Wars of the Roses. This apart, an examination of the evidence promises a contribution to our understanding of the financial position of the nobility in fifteenth-century England.

This study presents serious difficulties because so little of York's own financial records have survived, the absence of such documentation being especially marked for the decade that preceded York's death in the battle of Wakefield in

---

1 *RP* v. 255.
2 R.L. Storey, *The End of the House of Lancaster*, London 1966, p. 75.
3 C.D. Ross, 'The Estates and Finances of Richard, Duke of York', *Welsh History Review*, iii, 1966—7, 302.
4 The subject is touched on in R.A. Griffiths, *The Reign of Henry VI*, London 1981, esp. p. 674. See also J.R. Lander, *Crown and Nobility 1450—1509*, London 1976, 91.

December 1460. A complete valor[5] for his estates in Wales and the Marches exists for 1442—3. Unfortunately, there is no other financial record for these estates for the rest of York's life. A few receivers' accounts for two groups of his estates — those in Somerset and Dorset[6] and those in East Anglia and contiguous counties[7] — do survive but there are none after 1452. While the Welsh valor does provide a lists of the separate items of revenue in its respective lordships and manors, the receivers' accounts contain only summary figures of total manorial revenues paid to the receiver in the year of the account and these do not necessarily consist of the net annual revenues of the respective manors.[8] In the case of the duke's Yorkshire estates manorial accounts[9] survive for 1460—1; but, while these permit an assessment of manorial profits, they throw virtually no light on the disbursement of these revenues by the local receiver in the last months of York's life. For most of our information we have to rely on the records of the Crown.

Some solid information is available regarding the sources and size of York's income from his inheritance. When he secured livery of this in 1432, his net income in England and Wales must have been over £6,000. This estimate takes three items into account — the total at which York was assessed for the income tax of 1436 from his lands in England,[10] the value of his estates in Wales and the Marches provided in the valor of 1442—3[11] and annuities paid at the Exchequer and also from the customs of London and Hull.[12] Over the next dozen years or so he gained additional sources of income. In 1438 he was released for life from the payment of the fee farm of 85 marks a year payable to the Crown for the castle and land of Montgomery and the hundred of Chirbury.[13] In 1440 the manor of Cressage in Shropshire escheated to him as feudal lord.[14] In 1445 he obtained the manor of Crughowell from the Crown, having been deprived through fraud of its escheat some years earlier.[15] In 1447 he was given the manor of Great Wratting in Suffolk[16] and the castle and lordship of

5 PRO, Rentals and Surveys (SC 11), 818.
6 PRO, Ministers' Accounts (SC 6), 1113/11 (1451—2), BL, Egerton R., 8783 (1449—50) and 8784 (1452—3).
7 PRO, SC 6, 1113/10 (188—9). For accounts of receivers-general see BL, Egerton R., 8781—2 (1436—7 and 1443—4).
8 This point is not taken sufficiently into account in J.T. Rosenthal, 'The Estates and Finances of Richard, Duke of York (1411—1460)', *Studies in Medieval and Renaissance History*, ed. W.M. Bowsky, ii, 1965, 115—204.
9 PRO, Duchy of Lancaster, Ministers' Accounts (DL 29/8899/560 and SC6/850/26 and 28; 1115/1 and 6).
10 H.L. Gray, 'Incomes from Land in England in 1436', *EHR* xlix, 1934, 614. The figure was £2,569. Gray correctly added on annuities from the customs as well as the Exchequer. Cf. T.B. Pugh and C.D. Ross, 'The English Baronage and the Income Tax of 1436', *BIHR*, xxvi, 1963, 14.
11 Rents and farms (excluding Cressage, for which see below note 14) totalled £3,314 and administrative costs and repairs £942. In addition fines of sessions, gifts and tallages brought in almost £861.
12 An annuity of £104 19s. 4d. he held in 1433 (*RP.*, iv. 435.) was in 1435 joined by another of £68 1s. 2d. (PRO, Issue Rolls (E 403), 723 (11 July). The annuities from the customs amounted to £289 6s. 8d. from London and £400 from Hull.
13 *CPR, 1436—41*, 167.
14 *CCR, 1435—41*, 401—2.
15 *CPR, 1441—6*, 334.
16 *CPR, 1446—52*, 43. It had originally formed part of the Mortimer inheritance, having been forfeited by Sir Edmund Mortimer in the reign of Henry IV. It may, however, have been resumed by the Crown (*RP*, v. 339).

Hadleigh in Essex,[17] both grants taking effect on the death of Humphrey, duke of Gloucester in February of that year. Lastly, in October 1447 he received an additional annuity of £83 6s. 8d. which formed part of his inheritance but had been omitted from the inquisitions held on the death of his uncle Edward, duke of York.[18]

York's main sources of income from his inheritance were thus twofold — his lands in England and Wales and his various annuities from the Crown. Because of the absence of any sort of series of valors or accounts, it is quite impossible to attempt any assessment of the extent to which the duke's revenues from land were declining in the twenty years preceding his death. Manorial accounts for some groups of manors within the English estates do survive; and, while they are too few to permit any sort of well-founded overall impression, it is safe to say that there is nothing in them to suggest a serious, or even marked, decline in rents and farms.[19] Any conclusion about changes in the level of revenues on the estates in Wales and the Marches is totally dependent on inferences drawn from knowledge of other Welsh lordships in this period. But it is impossible to believe that York's holdings escaped the depression that struck those of the Stafford duke of Buckingham.[20] Indeed, the valor of 1442—3 demonstrates that 20.5 per cent of York's gross revenues in Wales and the Marches consisted of 'fines of sessions', gifts and tallages, all items that were especially susceptible to the consequences of the weakening of the lord's authority which was an endemic feature of the area following the rebellion of Owen Glendower. In addition, it must be said that there is no evidence to suggest that the consequences of agrarian depression were aggravated by inefficiency in the collection and administration of revenues. Indeed, there are indications to the contrary. An incident from the late 1450s is especially instructive, since it comes from a time when the duke's political problems might well have interfered with the collection of his revenues and his local authority. On 14 October 1458 the late receiver of the lordship of Denbigh was put in Shrewsbury gaol until he paid up his arrears.[21] The few groups of manorial accounts surviving from the decade or so preceding York's death contain nothing to indicate any slackening of efforts to secure the payment of arrears.

In analysing York's finances it is difficult to extract those parts of his inheritance that took the form of annuities paid out of royal revenues from the rest of his financial dealings with the Crown. To be sure, the annuities from the customs did not go through the Exchequer; but there were also annuities payable at the latter as well as his salaries for service in France and Ireland. The annuities from the customs were paid in cash by the collectors at London and Hull; but the Exchequer made its disbursements in tallies of assignment as

---

17 *CPR, 1446—52*, 79.
18 *CPR, 1446—52*, 117. Arrears since 1432 were included.
19 See the references provided in note 9. above.
20 *The Marcher Lordships of South Wales, 1415—1536: Select Documents* ed. T.B. Pugh, Cardiff 1963, esp. 145—83.
21 *CPR, 1452—61*, 570.
22 The most remarkable case of arrears concerned the manor of Cottingham in Yorkshire where in 1460—1 the farm for a pasture had been in arrears for eighteen years; but the farmer was Richard, earl of Salisbury (PRO, DL29/8899/560/m. 8).

well as cash, the former at this time forming the bulk of payments to substantial creditors. In practice these tallies often failed to yield cash when tendered at their places of assignment and were then returned to the Receipt of the Exchequer to be entered as 'fictitious loans' (*mutua per tallia*) on the Receipt rolls.[23] In their dealings with the Exchequer the task of York and his agents was thus a double one — to obtain primary payments and then to secure repayment in the case of those that had become 'fictitious loans'. Because payments of York's annuities at the Exchequer as well as those for his services in France and Ireland could produce 'fictitious loans', it is convenient to treat them together and give separate attention to the receipts from the customs collectors of London and Hull.

Table I[24] summarises York's receipts from the customs revenues. It is quite clear that the treatment he received, prior to his appointment as Protector, was erratic, there being no payments from Hull in 1431—40 or from London in 1447—53. In some measure the explanation must lie in the element of anachronism embedded in this portion of his inheritance which had been granted to his grandfather by Richard II at a time when the bulk of England's wool exports still went out in the form of sacks of wool that paid heavy duties. In part, at least, York may have been the victim of the switch to the export of manufactured cloth that was so marked a feature of the English economy in the late fourteenth and fifteenth centuries and led to some decline in customs revenues since cloth exports paid minimal duties.[25] In addition, York's annuities were only one of the demands imposed upon the customs collectors of London and Hull at a time when the government's finances were in a desperate condition; and no arrangements existed for the preferment of York over other creditors.[26] It is also possible that York was the victim of bureaucratic ineptitude. When he secured livery of his inheritance in May 1432, his annuities from the customs revenues were subject to the one-third dower-interest held by his grandfather's widow which accrued to him on her death in April 1434. But, despite letters patent of December 1439, it was not until 1450—1 that York began to secure the arrears due since her death from the customs revenues of Hull. At any rate, despite the vicissitudes of the treatment accorded York over this portion of his inheritance, it cannot be claimed that his situation worsened through the whole period 1432—60. He may well have suffered inconvenience and even at times embarrassment over the failure to secure regular payments. But the situation markedly improved once he became Protector in 1454. In the case of the London customs the total of payments in 1454—5 included five years' annuities from Michaelmas 1451. And the improvement in the case of London continued, even though in the years that followed he lost power over the government and events moved

---

23 See G.L. Harriss, 'Fictitious Loans', *Econ. Hist. Rev.*, Second ser., viii, 1955—6.
24 Based on PRO, Enrolled Customs' Accounts (E356), 18—21. For some surviving receipts from York and his receivers-general see PRO, Customs' Accounts, King's Remembrancer (E122); 61/61, 68, 72 and 75/34, 39, 48.
25 See, e.g., E.M. Carus-Wilson and O. Coleman, *England's Export Trade, 1275—1547*, Oxford 1963, *passim*.
26 *Cf.* those made by Edward IV in the case of the same annuities from the customs for his mother, duchess Cecily (cited in G.L. Harriss, 'Preference at the Medieval Exchequer', *BIHR*, xxx, 1957, 30).

TABLE I

Year	London £ s. d.	Hull £ s. d.
1431—2	5 0 0	—
1432—3	—	—
1433—4	—	—
1434—5	266 13 4	400 0 0
1435—6	—	—
1436—7	—	—
1437—8	199 0 0	—
1438—9	—	—
1439—40	237 8 5	—
1440—1	1146 11 0	533 6 8
1441—2	513 6 8	51 0 0
1442—3	50 0 0	—
1443—4	356 16 8	400 0 0
1444—5	43 6 8	—
1445—6	607 15 6	366 13 4
1446—7	11 13 4	—
1447—8	—	724 0 0
1448—9	—	—
1449—50	—	40 0 0
1450—1	—	639 8 1
1451—2	—	647 19 7
1452—3	—	530 0 0
1453—4	212 4 6	40 0 0
1454—5	1575 6 10	1075 5 0
1455—6	289 6 8	—
1456—7	289 6 8	—
1457—8	289 6 8	—
1458—9	—	—
1459—60	276 0 0	—

towards civil war. By his death in December 1460 almost 80 per cent of the London annuity due since Michaelmas 1447 had been paid. To be sure, the situation in the case of Hull was markedly different. By Michaelmas 1445 two-thirds of what was due had almost completely been paid; but the remaining third, the collectors still distinguishing between the original dower-interest and the rest, remained unpaid to the extent of just short of £400. No more was received from Hull after Michaelmas 1455.

Tables II and III[27] deal with the substance of York's complaints of 1454. In addition to the details of his pension payments at the Exchequer, they

---

27 Based on PRO, Receipt Rolls (E401), 744—875 and Issue Rolls (E403), 721—820.

The Financial Position of Richard, Duke of York 187

summarise his dealings with the Crown over his salaries for service in France and Ireland. He served in France as governor and lieutenant-general for two periods. He was retained for one year from February 1436, returning to England when his term ended; and then he served for five years from September 1440.[29] In September 1447 he began a term of ten years as the king's lieutenant in Ireland. Of these two offices, that in France and Normandy was the much greater burden on the finances of the government in England: York's salary was £20,000 a year, whereas his Irish office entitled him to 4,000 marks for the first year and £2,000 for each succeeding one. Table II provides details of both primary payments, distinguishing between cash and tallies of assignment, together with those of repayments of 'fictitious loans'.[30] The delays in such repayments could be substantial and might, indeed, lead to further 'fictitious loans'. Table III sets out the record of repayment that York managed to achieve.[31]

York's first period of service in France appears to have been quite adequately rewarded. The payments were extremely large; and the details of the contingent led by York provided in the Issue roll entries, indicating that complete payments were made, do not suggest that the Crown was in default to any serious extent. Moreover, York received the wages of himself and his men almost entirely in cash. It is true that in 1439 the Crown did not require the fees appropriate for the livery of part of his inheritance on the ground that he was still owed sums for his service in France.[32] But we hear no more of this; and, if there were still substantial amounts due, it is odd that York did not insist on a settlement before he accepted his lieutenancy in 1440.

His dealings with the Crown over his salary in the years 1440—5 present a more complicated problem. The first year went well, most of what was due being paid in cash: indeed, munitions were provided over and above the basic obligation of £20,000 a year. The second year was also one of more than adequate treatment. The Crown's total outlay in cash and assignments exceeded

---

29 Griffiths 541, n. 132 has suggested that he continued in office beyond the end of August 1445. The evidence indicating York's presence in Normandy is, in fact, more substantial than that cited by Griffiths (H. de Frondeville, *La Vicomté d'Orbec pendant l'occupation anglaise (1417—49)*, (Caen, 1936), pp. 57—8, 61—2 and 67). But a single reference in BN Paris, nouvelles acquisitions françaises, 7692, f. 297, can hardly outweigh the total silence in English financial and other records. In the documents cited by de Frondeville he was acting as the local *vicomte*. His presence in Normandy in 1446—7 can quite easily be explained in terms of his territorial interests there.
30 The years in Tables I—III start with the beginning of the Michaelmas term of the Exchequer.
31 It must be emphasised that the totals supplied in Tables II and III are crude additions of the entries in the Issue and Receipt rolls. Of the surviving rolls only the Treasurers' rolls that are complete for a whole term can provide an absolutely reliable record. And there are comparatively few of these. In consequence, the dates of the repayments of 'fictitious loans' have often to be supplied from a Receipt roll cancellation, and not from an Issue roll, while one of the latter might provide details of a repayment of a 'fictitious loan' that cannot be traced in the surviving Receipt rolls. A good illustration of the consequences of the absence of a Treasurer's roll is provided in the payment of £1,900 for the custody of Calais made to York of 17 June 1454 (PRO, Exchequer Memoranda Roll, King's Remembrancer (E159), 224, Easter, *rot*. 35). This is not entered on the surviving Chamberlains' rolls. Unfortunately, it is impossible to decide whether the payments summarised in Tables II and III minimise York's actual receipts to any appreciable extent; and payments missing from the surviving Issue rolls might well have produced 'fictitious loans' which are recorded. But it is difficult to believe that these considerations seriously affect any conclusions derived from Tables II and III.
32 *CPR, 1436—41*, 306.

TABLE II Exchequer Payments, 1435—60
£-s-d- to nearest penny

Year	Annuity In cash	Annuity In tallies	Service in France Normandy and Ireland In cash	Service in France Normandy and Ireland In tallies	'Bad tallies'	Repayment of 'fictitious loans' In cash	Repayment of 'fictitious loans' In tallies
1435—6	—	609- 5- 6	17,012-15- 1	68- 1- 2	—	—	—
1436—7	—	186-13- 4	—	—	—	—	—
1437—8	—	117- 2- 1	—	(766-13- 4)[28]	666-13- 4	—	—
1438—9	—	93- 0- 0	—	—	19-13- 4	—	—
1439—40	—	137-17- 0	—	—	92-16-10	—	—
1440—1	—	79-13- 4	20,254- 8- 0	165- 7-11	—	—	—
1441—2	—	102-11- 8	18,256-12-11	13,572- 6- 4	—	—	671-13- 4
1442—3	—	—	1,666-13- 4	(11,666-13- 4)[28]	13- 7- 1	—	13- 7- 1
1443—4	—	—	11,666-13- 4	—	8,223- 6- 5	—	13- 2-10
1444—5	—	745-19- 1	—	—	936- 5- 9	—	3,596- 0- 0
1445—6	—	87- 6- 8	—	26,000- 0- 0	11,164-19- 4	20- 0- 0	127-11- 6
1446—7	—	—	—	—	1,255- 0- 0	40- 0- 0	3,896-16- 9
1447—8	—	133- 6- 8	—	—	180-19- 2	410- 0-11	2,128-15- 8
1448—9	—	447- 3- 9	1,345- 0- 0	—	1,604- 9- 8	144-15- 0	6,432-13- 5
1449—50	—	—	—	1,200- 0- 0	—	—	60- 0- 0
1450—1	—	—	—	—	186- 0- 0	—	574-13- 4
1451—2	—	—	—	—	40- 0- 0	—	849- 6- 8
1452—3	—	—	—	—	—	—	267- 6- 8
1453—4	—	907- 6- 8	—	1,500- 0- 0	782-13- 4	—	1,249-12- 6
1454—5	—	113- 6- 8	—	—	565- 5- 0	447- 0- 8	2,810- 5- 8
1455—6	—	—	—	—	90-12- 0	147- 8- 8	1,116-19- 1
1456—7	—	—	—	—	100- 0- 0	—	1,431- 5- 4
1457—8	—	453- 6- 8	—	—	126-13- 4	40- 0- 0	718-11- 3
1458—9	—	84- 0- 0	—	—	—	40- 0- 0	184- 3- 4
1459 — Dec. 60	—	—	—	—	—	—	53-18- 4

28 This was the repayment of a loan.

TABLE III Repayment of 'Fictitious Loans', 1443—60

Year	Total of 'fictitious loans' for year:	1444—5	1445—6	1446—7	1447—8	1448—9	1449—50	1450—1	1451—2
1443—4	8,223- 6- 5	3,596- 0- 0	—	1,670- 0- 0	874-11- 9	932- 2- 9	—	—	230- 0- 0
1444—5	936- 5- 9	—	96- 5- 9	—	180- 0- 0	660- 0- 0	—	—	—
1445—6	11,164-19- 4	—	20- 0- 0	2,078- 0- 0	615- 9- 4	4,047-11- 8	10- 0- 0	186-13- 4	500- 0- 0
1446—7	1,255- 0- 0	—	—	100- 0- 0	428- 6- 8	350- 0- 0	—	—	—
1447—8	180-19- 2	—	—	—	—	—	—	134- 0- 0	—
1448—9	1,604- 9- 8	—	—	—	—	388- 0- 0	5- 0- 0	376- 0- 0	—
1449—50	—	—	—	—	—	—	—	—	—
1450—1	186- 0- 0	—	—	—	—	—	—	119- 6- 8	—
1451—2	40- 0- 0	—	—	—	—	—	—	—	—
1452—3	—	—	—	—	—	—	—	—	—
1453—4	782-13- 4	—	—	—	—	—	—	—	—
1454—5	565- 5- 0	—	—	—	—	—	—	—	—
1455—6	90-12- 0	—	—	—	—	—	—	—	—
1456—7	100- 0- 0	—	—	—	—	—	—	—	—
1457—8	126-13- 4	—	—	—	—	—	—	—	—
1458—9	—	—	—	—	—	—	—	—	—
1459—60	—	—	—	—	—	—	—	—	—

TABLE III (continued)

Year	1452—3	1453—4	1454—5	1455—6	1456—7	1457—8	1458—9	1459—Dec. 60	Total outstanding Dec. 60
1443—4	134- 0- 0	332- 0- 0	159-13- 4	71-11- 1	—	173-19- 3	—	50- 0- 0	—
1444—5	—	—	—	—	—	—	—	—	—
1445—6	—	277- 0- 0	1,661- 0- 8	735-16- 4	752-12- 0	40- 0- 0	40- 0- 0	—	200- 0- 0
1446—7	—	—	166-13- 4	—	200- 0- 0	—	10- 0- 0	—	—
1447—8	—	33- 5-10	—	13-13- 4	—	—	—	—	—
1448—9	66-13- 4	113- 6- 8	62-11- 8	149- 4- 8	298-13- 4	100- 0- 0	—	—	—
1449—50	—	—	—	—	—	—	—	—	—
1450—1	—	—	—	20- 0- 0	46-13- 4	—	—	—	—
1451—2	—	12- 0- 0	—	28- 0- 0	—	—	—	—	—
1452—3	—	—	—	—	—	—	—	—	—
1453—4	—	400- 0- 0	326- 0- 0	36-13- 4	—	—	20- 0- 0	—	—
1454—5	—	—	434- 6- 8	45-13- 4	33- 6- 8	—	48- 0- 0	3-18- 4	—
1455—6	—	—	—	66- 0- 0	—	344-12- 0	—	—	—
1456—7	—	—	—	—	100- 0- 0	—	—	—	—
1457—8	—	—	—	—	—	60- 0- 0	66-13- 4	—	—
1458—9	—	—	—	—	—	—	—	—	—
1459—60	—	—	—	—	—	—	—	—	—

its annual salary obligation by more than 50 per cent and just over 60 per cent of the total was in cash. On 7 December 1443, despite inadequate treatment in the preceding year, York felt confident enough about the situation to advance the Crown a loan of £11,666 13s. 4d. But the tallies of assignment in which this was repaid[33] the following 21 February left York with 'fictitious loans' to the extent of over two-thirds of this enormous loan. The deterioration of York's financial dealings with the Crown continued for the rest of his lieutenancy. The explanation lies in the decision to send the duke of Somerset as lieutenant and captain-general of Gascony and France in those parts where York's authority did not run, providing him with an advance of £25,000 on his wages. In the expectation that York's salary would fall into arrears, the council urged him to be patient.[34]

The consequences are best examined in the light of a writ of privy seal,[35] addressed to the treasurer and chamberlains of the Exchequer on 2 June 1446. This set out the terms of a settlement made with York over his arrears of salary for the last two years of his service in France and Normandy. It stated that £18,666 13s. 4d. was due for his fourth year, together with the full £20,000 for the fifth and final year. York had consented, 'consideryng the greet charges that we have in hand', to give the Crown a rebate of £12,666 13s. 4d., so that a total of £26,000 was now due. In the light of these details it is reasonable to assume that York had no complaint about arrears of his salary for his third year of service and that this settlement took into account all the payments, both cash and assignments, he had received since then. The repayments of 'fictitious loans' made from 1443 onwards that are summarised in Tables II and III leave no doubt that those still credited to York were not involved in the settlement and were a totally separate matter. Certainly in 1443—4 and succeeding years York failed to secure cash for many of the tallies of assignment he was given. And in the event not far short of half of the total of £26,000 promised in the settlement of 1446 had to be entered in due course as 'fictitious loans'. In 1444-5, to be sure, efforts had been made to clear almost 40 per cent of then outstanding 'fictitious loans'. But the failure to convert into immediate cash not far short of half of what had been agreed in final settlement meant that by the end of September 1446 a total of £16,610 in 'fictitious loans' was owed to York.

The Crown was even more delinquent in the payment of his Irish salary. In November 1448 he did receive in cash the first half of the £2,666 13s. 4d. due for his first year's service. This must have been done in order to persuade him to leave England to commence his duties. In December 1449 he obtained £1,200 in assignments, this falling short by £133 6s. 8d. of the whole of the second half year's instalment for his first year of service. No further payments were made after this. The treatment York received over the annuities payable

---

33 He was repaid in the form of assignments on the customs on February 21, 1444, the unusual step being taken of making a greant in the form of letters patent with the advice and assent of the council, presumably because the loan was on the security of royal jewels (*CPR, 1441—6*, 242). The comments of A. Steel, (*The Receipt of the Exchequer, 1377—1485*, Cambridge 1954, 22) are puzzling, since the figure stated in the Issue roll under February 21 and in the letters patent was that of the loan of the preceding December 7.
34 Storey, 72.
35 PRO, Exchequer Warrants of Issue (E404), 62/188.

at the Exchequer was erratic. At those times when efforts were made to clear arrears, it was always because he was in a politically advantageous position. In 1435—6 arrears were paid of the recently granted annuity of £104 19s. 4d., these payments obviously being intended as an encouragement to serve in France. Efforts were made to maintain payments through 1441—2. But in the two years 1442—4 the Crown defaulted; and the large payment of £745 19s. 1d. in 1444—5 fell short by almost £1,600 of the total due by Michaelmas 1445. In 1447 York obtained an additional annuity of £83 6s. 8d.; but the erratic treatment continued. There was an effort to bring payments up to date in 1448—9, clearly intended to encourage York's departure for Ireland. But no further payment of the annuities was made prior to his assumption of the Protectorate in April 1454.

In the absence of York's own financial records an assessment of the effects of this situation on his financial position is far from easy. He appears to have complained in the spring of 1450, since a writ[36] addressed in May of that year to the treasurer and chamberlains of the Exchequer ordered payment of arrears of both his Irish salary and his annuities at the Exchequer and from the customs. But the king's order resulted in no immediate relief and only a limited repayment of 'fictitious loans' over the next financial year. The total of the items mentioned in the writ was over £9,000; and over the next four years it continued to grow. Thus, when York assumed the Protectorate and Captaincy in April 1454, the Crown was heavily indebted to him in four separate categories. First, he had yet to secure repayment of 'fictitious loans' totalling roughly £5,750, though this area of debt had been markedly reduced in the course of 1446—9. Second, over five and a half years of his Irish salary was outstanding, a total of £11,133 6s. 8d. Third, pensions payable at the Exchequer were in arrears to a total of roughly £2,500. In so far as tallies of assignment in payment of these pensions could not be cashed, they contributed to the total of 'fictitious loans'. Fourth, the annuities from the customs of London and Hull were in arrears to a total of well over £5,000

It is tempting to attempt some comparison between this total and York's income from his lands in England and Wales. It is, of course, quite impossible to provide a precise calculation of the latter. But it can be said that it was not in excess of the total of 1436, since the manors that had been escheated to York as feudal lord and the grants he had received from the Crown since 1436 are unlikely to have compensated entirely for the losses incurred through the decline of revenues from his lands in Wales and the Marches. If we assume that York's gross income from his lands in 1454 was in the neighbourhood of £6,000, the total owing for York's services in France, Normandy and Ireland, including all outstanding 'fictitious loans', together with the arrears of the annuities payable at the Exchequer and from the customs, amounted to roughly four years of his gross landed income.

This conclusion must be placed in its proper perspective. *A priori* it must be argued that no magnate in late medieval England entered into the service of the Crown in war or in peace in the expectation that all the resulting financial

---

36 *Proceedings and Ordinances of the Privy Council of England*, ed. N.H. Nicolas (London, 1834—7), vi. 92—3). The total of the Crown's indebtedness mentioned in this writ was £9,133 6s. 8d. and over, not £20,000 (the total given in Storey, 65).

obligations to him would be met either speedily or even in their entirety. It is reasonable to assume that any agreement about financial compensation would both take this fact into account and ensure a margin of profit for him. Indeed, in York's case the settlement he made with the Crown in 1446 supports this view. The king's writ specifically stated that 'he hath promitted the lord capitaines and souldeours of oure garrisons withinne our said Royaulme and Duchie to contente them wages which he can not withoute he may have paiement of the said sommes'. York had not imposed hardship on himself by paying his garrisons. The writ's terms suggest that the reduction of York's claims on the Crown by roughly one-third would impose no hardship or embarrassment on York because it would enable him to pay the wages owed to his troops. To be sure, York did not immediately get all that was now promised; but there is no reason to believe that he paid all outstanding wages.

There are also considerations based on solid evidence. The salary of £20,000 a year from the English Exchequer did not embrace all the payments for his services. In addition, he received £4,000 a year from Norman revenues for the maintenance of his household while serving as the king's lieutenant.[37] When the English council considered in November 1441 the scale of the financial provisions made for York's lieutenancy, it took into account 'the grete taxes and imposicions that he hath put on the Kynges subgittes in the said cuntryes for the defense of the same' and assessed the grant he had received for the present year from the three estates of Normandy at £20,000 sterling.[38] In 1442 York had, with the assistance of the chancellor of Normandy, Sir Thomas Hoo, been able to divert to himself £9,000 in tallies of assignment from the English Exchequer intended for the receiver-general of Normandy: although the latter recovered this sum, apparently in the early months of 1447, its acquisition must have eased York's financial position at the time.[39] It is, of course, impossible to decide whether there was any truth in the accusations made by Adam Moleyns that York had embezzled monies intended for his troops; but this incident makes this charge seem more credible.[40] York and his son Edmund, earl of Rutland, were substantial landowners in Normandy.[41] It is not possible to estimate the value of their lordships; and it is not known how long York had held his. But in 1448, when he was no longer resident, York received £600 in net profits sent to England.[42] Lastly, in August 1445 he was granted the taxes due to the Crown from his lordships in Orbec, Beaumont-le-Roger and Breteuil. In the event pressure from Duchy officials led to the diversion of half of the total to the payment of soldiers' wages;[43] but even the remaining half must have been a useful windfall. Information about York's

---

37 *Letters and Papers illustrative of the Wars of the English in France during the Reign of Henry VI, etc.*, ed. J. Stevenson (RS, 1861—4, ii(2), [587]:36,000 francs at the rate of 9:£.
38 *Procs. Ords. Privy Council*, v. 171—2.
39 Collections Lenoir (Archives Nationales, Paris: 104 Mi), lxxiv. 183 (no. 30074).
40 BL, Harl. MS. 543, ff. 161—3. For the most recent discussion see Griffiths 506 and 542, n. 135.
41 The lordships were Evreux, Beaumont-le-Roger, Orbec, Conches à Bretheuil and St. Sauveur Lendelin (BN, Paris, MS. françaises, nouvelles acquisitions, 3624, no. 367.). York was granted the *vicomté* of Orbec between 29 September 1444 and 28 January 1445 (Frondeville, *La Vicomté d'Orbec*, p. 5). Rutland was holding St. Sauveur Lendelin by 15 September 1445 (Collections Lenoir, xxvii. nos. 29304 and 29343).
42 Collections Lenoir, xxvii. no. 29270.
43 PRO, Chancery Miscellanea (C47) 25/9/18.

The Financial Position of Richard, Duke of York 191

other sources of revenue during his Irish service is much more sparse. But he was entitled to all revenues while serving as lieutenant in addition to his salary from the English Exchequer. And he exercised all royal rights of patronage.[44] During the period of his personal presence there he received tribute from Irish chieftains.[45]

It is, then, quite clear that York enjoyed sources of profit that must have gone some way to mitigate financial hardship caused by the Crown's failure to meet its obligations during the periods of service in France and Ireland. But difficulties must have remained for him. A study of the details of payments and 'fictitious loans' set out in Tables I—III suggests that his financial position may have been a particularly pressing one in the years between his appointment to the Irish lieutenancy in September 1447 and his assumption of the Protectorate in April 1454. It is true that approximately 45 per cent of the 'fictitious loans' had been repaid by September 1447 and that a further improvement had occurred by September 1449. But then his French lordships were lost; and the arrears of his annuities from the Exchequer and the customs of London and Hull continued to grow. In fact, his complaint of 1454 gives a misleading impression. Most of the 'fictitious loans' that had accrued from his French service had been cleared by then. Except for the first year, his Irish office was unpaid; but it is legitimate to doubt whether York had spent any of his own resources there since his return to England in the autumn of 1450. Any difficulties he had emerged mainly from his failure to secure those revenues of his inheritance that issued from the Exchequer and the customs of London and Hull. But he did not mention these in 1454.

What truth, then, is there in York's story that his financial difficulties had forced him to pawn jewels and plate and sell lands? On the face of it this must arouse suspicion, since any landowner who wanted to clear pressing debts would normally sell moveable property before alienating land. In fact, the royal writ of May 1450, presumably echoing the language of York's petition, simply stated that 'for ye non payment of ye said wages he hath right greetly empoverisshed himself by chevysance of good and otherwise as it is said'.[46] There is certainly some evidence that York was pawning jewels. In the summer of 1450 when the rebels led by Jack Cade pillaged the house of the London merchant Philip Malpas, they took jewels worth £114 that belonged to the duke.[47] On 18 December 1452 York pledged jewels to Sir John Fastolf, it being agreed that he could redeem them for the payment of £437 by the following 24 June.[48] This did not happen and they were in Fastolf's possession at his death in November 1459. On 2 July 1461 they were recovered by Edward IV from John Paston and another of Fastolf's executors, the king paying a total of £466 13s. 4d. to redeem both them and an obligation for 100 marks in which

---

44 PRO, Exchequer, King's Remembrancer, Indentures of Retinue, (E101), 71/4/921 and 937.
45 E. Curtis, 'Richard, duke of York, as Viceroy of Ireland, 1447—1460', *Journal of the Royal Society of the Antiquaries of Ireland*, series vii, ii 1932, 167.
46 *Procs. Ords. Privy Council*, vi. 93.
47 The Issue roll entry is translated in F. Devon, *Issues of the Exchequer* London 1837, pp. 467—8. The privy seal warrant is PRO, E404/67/13.
48 BL, Add. Ch., 17242, printed in *The Paston Letters, 1422—1509*, ed. J. Gairdner, 6 vols., London 1940, v. 249.

his father had been bound to Fastolf.[49] Edward IV's redemption of these jewels within a few months of his accession, when his own finances were hardly prosperous, suggests that York had parted with especially treasured possessions. No other details of York's parting with jewels or plate have survived; but, in view of the absence of so much documentation, this is hardly surprising.

Much more information exists about his alienations of land. It falls into two categories. One consists of records of arrangements under which portions of York's inheritance were conveyed to feoffees in 1449 consisting of manors in Essex, Dorset, Somerset, Oxfordshire, Gloucestershire, Worcestershire and Suffolk.[50] If these conveyances were connected with financial difficulties, they must have involved mortgages or some other arrangements under which the lands were held temporarily by the feoffees as security for loans. A few of York's surviving financial records as well as details of the jointure conveyed by Edward IV to his mother and other grants shortly after his accession indicate that these lands were in York's possession at his death or some years earlier.[51]

The other category of landed transactions does, however, consist of permanent alienations. The first was in 1443 when the manor of Grays in Cavendish in Suffolk was given to one of his leading retainers in France, Sir Edmund Mulso.[52] In 1448 York conveyed the manors of Cressage in Shropshire and Arley in Staffordshire to feoffees to the use of William Burley and his wife[53] and in 1451 the manor of Easton in Gordano in Somerset to Thomas Young.[54] It would, however, be unwise to assume that these alienations in fee were simply made to raise ready cash. The grant to Mulso occurred at a time when York was not faring badly at the hands of the Exchequer and looks, therefore, like a reward to a trusted councillor and servant in his affairs in France.[55] The transactions with Burley and Young did fall within a period of financial difficulty. Even so, both men were trusted advisers. Burley was a feoffee to York's use and one of his stewards,[56] while Young as a member of the Commons in June 1451 petitioned that York be formally recognised as heir presumptive to the throne.[57] To be sure, York's language in 1454 does not preclude the

---

49 *CPR, 1461—7*, 96, printed in *Paston Letters and Papers of the Fifteenth Century*, ed. N. Davis, Part II, Oxford 1976, 243—4.
50 *Feet of Fines for Essex*, iv, Colchester 1964, 43—4; PRO, Feet of Fines, Series I (CP25[1], 224/118/28.
51 See especially *CPR, 1461—7*, 131. Southwold in Suffolk was definitely in York's hands in 1451—2 (PRO, SC6/1113/12). North Fambridge in Essex was granted by York's feoffees to a husband and wife for their lives on 15 October 1446, presumably as a reward for their services, and they were still in occupation in 1461 (*CPR, 1461—7*, 44).
52 *CCR, 1461—8*, 114.
53 *Descriptive Catalogue of the Charters and Muniments of the Lyttleton Family in the possession of the Rt. Hon. Viscount Cobham at Hagley Hall, Worcestershire*, ed. I.H. Jeayes, London 1893, 89—90 (nos. 351—5); *CCR, 1468—76*, 165.
54 *Pedes Finium commonly called Feet of Fines for the County of Somerset, Fourth Series, Henry IV to Henry VI*, ed. E. Green, Somerset Record Society, xxii: London 1906, 113: *CCR, 1468—76*, 165.
55 For Mulso see Griffiths, 671.
56 J.S. Roskell, 'William Burley of Broncroft: Speaker for the Commons in 1437 and 1445—6', *Transactions of the Shropshire Archaeological and Natural History Society*, lvi, 1960, 270.
57 Young was one of the duke's attorneys during his absence in Ireland (*CPR, 1446—52*, 245). It is also interesting to note that he was granted the stewardship of Easton in Gordano at Bury St.

interpretation that he sold some of his inheritance to retainers. And both Burley and Young were successful lawyers who may well have had profits to invest in land. At the same time there is circumstantial evidence to suggest that the grants of manors made to them by York were rewards to especially deserving supporters. The grant to Burley and his wife was made at the end of 1448, at a time when York's departure for Ireland was likely and he may have wished to encourage his retainer to watch his interests. The conveyance to Young was made less than six months before he took the risk of advocating in the Commons his lord's claim to the throne in the event of the king's death without lawful issue. It is, of course, by no means inconceivable that some of the help given York by Burley and Young may have been financial. Indeed, in the case of Easton in Gordano, there is some suggestion that the conveyance of 1451 involved a mortgage which was then converted into a absolute title, since the evidence of a manorial account shows that Young obtained a lease of the manor of 1449.[58] At any rate, these alienations did not reduce York's landed income to any remarkable extent. The gross value of Easton in Gordano was about £21 a year. In the case of the manors granted to Burley and his wife, Cressage had been in York's hands only since 1440, when it escheated to him as feudal lord. In 1442—3 both it and Arley were worth £51 a year in rents, farms and casualties.[59]

In the case of Sir William Oldhall there must be real doubt that York sold or even gave him a manor at this time. It has been assumed that he alienated the manor of Hunsdon in Hertfordshire to Oldhall some time in 1447—8.[60] Hunsdon was in the possession of a London alderman, Sir William Eastfield, in 1445. But it was described as York's in a writ and inquisition *ad quod damnum* in June and November 1446; and in 1447 York was given a licence to fortify the manor-house.[61] Oldhall, however, was in possession by 1448; and the lavish building-work he then had carried out must have been under the licence granted to York.[62] This body of information has to be interpreted in one of two ways. We must assume that, when York was recorded as owner of the manor, he was acting as a feoffee of Oldhall who had acquired the manor from Sir William Eastfield. Alternatively, it was York who purchased the manor, immediately planning building-work there; but he then conveyed it in fee to Oldhall. If the latter explanation is the correct one, it does not quite fit with the picture of alienations made under financial difficulties. It is possible that York purchased Hunsdon when he was still owed wages for the whole of his fifth year of service in France and for most of his fourth; and he planned building operations when he was still owed a very large total of 'fictitious

---

Edmunds on 26 February 1447, three days after the death of Humphrey, duke of Gloucester at the parliament held there (PRO, SC6/1113/9/m.14). Young was a member.
58 PRO, SC6/1113/16/m.6. The farm was £16 13s. 4d. a year; but rents, farms and casualties at the time of the least began amounted to just over £21. The farm had not been paid for the year of the account (1460—1) or for any previous year.
59 PRO, SC11/818.
60 For the most recent discussion see J.S. Roskell, 'Sir William Oldhall, Speaker in the Parliament of 1450—1', *Nottingham Medieval Studies*, v. 98, following *VCH, Hertfordshire*, iii, 327.
61 *VCH, Hertfordshire*, iii, 327; PRO, Chan., inq. *ad quod damnum* (C143), 450/32; *CPR, 1446—52*, 77. York was already engaged in building operations in Hertfordshire in 1446 (*CPR, 1441—6*, 402—3).
62 *CPR, 1446—52*, 233: William Worcestre, *Itineraries*, ed. J.H. Harvey, Oxford 1969, 48—51.

loans'. It is, of course, by no means inconceivable that he then decided that he had over-extended himself and sold the manor to Oldhall. But, if York did this, there is good reason, as in the case of the alienations to Burley and Young, to suspect that it was not a simple sale. Oldhall was York's chamberlain and feoffee. As probably the most trusted of York's followers, he already held grants of manors and lands for life, together with annuities, and was to continue to receive rewards from his lord.[63] There must be similar doubts in the case of the manor of Hambleton in Rutland which was alienated to Ralph, lord Cromwell in 1452.[64] The alienation occurred at a time when York's finances had improved; and Cromwell was an ally who had been York's annuitant for at least a decade.

There can, however, be no doubt that some manors were sold. In 1449 a group of manors in south-east England was conveyed to Thomas Browne — Southfrith, Deptfordstrand, Erith, Tong, Swanscombe, Kingsdown and Shilling in Kent, Shere Ebor and Pirbright in Surrey and Drayton in Sussex.[65] The key to the understanding of this transaction lies in the office held at this time by Thomas Browne — the undertreasurership of the Exchequer. Our knowledge of the background to his dealings with York in 1449 depends on the terms of a settlement between the duke and Browne, made on the duke's behalf in February 1451 by the bishops of Ely and Winchester, Ralph, lord Cromwell, Sir William Oldhall and Richard Quartermains.[66] It is clear that the duke had turned to Browne for help in securing repayment of 'fictitious loans' and the conveyance of a portion of his inheritance to Browne involved the expectation that prompt repayment would come from the Exchequer. At some stage York became dissatisfied and seized a collection of tallies in Browne's possession that included a substantial number belonging to other royal creditors. The settlement of their dispute laid down that these tallies should all be returned to Browne, with the exception of 5,500 marks' worth that belonged to the duke and another 1,000 marks' worth of his that remained unspent of a total of 2,300 marks' worth which had been given to seven (unnamed) persons in order to secure a patent (presumably a grant of lands, offices or revenues). In addition, Browne was to be given tallies to the value of 300 marks to compensate him for losses totalling 2,000 marks he had incurred

---

63 See J.S. Roskell, 'Sir William Oldhall', 96 and 98, and for additional information, J.S. Roskell, *The Commons and their Speakers in English Parliaments, 1376—1523*, Manchester 1965, 242, n. 1. At some date between 1441 and 1447 York also granted him the manor of Little Wratting *alias* Blunt's Hall in Suffolk (PRO, SC6/1114/2/m.5; West Sussex Record Office, Catalogue of Winterton, MSS, 1/17 and 28/77).

64 For the alienation see *CPR, 1446—52*, 218 and Leicestershire Record Office, DE 221/10/5/11 (the original of the royal license). The manor was one of those conveyed by lord Cromwell to feoffees in 1454 for the foundation of his college at Tattersall (*CPR, 1452—61, 200*). Cromwell was in receipt of an annuity of £66 13s. 4d. from the receiver-general in 1443—4 (BL, Egerton R., 8782). It is not inconceivable that York was contributing to the foundation of Cromwell's college. Some years later, presumably from Cromwell's feoffees after his death, the manor was purchased by Richard Quartermains (*CPR, 1461—7*, 40).

65 PRO, CP25(1), 116/322/715; and —293/71/343—4; *CCR, 1468—76*, 257. In addition $9\frac{1}{6}$ knights' fees in Essex and a half in Buckinghamshire were conveyed. For Browne, see J.C. Wedgwood, *History of Parliament. Biographies of the Members of the Commons House, 1439—1509*, London 1936, pp. 123—4.

66 PRO, Chan., Close Rolls (C54), 302/m. 25d. The abstract in *CCR, 1447—54*, 326—7 is accurate.

through the duke's 'hevy lordshipp'. York was to be permitted to buy back the manors of Erith and Swanscombe within the next five or six years[67] for the sum of 2,400 marks; but in that event Browne was to keep the rest of the lands conveyed to him. In the light of later evidence the alienations of 1449 have some puzzling features. There is the possibility that not all the manors were alienated in fee to Browne. Manorial accounts for 1463—4, together with the list of arrears in the early 1450s, indicate that some of these lands remained in York's hands.[68] But, when in 1465, as a result of Browne's execution and attainder, his estates were granted by Edward IV to his widow and her second husband, all the manors were included with the exception of Swanscombe and Erith; and at the same time it was stipulated that all other lands that had belonged to Richard, duke of York, were also excepted, although none of these was named. In 1472 Browne's son and heir quitclaimed all his interests in all the manors conveyed to his father by York to the latter's widow, duchess of Cecily, and her heirs.[69] It may well be, therefore, that the transaction of 1449 involved some mortgages as well as alienations in fee, a suggestion supported by the special treatment accorded Swanscombe and Erith in both 1452 and 1465. But it is also possible that York simply recovered some of the lands by force and managed to hold on to them.

The transaction with Thomas Browne shows that in 1449 York was compelled to take extraordinary measures to secure payment from the Crown. By this date the dwindling of revenues from his lands in Normandy may well have aggravated the consequences of the Crown's failure to meet its obligations. Yet it would be unwise to lay the blame for his financial difficulties squarely on these elements in the situation. On 10 August 1445 York had contracted to pay 4,500 marks as his eldest daughter's portion on her marriage to the heir of the duke of Exeter.[70] York made this arrangement at a point when the Crown still had failed to pay most of the salary due to him for his fourth and fifth years of service in France. The size of the marriage portion, the largest known to us from late medieval England, indicates the depth of York's anxiety to strengthen his connections with so important a match.[71] At the time he may well have been confident that the Crown would soon meet its obligations. But within the next four years the burden of paying the marriage portion must have exacerbated the hardships caused by the Crown's defaults and the dwindling of revenues from Normandy. In the event, although York was dissatisfied at the time and used force to assert his interest, the transaction

---

67 There is nothing to explain the absence of precision. 2400 marks would have amounted to roughly twenty years' purchase by these two manors' total value in 1463—4 (PRO, SC6/1114/10/m.5).

68 Deptfordstrand and Southfrith were in York's possession in 1451—2 and 1454—5 (PRO, SC6/1113/12—3). For the former, and also Pirbright, see *CFR, 1452—61*, 261 and 257. It should also be noted that none of these had been conveyed by fine. However, Drayton which was so conveyed, was farmed out in 1463—4 on a lease which had started at Michaelmas 1451. Because of the uncertainty over York's retention of some of these manors, it is impossible to assess the value of Browne's gains. But a decade or so later all the manors involved in the dealings of 1449 brought in net revenues of £130—40 (*CFR, 1452—61*, 261: PRO, SC6/1114/10).

69 *CCR, 1468—76*, 257.

70 *CPR, 1461—7*, 464—5 and 548—9; PRO, Duchy of Lancaster Miscellanea (DL41), 2/8.

71 *Fifteenth-century England, 1399—1509*, ed. S.B. Chrimes, C.D. Ross and R.A. Griffiths, Manchester 1972, 118n. 11, where the figure is wrongly given as 6500 marks. It remains, however, the largest known.

with Browne did improve his position. By Michaelmas 1449 the total of 'fictitious loans' owed to him had been reduced by roughly 69 per cent.

York's authority as Protector from April 1454 to February 1455 and the conditions he imposed for the acceptance of the Captaincy of Calais resulted in further improvement in his financial position. 'Fictitious loans' to a total of £3,400 were repaid;[72] and, while most of this sum was in the form of fresh tallies of assignment, the total of those that failed to yield cash was comparatively low. In addition, York secured assignments totalling £3,400 as the first instalment of his wages as Captain of Calais. Although no record survives of his efforts in this direction and he had made no complaint on this score, he also secured some reduction in the extent of the Crown's obligations to him in regard to his annuities at the Exchequer and from the customs revenues. In addition, on 19 July 1454 he was given at farm the keepership of the king's mines in Devon and Cornwall for ten years.[73] The extent of his profits cannot be determined and the chances of any must have been reduced in the years that followed by the political situation.[74] But he felt confident enough about his prospects to pay £110 for the first half-year.[75]

A complete and accurate account of York's financial position in the years between his loss of the Protectorate in February 1455 and his death in December 1460 is quite impossible. The victory gained by him and his allies at the first battle of St. Albans did give him a further short period of power in which the total of 'fictitious loans' was further reduced; and there were occasional further repayments in the years that followed.[76] At his death only £400 remained uncleared of the 'fictitious loans' that can be traced.[77] But beyond the meagre details in the Issue and Receipt rolls little is possible but educated guesswork. One piece of information certainly suggests that his financial position was reasonable satisfactory in the closing months of 1456 and that he felt confident about the future: a letter from Sir John Fastolf which must be dated to 15 November tells how 'here hathe ben my lady of York, and soore mevid me for ye purchase of Castre'.[78]

It is reasonable to assume that the struggle for power in the kingdom that led to York's laying claim to the throne in October 1460 and to his death in battle two months later forced him to recruit followers on a scale that cut deeply into

---

72 Only £1,500 is entered in the Issue roll and, therefore, in Table II. But in addition £1,900 was paid on 17 June 1454 (PRO, E359/Easter, *rot.* 35).
73 *CPR, 1452—61*, 158 and 291. On the latter occasion (12 May 1456) the grant was extended for twenty years and was defined as including all mines of gold and silver and other metals containing gold and silver. It is not possible to determine how the grant affected the tin mines that belonged to the Duchy of Cornwall.
74 It was not an area where York had territorial influence.
75 PRO, E401/854 (8 February 1457).
76 They were not, of course, necessarily made to York himself, since he may have handed the tallies concerned to his own creditors (see note 77). But those entered in Table II under 1459—60 were made on the eve of the campaign that ended in York's death and must have been intended to help the financing of this.
77 This sum comprises two tallies, both of £200, and issued on the same day — 21 July 1446. On 8 July 1462 one was repaid to John Snow of London 'broker' (PRO, E403/825). The other was repaid by order of Edward IV, dated 18 May 1462, to John Payne to whom York had given it in repayment of a debt (E404/72/21).
78 *Paston Letters and Papers*, Part II, p. 167.

his financial resources.[79] Nor can there be any doubt that for the five years preceding his death, although he fared extraordinarily well in securing the payments due to him from the customs of London, he saw hardly anything of the annuities payable to the Exchequer and the customs of Hull. In these years he must have been a classic case of a magnate whose expenditure on his retinue was growing while his income was declining. At the same time there is no evidence of land sales or mortgages in these years.

There is, however, evidence that York died heavily in debt. On 15 December 1461 the archbishop of Canterbury granted to Thomas Colt[80] a commission to administer the goods of the late duke who was presumed intestate as a result of his executors' refusal to act.[81] On 26 February 1462 Edward IV granted to Colt all his late father's lands in the counties of York, Essex and Dorset from the preceding Easter, together with £700 a year from the customs of wool and woolfells in London and three other ports from the preceding Michaelmas to hold until all the duke's debts had been paid.[82] It may well be that York's executors had felt daunted by the state of his finances; but it is probably more likely that Edward IV brought pressure to bear because he wanted complete control over his father's assets at a time when he had to finance the continuing struggle against the Lancastrians. Such an inference is supported by the absence of any mention of payments to Colt from the customs collectors concerned.[83] In the event Colt himself died in 1467. Whatever the true nature of his intentions at the time, the scale of Edward IV's arrangements certainly indicates that York's debts were considerable. Twenty years later a total of £681 was still owing. On 27 April 1480 Edward IV directed his treasurer and chamberlains of the Exchequer to pay a total of £396 13s. 4d. to a number of creditors,[84] each of them having agreed to rebate the amounts owed by rates varying between 50 and 30 per cent, presumably the only way they could recover their money.

There can be no simple or straightforward conclusion about the financial position of Richard, duke of York, since it depended on a number of disparate sources — the issues of his lands in England and Wales, the annuities paid from the customs of London and Hull, his annuities at the Exchequer, his salaries for service in France and Ireland, and, in the 1440s, his lands in

---

79 There is no evidence to suggest that York had an exceptionally large retinue before 1450. See, e.g., *Fifteenth-century England*, 108. After his accession Edward IV confirmed a mere total of six annuities for life granted by his father after 1450, totalling only £60 (*CPR, 1461—7*, 46, 53, 94, 97, 121, 129). It may be unwise to place much reliance on this, since by no means all of such confirmations may have been enrolled. Even so, if York's grants of fees and annuities for life had been on a remarkable scale, it is likely that more would be known. In this light it is reasonable to assume that a substantial part of York's expansion of his retinue after 1450 took the form of an enlargement of his household and of recruitment by means of daily wages and the wearing of his livery.
80 On Colt, see Wedgwood, *History of Parliament. Biographies*, pp. 208—9.
81 *Registrum Thome Bourgchier Cantuariensis Archiepiscopi, A.D. 1454—1486*, ed. F.R.H. Du Boulay, Oxford 1957, 200.
82 *CPR, 1461—7*, 107. In the event the payment of York's debts was not limited to the revenues from these estates. For example, some were paid from the receipts of the receiver of Herefordshire in 1469—70, including some connected with the household that had been repaid by Thomas Colt. The total of all the debts paid that year from this receiver, however, was only £52 (PRO, SC6/861/20).
83 PRO, E356/21. The whole of the first decade of the reign has been searched.
84 PRO, E404/77/1/13.

Normandy and other sources of profit there. The fact that roughly 15 per cent of his gross revenues came from the royal customs and the revenues of the Exchequer put York, unlike other magnates in the top reaches of landed wealth, at the mercy of the vicissitudes of government finance. Each of York's sources of income was in decline or proved unreliable during his active political life, one — the revenues from his French lands — disappearing completely. Even so, we know enough about his financial dealings with the government of Henry VI to conclude that the complaints he made in 1454 were exaggerated, even disingenuous. In particular, no direct and necessary connection existed between some of York's alienations of land and his financial difficulties in the late 1440s; and there is reason to believe that a special ambition — the marriage of his daughter —, and also, perhaps, rewards to followers in the form of permanent alienations of land, contributed to these difficulties. In the event the Protectorate of 1454—5 produced a marked improvement in his position. His short-lived hold on power after the first battle of St Albans produced some further improvement. Not all the sums owing to him had been paid; and his annuities payable at the Exchequer and from the custody of Hull fell into serious arrears. Nevertheless, his financial dealings with the Crown did not involve the problems of a decade earlier; and, if he continued to be in financial difficulties, the reasons cannot be traced to the Crown's delinquency.

The study of York's financial position can hardly support a simple correlation between indebtedness and rebellion. To be sure, his return from Ireland in 1450 coincided with a period of some financial difficulty; but this had been worse some years earlier. And the years in which he participated in a struggle that led to civil war cannot be regarded as a period in which his financial position worsened. For any explanation of York's conduct we must look beyond the state of his finances. It is unwise to forget that he was a prince of royal blood and not merely a leading magnate. Even when he served in France as Henry VI's lieutenant, only the life of a childless Humphrey, duke of Gloucester, at least in his own mind, separated him from the position of heir presumptive; and the proposal that his eldest son marry a daughter of the French king[85] could only strengthen such feelings. His relations with Thomas Young suggest that he was himself behind the proposal that he be formally declared heir presumptive to the throne. In his short stay in Ireland he acted more like a king than a royal lieutenant.[86] The years when his exclusion from the inner circles of government and thus of royal patronage was driven home coincided with ones of financial difficulty; and for a prince who felt deprived of a position he considered his right by birth the dealings he felt impelled to have with Thomas Browne must have seemed especially humiliating. In this light his failure to secure adequate treatment over the Crown's financial obligations to him served only to strengthen his resolve to secure his rightful position in the inner counsels of the realm.

---

85 J. Ferguson, *English Diplomacy, 1422—1461*, Oxford 1972, 26.
86 Curtis, 'Richard, Duke of York as Viceroy of Ireland . . .', 165—8.